The Lived Body

The Lived Body critically examines the notion of human embodiment in both classical and contemporary social thought. The ideas of a range of key thinkers from Marx to Freud, Foucault to Giddens, Deleuze and Guattari to Irigaray and Grosz are assessed in terms of the bodily themes and issues they address.

By using the notion of embodiment to transcend the dualist legacies of the past, this book argues that the body is not simply a 'textual effect' or 'discursive construct'. Rather, embodiment is the active basis of being in the world, and the foundation of self, meaning, culture and society. It is not therefore a question of choosing between experience and representation, but of exploring their dialectical relationship to one another, and the emergent properties contained therein.

These issues are illustrated through a variety of themes, including the 'fate' of embodiment in late modernity, sex, gender and the 'medicalisation' of the body, the sociology of emotions, pain, sleep and artistic images and representations of the body. An 'embodied' sociology is proposed, one that makes embodiment central rather than peripheral, and puts minds back into bodies, bodies back into society and society back into the body. *The Lived Body* will provide students and researchers in medical sociology, health science, cultural studies and philosophy with a challenging new way of thinking and clear, accessible coverage of the major theories and debates on the body in social theory, from basic issues to complex ideas.

Simon J. Williams is Senior Lecturer in Sociology at the University of Warwick. He is also Co-Director of the new Centre for Research in Health, Medicine and Society.

Gillian Bendelow is Lecturer in Medical Sociology and Social Policy at the University of Warwick.

The Lived Body

Sociological themes, embodied issues

Simon J. Williams and
Gillian Bendelow

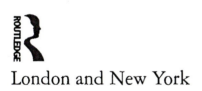

London and New York

First published 1998
by Routledge
2 Park Square, Milton Park, Abingdon, Oxon, OX14 4RN

Transferred to Digital Printing 2004

Simultaneously published in the USA and Canada
by Routledge
29 West 35th Street, New York, NY 10001

©1998 Simon J. Williams and Gillian Bendelow

Typeset in Garamond by Routledge

1005611245

British Library Cataloguing in Publication Data
A catalogue record for this book is available
from the British Library

Library of Congress Cataloging in Publication Data
Williams, Simon J. (Simon Johnson), 1961–
The lived body: sociological themes, embodied issues/Simon J.
Williams and Gillian Bendelow
p. cm.
Includes bibliographical references and index.
1. Body, Human – Social aspects.
2. Mind and body. 3. Dualism.
I. Bendelow, Gillian, 1956–. II. Title.
HM110.W53 1998
306.4—dc2198–16734
CIP

ISBN 0–415–19425–3 (hbk)
ISBN 0–415–19426–1 (pbk)

To the memory of a 'missing body':
something that never was but one
day may become

Contents

Conclusions   208

Illustrations

Plates

Figures

Tables

Acknowledgements

Thanks to Ann Oakley, Berry Mayall, Tim Holt, Nick Crossley, Ruth Charity, Margaret Archer, Robert Fine, Lynda Birke, Anna Maria Tota, Janice O'Brien and the two anonymous reviewers for helpful comments and discussions on earlier drafts and issues. Thanks also to our families, to Heather Gibson at Routledge, and to the Departments of Sociology and Applied Social Studies at the University of Warwick, who gave us the time and space, support and encouragement, to write the book. The result, we hope, does both them and us justice.

Introduction

This is a book about dualism and the associated problems it creates for an adequate sociology of embodiment. The separation of mind from body, nature from culture, reason from emotion has, as we shall see, been a consistent theme in Western thought, dating as far back as Plato's deliberations in the *Phaedo*, Aristotle's musings in *De Anima* (on the soul), and exemplified *par excellence* in Descartes' famous dictum *'Cogito ergo sum'*.[1] From this viewpoint, historically and even to the present day, the rational, objective, detached human mind, as the seat of truth, knowledge and wisdom, has constantly struggled to free itself from the 'shackles' of the human body and the slimy desires of the flesh. These dualisms have, in turn, been mapped onto the gendered division of labour in which men, historically, have been allied with the mind, culture and the public realm of production, whilst women have been tied to their bodies, nature and the private sphere of domestic reproduction.[2]

As an inheritor of these legacies, including the spectre of 'biologism', sociology, historically speaking, has neglected the body as an explicit theme in the analysis of social order, social change and social (inter)action. This, however, is clearly not the case today. Indeed, recent years have witnessed a veritable explosion of interest in the body within social theory, from Foucault's discursive body to Elias's civilised body, and from the reflexive body of late modernity to the post-structuralist celebration of the body ('without organs') as the nomadic site of desire. Seen in this new corporeal light, the body is not only deeply embedded in the core problems of sociology itself, from the bodily basis of social order to the embodiment of social action, but is fast becoming a 'core' problem in its own right.

On the one hand, this resurgence of interest suggests that the body, rather than being marginalised as an extrinsic biological factor/external constraint, is for the first time being taken seriously within sociological discourse. In addition, a series of fruitful debates is beginning to open up on the role of biology in sociological explanation: debates which are managing to sidestep the crude reductionism, dualism and 'naturalistic' legacies of the past.

On the other hand, however, it is equally possible to claim that, as a consequence of these very developments, the body is both everywhere and nowhere in social theory today. This is perhaps most graphically illustrated in recent post-structuralist thought where bodies are radically reconfigured as fluid, multiple, fragmented and dispersed. In this respect, a central paradox emerges, namely that, along with a range of other social and technological developments at the turn of the century, the recent upsurge of interest in body matters undermines still further our sense of what, precisely, the body *is*, and perhaps more troublingly, what it may *become*.

To put it bluntly, the more the body is studied and written about the more elusive it becomes: a fleshy organic entity and a natural symbol of society; the primordial basis of our being-in-the-world and the discursive product of disciplinary technologies of power/knowledge; an ongoing structure of lived experience and the foundational basis of rational consciousness; the wellspring of human emotionality and the site of numerous 'cyborg' couplings; a physical vehicle for personhood and identity and the basis from which social institutions, organisations and structures are forged. The body, in short, is all these things and much more besides. At best this has served to capture the multifaceted nature of the body in society. At worst it has led to a fragmentation of perspectives and a dispersal of approaches which, for the most part, talk *past* rather than *to* each other.

It is within this context that the present book is located, the central aims of which are fourfold. First, through the notion of dualism, we provide a critical (re-)reading of the body in classical and contemporary social thought. As we suggest, despite ritualistic cries of bodily neglect, corporeal concerns lie deeply buried at the heart of the sociological enterprise, from Marx to Bourdieu, Weber to Simmel and Elias to Goffman. Much of the sociological literature, therefore, just needs re-reading in a new, more corporeal, light. In developing this position further, we also chart a variety of other 'anti-Cartesian' traditions in which the body and associated problems of dualism have been more centrally addressed, from phenomenology to psychoanalysis, and from critical social theory to feminist scholarship.

A useful distinction can be made here between dual*ity* and dual*ism*. As the process of Cartesian dualism suggests, it is only through an act of conscious reflection ('*Cogito ergo sum*') that the split between mind and body is effected. To be sure, this duality represents a stage in the 'development' of human consciousness, but it is none the less founded on a series of problematic assumptions about mind/body relations. This stage of development (i.e. duality), in turn, leads to its own 'illusory' appearance, namely the problem of dualism. As a doctrine, dualism turns duality into an 'ism'; one in which the mind/body split appears somehow 'natural', rational and unconditioned. Moreover, it also spawns a number of other dualisms such as the nature/culture, reason/emotion, public/private divide, together with the associated ideological baggage this involves. The critique of dualism, as a critique of the illusions of duality, and the critique of duality as a critique of a certain stage in the development of human consciousness, must therefore look forwards rather than backwards to a 'third stage' of development which is, as it were, prepared for by the previous stage(s).

This, in turn, leads us to the second key aim of the book, namely, the need to develop an approach to the human body which 'overcomes' these dualistic legacies of the past. Despite the obvious appeal of neat, tidy analytical categories, bodies and minds, as we shall see, are never two entirely 'distinct' entities (*contra* Descartes), nor are they discrete attributes of a single monistic substance (*contra* Spinoza): things are much more 'messy' than that. Rather, as 'uncontainable' terms in any one domain or discourse, bodies and minds lie ambiguously 'somewhere in between', 'befuddling' traditional distinctions such as the nature/culture divide and a host of other conceptual oppositions besides. 'Destabilising' oppositional categories in this way does not, however, mean that we can dispense with them altogether. Rather, their analytical potential must be acknowledged and engaged with, so that new terms and different conceptual frameworks can be found in order to 'step outside' these traditional binary divisions and debates (Grosz 1994).

Here we return to the point raised above about the need to move 'forward' rather than backwards to a 'third stage' of conceptual development. *Embodiment*, we suggest, a term which lies ambiguously across the nature/culture divide, provides just such a means of doing so. Alongside other conceptual and analytical models such as Grosz's (1994) corporeal appropriation of the Möbius strip (an inverted three-dimensional figure eight), the 'inflection' of mind into body and body into mind can be grasped and the binary divide effectively overcome (without abandoning it altogether). Ultimately, however, as we readily acknowledge, there is no 'single', or 'final', solution to this knotty (philosophical) problem: even the idea of 'going beyond' the binary divide sets up its own duality (i.e. dichotomous versus non-dichotomous modes of thought). It is this central paradox, and the opportunities and constraints it affords, which fascinates us.

Having taken this position, the third main aim of the book is to chart some relatively new terrain in which a sociology of embodiment is central. Here, we look at a variety of corporeal themes and issues, including the 'fate' of human embodiment in the late modern age, the newly emerging sociology of emotions, pain and the vicissitudes of mind/body dualism, the 'dormant' body, and the relationship between art, the body and society.

Underpinning these issues is a fourth and final aim which threads throughout the book as a whole, namely, the need for an 'embodied' sociology; one which treats the bodily basis of social order and action as central, and takes the embodiment of its practitioners as well as its subjects seriously. This, in turn, necessitates a fundamental shift from the current tendency, so prevalent in social thought today, to theorise *about* bodies in a largely disembodied, typically male way (e.g. a sociology *of* the body, which 'objectifies' and 'subjectifies' the body from 'outside', so to speak), to a new mode of social theorising '*from*' lived bodies. Only on this basis, we claim, can a truly embodied sociology have any real hope of putting minds back into bodies, bodies back into society and society back into the body.

In stressing these four aims, it should, of course, be acknowledged that the focus of this book is primarily upon the adult body in contemporary Western (i.e. European and North American) society. Certainly, as we suggest at various points throughout the book, the newly emerging sociology of childhood is an important site from which to theorise the body, particularly as a biologically and socially 'unfinished' entity. At present, however, these developments remain largely embryonic. Indeed, whilst great emphasis has been laid on children as active social agents, sociologists of childhood have only recently begun to challenge the dominance of social constructionism, and to appreciate the importance of embodiment to the processes through which children participate in social life (Prout 1998, James *et al.* 1998). The theorisation of bodies in childhood, as opposed to adulthood, is therefore a relatively underdeveloped area of contemporary sociological thought. None the less, it constitutes a promising line of future development in evolving debates about human embodiment: an issue we discuss in both the first and last chapters of the book.

We also do not seek to discuss at any great length the important contribution which the study of religion can make to a newly evolving sociology of embodiment. To be sure, the role of religion in the social control of the body has been an abiding theme since the classical formulations of Marx, Durkheim, Weber and Freud. None the less, much of this theorising has again been flawed through the assumption of mind–body dualism; one in which the 'spirit', 'beliefs' and 'rituals', as legitimate topics of sociological inquiry, have been severed from the physical body, as the province of the biological and medical sciences. This, in turn, has led to recent calls for the 'rematerialisation' of the human body in the social sciences of religion, and acknowledgement of the fact that, 'believers' and 'non-believers' alike are never simply 'disembodied spirits', but embodied agents who experience the material and social world in and through their 'mindful' bodies (McGuire 1990). Again, a growing awareness of these corporeal issues has led to some promising new lines of research, including the relationship between embodiment, healing and ritual language in contemporary religious movements (Csordas 1990), together with other more general theoretical explorations of the relationship between religion and the body (Turner 1980, 1983; Mellor and Shilling 1997). To date, however, notwithstanding this handful of studies, it is fair to say that the sociology of religion remains a peculiarly 'disembodied' enterprise.

Essentially, the book constitutes what may be termed a 'meta-analysis' of the body in sociological theory, albeit one with an anti-dualist 'axe to grind'. It therefore builds upon and extends previous landmark texts in the area in important new ways, including Turner's (1984) *Body and Society*, now in its second edition (1996), and Shilling's (1993) *The Body and Social Theory*.

The book takes off in Chapter 1 with a preliminary examination of the nature and status of the body in classical and contemporary sociology. Here we examine the 'absent-presence' or 'secret *history*' of the body in classical sociology, including Marx's and Engels's accounts of working-class bodies in capitalist society, Weber's analysis of ascetic bodies, Durkheim's deliberations on sacred and profane bodies and Simmel's analysis of bodily gesture and the sociological significance of the glance for human sociality. We also reflect on some of the main reasons for the recent upsurge of interest in the human body within the social sciences, charting some of the most promising lines of present and future development in these corporeal debates to date.

This preliminary discussion serves as the basis for a more detailed exposition of the body in social theory in subsequent chapters. Thus, in Chapter 2, we consider the problem of bodily 'order' through a critical examination of Douglas's 'symbolic' body, Foucault's 'discursive' body and Elias's 'civilised' body. As we show, despite obvious differences in perspective, what these thinkers share in common – whether through ritualistic beliefs, disciplinary technologies of power/knowledge, or codes of etiquette and courtly behaviour – is a focus on issues of bodily conformity and the associated problems of corporeal transgression they raise in relation to the prevailing sociocultural and historical 'order'. Where they differ, of course, is in terms of their views on the nature of the human body they seek to analyse. Thus, whilst Douglas and Foucault emphasise the symbolic and discursive construction of the body, Elias, in contrast, offers a more subtle and sophisticated account of the dynamic interplay between biological and social factors across the long historical curve of the civilising process. As such, he provides, we suggest, a firmer, more satisfactory foundation than the shifting sand of social constructionism upon which to build a sociology of embodiment. These issues of corporeal conformity and transgression are consolidated in the final section of the chapter through a critical consideration of Turner's analytical typology of bodily 'order', together with Falk's recent account of the fate of (corp)orality, social solidarity and the ritualistic meal.

In contrast, Chapter 3 takes up the issue of social action through a focus on the problem of bodily 'control'. Here we consider Mauss's notion of body techniques, Merleau-Ponty's phenomenological analysis of the body-subject, and Goffman's more sociological focus on the body, the self and the carnal interchanges/ritualistic encounters of everyday life. In doing so, we seek to offer an alternative, more embodied approach, to the question of social agency and its institution-making capacities, one consolidated through Frank's typology of body use in action.

Building on these issues, Chapter 4 considers the changing nature and status of the body in late modernity. Taking as our point of departure the work of writers such as Giddens, Beck and Bauman, we suggest that social life is still fundamentally shaped by modern concerns – concerns that are only now becoming fully realised, with profound implications for human embodiment in late twentieth-century Western society. Here, key issues include the increasingly reflexive nature of the body and self-identity in late modernity, the changing parameters of risk, the salience of consumption and lifestyles in consumer culture, the uncertainties of embodiment in an increasingly mediated/technological age, and the problem of death for the modern individual. Alongside other key developments such as the transformation of intimacy and the salience of emotions in a rapidly expanding 'therapeutic' age, this points to a profound undermining of what bodies are and what they might become. Nowhere is this more so than in the technological clinic of late modern medicine and the glittering digital universe of cyberspace. Slipping the body is, however, an 'old philosophical trick' (Stone 1991), and these developments, no matter how complex, are ultimately grounded in and must return us to the inescapable fact of our human *embodiment*. Only on this basis, we suggest, can a truly 'human ethics of existence' emerge, one rooted in the 'life political agenda' of the 'real', not the 'virtual', world.

Having laid these sociological foundations, the next two chapters are taken up with a detailed exposition of a number of other alternative anti-Cartesian traditions which are, we claim, of central relevance to an 'embodied' sociology and the dissolution of former dualistic modes of thought. Thus, in Chapter 5, the 'libidinal body', we examine a variety of themes and issues, including psychoanalytic perspectives on the bodily ego, Schilder's analysis of body-image, and critical social theories of capitalism, sexuality and desire (e.g. the Frankfurt school, Deleuze and Guattari). Here, a line of theoretical continuity can be traced from Freud's and Lacan's analysis of the 'bodily ego' and 'imaginary anatomy', through Schilder's work on body-image, to Merleau-Ponty's notion of the 'body-subject' (Grosz 1994). As we suggest, what these perspectives share in common is a refusal to consider the body in binary terms. Rather, they point to the indeterminacy and mutual interconstituency of biological and psychosocial domains (Grosz 1994): views which are perhaps most radically, and problematically, expressed in Deleuze's and Guattari's attempt to reconfigure critically dualist ontologies of the body and the subject through a Nietzschean celebration of productive desire as a liberatory force.

Building on these anti-Cartesian traditions, Chapter 6 considers feminist reconstructions of bodily being and knowing, and the challenges they pose to dominant Western masculine modes of being and knowing. Here, critical debates surrounding 'sex' and 'gender' are traced through a number of key issues, including women's historical struggles to reclaim control of their bodies in the contested domains of sexuality and reproduction, the 'specular' theories of *différance* in French post-structuralist feminism, together with other recent attempts to reconcile materialist and constructionist approaches to the 'sexed' body. As we suggest, despite early signs of 'somatophobia', contemporary feminist writers are at the 'cutting-edge' of current social theorising around the body and desire, challenging previous (masculine) models of 'containment' through a reconstructed metaphysics of fluidity and flow.

Having laid the foundation for an anti-dualist ontology of the body, the remaining chapters seek to 'flesh out' this notion more fully through a critical exploration of a variety of other key aspects and 'predicaments' of human embodiment. Thus, in Chapter 7, we consider the issue of emotions, whilst in Chapter 8 we analyse the closely related issue of pain. As we suggest, not only are emotions central to the lived experience of our bodies and our selves, they also provide the existential basis for social reciprocity and exchange, and the 'missing link' between micro-processes and broader macro-issues of social structure. Seen in these terms, structure may, to paraphrase Giddens (1984), be fruitfully reconceptualised as both the *medium* and *outcome* of the *emotionally embodied practices* and *body techniques* it recursively organises. More generally, emotions throw into critical relief the dilemmas of modernity, from the tensions between love and sex to the resurgence of more sensual solidarities and the problems of authenticity in an 'inauthentic' age.

As with emotions, so with pain. In contrast to the dominant biomedical model, which prioritises sensation over emotion, pain, we argue, needs to be seen as a fundamentally *embodied* experience: one which combines both physical and emotional dimensions of human suffering. The ambiguous nature of pain, and the 'symbolic bridge' that culture and narrative provide between the immediate embodied disease as a disordered physiological process and its meaning-laden character as human experience (Kleinman 1988) provides, we suggest, a perfect example of how a foundational ontology of the body (as a pre-social, material entity) can profitably be combined with a social constructionist epistemology. The exploration of pain, in short, demands the dissolution of previous dichotomous ways of thinking which have impeded a more unified understanding of its social, cultural and biological significance. The medical discourse on pain is just one amongst a number of valid voices. By integrating medical and cultural discourse of pain in this way, we can transcend the false dualisms into which it has hitherto been forced, thereby 'reclaiming' pain from exclusive biomedical jurisdiction (Morris 1991).

Building on these issues, Chapter 9 considers the much neglected topic of sleep and its centrality to evolving sociological debates on the body and society. Reasons for this traditional sociological neglect are first considered, before proceeding to 'flesh out' some core features of this 'dormant' issue, including the biology/society divide, night-time and the sociocultural significance of dreams, the 'sequestration' and medicalisation of sleep, together with its social patterning across a variety of institutional domains. Far from being simply a biological or physiological imperative, sleep, it is argued, is a social role and practice that lies at the intersection of a number of pertinent divisions and debates, including the relationship between nature and culture, the public and the private, time and space, surveillance and control. Seen in these terms, the very meanings, motives and functions of sleep as an embodied activity, can only fully be understood when placed within the contexts, cultures and situational contingencies of everyday social and institutional life. Sleep, in short, is an *emergent* entity, located as it is at the nexus of physiological *need*, environmental *constraint*, and sociocultural *elaboration*.

Continuing in this anti-Cartesian vein, Chapter 10 explores the relationship between the body, art and society through a critical examination of Marxist, feminist and post-structuralist perspectives in art history. As we argue, art, in its manifold forms, is a central medium of communication regarding body/society relationships, including issues of power, surveillance and control within the broader sociocultural order. In particular, art expresses the tensions and dilemmas between 'experience' and '(re)presentation', 'aestheticism' and 'eroticism', 'resistance' and 'control'. Alongside performance art and other *praxical* modes of embodied expression such as dance, art provides a powerful 'visual narrative' of the embodied biographies of artists themselves, expressing fundamental features of the human condition. In doing so, the boundaries between art and social theory, reproduction and resistance, are (temporarily) destabilised, if not (permanently) effaced. These issues are vividly illustrated through a return to some of the key themes of the book, including modernity and identity, gender and sexuality, emotions and pain, illness, disability and death.

Finally, in a brief conclusion, we seek to draw the diverse strands of the book together and move toward a more 'integrated' theoretical approach to the body as a challenge to the dualist legacies of the past. In doing so, we return again to deep ontological questions concerning the nature and status of the body, and its relationship to the broader sociocultural order. In contrast to the prominence in social theory today of a passive, *representationalist* approach, one which finds its fullest expression in Foucauldian 'discourse determinism', we propose instead a more *experientially* grounded view of human embodiment as the existential basis of our being-in-the-world, one which overcomes past dualities, and in doing so helps us move outwards towards a broader understanding of the relationship between body and self, culture and society. From this viewpoint, meaning inheres in our bodily behaviour and its gestural significance rather than being the product of some prior disembodied 'cogito'. Culture, too, becomes a projection of the body into the world (Csordas 1994a).

In taking this position, we suggest a number of 'link' concepts, distilled from previous theoretical work in this area, which capture the complex, subtle and sophisticated relationship between the body and society, and the manner in which, through an imperceptible twist bodily 'interiority' becomes 'externalised' and social 'exteriority' becomes 'interiorised'. Seen in these terms, not only is meaning and culture an *active* product of human embodiment, but our body too is linked to the world through its socialised dispositions – dispositions which cons/train the body in certain historical and culturally pre/proscribed ways. In theorising the body, it is not, therefore, a question of choosing between order or control, materialism or constructionism, experience or representation, but of exploring their dialectical relationship to each other and the emergent properties contained therein.

We conclude, therefore, by suggesting that social institutions as well as micro-social processes cannot be understood apart from the real, lived experiences and actions of bodies, including practitioners of sociology themselves. *Embodiment*, in short, is central rather than peripheral to the sociological enterprise. The grounding of social theory should, therefore, be rooted in the contingencies and predicaments of human embodiment, and the links this provides to broader issues of social order and transgression, structure and action, agency and identity.

1   Sociology and the 'problem' of the body

A standard criticism in many texts on the body is that, until quite recently, sociologists have been reluctant to bring their 'skeletons out of the cupboard', so to speak, and give corporeal matters the proper airing they deserve. In this respect, it is claimed that the body, as an 'absent-presence', has stalked the sociological landscape in a largely ethereal fashion. Whilst the past history of the body may indeed be a 'secret' one, this is clearly not the case today. The deafening chorus of cries to 'bring the body back in' has now most surely been silenced by the recent upsurge of interest in the human body within the social sciences. In this chapter we take a closer look at these issues through a preliminary examination of the nature and status of the body in classical and contemporary sociology, together with a selective review of some of the areas and issues where recent sociological engagement with bodily themes appears most promising to date. In this respect, we build upon and extend previous discussions, 'incorporating' new material and insights along the way.[1] As we shall see, whilst there is certainly some truth in the 'absent-presence' thesis, the body can nevertheless be 'recovered' through a critical re-reading in a new, corporeal light, of much of the classical and contemporary sociological literature. Despite this promising start, however, much still remains to be done in order to develop a truly integrated sociological approach to the relationship between body and society and the 'problem' of human embodiment. It is this opportunity and challenge which informs the book as whole.

The body in classical sociology

As suggested above, a common point of departure in much of the contemporary literature on the body to date has been to highlight its neglected status in classical and, until quite recently, contemporary sociological theory. In this respect, sociology is said to compare unfavourably with other disciplines such as anthropology, where the human body has occupied a central place since the nineteenth century. Thus in philosophical anthropology (Gehlen 1988), for example, the body is considered in relation to the 'unchanging conditions of human changeableness' (Honneth and Joas 1988). From this viewpoint, one in which the Nietzschean ontology of Man as an 'unfinished' creature is central, human embodiment is never simply a constraint. Rather, it constitutes a set of opportunities which are endlessly elaborated through sociocultural and historical development (Honneth and Joas 1988). A concern with the human body has also been evident in physical anthropology, whereby social difference is seemingly 'naturalised' through appeals to its physical foundations. During the nineteenth century, for example, anthropologists and craniologists devoted great efforts to measuring, classifying and comparing almost every part of the human body, debating the social and political implications of the 'differences' they found, and assessing their significance for the 'equality' of the human species (Synnott 1993). Gradually, however, anthropology shifted from a nineteenth-century concern with 'measurement', to a twentieth-century concern with 'meaning' (Synnott and Howes 1992). Here, a view of the body as a 'surface' upon which the marks of culture and social structure are inscribed through ritual, symbolism, decoration, tattooing and scarification has been central (Polhemus 1978). More generally, anthropologists, from Hertz to Douglas, have emphasised the body as a potent natural symbol of society, including divisions such as the sacred and profane, good and evil, purity and danger, risk and taboo. Underlying many of these issues has been a broader set of debates within anthropology concerning the nature/culture divide, and the question of how so-called 'natural' facts, including the human body itself, are experienced differently according to culture, time and space.

Despite these anthropological legacies, the ontological status of social actors, and consequently the problem of human embodiment has, traditionally speaking, been a neglected theme within sociological discourse. To the extent that classical social theorists turned their attention to such issues, they have tended to define human actors in disembodied terms as rational agents who make choices through means/ends formulae, based on 'utility' criteria or 'general value' orientations (Turner 1991). Conscious ratiocination rather than the biological conditions of action was therefore seen as most important, with little room left for the 'lived' body as the primordial basis of human agency in the social world. In short, whilst the body entered anthropology at the fundamental level of ontology, the sociological stress upon rational economic action resulted in a failure to elaborate a fully sustained theoretical account of the body/society relationship. The body, in effect, became external to the actor who appeared, so to speak, as a rational, disembodied, decision-making agent (Turner 1991: 9).

Bodies then, at least according to standard accounts of their history, have tended to enjoy a rather ethereal, implicit existence within sociology. Reasons given for this apparent sociological neglect are manifold, including the predominant emphasis, by the founding fathers of the discipline, on social systems, their problems and their interrelationships rather than the ontological status or historical evolution of human beings; the suspicion of biological reductionism and its essentialist baggage; a conceptualisation of human agency linked with the capacities of the (rational) mind rather than the management of the body as a whole, and finally; the fact that these so-called 'founding fathers' were, of course, all men – the grand-*Masters* of their craft (Shilling 1993; Morgan and Scott 1993). Locating themselves amongst the *geisteswissenschaften*, sociologists have, in short, tended to perpetuate rather than challenge the dualistic legacies of Western thought stretching back to antiquity; legacies in which mind and body, nature and culture, reason and emotion, public and private have been artificially separated and rigidly reinforced.

Certainly sociologists, in the past, have greeted so-called 'naturalistic' accounts of the body – approaches which stress the unchanging pre-social or biological body as the foundation upon which social relations, hierarchies and inequalities are built – with a great deal of caution or scepticism, if not downright rejection; raising in their minds if not their bodies, the spectre of biological reductionism, not to mention racism and sexism.[2,3] None the less, despite their ideological associations and political biases, what 'naturalistic' views do at least take seriously, as Shilling (1993) rightly notes, is that human bodies not only form the basis for, but also contribute to social relationships. In contrast to many classical and contemporary sociologists, in other words, the human body and its biological constitution is accorded a central place in 'naturalistic' forms of inquiry. In this respect, shorn of its ideological and pseudoscientific baggage, the message of sociobiology and its legacy for sociology is that organic bodies do indeed make a significant contribution to social relations (Shilling 1993: 40).

To leave things here, however, would be to do both classical and contemporary sociology a gross injustice. As we shall see, bodily matters have their own (secret) history within sociology itself. Indeed, for some thinkers, bodily matters have been explicitly addressed, leading either to an acceptance or rejection of their sociological importance. For others, however, they remain largely implicit. In this respect, as with so much sociological inquiry, the work is 'already there', waiting to be mined through a corporeally sensitive re-reading (Morgan and Scott 1993). It is, therefore, to a fuller discussion of the vicissitudes of bodily matters in classical sociology that we now turn through a critical re-examination of corporeal themes in the writings of key thinkers such as Marx, Durkheim, Weber and Simmel. What then, did these 'founding fathers' have to say about the human body and emotions?

Marx's work, as Turner (1984) notes, is a constant reminder that, in order to exist, (capitalist) societies depend upon the continual (re)production of bodies across time and their allocation in social space. From this perspective, bodies become both the *means* and the *object* of human labour. For Marx, universal human nature is related to the fact that men, in the generic sense of the word, labour collectively on nature in order to satisfy their (organic) needs. In doing so, they thereby transform themselves into practical, conscious, sensuous agents (Turner 1984). Whilst nature exists as an independent reality, it is constantly appropriated and transformed through human labour and social praxis. Consequently, nature itself becomes a human product as the inorganic body of nature fuses with the organic body of the labourer. This is perhaps nowhere more clearly captured than in the following passage from Marx's 1844 *Economic and Philosophical Manuscripts*:

> The universality of man is in practice manifested precisely in the universality which makes all nature his (sic) inorganic body – nature, that is, in so far as it is not itself the human body. Man lives on nature – means that nature is his body, with which he must remain in continuous intercourse if he is not to die. That man's physical and spiritual life is linked to nature means simply that nature is linked to itself, for man is part of nature.
>
> (Marx 1959[1884]: 74)

Here, the convergence with philosophical anthropology is readily apparent. Man, as an 'unfinished creature', relates to the world on the basis of (organic) human need and the transformative potential of embodied social praxis. In doing so, Men, as social beings who enter into definite social relations of production with others, thereby 'complete' themselves. Marx's concern with social praxis and the dialectic arose from a critical reading of Feuerbach's sensualist materialism. Unfortunately, however, his commitment to historical materialism meant that ultimately Marx lost much of Feuerbach's original emphasis upon the sensual and emotional aspects of embodied human being (Turner 1984). None the less, Marx's views on capitalist bodies and the transformative potential of social praxis remain an important foundation upon which to build a truly sociological approach to embodied human agency within the material, social, political and economic world.

Perhaps the most direct and obvious illustration of the links between capitalism and the body, however, comes not from Marx, but from his lifelong friend and associate Engels. In a bold statement Engels likens *The Conditions of the Working Class in England* (1987/[1845]) to 'social murder' by the bourgeoisie. The combination of poor sanitary and environmental conditions, together with poor nutrition and long, arduous, health-risking forms of labour, resulted in a general 'enfeeblement' of the working-class body, which aged prematurely and died early. In Liverpool, for instance, in 1840, the average life span of the upper classes, gentry and professional men was 35 years; that of the business men and better-placed handicraftsmen, 22 years; and that of the operatives, day-labourers and serviceable class in general, just 15 years. As Engels points out, these chilling statistics were not uncommon. Indeed, Chadwick's *The Sanitary Conditions of the Labouring Population of Great Britain: Report 1842* (1965) contained a wealth of similar facts and figures.

In addition to sanitary and environmental conditions, Engels also provides graphic evidence of the bodily insults and injuries which capitalism inflicted upon the proletariat classes through poor working conditions and long arduous hours of repetitive work and laborious toil. For example, the lungs, hearts and digestive organs of men, women and children who worked in the mines were irrevocably damaged. Similarly, factory work had a number of detrimental consequences to the working-class body. In mill hands, for instance, malformations of the spine were common, some consequent upon mere overwork, others due to the effect of long work upon constitutions already feeble or weakened by bad food. Other common complaints and physical deformities included knees bent inwards and backwards, deformities and thickening of the ankles, bending of the spinal column either forward or to one side, flattening of the foot, pain in the back, hips and legs, swollen joints, varicose veins and large, persistent ulcers in the thighs and calves – conditions which were 'almost universal' amongst the operatives. As a consequence, most men were unfit for work by the age of 40, a few holding out until 45, with almost none by the age of 50 (Engels 1987 [1845]: 174–9).

The influence of factory work upon the female physique was also marked. Here, protracted work frequently led to deformities of the pelvis, partly through abnormal development of the hip bones and partly through malformations of the lower position of the spinal column. Consequently, female factory workers were more likely to suffer miscarriages or to undergo difficult confinements. Indeed, many pregnant women continued to labour up until the hour of birth for fear of lost earnings or a loss of employment, and the case was none too rare of children being delivered in the factory amongst the machinery. Children, too, were made to work long hours amongst dangerous machinery, thus giving rise to a 'multitude of accidents'. All in all:

> A pretty list of diseases engendered purely by the hateful greed of the manufacturers! Women made unfit for childbearing, children deformed, men enfeebled, limbs crushed, whole generations wrecked, afflicted with disease and infirmity, purely to fill the purses of the bourgeoisie.
> (Engels 1987 [1845]: 183–4)

Durkheim, too, paid greater attention to bodily matters than might first appear. Certainly his emphasis upon 'social facts' and society as a reality *sui generis* would seem, at first sight, to negate any such interest. Nevertheless, in an insightful essay entitled: 'The dualism of human nature and its social conditions', Durkheim does explicitly consider the nature of the human body and soul, their relationship to one another, and to the sacred and profane. As he states in classic Platonic style:

> It can even be said that although the body and soul are closely associated they do not belong to the same world. *The body is an integral part of the material universe as it is made known to us by sensory experience; the abode of the soul is elsewhere, and the soul tends ceaselessly to return to it. This abode is the world of the sacred.* Therefore, the soul is invested with a dignity that has always been denied the body which is considered essentially profane, and it inspires those feelings that are elsewhere reserved for that which is

divine. It is made of the same substance as are the sacred beings: it differs from them only in degree.

(Durkheim 1960 [1914]: 326, our emphasis)

The dual nature of human beings, what Durkheim refers to as *homo duplex*, stems directly from these fundamental divisions of body and soul, sacred and profane. Indeed, for Durkheim, our inner life had something like a 'double centre of gravity'. From this perspective, a 'true antagonism' exists between, on the one hand, our individuality and the body in which it is based, and, on the other, everything in us which expresses something over and above ourselves. The result, for Durkheim, was that we are never completely at peace with ourselves, for we cannot follow one of our two natures – one rooted in morality, the other in the instincts and penchants of the body – without throwing the other one out of kilter. Our 'joys', in other words, can 'never be pure' (Durkheim 1960 [1914]: 328–30). The traditional division of body and soul is, therefore, no mere flight of fancy for Durkheim. Rather, we are the direct realisation of this fundamental antinomy. Indeed, in a manner directly echoing Freud, Durkheim predicted that the struggle between these 'two beings' would increase rather than decrease with the growth of civilisation: the rationalist Enlightenment project, in short, will never achieve total control over the 'extra-rational' senses and sensualities of embodied human beings.[4]

If the body is central to Marx's and Engels's work, yet ambiguous for Durkheim, it certainly does not require too much re-writing to bring it 'back in' to Weberian sociology. *The Protestant Ethic and the Spirit of Capitalism*, for example, is predicated upon the notion of the ascetic body in which the pleasures of the flesh are denied through thrift and hard work in one's 'calling' as a sign of God's grace. Certainly, as Weber shows, Protestant writings at this time were dominated by the continual, passionately preached, virtues of hard work and unrelenting mental and physical labour (Weber 1974: 158). Here, loss of time through sociability, idle talk or luxury was considered worthy of utter condemnation. Indeed, every hour wasted was considered labour lost for the glory of God. In this respect, the denials of the flesh and the sexual asceticism of Puritanism differed in degree only, not in principle, from that of monasticism:

> Sexual intercourse is permitted, even within marriage, only as the means willed by God for the increase of His glory according to the commandment 'Be fruitful and multiply'. Along with moderate vegetable diet and cold baths, the same prescription is given for sexual temptations as is used against religious doubts and a sense of moral unworthiness: 'Work hard in your calling'.
>
> (Weber 1974: 158–9)

Whilst it was acceptable to labour to be rich for God, one could not do so for the flesh or sin. Asceticism therefore turned with all its force against one thing: the spontaneous enjoyment of life and all it had to offer. For Weber, this religious valuation of relentless work in a worldly calling as the surest proof of genuine faith and spiritual salvation, served as the most 'powerful conceivable lever' for the expansion of that attitude toward life he termed the 'spirit of capitalism' (Weber 1974: 172).

Once capitalism developed, however, its prioritisation of formal ratio-nality left little room for human feelings and sentiments. Capitalism, both past and present, requires the rational management and control of the body and emotions: if and when the latter are experienced, they are to be kept in private spheres of the individual's life or else manipulated for commercial ends (see Chapter 7). This, in turn, contributes to the 'disenchantment' of the modern Western world as rationality infuses organisations, bureaucracies, and the routinised structures of everyday life.

As Turner (1992) rightly argues, there are important points of theoretical convergence here between Weber's analysis of the rationalisation and Foucault's work on disciplinary technologies of power/knowledge. Certainly, it is clear that much of Weber's writing is about the rationalisation of bodies across time and space and the management of emotions; even religion and emotionality were subject to the pressures of rationality and science (Weber 1948: 286–97). Bureaucracies, for example, are embodied institutions, predi-cated on the rational control of official as well as 'client' bodies and emotions. Certainly the rationale of most, if not all, state bureaucracies, is ultimately to do with the surveillance and control of individual and collective social bodies. In this sense, bureaucratic bodies both derive from and give organisa-tional expression to the formally encoded rules and official hierarchies which characterise this rational, ideal–typical, complex (Morgan and Scott 1993: 16; see also, Albrow 1992). The more capitalism infuses itself in bureaucratic structures, the more 'dehumanising' it becomes, and the more 'disenchanted' the modern individual feels, locked in its 'iron cage'.

Moving from Weber to Simmel, it is clear that he too had much to say about bodies, particularly the senses and human emotionality. Public order, based as it is on the mutual exchange of expressive gestures, is bodily through and through for Simmel (Denzin 1984: 38). Of all the special sense organs, it is the eye, Simmel stresses, which has a uniquely sociological function.[5] The union and interaction of individuals is based upon the mutual exchange of glances which is perhaps the most direct and purest social reciprocity of all:

> By the glance which reveals the other, one discloses himself. . . . The eye of a person discloses his own soul when he seeks to uncover that of another. What occurs in this direct mutual glance represents the most perfect reciprocity in the entire field of human relationships.
>
> (Simmel 1969: 358)

In stressing this view, Simmel links the sociological significance of the eye to the expression of the face as the first object of vision between two individuals. Whilst the eye discloses the soul, the face is the depository of past experience and the embodiment of personal meaning, crystallised into permanent features. From this position, Simmel goes on to argue that a greater perplexity characterises the person who only sees, as opposed to one who only hears, and that social life in the large city (i.e. the metropolis), as compared with towns or rural settings, shows a greater preponderance of occasions to see rather than to hear people. In doing so, Simmel confronts the heart of the problem of modern social life, namely, 'the lack of orientation in the collective life, the sense of utter lonesomeness, and the feeling that the individual is surrounded on all sides by closed doors' (Simmel 1969: 361).[6]

Finally, bodily themes were also, of course, central to Spencer's sociology; in particular his 'evolutionary biologism' and organic analogy of society. Whilst Spencer continued to shuttle back and forth between organic and 'super-organic' bodies (i.e. social systems) in his analysis of structural differentiation (J. H. Turner 1985), it was left to Parsons to push these organic analogies to their ultimate functionalist conclusions. For Parsons, however, the body is treated simply as a behavioural system or biological organism which performs the (A) adaptive function, thereby erecting a rigid distinction between this and the other components of this general action system (i.e. the personality system (Goal), the cultural system (Latency), and the social system (Integrative)). As such, despite or perhaps because of his abiding interest in biology, Parsons's treatment of the organism and its relationship to the other components of his general action system, provides an inadequate basis from which to develop a truly sociological approach to human embodiment (Turner 1984).[7]

To summarise, even the briefest exegesis of classical sociology serves to highlight the wealth of bodily insights which can be mined from the writings of the so-called 'founding fathers' of the discipline. Seen in these terms, classical sociological themes such as stratification, the sacred and the profane, rationality, bureaucracy, and human sociability, may fruitfully inform the sociology of the body, just as the sociology of the body can 'breathe new life' into these classical sociological themes.

Ferment and change: recent developments in the sociology of the body

As we have argued, a great deal can be learnt about the body and society through a critical re-reading of both classical and contemporary sociological literature. Given this fact, what really needs to be asked is why the sudden 'explosion of interest' in bodily matters at the end of the twentieth century – 'why bodies', 'why now'? – and where do the most promising lines of current and future development in these corporeal debates lie? Reasons for this reversal of corporeal fortunes are now well-rehearsed – from long-standing debates in feminism to the growth of consumer culture, and from shifting demographic patterns (i.e. the burden of chronic illness and the 'greying' of the Western population) to the advent of postmodernism and the 'crisis of meaning' surrounding the body, both inside and outside the academy (Shilling 1993).[8]

It is not, however, our intention to repeat these arguments again here. Suffice it to say that a plethora of recent publications can be cited as confirmation of this trend, from Turner's (1984) landmark book *Body and Society*, now into its second edition (1996), to Shilling's (1993) *The Body and Social Theory*, Falk's (1994) *Consuming Body* and Martin's (1994) *Flexible Bodies*.[9] In addition, 1995 also marked the foundation of a new journal *Body & Society*, edited by Featherstone and Turner, designed to cater for this recent upsurge of interest in the social and cultural analysis of the human body. If we add to this growing 'corpus' the writings of Foucault (1977, 1979, 1980, 1987, 1988a,b) on the 'discursive body' and 'technologies of the self', Merleau-Ponty (1962, 1963, 1965, 1968) on the 'phenomenological' body, and Baudrillard (1983a,b, 1988) on the 'hyperreal' body, one can readily appreciate this recent burgeoning interest in bodily matters within contemporary sociology.

Despite this growth of interest, including recent attempts toward analytic integration (Turner 1984, 1992; Frank 1991a; Falk 1994), we do not, as yet, have a general theoretical framework within which to satisfactorily address the broad range of ontological and epistemological questions surrounding the body and its relationship to the broader sociocultural and historical order. Rather, as suggested earlier, the body remains as elusive, if not elusory (Radley 1995), as ever. Some theoretical perspectives, indeed, are premised upon just such a view. Alongside a sustained critique of the dualist legacies of the past, one of the central aims of this book is to go some way towards meeting this analytical challenge through an approach which combines what Turner (1992) usefully refers to as a foundationalist ontology (i.e. an 'organic', pre-social, body as a material entity which exists beyond discourse) and a social constructionist epistemology (i.e. the body as a product of power/knowledge), via a number of conceptual 'links' between different levels of corporeal analysis.

For the moment, however, it is to a preliminary consideration and selective review of certain key areas where, in our view, recent explorations of the body or related issues are proving most promising, that we now turn. In doing so, we hope to convey something of the thriving culture of body-oriented discourse both within and outside the sociological domain. Perhaps the first of these issues concerns the 'problem' of biology. Whilst the 'limits' of sociobiological explanations are now well recognised,[10] there have in recent years – partly in response to the 'worst excesses' of postmodernism and its 'writing in/out' of the body – been a growing number of calls or attempts to rethink the biological in non-reductionist terms. Benton (1991), for example, suggests that new ways of understanding science and its relationship to culture, alternative ways of philosophically ordering scientific knowledge, and newly influential social movements – from ecology to animal rights – have all combined in recent years to facilitate or compel new ways of thinking about biology and the human sciences. The choices, as he states:

no longer have to be seen (in reality they never did) as limited to an intellectual imperialist, politically conservative biological reductionism, on the one hand and an idealist or dualist anthropocentrism, on the other. The state of biological science is fluid, *there are numerous competing conceptualisations within biology, and there are several well-articulated alternatives to reductionist materialism available for use as philosophical means in the attempt to re-think the biology/social relationship.*

(Benton 1991: 18, our emphasis)

Seen in these terms, existing networks of conceptual oppositions such as mind/body, culture/nature, society/biology, reason/emotion, object/subject, human/animal, meaning/cause, are beginning to be seen as 'intellectual obstacles' in the way of meeting these challenges. As such, we may indeed need to give the biological an, albeit cautious, 'welcome back in': a re-alignment which in no way implies 'reductionism' or a defence of 'genetic determinism' (Benton 1991).

These views, in turn, have more recently been endorsed by Archer (1995) who, in her morphogenetic approach, draws on the work of writers such as Bhaskar (1989) and Sayer (1992) in order to develop a realist social theory. Human beings, as she notes, must have a particular physical constitution for social influences to consistently 'do their work', so to speak (as in learning, tool making, and use, etc.). The human hand, for example, is a remarkable example of evolutionary engineering: a single tool which manipulates an astonishing variety of objects of different shapes, weights and sizes, each of which needs a precise combination of muscle tensions that mould it into the right shape for the 'task-in-hand' (Pinker 1998; Turner 1992). Even in those cases where human biology is 'mediated' in almost every way, 'this does not mean that the mediated is not biological nor that the physical becomes epiphenomenal'. Seen in these terms, 'sociobiology can make valid points, without over-reaching itself if the realist principles of stratification and emergence are respected' (Archer 1995: 288).[11]

Discussion of these biological questions and the realist issues they raise, in turn, leads us into the second major area where recent corporeal developments are proving particularly promising. As we argue in Chapter 6, feminist scholarship, taken as a whole, constitutes one of the most sustained and systematic attempts to take 'gendered' embodiment and the problem of sexual 'difference' seriously – a concern which, it should be stressed, predates the recent 'faddish' interest in body matters. In particular, femin*isms* have 'problematised' the body through critical debates over the nature of gender, sexuality and sexual 'difference'. In doing so, feminists have pointed to the multiple ways in which women's bodies, past and present, are implicated in social relations of inequality, domination and oppression: thereby 'destabilising' male-stream social theory and its seemingly rigid and reified conceptual forms. Post-structuralist feminists, for example, drawing critically on the work of Foucault and others, have sought to question the notion of power/knowledge operating 'externally' upon a pre-figured or pre-social body, preferring instead to see it as 'constitutive' of 'sex', gender and subjectivity (Butler 1990, 1993a; Sawicki 1991; Diamond and Quinby 1988). This, in turn, has inspired many subsequent approaches to the historical (re-)making of 'sexed' bodies, from the Greeks to Freud (Lacquer 1987, 1990). Others, however, have chosen to question the determinative power of discourse, arguing instead for a feminist 'body/politics' which allows women to challenge prevailing representations of the body through processes of 'resistance' and 're-inscription' in less 'alienating' terms (Jacobus *et al.* 1990).

More recently, however, the male body has become increasingly prominent as an explicit topic of investigation for theorists and empirical researchers alike. Certainly, from what has been said above, it is clear that feminist scholarship, whilst by and for women, has never simply been about women to the exclusion of men. None the less, the explicit focus on men in recent years has, as Morgan (1993) notes, enabled at least three basic assumptions to be challenged, namely: the tendency to see men and masculinity as '*the*' body; the tendency to deny or undertheorise men's bodies; and the tendency to see men and masculinity as separate, such as 'minds' using 'bodies'. Underlying these issues is a broader commitment to counter the dangers of reification, essentialism and reductionism when using terms such as 'men' and 'women', 'masculinity' and 'femininity'.[12] Preliminary theoretical moves in this respect have been to argue that terms such as 'men' and 'masculinity' are socially constructed entities and that there needs to be a *pluralisation* of terminology such that we speak of 'masculinit*ies*' rather than 'masculinity' (Hearn and Morgan 1990a: 8–10).

Alongside an abiding concern with the 'crisis' of masculinity and the problems of male 'body-image', an important line of research here has been to focus on the relationship between sexuality, power and 'hegemonic' forms of masculinity. Drawing upon Gramsci's use of the concept, the notion of hegemonic masculinities serves to highlight the dominance within any given society of certain forms and practices of masculinity, including particular forms of (il)legitimate bodily deployment and physical aggression, which in turn are historically conditioned and open to change (i.e. white, heterosexual, middle-class, Anglophone, etc.) (Connell 1995, 1987). As this suggests, within patriarchal societies, men as well as women, children and 'other' groups may be subordinated, marginalised and stigmatised in relation to these dominant forms of masculinity as a consequence of their sexuality, class position, religious affiliation or marital status. Homophobia, for example, is a vital component of heterosexual masculinity (Herek 1987). In particular, the interplay between hegemonic and subordinate masculinities suggests the experience of masculinity is far from uniform and that new ways of theorising these differences need to be developed (Hearn and Morgan 1990a: 11).

This, in turn, draws attention to the fact that there are many ways, just as there are many sites, where gender, power and the body intersect and interact. Consequently, it cannot, as Morgan (1993) argues, simply and unproblematically be maintained that women are more embodied than men or *vice versa*. Rather, the relationships between men, women and embodiment are different in character rather than degree, and this 'difference' lies in the 'complex interplay and triangular relationship between gender, power and embodiment' across differing social sites and locations, and not in terms of any 'simple, straightforward notions of physiological determination' (Morgan 1993: 84).

To these developments, both within and outside feminism and sociology, we may also add the recent more interdisciplinary focus of 'queer theory' (Burston and Richardson 1995). Drawing from the critique of unitary identity politics by people of colour and sex rebels, queer theory – though often indistinguishable from social constructionist perspectives on sexuality – has sought to shift the debate away somewhat from an exclusive emphasis on homosexuality to a focus on heterosexuality as a 'social and political organising principle', and from a politics of minority interest to a politics of 'knowledge and difference' (Seidman 1995). In doing so, the emphasis has been firmly placed on 'identities which are always multiple, or at best composites, with an infinite number of ways in which "identity-components" can intersect and combine' (Seidman 1996: 6). In this way, new opportunities and alliances have 'opened up', not simply surrounding questions of sexual identity and the celebration of 'perverse' desire (Grosz 1995; Grosz and Probyn 1995), but also in terms of the relationship between queer theory and sociology.[13]

Running parallel, and to a certain extent overlapping with these corporeal developments in gender studies, has been a third promising strand of recent work centred, implicitly or explicitly, on body matters, namely; the increasing focus on children and the sociocultural construction of childhood (James 1993; James and Prout 1990; Aries 1976). Certainly, as suggested in the introduction to this book, the sociology of childhood is an important site from which to theorise the body, particularly as a biologically and socially 'unfinished' entity. However, it is only relatively recently that sociologists of childhood have begun to appreciate the importance of embodiment to the processes through which children actively participate in social life (James *et al.* 1998; Mayall 1996; Hill and Tidsall 1997). Prout (1998), for example, drawing upon actor-network theory and the sociology of translation, sees childhoods and bodies as constructed not only from human minds and their interactions, not only from human bodies and their interactions, but also through an unending, mutually constituting interaction of a vast array of material and non-material resources. Examining childhood bodies in this way, he suggests, becomes a matter of tracing through the means, the varied materials and practices (both discursive and non-discursive) involved in their construction and maintenance – as well as their potential unravelling and dissolution. The emphasis here is on children as active creators of social life rather than powerless products of society, and on childhood itself as something full of 'reversals', 'transformations' and 'inversions', rather than being a progression towards an 'ever closer copy' of adulthood (Prout 1998). Attention to children's bodies, therefore, constitutes a 'critical test case' and promising line of future development in evolving sociological debates on the nature and status of human embodiment: an issue to which we shall return in the concluding chapter of this book.

Perhaps the fourth key area in which corporeal issues are increasingly coming to the fore concerns the sociology of sport: an arena in which the machine-like body, as a fine-tuned reified product of ever more complex equipment and training techniques, is a central concern (Brohm 1978). In particular, writers such as Bourdieu (1978, 1984) have systematically addressed the relationship between the body, sport and social class, including the structure and dynamics of sporting fields.[14] The body, as Blake (1997) notes, is continually being reconstituted and reshaped through the rules and technologies of sports performance, and through the apparatuses of sporting consumption. What then, he asks rhetorically, are the implications for the public world of sport of:

> an increasingly cybernetic sporting elite, reliant for competitive success on the external design technologies of sports clothing and machinery, and internally on the artificial reconstructions of minds and bodies produced by drugs, genetic programming, microsurgery and even microcircuitry?
>
> (Blake 1997: 162)

Answers to such questions clearly lie in the future. What they do suggest, however, is that the 'rules of the game', including the very nature of 'sporting bodies' and the meaning of 'competition', are likely to change in the increasingly 'cyborg-driven' world of sport. Building on these developments, sociologists have also been interested in the various ways in which sport provides opportunities for spectators as well as participants to spontaneously 'lose their bodies'. In this respect, the quest for excitement and intensity of involvement in sporting events, facilitates what Elias and Dunning (1986) have usefully termed a 'controlled de-controlling of the emotions', and a blurring of the boundaries between individual and collective bodies.[15]

Another promising line of development here has been the examination of young people's own constructions of their bodies and identities in and around physical education lessons and the science curriculum. Certainly school provides a key site for the disciplining, normalisation and control of children and young people's bodies (Kirk 1993; Shilling 1991). Until recently, however, sociologists have tended to neglect the role of physical education lessons in these vital processes. As Kirk and Tinning (1994) argue, in physical education classes, physical culture is instantiated in a most immediate, visible and visceral fashion. More precisely, engagement with physical tasks in physical education, itself a key site of health promotion, exposes the adolescent body and thus places self-identity at risk. As a consequence, many young people, particularly girls, experience varying degrees of estrangement or disembodiment both in their physical education lessons and other encounters with popular physical culture as a strategy for protecting or defending their self-identities. The upshot of these processes, as Kirk and Tinning suggest, is that many young people are hindered in appropriating the resources of popular physical culture in order to lead healthy, active, lives.[16]

This, in turn, leads us nicely into the fifth major area in which corporeal themes and issues are currently being profitably addressed, namely, the sociology of health and illness. Far from being merely a matter of personal significance to an 'ageing' sociology profession, bodies constitute the 'staple diet' of medical sociologists, young or old, fit or frail. Medical sociology, in other words, is a particularly fertile terrain upon which to explore the ontological status of the body, dealing as it does with key aspects of human embodiment. Indeed, from social constructionist accounts of medical knowledge and the metaphorical nature of disease, to social inequalities in health and the phenomenology of pain and suffering, sickness, disability and death, the body has been an implicit, if not explicit, theme in medical sociology. In addition, medical sociologists have also been instrumental in highlighting the intersections between health, risk and consumption, the medicalisation, surveillance and control of (women's) bodies, the dilemmas of high-technology medicine, and the gendered/emotional division of labour in health care.[17] In doing so, the sociology of health and illness again raises in acute form the ambiguous status of the body in relation to traditional nature/culture, biology/society divisions. In these and many other ways, in short, medical sociology is proving to be central to the theoretical and empirical elaboration of the relationship between body, self and society. Indeed, as Turner (1992) boldly proclaims, medical sociology may, given these corporeal trends, prove to be the 'leading edge' of contemporary social theory.

Overlapping with these developments, perhaps the last main arena in which corporeal matters are being given the proper 'airing' they deserve, concerns the dilemmas of technology. On the one hand, as we shall see in Chapter 4, a broad range of technological advances, from organ transplantation surgery to the Human Genome Project, plastic surgery to virtual medicine (Davis 1994; Waldby 1997) mean that our ability to 'control' the human body continues to grow exponentially (Williams 1997). Indeed, there are now few parts of the human body which modern technology cannot reconstruct or reconstitute in some way or other. Moreover, as a recent television documentary entitled 'Test-tube bodies' suggests, 'cutting edge' scientific and medical research is now involved in the growth and cultivation of new human tissue, organs and other body parts such as the ear. Here we return, *par excellence*, to the age-old Cartesian view of the body as a 'faulty machine': albeit one which, this time, can be fine-tuned and reconstructed in a myriad of technologically sophisticated ways. On the other hand, however, it is these very processes of control which have served to reduce our certainty of what the body is, what it can become, and where precisely the boundaries between one body and another lie (Shilling 1993; Turner 1996 [1984]).

This, in turn, keys into the 'birth of the cyborg' (Haraway 1991) and the advent of new forms of computer technology, including virtual reality and digitalised cyberspace. Here, in this glittering world of computerised sights and sounds, what Heim (1991) refers to as the 'erotic ontology' of cyberspace, postmodern minds, it is claimed, cease to be anchored in fleshy modernist bodies as new forms of community, social bonds, trust and emotional intimacy, including the advent of so-called 'cybersex', begin to emerge. According to this line of reasoning, bodies and bodily contact, in the shadow of AIDS, become 'optional' as the 'virtual' body reveals as much or as little of ourselves as we wish to disclose (Stone 1991). For some this constitutes the ultimate Platonic dream, for others, however, a chilling Baudrillardian nightmare of monstrous proportions; one which ultimately results in an evasion of our responsibilities in the 'real' world (Slouka 1995; Williams 1998a; see Chapter 4, this volume).

In drawing the diverse themes of this chapter together, one crucial issue remains to be addressed, namely: the theoretical tension between what, broadly speaking, might be termed a sociology *of* the body on the one hand, and an *embodied* sociology on the other: a distinction, as noted in the introduction to the book, which resonates with that between a 'sociology of postmodernity' and a 'postmodern sociology' (Bauman 1992a). Whilst the former translates, in corporeal terms, into a treatment of the body as simply one amongst many topics which sociologists can study from 'outside' so to speak, the latter, in contrast, refuses to slip into this deceptive Cartesian view of the world – one which treats mind and body as distinctly separate entities – taking the embodiment of its practitioners as well as its subjects seriously through a commitment to the lived body and its being in the world, including the manner in which it both shapes and is shaped by society. From sleep to death, pain to emotions, this book, we hope, is contribution to the latter enterprise.

Conclusions

In this chapter we have preliminarily reviewed a critical selection of corporeal themes and issues pertaining to the nature and status of the body in both classical and contemporary sociology. As we have argued, despite a largely 'secret *his*tory', it is none the less possible to 'recover' the body through a critical re-reading in corporeal terms of classical sociological thinkers such as Marx, Weber, Durkheim and Simmel. To be sure, one of the prime reasons for this relative neglect of the body in the past has been the 'spectre of biologism' and the fear of reductionism. However, in contrast to these past trends, the body has recently enjoyed a reversal of fortunes. Reasons for this upsurge of interest, as we have seen, include feminist critiques of 'sex' and 'gender', the dilemmas of masculinity, the rise of the (postmodern) body in consumer culture, shifting demographic trends, and finally, the so-called 'crisis of meaning' surrounding the body in an increasingly technological, digitalised age: themes to which we shall return in subsequent chapters.

As regards recent lines of corporeal development, six in particular appear most promising: the 're-thinking' of the biological in non-reductionist terms; the focus on men's as well as women's bodies; the sociology of children and childhood; work centred around sport and the changing nature of 'sporting bodies'; the sociology of health and illness; and finally, the dilemmas of technology, including the advent of so-called cyberspace. In this respect, we have advocated an approach to these corporeal challenges which is less about a sociology *of* the body than it is an *embodied* sociology: one which takes the embodiment of its practitioners as well as its subjects seriously, rooted as it is in the 'lived' body. Despite this promising start, however, much still remains to be done in order to fully develop such an approach; one which not only overturns the dualist legacies of the past, but also satisfactorily addresses the relationship between bodily 'order' and 'control'. It is to a critical exploration of this core sociological problematic that the next two chapters are devoted.

2 Bodily 'order'

Cultural and historical perspectives on conformity and transgression

Introduction

In a now classic paper, Dawe (1971) explores what he sees to be the two main alternative sociological traditions to the question of society, both of which emerged from a reaction to the Enlightenment. The first takes as its problem the establishment of *order* and asserts the ontological primacy of social systems over social actors. To the extent that individual intention is theorised, it is said to derive from the central societal value system. Within this paradigm, the spectre of the 'over-socialised' conception of 'man' looms large (Wrong 1961). The second tradition, in contrast, is premised on the alternative notion of 'autonomous man' and takes as its problematic the libertarian question of how humankind can assert *control* over the institutions it creates. Thus a vocabulary of social action, will and agency follow: society is the creation of its members, not an abstract, reified, reality *sui generis*.

Underpinning these issues are deeper corporeal questions concerning the relationship between the body and society. Whilst social 'order' is ultimately concerned with the regulation and restraint of individual and collective bodies across time and space, social 'control', on the other hand, is premised upon the alternative problematic of bodily *use* and the embodiment of social action. In this chapter, we take a closer look at these issues through the notion of bodily order and the related problem of corporeal 'transgression'. In doing so, we examine a selection of key thinkers who, from different vantage points, have taken the problems of bodily order and corporeal transgression as their implicit, if not explicit, starting point. These include Hertz and Douglas on the symbolic aspects of bodily order, Foucault on disciplinary technologies of power/knowledge, and Elias on the 'civilised' body. In addition, we also consider Turner's analysis of 'bodily order', together with Falk's recent attempt to theorise corporeality as a transgressive mode of bodily being; one which is endlessly elaborated through the broader socio-cultural order. Seen in these terms, bodily order and corporeal transgression are intimately related. Hence it is to the first of these issues, the 'symbolic' body, that we now turn.

The 'symbolic' body

One of the main ways in which bodies are socially ordered, sorted and segregated is through the use of ritual and symbolism. Indeed, this constitutes one of the primary routes to the 'completion' of the body within the broader sociocultural order. Whilst the central concern here is with issues of *representation* rather than *experience*, symbolic approaches to the human body none the less provide a powerful means of grasping its socially constructed nature as a 'natural symbol' of society. In particular, anthropologists have drawn attention to the manner in which bodies are 'good to think with', ritually transforming and symbolically resolving dangers, threats and risks within the broader body politic.

An early exploration of these issues in relation to the sacred/profane distinction is to be found in the work of Durkheim's nephew, Robert Hertz. In *Death and the Right Hand* (1960 [1909]), Hertz considered the question of 'handedness', or more precisely, the extent to which the universal predominance of right-handedness is biologically or socially determined, concluding that it was in fact a product of both physical and cultural factors. Whilst, for Hertz, there was no reason to deny the organic basis of body asymmetry, these vague dispositions to right-handedness could not account for the absolute preponderance of the right hand if this were not reinforced or fixed by other influences which were extraneous to the organism itself.

Although Hertz's approach rejected the either/or of biological and sociological approaches to the human body, it is none the less clear that his approach followed the tradition set by Durkheim and Mauss (1975 [1902]) on primitive systems of classification. Seen in these terms, the predominance of the right hand is a social fact; one which expresses the traditional division of the world into the sacred and profane. As Hertz states:

> How could man's body, the microcosm, escape the law of polarity which governs everything? Society, and the whole universe have a side which is sacred, noble, precious, and another which is profane and common: a male side, strong and active, and another, female, weak and passive; or, in two words, a right and a left side.
>
> (Hertz 1960 [1909]: 98)

Despite Hertz's seminal contribution to the problem of body symbolism, it is Douglas who, perhaps more than anyone else, has done most to demonstrate the symbolic properties of the body, including its orifices, pollution and waste. For Douglas:

> The social body constrains the way in which the physical body is perceived, and the physical experience of the body, which itself is always mediated and modified through the social categories with which it is known, sustains a particular view of society. There is a continual exchange of meanings between the two kinds of bodily experience so

that each reinforces the other. The forms it adopts in movement and repose express social pressures in manifold ways. The care that is given to it, in grooming, feeding and therapy, the theories about what it needs in the way of sleep and exercise, about the stages it should go through, the pains it can stand, its span of life, all the cultural categories in which it is perceived, must correlate closely with the categories in which society is seen in so far as these also draw upon the same culturally processed idea of the body.

(Douglas 1970: 65).

This leads Douglas to argue that everything, in fact, symbolises the body, and that the body symbolises everything else. Indeed, the body is a model which can stand for any bounded system and its boundaries can represent any boundaries which become threatened or endangered. Whenever the boundaries of a social collectivity or people are threatened, these anxieties are mirrored in the degree of care exercised over the physical body. In contrast, if there is no concern to control social boundaries, then there is unlikely to be a concern to control bodily boundaries. Seen in these terms, the powers and dangers accredited to social structure are reproduced in small upon the human body.

Any structure of ideas, Douglas argues, is vulnerable at its margins. 'Dirt', for example, as a cultural category, exerts pressure at socially defined and ritually proscribed boundaries and margins. Similarly, bodily orifices, together with 'marginal' matter issuing from them, are potent symbols of power and danger, pollution and taboo (Grosz 1994). Simply by issuing forth, bodily fluids such as spittle, blood, milk, urine, faeces, sweat or tears have 'traversed the boundaries of the body'. Ideas about demarcating, separating and punishing transgression have, therefore, as their main function, the imposition of a system of symbolic order on what is in effect an inherently 'messy' or 'untidy' experience: symbolically (re)ordering this 'matter out of place' as means of ritually protecting the vulnerable margins and threatened borders of the broader body politic. Reflections on dirt and pollution, in other words, involve reflection on the relation of 'order to disorder, being to non-being, form to formlessness, life to death' (Douglas 1966: 6).

The implications of Douglas's analysis for our understanding of bodily symbolism and its relationship to the problems of social order and corporeal transgression are perhaps most clearly spelt out in her rather incongruous sounding paper: 'Do dogs laugh?: a cross cultural approach to body symbolism' (Douglas 1971). Here she argues that we have unduly privileged the spoken channel of communication and should see the body as an expressive medium of communication in its own right, distinct from, yet closely connected with words which emanate from the mouth. In particular, having argued that there is, in fact, a universal language of bodily interruptions and that human laughter is a unique form of communication, Douglas draws attention to the thresholds of tolerance concerning bodily relaxation, expression and control, and their intimate connection with the strength and permanence of social relations. Bodily expressions, in other words, are organised along a continuum from strong to weak control, according to whether social demands are strong or weak, acceptable or not. If general social controls are slack, then the thresholds for bodily expression and eruptions will be set higher. Conversely, if general social controls are strong, then the thresholds for bodily expression and eruptions will be set lower. The more tightly controlled and rigidly hierarchised a society or sub-cultural group, the more strictly defined and the less variable bodily responses and expressions are likely to be. Natural expression is, therefore, culturally determined, and bodily control, in turn, is an expression of social control.

The body, in short, provides a potent metaphor for social (dis)order; one which implies a reciprocal thinking of society through the body and the body through society. Seen in these terms, ritual works upon the body politic through the symbolic medium of the body (Douglas 1966: 129). Here fundamental categories such as the sacred and the profane, purity and danger, risk and taboo are thought and expressed through the reciprocal interplay between the physical and social body. This, in turn, points to the ambiguous nature of the body and its endless elaboration through the sociocultural and symbolic order of society. On the one hand, as a potent symbol of society, the human body is inherently 'ordered' and 'orderly'. On the other hand, however, bodily orifices, seepages and flows attest to a certain irreducible 'dirt', 'horror' or 'disgust'; something which not only befuddles cultural categories and trangresses the symbolic boundaries of the broader body politic, but also highlights the impossibility of the 'clean', the 'pure' and the 'proper' (Grosz 1994: 194). The symbolic ordering of the body is therefore double-edged, depending for its very existence upon the darker, transgressive, side of human corporeality. Bodies, in short, are Janus-faced: both sacred and profane, purity and danger, order and chaos.

Despite these useful insights on the body as a classificatory system and the symbolic basis of social order, these anthropological perspectives are not without their problems. In particular, in concentrating on the *representational* aspects of the body, there is a lack of attention to issues of *lived experience* and the problems of human embodiment. Relatedly, there is little regard for issues of social *praxis*, including the 'use' to which bodies are put in society and the learnt 'techniques' they draw upon in the conduct and negotiation of everyday life. Bodies, in short, appear relatively inert, *tabulae rasae*, upon which society stamps its indelible symbolic imprint. As we shall see below, similar problems are also encountered, albeit from a different epistemological vantage point, in Foucault's historical writings on power/knowledge and the 'discursive' body.

Power/knowledge and the 'discursive' body

For Foucault, the body occupies a central place in the strategic configuration, and historically contingent relations, of power/knowledge within society. Indeed, so central is the body to Foucault's epistemological project that he has described his work as constituting a: ' "history of bodies" and the manner in which what is most material and most vital to them has been invested' (Foucault 1979: 152). In particular, Foucault's genealogical analysis serves to highlight the location of the body within a political field of investment and power relations; one characterised by a substantive preoccupation with those 'carcereal' institutions which seek to discipline the body, thereby rendering it 'docile', productive and economically useful. Underlying this is an epistemological stance which views the body itself as a 'discursive' product of power/knowledge and shifting forms of political investment. These issues of power, epistemology and the body can be usefully grouped, for clarity of exposition, around two main themes: first, the 'regulation' of bodies, and second, the problem of 'resistance'.

Regulation

In *The Birth of the Clinic* (1973) Foucault documents the transformations which took place towards the end of the eighteenth century concerning the way in which medicine analysed, inscribed and read the body. In particular, he stresses how a new 'anatomical atlas' of the body began to emerge at this historical juncture; one which was 'read' through the 'clinical gaze' of the doctor and a new set of hospital-based methods which emphasised clinical observation, bedside teaching and physical examination for the 'clue' to disease (Armstrong 1983). The advent of this clinical gaze, together with developments in pathology, meant that diseases became localisable to specific organs and tissues rather than being seen, as before, in terms of more generalised disturbances of the patient's body. As a consequence, the patient's role in the diagnosis of disease diminished and the 'sick-man' disappeared from medical cosmology, dissipating at first into a 'clinical case', and later still, through the advent of laboratory medicine, into a 'complex of cells' (Jewson 1976). From this moment on, the deployment of medical techniques, including the introduction of the humble stethoscope in 1819 and the treatment of disease, drew out a particular anatomy of the clinical body. In short, new forms of knowledge (i.e. pathological medicine), served new social practices (i.e. clinical medicine), which, in turn, served to fabricate 'real' objects of study (i.e. the body of the patient) (Armstrong 1994).

As Foucault suggests, this analysis of the various ways in which the body is seen, described and constructed may profitably be termed 'political anatomy'. It is political because the changing ways in which the body has been viewed and described are not simply the product of some 'random effects' or 'progressive enlightenment', rather, they are based upon certain forms of knowledge and mechanisms of power which, since the eighteenth century, have served increasingly to penetrate and inscribe the body. Seen in these terms, medicine, far from standing outside social relations, is itself a moral and political enterprise (i.e. bio-power) concerned with the regulation, surveillance and control of bodies through the medical regimen: a situation both consolidated and extended in the twentieth century through the advent of 'biographical medicine' and the 'psycho-social' model of disease (Armstrong 1983).

These changes were not, however, simply confined to the hospital. Rather, as Foucault convincingly demonstrates, they occurred throughout European society towards the end of the eighteenth century. Thus, the view of the body as something 'docile', that could be surveyed, used and transformed, was increasingly evident not only in the clinical examination, but also in the school test, the factory, and the military inspection. It was also reflected in the changing regime of criminal punishment, which shifted from torture, pillorying and public display to the use of continuous surveillance behind the high walls of the prison, the epitome of which was Bentham's panopticon, a model which dispersed itself throughout society in the form of a 'carcereal network' (Foucault 1977). Thus, from the organisation of architectural space to the temporal ordering of individuals through the timetable, the body became increasingly surrounded and invested by various techniques and technologies of power which served to analyse, monitor and fabricate it in useful, productive ways. Together, these procedures served to ensure that the person under analysis was subject to detailed and continuous surveillance from the 'disembodied gaze' of an omniscient, omnipotent, omnipresent eye.

In analysing this shift from sovereign power – one in which the body of the king symbolised the concentration of a centralised power that was physically, sometimes brutally, inscribed upon its subjects – to the more pervasive system of disciplinary power, Foucault is able to highlight its *productive*, *constitutive* nature. As he explains, disciplinary power is a power which is 'given over to the classification, documentation and placement of individuals'; a power attuned to the 'minutest detail', one which places 'everyday behaviour, identities, seemingly unimportant gestures, under continuous forms of surveillance'; a power which is exercised 'regularly and evenly rather than spectacularly and unevenly in outbursts of force'; a power which is geared to the 'training and "dressage" of individuals'; a power which 'turns its subjects into objects of power/knowledge'; and a power which is 'not a property of pre-given individuals but permeates a large array of apparatuses' (Foucault 1977: 77–8). At the centre of disciplinary power/knowledge lies the notion of 'docility'; a term which joins the analysable body to the 'manipulable' body, a body that may be 'subjected, used, transformed and improved' through an ever finer net of surveillance, regulation and control (ibid.: 136).

These issues of power/knowledge and the discursive production of bodies are well illustrated in Foucault's three-volume study of the *History of Sexuality* (1979, 1987, 1988a). In the opening pages of volume one, Foucault begins by attacking the hitherto widely accepted 'repressive hypothesis', which depicts the history of European societies since the seventeenth century as one involving a series of restrictions, prohibitions, censorships and taboos upon the 'sexual' body. This conventional history of bodies and pleasures has, in turn, been incorporated into broader theories concerning the development of capitalism in which the repression of sexuality is viewed as a requirement of the capitalist mode of production and its class relations. In contrast, Foucault draws attention to the fact that:

> since the end of the sixteenth century, the 'putting into discourse of sex', far from undergoing a process of restriction, on the contrary has been subjected to mechanisms of increasing incitement; that the techniques of power exercised over sex have not obeyed a principle of rigorous selection, but rather one of dissemination and implantation of polymorphous sexualities; and that the will to knowledge has not come to a halt in the face of a taboo that must not be lifted, but has persisted in constituting – despite many mistakes, of course – a science of sexuality.
>
> (Foucault 1979: 11)

As this quotation suggests, what is at issue here is the overall discursive way in which sex is 'put into discourse'. In keeping with his general theoretical stance, Foucault's main concern here is to locate the forms of power, the channels it takes, and the discourses it permeates in order to reach the most 'tenuous and individual modes of behaviour'; the paths that allow it access to the 'rare or scarcely perceivable forms of desire'; the manner in which it 'penetrates and controls everyday pleasure', entailing effects which may not only 'refuse, block and invalidate', but also 'incite and intensify'; in short, the 'polymorphous techniques of power' (ibid.: 11). Here we see the productive nature of power/knowledge in all its resplendent glory. As a form of political investment, power/knowledge is never simply repressive, but also inherently creative.

In the nineteenth century, sexuality was increasingly constituted in scientific terms, the objective of which was to produce a true discourse on sex, the 'truth' of sex so to speak. At the centre of this *'scientia sexualis'* was a technique or procedure for producing the 'truth' of sex, namely the confession. As Foucault argues, from Christian penance to the psychoanalyst's couch, sex has been the central theme of the confession. Truth and sex were therefore joined, and from this a knowledge of the 'sexual subject' emerged. In particular, there was a shift in the object of discourse as the locus of sexuality began to move from the body to the mind, a shift in which people's intentions as well as their actions became the focus of inquiry. Paralleling this diffusion of disciplinary technologies of individualisation, Foucault argues that the technology of the confession spread out beyond its ritual Christian confines into a diverse range of social relations such as that between parent and child, teacher and pupil, psychiatrist and patient, and so on, the effect of which was the constitution of 'archives of truth' concerning sex which were inscribed in medical, psychiatric and pedagogical discourses (Smart 1985).

This intersection of the technology of the confession with scientific discourse constituted the domain of sexuality as 'problematic' and thus in need of interpretation, therapy and normalisation. In short, sex became not merely another object of power/knowledge, but the very secret and privileged locus of our being, our truth.

Associated with this production and proliferation of discourses on sex in the nineteenth century, Foucault identifies four great strategic unities which comprised mechanisms of power/knowledge centred upon sex and, as a corollary, the figures of four 'sexual subjects'. First, there was the 'hystericisation of women's bodies', the sexual subject of which, was of course, the hysterical woman; second, a pedagogisation of children's sex in which the sexual subject was the 'masturbating child'; third, a socialisation of procreative behaviour occurred in involving the 'Malthusian couple'; and finally, there was a psychiatrisation of perverse forms of pleasure which constituted the 'perverse adult' as its sexual subject. For Foucault, these four strategic unities did not regulate a pre-discursive realm of sexuality. Rather, they constituted an effective 'deployment' of sexuality on, over and within the bodies of men, women and children, and the fabrication of 'new' sexual subjectivities (Smart 1985). The deployment of sexuality therefore, as the very 'secret' and 'truth' of life itself, fabricates and extends the regulation, surveillance and control of bodies within the broader body politic (see also Mort 1987). As Foucault states, sex:

> was at the pivot of two axes along which developed the entire political technology of life. On the one hand it was tied to the *disciplines* of the body: the harnessing, intensification, and distribution of forces, the adjustment and economy of energies. On the other hand, it was applied to the *regulation* of populations, through all the far reaching effects of its activity. It fitted in both categories at once, giving rise to infinitesimal surveillances, permanent controls, extremely meticulous orderings of space, indeterminate medical or psychological examinations, to an entire micro-power concerned with the body. But it gave rise as well to comprehensive measures, statistical assessments and interventions aimed at the entire social body or at groups taken as a whole. Sex was the means of access both to the life of the body and the life of the species. It was employed as a standard for the disciplines and as a basis for regulations. . . . Spread out from one pole to the other of this technology of sex was a whole series of different tactics that combined in varying proportions the objective of disciplining the body and that of regulating populations.

> (Foucault 1979: 145–6)

Here we arrive at a general conclusion. The significance of sexuality for Foucault lies in the pivotal political role it plays in both the discipline of individual bodies and regulation of populations. On the one hand, we have an *'anatomo-politics'* of the body 'centred on the body as machine, its disciplining, the optimisation of its capabilities, the exhortion of its forces, the parallel increase in its usefulness and its docility, its integration into systems of efficient and economic controls'. On the other hand, we have the *'bio-politics* of the population' focused on the:

> species body, the body imbued with the mechanisms of life and serving as the basis of the biological processes; propagation, births and mortality, the level of health, life expectancy and longevity, with all the conditions that can cause these to vary.
>
> (ibid.: 139).

Foucault's earlier institutional analyses of the asylum, clinic and prison are therefore complemented by his later focus on the seemingly more personal, yet highly political, issues of sex, pleasure and power. Underlying this shift of focus, lies a deeper concern with the problems of 'resistance' to the 'normalising' powers which Foucault had earlier sought to chart. Hence it is to these issues of 'resistance' that we now turn.

Resistance

In his later writings Foucault became much more interested in the ways in which individuals act on their bodies, souls, thoughts and conduct, so as to 'transform themselves in order to attain a certain state of happiness, purity, wisdom, perfection, or immortality' (Foucault 1988b: 18). More precisely, it was through the formation of a 'critical ontology of self' that he thought it possible to formulate an alternative ethical standpoint of 'resistance' to the 'normalising' power and government of the individual. In this way, Foucault was able to develop the concepts of autonomy, reflexivity and critique as a means of overcoming some of the more negative implications of his earlier work on disciplinary technologies of power/knowledge and the production of 'docile' bodies, a shift succinctly summarised in the move from the 'objectivisation' to the 'subjectivisation' of the subject (McNay 1994: 133).

Foucault illustrates these processes in volumes 2 (1987) and 3 (1988a) of the *History of Sexuality*, through an analysis of Ancient Greek and Hellenistic Roman 'arts of existence' and the 'desiring subjectivities' to which they gave rise. 'Arts of existence' for Foucault are those 'intentional' and 'voluntary' actions – from the cultivation of diet and friendship to the enjoyment of sexual liaisons – in which individuals not only set rules of conduct, but in doing so, critically 'transform themselves', making their life into an aestheticised and stylised 'work of art'. In particular, what Foucault appeared to value most in Ancient Greek culture was the fact that they were free from the 'normalising' pressures of modern life. In other words, they were able to exercise a certain 'liberty' or 'autonomy' of practice, one which sought to maximise the pleasure, beauty and power derived from life itself. This, for

Foucault, suggests the need to distinguish between *morality* as an imposed set of rules and prohibitions and *ethics* as the actual actions and practices of individuals with respect to these rules and values. It is at this second level of ethics that his 'arts of existence' are located (McNay 1994).

It is this Ancient Greek principle of autonomous, reflexive conduct and the aesthetic stylisation of existence it implies, which Foucault draws upon as an 'antidote' to the 'normalising' tendencies of modern societies, one in which the modern individual is involved in a 'struggle against forms of subjection' which regulate identity and sexuality (McNay 1994: 142). As Foucault suggests, in a secularised era of 'psy' disciplines which increasingly 'govern of the soul' (Rose 1990), the imperative must now become the promotion of: 'new forms of subjectivity through the refusal of this kind of individuality which has been imposed on us for several decades' (Foucault 1982: 216). More precisely:

> the critical ontology of ourselves has to be considered not, certainly as a theory, a doctrine, nor even as a permanent body of knowledge that is accumulating: it has to be conceived as an attitude, an ethos, a philo-sophical life in which the critique of what we are is at one and the same time an historical analysis of the limits that are imposed on us and an experiment with the possibility of going beyond them.
>
> (Foucault 1984a: 50)

'Becoming', 'overcoming' 'reflexivity' and 'resistance' are thus the leitmotifs of Foucault's later writings, themes which involve and necessitate a continual interrogation of who we are and what we may become. In this respect, not only does Foucault further the Sartrean theme of existence preceding essence, his notions of a 'critical ontology of self' and the 'aesthetic stylisation of life' bear some interesting resemblances to later notions of the body and self as 'reflexive projects' in late modernity (Giddens 1991).[1] (See Chapter 4, this volume.)

To summarise, from the clinic to the confessional, and from 'normalising' power to the (ancient) 'arts of existence', Foucault's genealogical analysis of power/knowledge has become an important resource for social theorists interested in examining the socially constructed nature of the body and the technologies of self they foster. In contrast to so-called 'naturalistic' theories, Foucault does not view bodies as pre-socially 'different'. Nor does he accord biology a determining or constraining role in relation to human capabilities. Rather, bodies are historically contingent, malleable products, of shifting power/knowledge relations. From this viewpoint, far from standing outside of social relations, the biological body is simply a further manifestation of 'the social'. As we shall see in Chapter 6, this volume, this 'discursive' approach to the human body has proved particularly useful to certain strands of feminism in challenging notions of 'natural' difference and destabilising the 'fixity' of 'sex' and gendered identities.

Nevertheless, despite these obvious advances on naturalistic views, a number of problems still remain in Foucault's writing. In particular, Foucault's post-structuralist approach to the human body is ultimately unable to overcome the problem of dualism. Instead, he simply substitutes one form of essentialism (i.e. biological) for another (i.e. discursive). Certainly it is possible, as Shilling (1993) points out, to see in Foucault's writing a critical engagement with the 'real' body. This, for example, is clearly evident in his analysis of the clinic, and the 'real', 'material' effects which disciplinary technologies of power/knowledge have on the body.

On the other hand, however, Foucault's epistemological view of the body means that it effectively disappears as a *material* or *biological* entity. We can never know the biological or material body in the 'raw', so to speak, only through the filter of this or that discourse. As we shall see in Chapters 5 and 6, this volume, a similar fate befalls Lacan, who insists that the 'real' is unreachable, except through the 'symbolic' construction of language. The upshot of this is a somewhat dematerialised, disembodied notion of human corporeality as a 'discursive' product. Once the body is contained within the network of modern disciplinary systems of power/knowledge, it is the mind which becomes the 'true' locus of power. The Platonic terms of reference are therefore simply reversed rather than transcended: the soul now becomes the prison of the 'docile' body (Falk 1994).

Following directly on from this first point, there is also little interest here in the materiality of the phenomenal body as an *active*, experiencing, intentional entity (Turner 1984). Indeed, from a Foucauldian perspective, the praxical, sensual relation we have to the world, and the powers of bodies to produce, appear limited to those invested in them by discourse. The body as an active producer of meanings, in other words, falls by the wayside in Foucault's desire to discursively construct anything and everything. As such, it becomes extremely difficult to conceive of the body as a material component of social action (Shilling 1993: 80).[2]

This, in turn, leads us to a final criticism, namely, the inability to satisfactorily explain 'resistance'. Not only does Foucault's (early) 'discourse determinism' (Turner 1984) lead to a fairly pessimistic view about the possibilities of radical resistance, his (later) focus on technologies of self can also be read as an 'amoral project' of relevance only to the privileged few (McNay 1994). To be sure, Foucault argues that 'wherever there is power there is resistance', but this amounts to little more than a slogan without an adequate theory of the material body from which this resistance must ultimately flow. Indeed, despite his increasing concern with issues of 'resistance', the physical limits which the material body imposes on our ability to endlessly 'become'/'overcome' remain a seriously neglected issue in Foucault's writings, issues which are thrown into critical relief through the obdurate physical effects and deleterious consequences of ageing, sickness, disability and death (Williams and Bendelow 1998). Here we return to the underlying problems in all of Foucault's work, namely, the ontological status of the body and the overemphasis on the 'holy trinity' of power/knowledge/discourse. In short, 'regulation' (i.e. bodily 'order'), rather than 'resistance' (i.e. bodily 'control'), ultimately wins out in the dematerialised world of Foucauldian discourse determinism.

The 'civilised' body

So far in this chapter we have chosen to focus on the problems of bodily order/transgression through dominant representationalist approaches; perspectives which serve to highlight the socially constructed nature of bodies, both historically and cross-culturally. In contrast, an alternative approach, one which stresses the interlocking of biological and social factors across the long historical curve of the 'civilising process', is to be found in the work of Elias.

As Shilling (1993) notes, although perhaps not a central concern, Elias's work none the less contains within it an implicit, if not explicit, theory of 'civilised' bodies as unfinished biological and social entities. More specifically, Elias's approach to the body is, he suggests, manifest in at least three main ways. First, civilised bodies develop in 'figurations' whose shape is constantly changing as a result of fluctuating social relations, tensions and power balances which individuals enter into in the course of their everyday lives (Burkitt 1991). As Elias stresses, figurations are not simply abstractions which exist beyond individuals, but the network of interdependencies which individuals constantly forge and foster. Plans and actions, rational and emotional impulses, constantly interweave, forming an order more powerful and compelling than the will and reason of the individuals comprising it. The civilisation process, in other words, is not rationally planned (Elias 1982 [1939]: 230). As social figurations change through the ebbs and flows of the civilising process, so too do the influences which are brought to bear on the development of human bodies.

Second, in studying the development of 'civilised bodies', Elias's approach is both *sociogenetic* and *psychogenetic*, including not only broad long-term processes underlying society's development such as transformations in the division of labour, but also transformations in the personalities and drive economies of individuals together with changes in their actual behaviour (Shilling 1993). As Elias states:

> In order to understand and explain civilising processes one needs to investigate . . . the transformation of both the personality structure and the entire social structure. This task demands, within a smaller radius, *psychogenetic* investigations aimed at grasping the whole field of individual psychological energies, the structure and form of the more elementary no less than the more self-steering functions. Within a larger radius, the exploration of civilizing processes demands a long-range perspective, *sociogenetic* investigations of the overall structure, not only of a single state society but of the social field formed by a specific group of

interdependent societies and of the sequential order of its evolution.
(Elias 1982: 287–8)

Third, as suggested above, Elias approaches the human body as both a biological and a social entity. In this sense, as Shilling (1993) rightly observes, biological and social factors mesh closely together in his work in terms of evolutionary processes. As Elias stresses, despite the inescapable fact that human bodies are essentially biological, evolution has none the less equipped them with higher-order capacities such as speech and thought which, in contrast to all other species and earlier times, release them from the necessity of further biological change. More specifically, it is the biological capacity of human beings for learning which has emancipated them from dependence upon further biological change: something which Elias refers to as *symbol emancipation* (Elias 1989a,b,c, 1991). That is to say, the extraordinary capacity of human beings for learning, their unique capabilities for synthesis and their ability to transmit accumulated stocks of knowledge from generation to generation via symbols, make possible rapid social differentiation and adaptation to new circumstances *independently of further biological change.*

Not only have these evolutionary processes of symbol emancipation resulted in the dominance of human beings over all other species, they have also facilitated the historical development of civilised bodies; a process in which individuals increasingly *learn* to control their emotions, drives and instincts. As Elias (1991) argues, no human emotion is ever an entirely unlearned genetically fixed reaction pattern. Rather, like language itself, human emotions result from a merger of learned and unlearned processes. Whilst humans share certain reaction patterns such as the fight–flight response with non-human species, there are also marked differences in that humans are capable of far greater diversification in accordance with different situations and antecedent experiences.

In analysing these civilising processes, Elias is not concerned with making any simple value judgements regarding the relative merits or comparative worth of differing societies. Rather, civilisation, needs to be seen in *relational* terms as an *ongoing* process without a beginning or an end point. From this perspective, civilising processes constitute an interrelated set of developments which include the internal pacification of society, the refinement of customs, advances in the thresholds of shame and repugnance, the growing degree of foresight and self-restraint in social relations, and the increasing distance between the behavioural and emotional standards of adults and children (Kuzmics 1987).

Although Elias stresses that there is no absolute zero-point in the civilising process, the period between medieval warrior nobility and court absolutism is particularly important for the long-term transformations he seeks to identify. In comparison with later times, the medieval personality structure was highly volatile, unpredictable and liable to frequent outbursts; fluctuating between extremes for seemingly minor reasons. Within this context, life was short, violence was an everyday occurrence, and pleasure was taken in torture, mutilation and killing. Indeed, not only was the pleasure of killing and torture great, it was also socially permitted and expected.

For example, Elias (1978: 194) cites the case of a knight who spends his life plundering and destroying, mutilating and killing innocent victims, and his wife who is just as cruel, helping with his executions, and revelling in the torture of poor women. Even in sixteenth-century Paris, considerable pleasure was still, it seemed, derived from torture and killings, as witnessed, for instance, in the Midsummer Day festivity of burning one or two dozen cats alive (ibid.: 203). Given these brutal ways of life, people had to be constantly on guard, ready to protect themselves, their property and possessions, at all times of the day and night.

Certainly, in comparison with later periods, bodily impulses and inclinations at this time were far less restrained and early standards of behaviour were relatively simple, naive and undifferentiated. Consequently, early books on manners and etiquette were largely concerned with basic matters of bodily (im)propriety; things which later, as the civilising process unfolds, it would become embarrassing and disgusting to talk about. For example, these early texts instruct their readers on how to handle food and conduct oneself at the table (don't slurp your soup, use a spoon, don't put gnawed bones back into the dish); how and when it is (im)proper to fart, burp or spit (cough in order to hide the sound of a fart, do not spit over or on the table); how to blow one's nose (refrain from blowing your nose on the tablecloth, or with the same hand with which you hold meat); how to behave when passing someone in the street who is in the act of urinating or defecating (it is impolite to greet someone who is urinating or defecating); how to behave when sharing a bedroom, or even a bed, with a stranger at an inn (lie quietly, do not toss and turn your body, don't annoy or wake your companion) and so on (Mennell 1989). As Elias argues, the very fact that these texts took such pains to emphasise what they subsequently condemned provides powerful evidence for the existence of such conduct at this time.

Further evidence in support of this contention comes from the writings of Rabelais on the grotesque realism of popular carnival culture. As Rabelais shows, in contrast to official feudal hierarchies and dichotomies, the grotesque realism of medieval carnival culture focused upon the principle of 'degradation' and the 'excrescences' and 'orifices' of the natural body. The imagery here is of an open, collectivised body of the people, a material bodily whole, which 'transgresses its own limits, fecundates and is fecundated, gives birth and is born, devours and is devoured, drinks, defecates, is sick and dying' (Bakhtin 1968: 318–19). Carnival culture, in other words, was essentially *dialectic*, emphasising *process* rather than *product*, a view in which the 'excessive'/'transgressive' body as an unfinished metamorphosis of birth and death, growth and becoming was central to the overturning and parody of official feudal culture.

At the time of the Renaissance, however, certain changes become perceptible, changes in behaviour and bodily modes of conduct which were closely connected with the development of court societies, achieving central significance in seventeenth-century and eighteenth-century Europe. As Elias (1983) shows, these court societies institutionalised highly detailed codes of bodily de/comportment and emotion management, codes which served to distinguish people in terms of their relative social worth. As a consequence, bodies were central to the value system of courtly etiquette and pressures for foresight and self-containment therefore increased (Shilling 1993). Here, within these courtly circles, survival depended less upon the bodily strength or physical force of warrior nobility, and more upon the rationally calculated adherence to certain behavioural codes and the increasingly intricate arts and skills of impression management (Kuzmics 1987). The earlier clashing of 'affect with affect', therefore gave way to the courtly meshing of 'calculation with calculation' (Elias 1982 [1939]: 273).

Gradually, these processes diffused throughout the entire structure of society, changes which included: the gradual decline in people's propensity to obtain direct pleasure from acts of violence; a decrease in sudden swings and fluctuations of behaviour; the placing of ever stricter taboos on natural bodily functions such as urinating, defecating, spitting and blowing one's nose; the rationalisation of sleeping cycles, places and spaces; and the gradual removal of sexuality behind the scenes of social life. Again, these changes are succinctly captured in the manners books of the time, a difference, Elias suggests, which is partly discernible in *what no longer needs to be said*. Many bad manners and bodily functions originally dealt with at length in these texts are now only briefly mentioned in passing. Indeed, it is this 'conspiracy of silence' – one involving a 'hiding behind the scene' of all that is natural or distasteful, including the suppression of the 'animal' in food – which constitutes one of the major features of the civilising process in Europe (Mennell 1989). Civilising processes, in other words, depend as much on unspoken assumptions about past achievements, as they do on spoken proscriptions about future ones.

As suggested earlier, Elias is not, however, simply concerned with the outward manifestations of behaviour, but also with the corresponding transformations taking place in people's feelings (i.e. their 'drive economy' and their 'psychological make-up'). In other words, the social dynamism which Elias identifies, goes hand in hand with a psychological dynamic and an advancement in the thresholds of shame and embarrassment. Gradually, controls become much more internal, unconscious and automatic, a process which Elias refers to as a tilting of the balance from *external constraints* to *internal restraints*. At first, many of these new standards required conscious effort amongst adults and were largely conditional upon circumstance, especially with respect to the company one was in and their social standing. However, in due course, not only was conformity regarding behaviour instilled in children by adults, but so, too, were feelings of shame, embarrassment and disgust, feelings that henceforth would arise automatically and unconsciously in circumstances which, only a few generations earlier, would simply not have been felt, even amongst adults (Mennell 1989).

As a consequence, an increasing psychological distance between adults and children develops across the span of the civilising process. Clearly, the amount that the child has to learn in terms of behavioural codes and self-control in order to attain adult standards has greatly increased over time. For us, the toilet habits and table manners of the child resemble those of medieval adults, whilst the difference between the latter and their offspring was certainly much less than it is today. In this respect, the changes taking place in manners books over the centuries closely mirror those required in the life of each individual child in the process of 'growing up'. The psychogenesis of the adult personality cannot, therefore, be understood in isolation from the sociogenesis of our civilisation. Indeed, this very principle constitutes what Elias terms the sociogenetic ground rule, namely that: 'the individual, in his [*sic*] short history, passes once more through some of the processes that his society has traversed in its long history' (Elias 1978 [1939]: xii).

In drawing these themes together, Shilling (1993) usefully summarises Elias's approach to the civilising of bodies under three main headings. First, bodies become increasingly *socialised* across the historical curve of the civilising process. Not only are the natural rhythms and function of the bodies subject to ever tighter social controls and restrictions, but human bodies themselves are transformed into a location for the expression of civilised codes of behaviour, thereby providing the basis for the social differentiation of individuals according to 'bodily worth'. Manners, in other words, become key embodied markers of social value and self-identity. In this regard, Elias's historical analysis of civilised bodies mirrors Goffman and Bourdieu's more contemporary focus on the body as a bearer of symbolic value and its relationship to the (performing) self (see Chapters 3 and 4, this volume).

Second, this process of socialisation is also, Shilling notes, accompanied by an increasing *rationalisation* of the body in time and space. As we have seen, in medieval times desires and impulses were freely and directly expressed in conscious thoughts and actions. However, with the subsequent development of civilised bodies, a growing division occurs between consciousness and drives. As Elias explains:

> The autonomous individual self-controls produced in this way in social life, such as 'rational thought' or 'moral conscience', now interpose themselves more sternly than ever before between spontaneous and emotional impulses, on the one hand, and the skeletal muscles, on the other, preventing the former with greater severity from directly determining the latter (i.e. action) without the permission of these control mechanisms.

> (Elias 1978 [1939]: 257)

Echoing Freud, Elias points out that these processes of rationalisation and psychogenetic transformation are not without their costs. The passionate affects struggle no less violently within the individual against the 'supervising part' of themselves, and the relationship between drive satisfaction and drive control does not always find a happy resolution. In short, the civilising process is never entirely without pain: 'it always leaves scars' (Elias 1982 [1939]: 244).

Third, in conjunction with these two factors, there also occurs a progressive *individualisation* of the body and self (Shilling 1993). As Elias notes, the idea of the *homo clausus* (the individual as a self-contained entity, a little world in themselves), or the 'self in a case' is a recurrent leitmotif running through Western thought from Descartes's *Cogito*, Leibniz's windowless monads and the Kantian thinking subject, to the more recent extensions of this idea of the entirely self-sufficient, 'autotelic' individual (Giddens 1994). Yet, as Elias clearly shows, this very experience of being 'separate' and 'isolated' from others is actually the result of the civilising process itself, not some natural, pre-social state which is universally experienced by each individual. As the civilising process develops individuals become far more aware of themselves as separate entities. As a consequence they begin to exert a greater degree of control over their bodies:

> The firmer, more comprehensive and uniform restraint of the affects characteristic of this civilizational shift, together with increased internal compulsions . . . these are what is experienced as the capsule, the invisible wall dividing the 'inner world' of the individual from the 'external world' . . . the subject of cognition from its object, the 'ego' from the 'other', the 'individual' from 'society'.
>
> (Elias 1978: 258)

Here we return full circle to the emphasis upon figurational sociology. For Elias, it is not particularly helpful to conceive of 'men in the image of man' (ibid.: 261). Rather, it is more appropriate to envisage numerous interdependent people forming figurations (i.e. groups or societies of different kinds) with one another, processes which, paradoxically, may promote a growing sense of individualisation.

According to Elias, the civilising process cannot be explained in terms of material factors, nor indeed according to matters of health and hygiene, or reasons of respect. Rather, in each particular case, as he convincingly shows, codes of behaviour and standards of restraint arose *first*. Only later was it possible to attribute *retrospectively* these reasons to such changes. The answers must therefore lie elsewhere. In this regard, Elias identifies three main factors as the driving force behind these historical changes: first, the search for (courtly) distinction, one which facilitated the growth of foresight and the gradual internalisation of external behavioural controls; second, an increasingly complex division of social functions which led to lengthening chains of interdependence amongst people; finally, the formation of increasingly effective (state) monopolies of violence and taxation, which in turn led to the internal pacification of society. More than anything else, Elias argues, it was these three factors which allowed civilised codes of conduct to flourish in Europe from the sixteenth century onwards. As he states:

> The closer the web of interdependence becomes in which the individual is enmeshed with the advancing division of functions, the larger the social spaces over which this network extends and which become integrated into functional or institutional units – the more threatened is the individual who gives way to spontaneous impulses and emotions, the greater is the social advantage of those able to moderate their affects, and the more strongly is each individual constrained from an early age to take account of the effects of his [*sic*] own or other people's actions on a whole series of links in the social chain. The *moderation of spontaneous emotions*, the tempering of affects, the extension of mental space beyond the moment into the past and future, the habit of connecting events in terms of chains of cause and effect – all these are different aspects of the same transformation of conduct which necessarily takes place with *the monopolisation of physical violence, and the lengthening of the chains of social action and interdependence*. It is a 'civilizing' change of behaviour.
>
> (Elias 1982 [1939]: 236, our italics)

Clearly, as we have seen, Elias's theory of civilised bodies represents a significant advance on social constructionist approaches and perspectives. In seeking to interlock biological and social factors in a historically dynamic way, one which relates to broader processes of state formation and the monopolisation of physical violence, Elias provides a complex, subtle and sophisticated sociological perspective on the problem of bodily order (Shilling 1993). From this perspective, emotions assume a central rather than peripheral role, highlighting the considerable analytical purchase which can be gained from a sociological approach which is, at one and the same time, both sociogenetic and psychogenetic. Moreover, despite a predominant focus on 'civilized' bodies, Elias also pays considerable attention to the 'unruly', 'transgressive' features of 'natural' bodies; bodies in need of 'completion' and 'acceptance' by the prevailing sociohistorical order. Seen in these terms, the civilising process is forged out of a tensionful balance between natural drives and social controls.

Despite these obvious merits, Elias's approach is not, however, as Shilling (1993) rightly notes, without its drawbacks. First, whilst acknowledging the evolutionary role of biology in symbol emancipation and the civilising process, his analysis of the latter is ultimately achieved at the expense of the former. That is to say, post-symbol emancipation, the biological constitution of human action tends to recede from Elias's view in favour of an approach which stresses the social 'completion' of the individual through the civilising process (Shilling 1993). Elias, therefore, misses the opportunity to fully bring the biological body 'back in' to sociological explanation, in a non-reductionist way.

Following directly on from this first point, the body in Elias's analysis becomes a more or less *passive* recipient of civilising processes; a process which involves, *inter alia*, the 'regulation' of instinctual urges, and the 'restraint' of individual gestures. As such, the notion of the *embodied* social agent, one who 'selectively applies' standards of civilised behaviour according to varying social roles and situational circumstances, remains an underdeveloped aspect of Elias's work (Shilling 1993). If this is true of bodies in general, then it is particularly true of children's bodies. There is little recognition here, for example, as Prout (1998) rightly observes, of the possibility that children actively appropriate and transform as well as absorb. Nor is there a sense of childhood and growing up as processes full of 'reversals' and 'transformations'. What is missing, in short, is a sense of childhood as *'being* as well as becoming', childhood as *'staged* and *enacted'*, and children as 'active, creative *performers'* who exhibit 'difference' at the level of embodied social conduct (Prout 1998; James *et al.* 1998).

In this respect, Goffman's dramaturgical approach to social life, with its front-stage/back-stage metaphors and its emphasis on strategic forms of interaction, can be seen as a necessary complement or antidote to Elias's 'over-socialised' analysis of civilised bodies (see Chapter 3, this volume). As Goffman shows, not only do individuals, in their back-stage regions engage in a range of 'uncivilised' behaviours, from nose picking to burping, farting and belching, they are also 'a-social creatures, of variable mood and impulse', who lapse into moments of 'silent irritability' (Goffman 1959: 63; Lofland 1980).

Related to the above points, there is also a major discrepancy in time periods concerning the 'building up' and 'breaking down' of these civilising processes (Mennell 1989). Processes of 'informalisation' (Wouters 1986, 1987, 1990) and the 'controlled de-controlling' of emotional behaviour (Elias and Dunning 1986) notwithstanding, this rapid ability of individuals to 'de-civilise' modes of conduct sits uneasily, Shilling argues, alongside Elias's emphasis on their stable internalisation.

Finally, Elias's figurational sociology leaves little room for the possibility of embodied actions resulting in intended rather than unintended social outcomes (Shilling 1993). As we have seen, figurations weave webs, and produce social consequences, which no body had intended. Indeed, the civilising process is an order 'more compelling and stronger than the will and reason of the individual people comprising it' (Elias 1982 [1939]: 230). The intended is therefore dominated by the unintended in Elias's work (Haferkamp 1987). Here we return to the problems identified earlier, namely the production of 'docile' bodies and the sociological prioritisation of (bodily) 'order' over 'control'.

Bodily order/corporeal transgression: towards an analytical framework

A notable feature of the chapter so far has been the manner in which various theoretical perspectives and approaches to the problem of bodily order have been presented with little or no attempt at analytical integration. Indeed, to date there have been few attempts to produce an integrated theory of the body in society. An early attempt to rectify this lacuna can, however, be found in the pioneering work of Bryan Turner (1984).

In keeping with the bodily themes presented in this chapter, Turner's point of departure is a reworking of the classical Hobbesian problem of social order, one which starts out from the problem of the regulation of bodies in society. Here, Turner follows Foucault (1979) in making a distinction between the regulation of populations and the discipline of bodies. In addition, he also draws upon Featherstone's (1991) distinction between the interior body as an environment and the exterior body as a medium for the representation of a public, performing self. In making these distinctions Turner's argument is that the Hobbesian problem of order – one involving the geometry of bodies – has four interrelated dimensions. At the population level, these concern the *reproduction* of bodies through time and their *regulation* in space. At the individual level, they relate to the *restraint* of desire as an interior problem, and to *representation* as an exterior (i.e. surface) problem of the body in social space. Drawing upon Parsonian terminology, Turner states that these four 'societal tasks' are problems which every social system has to confront and solve.

Turner then proceeds to delineate a dominant social theorist of each specific societal task, a paradigmatic illness in which bodies break down as a consequence of their imposition, and finally an institutional sub-system for dealing with these societal tasks. For example, whilst Malthus was concerned with the reproduction of populations and their control through natural or moral constraint, Weber serves as the classic theorist of asceticism and its bearing upon the moral regulation and rational control of the interior body. In contrast, Rousseau epitomises what became a persistent motif of nineteenth-century social thought, namely a concern with the moral consequences of urbanisation, whilst Goffman captures, *par excellence*, the problems of representation and the dilemmas of impression management in contemporary society; a view in which individuals, as 'a-moral merchants of morality', are preoccupied with 'surface' appearances which are only 'skin-deep'.

In delineating his four paradigmatic types of illness, Turner makes explicit reference to Foucault's analysis of medical history and sexual deviance, a view in which all illness is social illness. Thus, in historical terms, Turner suggests that the paradigmatic expression of disease regarding the reproduction of populations across time, was onanism. Masturbation became an object of severe moral condemnation in the second half of the eighteenth century, and by the nineteenth century a cluster of medical categories such as 'masturbatory insanity' or 'spermatorrhoea' emerged in order to classify the negative consequences of this 'unproductive' form of sexuality. Hysteria, in contrast, was seen as a metaphor for the social subordination of women, particularly middle-class women who, in the Victorian period, were attempting to express their independence through professional employment. Women, at this time, were caught in a contradictory set of circumstances. On the one hand they were regarded as being 'over-charged' with sexual energies, yet marriage, as their only legitimate outlet, was often delayed in European marriage patterns. On the other hand, women who delayed marriage in late Victorian society in order to pursue careers in nursing or teaching were seen to be especially prone to a hysterical attack of the 'vapours'. Hysteria, therefore, served as a potent metaphor for problems concerning the internal restraint of the body in patriarchal society. Similarly, with respect to the regulation of populations in space, Turner argues that nineteenth-century anxieties about seductive intimacies between anonymous strangers in urban life found their symbolic expression in female agoraphobia. Finally, as women from the middle classes entered public employment in the twentieth century, 'female complaints' took on an increasingly symbolic or 'representational' character focused upon the surface or exterior body, anxieties that crystallised in the form of anorexia nervosa and clearly express the ambiguities of female gender in contemporary Western societies (see Chapters 4 and 6, this volume).

As Turner suggests, these illnesses of women have one important thing in common, namely the fact that they are all, sociologically speaking, illnesses of dependence: conditions which express the separation of the public world of (male) authority from the private world of (female) feeling (Turner 1984: 113). The institutional sub-systems which Turner delineates as the societal means for the management of these corporeal problems are, therefore, patriarchy for the reproduction of populations over time, asceticism for the internal restraint of bodies, panopticism for the regulation of bodies in social space, and finally, commodification for the representation of the exterior body. The full typology is presented in Table 2.1.

Clearly Turner's analysis of 'bodily order' has a number of merits, being the first attempt to systematically integrate these diverse theories of the

Table 2.1 Turner's model of 'bodily order'

	Populations	*Bodies*	
Time	Reproduction	Restraint	Internal
	Malthus	Weber	
	Onanism	Hysteria	
Space	Regulation	Representation	External
	Rousseau	Goffman	
	Phobia	Anorexia	

Source: Reprinted from Turner (1984: 91)

body into a coherent analytical framework. However, it also suffers from a number of limitations. In particular, as Frank (1991a) points out, a tacit functionalism pervades this framework in which, via a 'top-down' model, the body is considered from the viewpoint of society, its tasks and its problems of government. In contrast, as we shall see in the following chapter, an alternative approach is to start in a 'bottom-up' manner, with bodies and their action-oriented problems as the core analytical issue. Seen in these terms, Turner's analytical typology represents the final level of abstract systems theorising about the body, not its starting point.

In response to these criticisms, Turner's (1992) more recent work has attempted to 'flesh out' a more 'grounded' approach to the 'lived' body; one which is rooted in the predicaments of human *embodiment* through a critical (re)reading of phenomenology and philosophical anthropology. Underpinning this is a broader commitment to what Turner refers to as 'epistemological pragmatism'; a strategy which, given the embryonic state of the sociology of the body, seeks to maximise rather than prematurely foreclose our theoretical options.

We shall return to these problems of embodiment and social action in subsequent chapters. For the moment, however, it is to another, albeit closely related problem, that we turn, namely, the issue of corporeal 'transgression'. As we have seen, the dominant theme of this chapter has been a concern with bodily order; a position crystallised in Turner's analytical typology and his 'corporealisation' of Hobbes. Yet in elaborating on his 'four R's', Turner fails to bring out adequately the fact that bodily order is itself predicated on the problem of bodily 'transgression'. From Weber to Foucault, Douglas to Elias, Bakhtin to Bataille, it is possible to recover a view of the body as a recalcitrant, excessive/transgressive entity, one in need of (continual) regulation and restraint through the prevailing sociocultural and historical order. Indeed, this emphasis on transgressive bodies is further reinforced by Turner, albeit implicitly, through his four paradigmatic types of illness – illnesses that themselves arise from the social ordering of (female) bodies.

This, in turn, leads us to a deeper set of ontological reflections on human nature. In this regard, Gaston Bachelard's (1987 [1964]) deliberations on human beings as creatures of *desire* rather than *need*, together with George Bataille's (1985) reflections on excessive bodies, provide the basis for a very different approach to the question of bodily order – one that is rooted, first and foremost, in the problem of corporeal transgression.

These issues have recently been taken up and developed by Falk (1994) in his analysis of the 'consuming' body. As Falk argues, his primary focus is on the *historicity* of the body, specified, on the one hand, into the changing modes of thematisation (i.e. something to be subsumed into the socio-cultural order) and, on the other hand, to the fates of *corporeality* or bodiliness as the *experientiality* of the body which is always related to the former (Falk 1994: 2).

In this regard, Falk echoes Bachelard and Bataille's suggestion that, as a sensual being, (wo)man's corporeality is inextricably bound up with (human) desire as opposed to (animal) need. From this it follows that the human body, through its corporeal flows and libidinal intensities, is itself excessive/transgressive, as witnessed, for example, in the 'liminality' of collective festivals (cf. Bakhtin 1968) and the eroticism/'perversion' of sexual acts (cf. Bataille 1985). To be excessive/transgressive, however, implies the crossing or breaking of historically set and socioculturally elaborated boundaries which de/confine the body in certain specific ways (cf. Douglas 1966). Indeed, transgression itself needs 'limits', just as limits need points of transgression. Here we return to the old Durkheimian insight that deviance is necessary for the symbolic (re)affirmation of collective sentiments and the ritual (re)enforcement of moral boundaries.

This, in turn, points to the historical, social and cultural relations within which human corporeality is entwined. Corporeality, in other words, as a form of trangression, is itself a cultural and historical category, one that demands the existence of 'limits' and is never lived in the 'raw'. Eroticism, for example, like dirt and pollution, is universal, yet the transgressions it embraces have their own historicity (Falk 1994). Similarly, the manner in which corporeal flows are (sexually) coded, and the ritually guarded boundaries they transgress, are products of the sociocultural relations within which human corporeality is itself de/confined. Seen in these terms:

> The increase in the density of limits, categories and norms related to corporeality produces a multiplicity and diversification of transgressions as a complementary opposition, though primarily in the *experience* [as opposed to the *expressive*] dimension of corporeality. . . . The more articulated and multifarious the restrictions on corporeality, the more sophisticated the forms of transgression become. Lack of restraint emphasising corporeal expression is replaced by a diversification of the scale of sensory pleasures.
>
> (Falk 1994: 65, our emphasis)

Given this view, Falk is able to interpret the historical 'fate' of corporeality across the long historical curve of the civilising process as a paradoxical combination of both discipline and emancipation: one involving a shift from the relatively 'open' body and 'closed' self of pre-modern times, to the 'closed' body and 'open' self of contemporary consumer culture. As the scale of human corporeal *expression* becomes restricted through the 'shielding' and 'instrumentalising' of the body, the field of *experience* widens, diversifies and becomes more sensitive. In other words, an increase in the quantity of restrictions placed on the direct expression of corporeal pleasures is accompanied by a diversification and intensification of the quality of human sensual experience.[3] As a consequence, transgressions themselves multiply and become ever more complex.

To summarise, Falk's analysis of the consuming body represents a significant advance on Turner's account of bodily order in at least three respects.
First, Falk provides a far more *dynamic* view of the human body and its role
in the historical web of sociocultural relations. Second, his analysis displays a
subtle concern with the effects of these broader sociocultural relations on the
experiential and expressive aspects of the body (i.e. the body as a sensory and
sensual, as well as a sensible, being). Finally, the body, for Falk, is first and
foremost an excessive/*transgressive* entity, both expressively and experientially,
an issue that returns us, full circle, to the dynamic role of human corporeality in the historical web of sociocultural relations. Seen in these terms,
bodily order and corporeal transgression are intimately related.

Conclusions

Taking as its point of departure the sociological problem of 'order', this
chapter has explored the corporeal implications of this question through a
critical account of the 'symbolic' body (Hertz and Douglas), the 'discursive'
body (Foucault) and the 'civilized' body (Elias). As we have argued, what
these perspectives share in common – whether through the symbolic
medium of ritual, disciplinary technologies of power/knowledge, or (courtly)
codes of etiquette and internalised restraints – is a largely *passive* view of the
body, one that is dominated by the social order. Where they differ, however,
is in their view of the constitution of the body itself. In this respect, qualifications apart, Elias's approach represents a significant advance on social
constructionist perspectives, linking as it does biological and social factors
in a dynamic, evolutionary way, across the long historical curve of the civilising process.

More generally, in seeking to draw these analytical issues out more
clearly, we have sought to show, through a critical reading of Turner and
Falk, how the question of bodily order itself ultimately rests on the problem
of corporeal transgression. Bodies, in other words, through their corporeal
flows and libidinal intensities, are first and foremost, 'excessive/transgres-
sive' entities. To be transgressive, however, implies the crossing or breaching
of historically set 'limits' and sociocultural boundaries. Corporeal transgression, therefore, depends on social order, just as social order depends on
corporeal transgression. We will return to these issues of corporeality, desire
and transgression in Chapter 5 on the 'libidinal' body, and Chapter 6 on
feminisms and the body. For the moment, however, it is to the more
pressing sociological question of bodily 'control' and the embodiment of
social action that we turn in the next chapter.

3 Bodily 'control'

Body techniques, intercorporeality and the embodiment of social action

> It is through the *skin* that metaphysics will be made to re-enter our minds; only the *flesh* can supply a 'definitive understanding of Life'.
>
> (Artaud 1988)

In the previous chapter we argued that questions of social 'order' ultimately rest on problems of bodily conformity and transgression. In this chapter, we take up these issues from the alternative sociological vantage point of bodily 'control'. From this perspective, the key question is not how bodily 'order' is possible, but how individuals, as embodied agents, begin to reassert control over the (reified) social institutions they have created. From this stance, a vocabulary of will, motives and human intentionality follow; terms which are rooted in the ontological primacy of social actors over social systems. Key issues here include the notion of body techniques (Mauss), the lived experience of the body-subject as the existential basis of our being-in-the-world (Merleau-Ponty) and the intercorporeal/intersubjective nature of everyday social life as a praxical and symbolic accomplishment (Goffman). In stressing these issues, we begin to flesh out a more embodied form of sociology, one grounded in the corporeal problems of agency and control. It is to a fuller exploration of these particular issues that this chapter is devoted.

Body techniques and the habitus

In a seminal paper on 'body techniques', Marcel Mauss (1973 [1934]) provides us with a pioneering statement on the practical and social uses to which the body is put by members of society. In doing so, Mauss makes at least two significant contributions to our understanding of body techniques as a viable topic of social scientific inquiry. First, he provides us with a definition of the concept as: 'the ways in which, from society to society men [*sic*] know how to use their bodies' (ibid.: 70). Second, having done so, he then proceeds to extensively catalogue a broad range of differing types of body techniques, from walking to swimming, digging to spitting, sleeping to making love.

As Mauss argues, each society has its own habits, and body techniques identified in one society or historical period may have no equivalent in another. For example, Mauss recounts how English soldiers during the First

World War did not know how to use French spades – a situation which resulted in the change of 8,000 spades per division – and how he had to teach the members of one society he encountered how to spit. Another powerful illustration of these culturally variable techniques is provided by the Maori women of New Zealand, who adopt a peculiar gait – one drilled into them at an early age by their mothers – characterised by a loose-jointed swinging of the hips: something which, at first sight looks ungainly, but is in fact admired and valued by the Maori people themselves.

Body techniques display three fundamental characteristics. First, as the name implies, they are *technical* in that they are constituted by a specific set of bodily movements or forms: 'The body is man's [*sic*] first and most natural instrument'. Second, they are *traditional* in the sense that they are learnt or acquired by means of training and education: 'There is no technique and no transmission in the absence of tradition'. Finally, they are *efficient* in the sense that they serve a definite purpose, function or goal (e.g. walking, running, dancing or digging) (Mauss 1973 [1934]: 75).

In order to more fully flesh this notion of body techniques out, Mauss argued that it is necessary to have what he termed a 'triple viewpoint' of the 'total [*sic*] man'; one which combines physical, psychological and sociological considerations:

> we are everywhere faced with the physio–psychosociological assemblages of series of action. These actions are more or less habitual and more or less ancient in the life of the individual and the history of society. . . . In group life as a whole there is a kind of *education of movements* in close order. . . . Hence there is a strong sociological causality in all these facts. . . . On the other hand, this all presupposes an enormous biological and physiological apparatus. . . . I think that the basic education in all these techniques consists of an adaptation of the body to their *use*.
>
> (Mauss 1973: 85–6, our emphasis)

A key concept here for Mauss is the 'habitus', as a more-or-less ingrained sociocultural–cultural relation to the body and its movements. Indeed, for Mauss, there is perhaps no such thing as a 'natural way' for the adult. Rather, in every society; 'everyone knows and has to know and learn what he [*sic*] has to do in all conditions' (ibid.: 85). In stressing this notion of 'habitus', Mauss's account of body techniques bears some interesting resemblances to Bourdieu's later use of the term. For Bourdieu, as for Mauss, the very ways in which people relate to and treat their bodies reveal the 'deepest dispositions' of the habitus at work. This, in turn, is underscored through Bourdieu's use of the term 'bodily hexis' to denote the socially inscribed manner in which individuals 'carry themselves'. Bodily hexis, in short, is 'political mythology realised, *em-bodied*, turned into permanent dispositions, a durable manner of standing, speaking, and thereby of feeling and *thinking*', principles which are placed beyond the conscious reach of the mind (Bourdieu 1977: 94).[1]

Despite Mauss's important contribution to 'bringing the body back in', his approach can be criticised on at least four counts. First, whilst suggestive, Mauss's paper is descriptive in nature and primarily concerned with the cataloguing and classification of body techniques according to his own personal experiences and reflections (as a soldier, an anthropologist, a traveller and a sportsman). Second, as with Bourdieu's notion of the habitus, Mauss paints an overly deterministic picture of the individual who acts in a largely unthinking or unreflective way (what Bourdieu terms the 'logic of practice') on the basis of their corporeal–cultural body techniques. Third, Mauss may also be criticised for unproblematically equating the social conditioning of body techniques with the rationalist enterprise and neglecting the important role that emotions play in their acquisition, use and consequences. Finally, Mauss's analysis of body techniques tends to posit them as abstract entities independently of the concrete social situations, circumstances and (political) contingencies of their exercise. The upshot of this is that issues of power, conflict and control in the acquisition and exercise of body techniques are minimised. All in all then, despite his emphasis on the practical aspects of body *use*, Mauss's agents once again appear to be 'over-socialised' products of society – an order that appears to operate in a largely unthinking fashion through the durable dispositions and sedimented traits of an inflexible habitus. There are, in short, as Shilling (1997a) has recently argued, good reasons for rejecting attempts to ground notions of the embodied agent in dominant, static notions of the habitus which minimises creativity and in doing so makes it difficult to conceive of social change.

In order to recover this more critical notion of embodied human agency, we need to turn instead to the work of other writers such as Merleau-Ponty and Goffman, writers whose emphasis on the *sentient body-subject, intercorporeality* and the *intersubjective* nature of social life as a dynamic, situationally contingent set of carnal relations, provide the foundations for a truly embodied non-dualist, sociology.

The 'body in the mind': phenomenology, carnality and the 'flesh'

Of all the figures in the history of Western thought, it is perhaps the philosopher Maurice Merleau-Ponty who has done most to overturn the Cartesian dualist legacies of the past. In particular, it is possible to highlight at least two major contributions which Merleau-Ponty has made to our understanding of the problems of mind/body dualism, and the need for a 'carnal' sociology. First, through his phenomenological critique of perception as an embodied experience, Merleau-Ponty (1962) provides us with the philosophical foundation for a truly non-dualist ontology of the body. Second, in doing so, he is also able to, albeit philosophically, resolve the problem of intersubjectivity through an approach which stresses the intercorporeal nature and carnal roots of our being-in-the-world (Crossley 1995a). Seen in these terms, mind and body are thoroughly interfused as Descartes's *cogito* is replaced by Merleau-Ponty's sentient body-subject

Taking each of these issues in turn, perception, for Merleau-Ponty, is first and foremost an embodied experience. Even our 'higher' perceptual experiences cannot escape our primordial embodiment. The theory of the body, in other words, is always 'already a theory of perception'. In this respect, Merleau-Ponty raises a number of doubts and objections to Cartesian thought, including the fact that the ontological separation of mind and body leaves unresolved the question of how precisely mind engages with body and world during the act of perception itself (Crossley 1995a). On this point Descartes provides only a limited and philosophically quite unsatisfactory answer.[2] Cartesianism defines perception as an inner representation of an outer world of given objects, thus giving rise to the subject/object dualism and all the problems this involves. According to Merleau-Ponty, these and many other problems cannot be adequately resolved within a Cartesian/mentalistic framework. Rather, perception must be radically rethought, and it is this critique which serves as Merleau-Ponty's point of departure in developing a phenomenology of embodiment (Crossley 1995a).

Instead of mistakenly beginning with the world as an already pre-constituted realm of cultural objects and forms, Merleau-Ponty stresses instead that the central phenomenological task is to 're-establish the roots of the mind in its body and in its world' (Merleau-Ponty 1963: 3). In doing so, he reminds us that, phenomenology is a descriptive science of 'existential beginnings' which, in turn, need to be located in the world of embodied subjects (Crossley 1995a). The phenomenological reduction, in other words, is never a complete reduction due to our existential being-in-the-world (Langer 1989). In breaking with the subject–object distinction – itself a product of conscious reflection and analysis – Merleau-Ponty seeks to 'reflect' upon the 'unreflected', the aim of which is to recover or bring back to the centre of our attention and awareness that *pre-objective*, primordial relationship we have to our bodies and the world, one which objective thought loses sight of (Crossley 1995a). The power of the *pre-objective*, in other words, lies in its ability to distinguish from 'every modality of the *res extensa*, as from every *cogitatio*' and to 'effect the *union* between the "psychic" and the "physiological"' (Merleau-Ponty 1962: 80).

From this viewpoint, perception is not some (private) 'inner' representation of an 'outer' (public) world, rather it is, in a fundamental sense, an 'openness to being' that occurs in-the-world (Crossley 1995a). The perceiving mind, in other words, is an 'incarnate body':

> we are in the world through our body, and . . . we perceive that world within our body . . . by thus remaking contact with the body and with the world, we . . . also . . . rediscover ourself, since, perceiving as we do with our body, the body is a natural self and, as it were, the subject of perception.
>
> (Merleau-Ponty 1962: 206)

From this it follows that perception is 'perspectival' – one always observes from somewhere (above, below, left, right, close or at a distance), never from nowhere (i.e. a 'God's eye view'). The perspectival nature of perception, in other words, is a primary expression of our embodiment, involving as it does the articulation of both body and world through a 'spontaneous synthesis' of our senses (Langer 1989). It is also, as Merleau-Ponty stresses, rooted in behaviour (i.e. seeing, looking, touching) as a *practical* relationship to and involvement in the world. This, in turn, suggests that perception is an *active* process, one involving a sentient body-subject who points 'outwards' and is directed towards a common world of learnt practical skills and existential understandings (Crossley 1995a).

This concern with a common world of practical skills and shared under-standings leads us to the second major legacy that Merleau-Ponty provides, namely, his 'corporeal resolution' of the whole intersubjectivity question (i.e. how mind can know of the existence of other minds). For Merleau-Ponty, the answer to this question is simple. The body's intimate relationship with the world means that it is part of single *reversible* fabric or *flesh*. The flesh of the body and the flesh of the world are inextricably intertwined – what Merleau-Ponty refers to, using a biological term, as a chiasma (i.e. the crossing-over or intersection of things). In particular, the body's 'openness' of being suggests a shared world of *intermundane* space which crosses over and intertwines with that of similarly embodied human beings. Given such a view, the division of the world into perceiver and perceived, sentient and the sensible, toucher and touched, can never be absolute. Rather, as both sentient and sensible beings, we can see and be seen, hear and be heard, touch and be touched (Grosz 1994). As Merleau-Ponty states: 'he [*sic*] who sees cannot possess the visible unless he is possessed by it, unless he is of it, unless . . . he is one of the visi-bles, capable of a singular reversal, of seeing them – he who is one of them' (1968: 135). The problem of intersubjectivity is, therefore, as Crossley (1995a) notes, resolved through the primordial carnal bonds and meaningful relations that exist between embodied human beings. Intersubjectivity, in short, is carnal through and through, forged as it is by the *intercorporeal* rela-tions of sentient body-subjects and their primordial bonds with a common reversible world.

This notion of carnal intersubjectivity is further reinforced through Merleau-Ponty's emphasis on the active body as the expressive basis of meaning and ideas. In keeping with his non-dualist ontology, meaning for Merleau-Ponty is not the product of some inner mental state. Rather, it resides in the actual concrete behaviour of the sentient body-subject: embodied gestures which are, so to speak, 'publicly available' through our participation in a common visible world of intermundane space and shared understandings (Crossley 1995a). Anger, for example, does not refer to some prior inner emotional state, rather it is expressively embodied in the shaking of my fist. If we add to this the fact that our bodily engagement with the world is derived from a cultural stock of acquired (practical) skills, techniques and shared understandings, and that space and time are actively taken up and transformed in the process, then we have a view of the body-subject as a corporeal agent of 'cultural praxis'. Indeed, it is on this basis, as Crossley (1995a) notes, that Merleau-Ponty is able to posit a 'carnal version' of Bourdieu's habitus – one which includes the acquired perceptual and linguistic schemas, and affective modes of conduct of the active body-subject.

Clearly, in considering the work of Merleau-Ponty, we have come a long way from Platonic thought and Cartesian dualism to a view in which mind and body, subjectivity and materiality are not in fact split, but are instead thoroughly interfused. Seen in these terms:

> Man [*sic*] taken as a concrete being is not a psyche joined to an organism, but the movement to and fro of existence which at one time allows itself to take corporeal form and at other times moves towards personal acts. . . . *The union between soul and body* is not an amalgamation between two mutually external terms, subject and object, brought about by arbitrary decree. It *is enacted at every instant in the movement of existence.*
>
> (Merleau-Ponty 1962: 88–9, our emphasis)

Meaning, in short, resides in the body, and the body resides in the world.

These issues have recently been taken up and further explored in Johnson's (1987) compelling account of the bodily basis of meaning, imagination and reason. For Johnson, any adequate account of meaning and rationality must accord a central place to human embodiment as the basis from which knowledge and understanding of the world and the conceptual structures for grasping it occur.[3] In particular, Johnson draws our attention to the ways in which imagination links cognitive and bodily structures, and how basic concepts of experience such as balance, scale, force and cycles emerge directly from our physical and corporeal experience as 'contained' embodied beings; concepts which, in turn, can be metaphorically and metonymically extended in order to create more abstract meanings and rational connections.

The 'verticality' schema, for instance, arises directly from our tendency to employ an 'up–down' orientation in picking out meaningful structures of experience – a structure that is grasped repeatedly on a daily basis from perceiving a building and standing upright, to climbing stairs. This schema is an abstract representation or analogue of our embodied verticality experiences that are grounded in our everyday lives and being-in-the-world (Johnson 1987). For Johnson, it is these *experientially based* imaginative structures of the image–schematic sort that are integral to meaning and rationality, *grounded as they are in the body*. Similarly, through metaphor, we make use of patterns that obtain from our direct physical experience in order to organise our more abstract understanding. The fundamental notion that 'more is up', for example, involves a process of metaphorical projection from 'up' to 'more', which is based directly on human bodily experience and the image schemata it involves. More and up, in other words, are metaphorically connected in our experience in a way that provides a physical basis for more abstract understandings of quantity (Johnson 1987).

These and many other examples suggest that our understanding of the world and the way it works contains many 'pre-conceptual' and 'non-propositional' structures of experience that are rooted in our bodies – structures that can be metaphorically projected and propositionally elaborated in order to constitute a rich network of human meaning and significance. This, in turn, necessitates a fundamental rethinking of human *'experience'*, one that includes our bodily, social, emotional and linguistic as well as our intellectual being: everything, in fact, which makes us human (Johnson 1987). It is on this basis that Johnson is not only able to effectively argue that the body is 'in' the mind, but also to further our understanding of how, precisely, the body *is* in the mind; how it is possible and necessary for abstract meanings and for reason and imagination itself to have a bodily basis. In doing so, he provides an implicit, if not explicit, critique of discourse as a more or less 'free-floating' force in the social construction of reality. Discourse, from this perspective, does not simply fabricate bodies, rather, bodies shape discourses and the (rational) structures of knowledge we use to understand the world.

To summarise, together, Merleau-Ponty and Johnson provide a profound critique of Cartesian dualism. Not only do they highlight the impossibility of treating mind and body as separate entities, they also draw attention to our practical engagement with the world and the bodily basis of meaning, imagination and reason. This, coupled with the stress upon intercorporeality, intermundane space and the culturally acquired skills and dispositions of the sentient body-subject, suggests a position that builds on Mauss's discussion of body techniques and Bourdieu's notion of the habitus in significant new ways. Ultimately, however, as phenomenologists, their work remains rooted in a philosophical framework which is sociologically unsatisfactory for the broader exploration of social action and the problem of 'control'. In order to recover these possibilities we need to turn instead to the work of Erving Goffman on the vicissitudes of the embodied self and the carnal interchanges of everyday life.

The vicissitudes of the embodied self/the carnal interchanges of everyday life

No account of the problems of bodily action and control would be complete without explicit mention of Goffman's dramaturgical perspective on social life. Rooted as it is in the interactional dilemmas of embodied selfhood and the carnal interchanges of everyday life, Goffman's writings, taken as a whole, make at least three major contributions to the sociology of the body. First, through his keen Chicago-trained eye for sociological detail, Goffman is able to demonstrate the corporeal basis of micro-public order as a *praxical* accomplishment of embodied social agents (Crossley 1995b). Second, through his focus on issues such as stigma and embarrassment, Goffman provides us with a clear understanding of how the body mediates between social identity and self-identity (Shilling 1993). In doing so, he is also able to highlight the important role of human emotions, feelings and sentiments, and the 'circuits of selfhood' they involve. Finally, contrary to many standard accounts of his work, Goffman demonstrates an abiding interest in the bodily *production* of social hierarchy, dominance and control, from symbols of class status to the arrangement between the sexes.

Taking each of these issues in turn, Goffman's analysis of micro-public order, as Crossley (1995b) has recently argued, serves not only as a partial corrective to Mauss's analysis of body techniques, but also extends and develops Merleau-Ponty's concern with intersubjectivity and intercorporeality in significant new ways which are of more general relevance to a corporeal sociology. In particular, it is in *Relations in Public: Microstudies of the Public Order* (1971), that Goffman, although making no explicit use of the terms, demonstrates most clearly the *interdependency* and *relational* constitution of body techniques and intercorporeality. In doing so, he goes beyond Mauss's descriptive, decontextualised, cataloguing of body techniques in order to consider the socially situated nature of bodily activity and its location within the 'interaction order' (Crossley 1995b).

For Goffman, successful passage through public space, whether it be the street, the supermarket, or a busy shopping mall, is both a practical problem and skilful accomplishment for the human agent, involving specific social rules and rituals which facilitate this passage and 'repair' disruptions to the micro-public order of social interaction. For example, Goffman refers to individuals as 'vehicular entities' or 'human ambulatory units' who have to manage their bodies in public places through pedestrian 'traffic rules' (e.g. 'routing', 'scanning', 'body checking') – rules that are socially organised in time and space through conventions such as queues, files, processions and marches. In this respect, Goffman's sociology is sensitively attuned to the different settings in which we walk, the pedestrian rules and values that this embodies, and the manner in which specific obstacles and events, both physical and social ones, are negotiated in the process. The social view of walking that this entails extends, Crossley (1995b) suggests, beyond Mauss's notion of different walking styles, to encompass the socially situated nature of walking, the accommodations this involves and the formal structures of 'interactional orderliness' that emerge as a consequence.

In stressing such issues, Goffman reminds us that social order rests on these micro-public foundations, and that these foundations, in turn, are dependent on the corporeal competences (i.e. body techniques) and practical know-how (i.e. habitus) of the sentient body-subject *qua* embodied social actors (Crossley 1995b). In this way, Goffman is able to highlight the various ways in which social space and time are taken up and actively transformed according to the specific purposes, meanings and functions of social action (Crossley 1995b). On a darker note, Goffman also draws attention, through the notion of the *umwelt*, to the territorial contingencies and vulnerabilities that our bodily being involves. The individual must be 'there in the flesh' to be there at all, and the body, as a piece of 'consequential equipment', is therefore continually 'put on the line' by its owner (Goffman 1967: 167). Thus, in an exercise of paranoid logic, Goffman talks of 'safe' and 'dangerous' places, of 'normal' appearances – themselves the most troubling of all – and of 'lurk lines' in which those who may wish to harm us, from muggers to rapists, lie in wait, ready to 'pounce'. In this sense, Goffman provides us with a protean micro-politics of personal and lived space – one that includes (potential) hazards and threats to our corporeal selves and fleshy bodies. Bodies, in short, just like selves to which they are so closely tied, are continually 'risked' or 'put on the line' in the ritualistic encounters and public spaces of everyday life.

Goffman also draws attention to the fact that this micro-social interaction order is dependent on the perceptible, 'readable' intentions, involvement and dispositions of its members that, in a fundamental sense, must be taken at 'face value' (Crossley 1995b). Actors must therefore 'scan' the scene in order to pick up the positional, gestural and linguistic clues regarding potential lines of action of their (fellow) participants in the interaction order. Within routine social interaction, bodies are constantly 'giving off' and receiving information – a process which includes both 'scanner' and 'scanned' alike – and this has a crucial bearing on how encounters are managed and the smoothness with which they proceed. Here we return to the sociological significance of the Simmelian 'glance' and the expressive nature of the bodily senses. In particular, Goffman stresses how issues such as eye contact, 'civil inattention' and rules concerning involvement propriety play an essential part in the maintenance of face-to-face encounters and the smooth routine flow of social interaction. As he states:

> always in the interaction order, the engrossment and involvement of the participants – if only attention – is critical. . . . Emotions, mood, cognition, bodily orientation, and muscular effort are intrinsically involved, introducing an inevitable psychobiological element. Ease and unease, unselfconsciousness and wariness are central. . . . It is not only that our appearance and manner provide evidence of our statuses and relationships. It is also that the line of our visual regard, the intensity of our involvement, the shape of our initial actions allow others to glean our immediate intent and purpose, and all this whether or not we are engaged in talk with them at the time.
>
> (Goffman 1983: 3)

This 'gleaned' character of performances and observations is facilitated by the central process of social ritualisation (i.e. the standardisation, through socialisation, of bodily and vocal behaviour, affording such behaviour a specialised communicative function) (Goffman 1983: 3). It is here, Goffman suggests, that shared vocabularies of 'body idiom' play a crucial symbolic role. Indeed, the understanding of body idiom as a 'conventionalised discourse' is one reason for calling 'an aggregate of individuals a society' (Goffman 1963: 35). As a conventionalised discourse, body idiom is also inherently normative, in the sense that there is typically an obligation to convey certain information of this nature when in the presence of others and an obligation not to convey other impressions. Whilst an individual can refrain from speaking, s/he cannot stop communicating through body idiom – one must either say the right or wrong thing, one cannot say nothing. Paradoxically, this results in a situation in which the best way to give the least amount of information is to 'fit in' and be the kind of person one is socially expected to be.

A particularly interesting type of body idiom concerns what Goffman terms 'body gloss' (i.e. the use of over-all body gesture to make facts otherwise unavailable 'gleanable' (Goffman 1971: 11)). This, he further sub-divides into three distinct types of body gloss. The first, 'orientation gloss', concerns the manner in which individuals, through body language, attempt to convey that their actions are orientated towards some untroubling, everyday purpose. When in public places, for example, an individual may continually check their wrist watch and scan the surrounding area in order to indicate to anyone who cares to be watching that they are in fact waiting for somebody and not loitering with intent. In contrast, 'circumspection gloss', whilst having the same purpose of disarming the suspicious onlooker, involves the conversion of a misdemeanour into something similar but less offensive such as the replacement of a stare by a scanning glance. Finally, 'over-play gloss' occurs when the individual 'throws himself [*sic*] into what would thus become of him, but does so in an unserious manner, thereby covering any real constraint by much larger unserious ones of the same kind'. In lifting a heavy object, for instance, one which might expose the person's naked effort, the individual may choose instead to enact 'utter strain unseriously' (ibid.: 135).

Underlying many of the issues discussed so far is, of course, Goffman's sociological treatment of the self. For Goffman, face and body work are crucial not only to the maintenance and smooth flow of interactional encounters, but also to the maintenance and integrity of social roles and identities. Here we arrive at what is perhaps the second key legacy which Goffman provides for the sociology of the body. The self, for Goffman is a 'ceremonial thing, a sacred object, which must be treated with proper ritual care' (ibid.: 91). Individuals must ensure that their proffered selves are maintained through appropriate social conduct and the necessary ritual 'repair work' in the face of (minor) derelictions of interactional duty. An apology, for example, may suffice, not only to demonstrate awareness that a rule has been broken, but also to indicate that one is not the sort of person who wilfully breaks rules. Alternatively, we may simply 'slap our thighs, roll our eyes, hold our hands in the air, or swear', in order to prove our awareness of the 'fool we have been', and that we are 'not the same fool now'. In each particular case, our embodied gestures and the ritualistic behaviours they involve serve as moral tokens of our own self-worth.

These issues are clearly illustrated in Goffman's analysis of embarrassment. As Schudson (1984) observes, Goffman's sociology is anchored in the assumption that embarrassment is of fundamental social and moral significance. Echoing Darwin's (1955 [1895]) earlier observation that blushing is a distinctively human manifestation of emotion and that this is intimately bound up with our feeling concerning what others think of us, Goffman identifies two main sources of embarrassment, namely: inconsistencies in character and discontinuities of social interaction. In both cases, the body is central, providing as it does an indexical sign of interactional unease, the correlates of which include:

> blushing, fumbling, stuttering, an unusually low- or high-pitched voice, sweating, blanching, blinking, tremor of the hands, hesitating or vacillating movement, absent-mindedness, and malaproprisms . . . there may be a lowering of the eyes, bowing of the head, putting of hands behind the back, nervous fingering of the clothing or twisting of the fingers together, and stammering, with some incoherence of idea as expressed in speech. There are also symptoms of a subjective kind: constriction of the diaphragm, a feeling of wobbliness, consciousness of strained and unnatural gestures, a dazed sensation, dryness of the mouth, and tenseness of the muscles. In cases of mild discomfiture these visible and invisible flusterings occur but in less perceptible form.
>
> (Goffman 1967: 97)

Even when an individual appears poised according to certain bodily signs, other signs such as shaking hands or facial tics, may none the less display the individual's feelings of nervousness and embarrassment – a case of 'bodily betrayal' *par excellence*.

Perhaps the classic handling of these issues comes in Goffman's (1968 [1963]) analysis of stigma and the management of spoiled identity. As Goffman states, whilst stigmata are of many different types, including 'abominations of the body', they all share one central characteristic, namely, a crucial *discrepancy* between one's *virtual* and *actual* social identity. This discrepancy may be 'known about' beforehand, or it may become evident as the individual presents him/herself before others. In Goffman's terms, these individuals constitute the 'discredited', who have special reasons for feeling that 'mixed contacts' with 'normals' will be 'tensionful': a situation that, unhappily, can lead to 'avoidance, rejection or withdrawal by either party'. This, again, serves to highlight the earlier, more general point that embodied, expressive signs – including 'stigma symbols' such as the wrist markings of an attempted suicide or pock marks on a drug addict's arms – may serve to qualify whatever an individual attempts to convey to others by verbal means alone.

In contrast, for those whose 'differentness' is not immediately apparent or known about in advance (i.e. the 'discreditable'), the dilemma is 'to display or not to display; to tell or not to tell; to let on or not to let on; to lie or not to lie; and in each case, to whom, when and where' (Goffman 1968: 57). The degree of *visibility* or *evidentness* (i.e. how well or badly the stigma functions as a means of communicating the individual's possession of it) *known-about-ness* and *obtrusiveness* of a discrediting attribute serve, therefore, as an important interactional baseline from which the individual works in stigma management and the negotiation of spoiled identity. Within all this, the body clearly plays a central role. In this sense, Goffman's analysis of stigma can be read as a corporeal treatise on the various ways in which the body and the norms regarding its presentation mediate between an individual's social identity and self-identity (Shilling 1993).

Finally, moving beyond the issue of body techniques and the vicissitudes of embodied self-identity, Goffman (1983) also displays a keen interest in how key features of social structure gear into the interaction order. For example, in his discussion of symbols of class status, Goffman draws attention, in a strikingly similar manner to Bourdieu, to the fact that these symbols are literally *embodied* and *enacted* during routine social interaction. From this viewpoint, symbols of class status consist of:

> the kind of acts which impress others with the suitableness and likeableness of one's general manner. In the minds of those present, such a person is thought to be 'one of our kind'. Impressions of this sort seem to be built upon a response to many particles of behaviour. *These behaviours involve matters of etiquette, dress, deportment, gesture, intonation, dialect, vocabulary, small bodily movements* and automatically expressed evaluations concerning both the substance and details of life. In a manner of speaking, these behaviours constitute a social style.
>
> (Goffman 1951: 300)

As Goffman argues, the fact that many of these symbols of class status are anchored in the body (i.e. have 'organic moorings'), serves as an important *restrictive* mechanism, thereby enhancing and preserving their prestige value (cf. Bourdieu's notion of the habitus and physical capital). Similarly, in his discussion of the arrangement between the sexes, Goffman notes how institutionalised arrangements do not so much allow for the expression of natural differences between the sexes as for the *production* of them. In this respect, he suggests a kind of 'institutional reflexivity' in which:

> deep-seated institutional practices have the effect of transforming social situations into scenes for the performance of genderisms by both sexes, many of these performances taking a ritualised form which affirms beliefs about the differential human nature of the two sexes even while indications are provided as to how behaviour between the two sexes can be expected to be intermeshed.
>
> (Goffman 1977: 325)

From this perspective, even simple expressions of bodily deference such as a man opening a door for a woman, can be seen not merely as symbolic but as *constitutive* of gender inequalities. Indeed, in treating women as 'faulted actors', male domination can be 'carried right into the gentlest, most loving moments without apparently causing strain' (Goffman 1979: 9). These issues are perhaps most graphically illustrated in Goffman's sociological analysis of *Gender Advertisements* (1979). In analysing general features of the body like stature, lightly touching and caressing versus grasping and manipulating, mental drifting versus mental presence, appeasement and submission postures, and proprietary gestures, Goffman enables us to render the implicit message of these pictures explicit. Advertisers, in short; 'conventionalize our conventions. . . . Their hype is hyper-ritualization' (ibid.: 84).

To summarise, whether we are talking about the routine organisation of social interaction or the micro-politics of public order, the relationship between social identity and self-identity or symbols of class status and the arrangement between the sexes, Goffman's sociology is anchored in the fundamental problem of human embodiment. In this respect, as Crossley (1995b) rightly argues, Shilling's (1993) 'social constructionist' reading of Goffman as a 'dualist' and 'subjectivist idealist' appears to be problematic. Goffman's studies of meaningful social behaviour do not in fact subordinate the body to the mind or to social symbolism. Rather, his primary concern, as we have seen, is with *what the body does* in the social world, *how it works to construct and reproduce that world* and how *it acts* through its sentient, embodied praxes. Seen in these terms, Goffman prepares the ground for a truly 'non-dualist' or 'carnal' version of sociology: one that both consolidates and extends the notion of body techniques, intercorporeality, and the embodied nature of our being-in-the-world (Crossley 1995b: 148).

Body and self, seer and seen, class and gender, dualistic concepts are thus well and truly sunk within Goffman's 'embodied' interaction order.

The embodiment of social action: an analytical framework

As in the previous chapter we have, until this point, concentrated on different theories of body use and the associated problems of agency and control, with little attempt at theoretical synthesis or integration. Whilst there have been few attempts to do so to date, Frank's (1991a) typology of 'body use in action' represents a significant advance on Turner's earlier analysis of bodily order. As suggested in Chapter 2, Frank's point of departure is to reverse Turner's terms of reference and to start instead in a 'bottom-up' manner, with bodies and their problems as the core analytical issue (i.e. an *action* rather than a *system* problem). From this perspective, the central theoretical issue is to show how societies themselves are built up from the tasks of bodies, not *vice versa*.

To this end, Frank, in an interesting adaptation of Giddens's (1984) structuration theory, proposes an approach in which the body is seen as both the *medium* and *outcome* of social 'body techniques' (cf. Mauss), and society is both the medium and outcome of the sum of these techniques. More specifically, Frank suggests that 'the body' is in fact constituted at the intersection of an equilateral triangle composed of *institutions, discourses and corporeality*. Here, discourses are used to signify the 'mappings' of the body's possibilities and limitations, providing the 'normative' framework within which bodies can, as it were, 'understand' themselves. Institutions, in contrast, are those places and contexts within which these discursive practices occur. Finally, corporeality, as third dimension to the constitution of 'body', refers to the obdurate physical facts of the body: a fleshy, material, body which is 'formed in the womb, transfigured through the life course, dies and decomposes' (Frank 1991a: 49).

It is within this triangular framework that Frank seeks to elucidate his typology of body use in action. As we argue in Chapter 8, bodies become most conscious of themselves when they encounter resistance of various kinds. In this respect, Frank suggests that the body confronts four central questions that it must ask itself as it undertakes action in relation to some object. First, there is the dimension of social control. Here the body must ask itself how predictable its performance will be (i.e. the issue of *control*). Whilst we may know what we want the body to do, it none the less retains some contingent will of its own, and it is this issue of control which needs to be resolved. Second, the body must also constitute itself on a dimension of *desire* according to whether or not it is producing or lacking. Third, the body must also, of course, take up a *relationship to others*. The central question here revolves around whether the body relates to itself in a monadic, closed, or dyadic, open, manner – one involving a mutually constitutive relationship with others. Finally, the fourth dimension of the body that Frank identifies concerns the issue of *self-relatedness*. Here, the key question concerns whether body consciousness associates itself with its own being, in particular its surface, or instead, dissociates itself from that corporeality?

From these four dimensions of control, desire, other-relatedness and self-relatedness, Frank is able to generate a matrix of four cells which are filled by what he terms the 'disciplined' body, the 'mirroring' body, the 'dominating' body and the 'communicative' body. These four types represent *body use in action*. As the body responds to these four questions concerning its object relatedness (e.g. is it predictable or contingent, dissociated or associated, etc.), a typical style of body usage emerges. However, these empirical bodies will not stay long with any one type of usage: in reality, 'the truth is a mess' (Frank 1991a: 52–3).

Seen from this vantage point, there is no Hobbesian problem of order, only action problems: how predictable am I, do I lack or produce, am I associated or dissociated from my corporeal body, am I monadic or dyadic towards others? For Frank each type of body usage resolves these problems through a particular mode of activity. Thus, for the disciplined body, the specific medium of activity is regimentation, the model of which is the rationalisation of the monastic order; for the mirroring body in contrast, the specific medium is consumption, the model of which is the department store; for the dominating body, the medium of activity is force and the model is warfare; finally, for the communicative body, the medium is what, in general terms, may be referred to as 'recognition', the models of which are dance, community rituals, shared narratives, and the care of the young, the old, the sick and disabled.

Looking at each of these bodies in more detail, the problem of control for the disciplined body is resolved, Frank suggests, by making itself predictable through its regimentation. With respect to desire, the disciplined body understands itself as lacking, whilst its other-relatedness is monadic due to the fact that the body becomes isolated in its performance. Even in military drill, Foucault reminds us, the body performs amongst others, not with them. Finally, the disciplined body is dissociated from itself: the ascetic is in but not of the body, whilst monastic mortification practices and the military instil in their adherents a sense of bodily dissociation. Here, as suggested above, the theorist of the disciplined body *par excellence* is, of course, Foucault.

As with the disciplined body, the mirroring body remains predictable, but for different reasons. Whilst the disciplined body achieves predictability through regimentation, the mirroring body's predictability is to be found in the manner in which it *reflects* all that is around it. Based upon consumption, the body becomes as predictable as the objects made available to it. The other-relatedness of the mirroring body also remains monadic, but again for different reasons. Whilst the mirroring body is open to the external world, it is none the less closed in its appropriation of that world, constituting its objectives in relation to its own self-reflection. As Frank argues, consumption involves the 'endless assimilation of a world of objects to one's own body and of one's own body to the world of objects' (1991a: 62). The mirroring body is also endlessly producing desires through the paradigmatic medium of consumption. What it sees it desires, and seeks to make part of its own self-image in an endless cycle of appropriation. Thus the object becomes a mirror in terms of which the body sees itself reflected. Finally, the mirroring body is also, of course, associated with its own surface – a situation classically captured in Lasch's (1979) *The Culture of Narcissism*, but also more generally in the writings of social theorists from Baudrillard to Bourdieu (see Chapter 4).

The dominating body, as Frank rightly argues, is impossible to theorise without giving due weight to issues of masculinity and lack. Thus, when a dyadic other-relatedness is combined with a fundamental sense of lack, the body turns to domination as its expressive mode of relating to 'others': others who are sought out as 'subhuman entities' which can be fought, crushed and destroyed, for the dominating body's 'lifeblood'. The world of the dominating body is a world of warfare which, by definition, is contingent. The dominating body must, therefore, be dissociated from itself in order to be able to absorb and inflict punishment. In illustrating these issues, Frank draws heavily on Theweleit's *Male Fantasies* (1987 [1977], 1989 [1978]), an intriguing two-volume study of the German *Freikorps* (i.e. the private volunteer armies that roamed Germany in the inter-war years serving the cause of domestic repression), and ultimately the whole problem of fascism (see Chapter 10, this volume). In particular, using a variety of documentary evidence including novels, letters and autobiographies, Theweleit is able to show how the masculine identity of these pro-fascist officers was ultimately shaped by a dread of women and a fear of dissolution – a fear intimately related to their aggressive racism and anti-communism. For the *Freikorpsmen*, the 'only real thing was fighting' and the reduction of 'others' to a 'bloody mass' or 'pulp' (Theweleit 1987 [1977]: 395). As a consequence, the whole problem of human contingency and the ceaseless motion of 'desiring production' was ultimately transformed by these men into the 'production of death itself' (Ehrenreich 1987: xii).

Whilst disciplined, mirroring and dominating bodies are clearly related to certain corporeal types at the empirical level, the communicative body, in contrast, is 'less a reality than a praxis' (Frank 1991a: 79). Although it is quite possible to look back in time for examples of communicative bodies (e.g. the Rabelaisian carnivalesque bodies of medieval popular culture (Bakhtin 1968)), Frank chooses instead to look forward to the paradigmatic examples of dance and performative art, together with the caring practices of medicine. As he explains, the quintessential feature of the communicative body is that it is a body in the *process* of creating itself. Here the body's contingency is no longer a problem but a creative opportunity. Indeed, it is only when contingency and dyadic other-relatedness intersect with a *producing* form of desire (cf. Deleuze and Guattari in Chapter 5, this volume) and a self-relatedness which is associated, that dyadic relations are no longer premised upon domination, and contingency no longer becomes threatening.

In this sense, discourses and institutions now *enable* more than they constrain the communicative body, a situation that is reversed with respect to the other styles of bodily usage. Here Frank discusses a range of literature from Hanna's *Dance, Sex and Gender* (1988) and Sayre's *The Object of Performance* (1989), to Murphy's *The Body Silent* (1987) and Kleinman's *The Illness Narratives* (1988). In doing so, he is able to illustrate the fundamental point that what communicative bodies are really about is expression, sharing and mutual recognition through a diverse array of human experiences from dance to illness (see Chapters 8 and 10, this volume).

These dimensions of action problems, types of bodily activity and their media, are schematically reproduced in Figure 3.1.

To summarise, Frank's fundamental point is that the grounding of social theory must first and foremost be the body's consciousness of itself; only from this basis can theory put selves into bodies and bodies into society. Whilst bodies certainly do have problems with each other, the fundamental issue to hold on to is the 'embodiment of these problems' rather than allowing them to be 'abstracted from the need, pains and desires of bodies' (Frank 1991a:

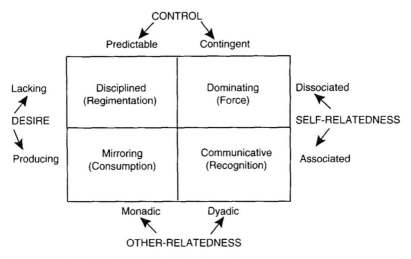

Figure 3.1 Frank's typology of body 'use' in action
Source: Reprinted from Frank (1991a: 96)

91). In this regard, the core problem is not the 'social ordering' of bodies – the term 'order' implies a 'looking down on bodies' instead of experiencing their own problems of contingency and alignment – but rather their 'communication' (i.e. the problem of how individual bodies 'come to terms' with one another). In building this approach up to that at which Turner's typology begins, bodies can be seen as the *foundation* as well as the product of both discourses and institutions. Discourses, in other words, are embodied, and social institutions cannot be understood apart from the real, lived experiences and actions of bodies. The grounding of social theory must, therefore, be the body's consciousness of itself. In short, what is required is not so much a sociology of the body, as an *embodied* sociology, one which includes its practitioners as well as its subjects. Only on this basis can theory put selves back into bodies, bodies back into society and society back into the body (Frank 1991a).

Conclusions

In this chapter we have sought to reverse the terms of debate considered in Chapter 2 and to concentrate instead on the (related) problem of bodily 'control'. In doing so, the analytical emphasis has shifted from a concern *about* bodies (i.e. the problem of order and representation) to one which emerges *from* bodies (i.e. body *use*, the embodiment of social action). Here, as we have seen, key issues include Mauss's notion of body techniques, Merleau-Ponty's non-dualist ontology of the sentient body-subject as a *praxical* being-in-the-world, together with Goffman's 'carnal' sociology of the embodied self and the intercorporeal nature of everyday social life/the micro-public order. These issues, in turn, have been extended and developed through Frank's typology of body use in action: one in which the body is constituted at the intersection of an equilateral triangle of *discourses, institutions* and *corpo-reality*, and society itself is seen as both the *medium* and *outcome* of the social body techniques it recursively organises (cf. Giddens). Only on this basis, we suggest, can a truly *embodied* sociology (*vis-à-vis* a sociology *of* the body) be developed.

These are issues to which we shall return in subsequent chapters. For the moment, however, it is to a fuller exploration of the 'fate' of human corpore-ality in late modernity and consumer culture (i.e. the vicissitudes of Frank's 'mirroring body'), that we turn in the next chapter. In doing so, we aim to probe further the relationship between the body and self-identity, together with the corporeal 'crisis' of meaning, in an increasingly reflexive, technolog-ical age.

4 The body in 'high' modernity and consumer culture

A key theme running through many of the chapters so far has been the uncertain nature and status of the body in contemporary Western society. In this chapter, we take a closer look at these issues through a consideration of the body in 'high' modernity and consumer culture. Taking our lead from writers such as Giddens, Bauman and Beck, we shall argue that whilst intimations of a postmodern world may indeed be occurring, social life is still fundamentally shaped by modern concerns, concerns that are only now becoming fully realised. Key issues here include the reflexive nature of social life, the problems of risk and consumption, the challenge of technology, and the dilemmas of death in a secular age. In raising these issues, we return once again to one of the fundamental questions underpinning this book as a whole – what is the body? This, in turn, relates to a broader set of questions concerning the 'fate' of human embodiment at the turn of the century. Central to these developments has been the growth of social reflexivity. Hence, it is to a brief discussion of this key issue, as a backdrop to the chapter as a whole, that we first turn.

The 'reflexive body'

Contra-postmodernism, we are now, Giddens claims, living in the age of 'high' modernity, a post-traditional order in which *modern* trends have become radicalised and universalised. From this viewpoint, neither modernity nor the self are redundant themes. Rather, social life is still fundamentally shaped by modern concerns even though the consequences are only now becoming fully realised. Modern institutions differ from all preceding forms in terms of their dynamism, the degree to which they undercut tradition, and their global impact. In this respect, 'late' modernity displays an ever increasing degree of social *reflexivity*, involving not only the 'routine incorporation of new knowledge into environments of action which are thereby reconstituted in the process', but the reflexive (re)organisation of social relations and aspects of nature (e.g. the 'socialising of biological mechanisms') in terms of criteria which are 'internally referential' to late modernity itself (Giddens 1990, 1991). Modernity, in short, becomes its own theme (Beck 1992).

Whilst modernity is a post-traditional order, the 'sureties of custom' and tradition have not been replaced by the 'certainties of rational knowledge'. Rather, late modernity, Giddens (1991) argues, institutionalises the principle of radical doubt by insisting that all knowledge is tentative and corrigible, taking the form of hypotheses rather than absolute statements of fact which are subject to critical scrutiny and systematic revision in the light of ever changing social circumstances. Within this context, systems of accumulated expertise become pluralised, contested and divergent in their implications: even the most 'reliable' authorities can only be trusted 'until further notice'. More generally, the increasing dislocation of knowledge and control leads to a multiplication of 'manufactured' risks and uncertainties. *Active* forms of trust therefore vie with *radical* forms of doubt and uncertainty as general existential features of life in reflexive modernity (Giddens 1994).

These transformations, together with the increasingly 'mediated' nature of contemporary experience and the re-ordering of time–space boundaries in which the 'local' and 'global' are realigned, mean that the self undergoes 'massive changes' through the reflexive (re)organisation of the life span and a continuous, yet revisable, biographical narrative of self-identity (Giddens 1991). The body too becomes less an extrinsic 'given' which functions outside the internally referential systems of late modernity, and is instead reflexively (re)made amidst a puzzling diversity of options and possibilities (ibid.). Thoroughly penetrated by modernity's reflexive systems and abstract knowledge, the body, like the self:

> becomes a site of interaction, appropriation and reappropriation, linking reflexively organised processes and systematically ordered expert knowledge. Once thought to be the locus of the soul, then the centre of dark perverse needs, the body has become fully available to be 'worked upon' by the influences of high modernity. As a result of these processes, its boundaries have been altered. It has as it were, a thoroughly permeable 'outer layer' through which the reflexive project of the self and externally formed abstract systems routinely enter.
>
> (Giddens 1991: 218)

This, in turn, sets up something of a paradox, namely: the greater our ability to control the human body, the more *uncertain* our sense of what precisely it is, what is 'natural' about it and, perhaps most worryingly of all, what it might become (Shilling 1993). As the boundaries between the natural and the social begin to blur through the 'socialising of biological mechanisms', science runs ahead of our ability to make informed moral judgements and choices about whether bodies should in fact be reconstructed in this way or that, and the extent to which our humanity is being compromised in the process.

These are issues to which we shall return throughout the chapter. For the moment, however, it is worth noting, at an early stage, that this emphasis on the socially reflexive body and self, whilst important, is not without its problems. As Shilling and Mellor (1996) rightly point out, people comprise both minds and bodies in Giddens's analysis, but are *essentially* minds for most of their lives, tending only to be shaped by their sensual bodily responses when their attempts to reflexively understand and engage with the world break down. This, in turn, has three major consequences. First, in terms of ongoing debates over structuration theory, it provides only a very limited understanding of how people's experiences and responses to social structures are shaped by their sensory/sensual embodied selves. Second, in doing so, it prioritises *cognitive* reflexivity and mental engagement, thereby marginalising the more carnal and sensual dimensions of close personal relations, so central to Giddens's (1992) analysis of the transformation of intimacy (Shilling and Mellor 1996).[1] Finally, this general stress on social reflexivity as an all-pervasive force in late modernity fails to acknowledge the fact that a new conception of 'fitness' is being forged, one in which, just as surely as nineteenth-century social Darwinism, some will 'succeed' and others will fail due to 'inflexible bodies' and 'unresponsive selves' (Martin 1994).

'Risky' bodies/'panic' sex?

Closely linked to these issues of reflexivity and uncertainty, is another core feature of life in late modernity, namely, the dilemmas of 'risk' culture at the turn of the century. To be sure, life has always, in an important sense, been a 'risky business' – from the battles of medieval warrior nobility to the great plagues of past centuries. None the less, the nature, scope and dimensions of contemporary risks have all profoundly altered in the late modern era. Whilst misfortunes and disasters in pre-industrial times were attributed to fate(s), God(s) or natural disasters, modern risks, as mentioned above, are increasingly 'manufactured' through human intervention of many different sorts – something which is systematically intensified as a consequence of the globalising process (Giddens 1994). 'Danger', in short, lurks everywhere, as risks of many different sorts, 'clamour for attention' (Douglas 1986: 59). The nature of modern risks can also no longer be understood simply in class terms. Rather, in 'risk' society, we are all ultimately confronted with a similar fate from which it is difficult if not impossible to escape. As Beck (1992) succinctly puts it: 'poverty is hierarchic, smog is democratic'. Risks, in other words, display a 'boomerang effect' in which even the rich and powerful are *ultimately* not safe. Slowly but surely, a 'victimisation by risk' is beginning to take place (Beck 1992).

Not only does modernity *create* risks through our ways of living, working, systems of transportation and the like, it also seeks to *compensate* for them by means of calculation and political regulation (Beck 1992). In an increasingly 'decisionist' culture, the 'profiling of risks' becomes an important means of 'colonising the future', instilling a sense of calculability in what is fast becoming a 'runaway world' (Giddens 1991). Yet risk assessment is also, by definition, imperfect, not least because the nature of modern risks is largely invisible and their central locus lies in the future. Indeed, in many respects, the nature of modern risks – including nuclear, chemical, genetic and ecological mega-hazards – abolishes the 'calculus of risk' as there are simply no statistical bases from which to assess the probability of their occurrence (Giddens 1991). This, coupled with the difficulty of establishing blame or culpability, and the neglect of multiplicative effects, points to the complex and contradictory nature of contemporary risk assessment.

Given these difficulties, the divisions between social and scientific rationality become ever more apparent as social movements raise issues which are not addressed by experts and *vice versa*. As the 'legitimating patrons' of global industrial pollution and contamination, the sciences are prominently involved in the origin and growth of these very risks. In this sense, lay consciousness and public perceptions of the risks of modernisation have established themselves against the resistance and demystification of scientific rationality (Beck 1992). Risks, in other words, display the limits of modern systems of expertise and sources of authority, exposing gaps in knowledge which compromise the very notion of 'expertise' itself (Giddens 1991). Social and scientific rationality are also, however, closely interwoven. Technical discussions of risk rely on social expectations and value judgments, whilst social discussions and perceptions of risk increasingly come to depend upon scientific evidence and arguments: a 'dialectical' relationship of 'expertise and counter expertise' (Beck 1992).

One of the principal ways in which these discourses of risk and moral danger are articulated and expressed is through public health campaigns and the forms of 'surveillance medicine' they spawn. Armstrong (1993), for example, has described the changing configuration of medicalised topography, risk and hygiene over the past two centuries in terms of four models of public health space. In the first, 'quarantine model' of hygiene, a *cordon sanitaire* was erected between healthy and unhealthy spaces such as houses, towns or ships. Within this model, risks to health were located in places. The next model, one which emerged in the mid-nineteenth century in the form of 'sanitary science', was primarily concerned with monitoring the passage of substances such as air, water, faeces and semen across the boundaries of the body. Here, the late nineteenth-century focus on sewage, air and water pollution identified risks as being located between physical bodily space and 'non-corporeal external space' – a model of transmission characterised by a physical exchange between the body and the outside world. The third model of 'personal hygiene' was one that emerged in the twentieth century. In contrast to the previous two approaches, this model focused on personal cleanliness and behaviours such as exercise, eating and smoking. Within this framework, risks to health were located in a space defined by the 'boundaries between people' and the individual's health status was thought to be threatened by their interactions with other individuals. Finally, within the late twentieth-century 'new' public health paradigm, risks to health are no longer simply conceptualised as existing in places or spaces, nor in terms of personal hygiene. Instead, the contemporary emphasis on health promotion, lifestyles and the 'green response' to ecological dangers has meant that risks are located anywhere and everywhere (Armstrong 1993). Seen in these terms, a 'new regime of disease' is beginning to emerge – one involving a critical reconfiguration of corporeal space and bodily boundaries (Turner 1995).

In Foucauldian terms this shift to an all-encompassing notion of risk can be seen as constituting a new form of surveillance – one that seeks to reconfigure individuals through their constant and pervasive observation'. Thus, whilst hospital medicine operated with the 'three-dimensional corporeal volume of the sick patient', surveillance medicine, in contrast, focuses on the 'risk factor network', which is read across an 'extra-corporal and temporal space' – a space represented by the notion of 'lifestyle' – to identify the precursors of future illness (Armstrong 1995). Here individuals are advised, cajoled and encouraged by health promoters to assess critically their risks of succumbing to disease and to change their behaviours accordingly. In doing so, a 'victim blaming ideology' develops – one in which individuals are instructed to take responsibility for their health at a time when they are least able to do so (Crawford 1977, 1980).

As this suggests, risk discourse at the turn of the century – from the threat of chemical warfare to the destruction of our natural habitat and the 'greying' of the Western population – increasingly target the body as an apocalyptic site of 'contamination' and 'catastrophe', 'toxicity' and 'waste' – one that is needful of constant surveillance, regulation and control. From this viewpoint, the powers, dangers and risks of the social body are symbolically mirrored and reproduced in small on the human body (see Chapter 2, this volume). These issues are clearly illustrated in relation to HIV/AIDS. Indeed, it is HIV/AIDS that, perhaps more than any other modern disease, displays analogies between bodily pollution beliefs and the threats and dangers to the social order.[2]

Certainly the AIDS epidemic, particularly in its early stages, has been matched by an epidemic of fear, anxiety and moral concern: what Strong (1990) has appositely referred to as 'epidemic psychology'. Here, metaphors of 'invasion', 'pollution', 'alien takeover' and 'attack' are frequently encountered (Sontag 1991). Within this discourse, the source of AIDS always lies 'elsewhere': either in different countries or in 'different' and therefore 'deviant' social groups. This, in turn, reinforces a moralising discourse on AIDS as punishment or divine retribution for 'lax lifestyles' – one in which gay men, bisexual men, prostitutes and IVDUs are viewed as 'guilty', whilst haemophiliacs, recipients of blood transfusions, and children born to mothers with AIDS are seen as 'innocent victims'. The upshot of this is a new 'cultural politics' for reconstructing the self in conformity with intensified mandates for self-control and bodily discipline (Crawford 1994). AIDS, in short, intensifies concerns and anxieties surrounding rationality, the maintenance of bodily boundaries, the contamination of body fluids and the robustness of one's immune system.[3]

Kroker and Kroker (1988) refer in this context to the emergence of 'panic' bodies, a situation in which a corporeal politics of 'Body McCarthyism' seeks to distinguish between the 'clean' and 'unclean' according to the 'purity' of bodily fluids. In particular, they note a striking resemblance between medical and military rhetoric in relation to AIDS, drawing parallels between the fear of AIDS and a generalised fear of the breakdown of immunological systems. Everywhere today it seems, from the immunology labs to the corporate training sessions of multinational companies, people are actively using and pushing the immune system to organise and comprehend their lives. Indeed, the immune system has emerged as a field of terms in which all manner of questions and definitions are given meaning and measured. Here, we return again to the new ideal of 'flexible' bodies as the passport to success in all walks of life (Martin 1994; Haraway 1991).

In contrast to this focus on 'panic bodies', particularly in the era of HIV/AIDS, other writers and researchers have pointed to the considerable degree of scepticism that exists within the lay populace regarding the dangers of so-called 'unhealthy' lifestyles. To be sure, public health campaigns and risk discourses may seek to engender a heightened sense of 'health consciousness' amongst the lay populace, but in no way should this simply and unproblematically be equated with the emergence of 'panic bodies'. Rather, a perennial conundrum for health promoters, the medical profession and the government alike is the extent to which 'advice' about health, risk and lifestyles remains unheeded at the level of everyday beliefs and practices. Even in the field of HIV/AIDS prevention, the translation of messages about 'safe(r) sex' into action remains a fundamental stumbling block, particularly for young women who do not approach the sexual encounter as equal partners (Holland *et al.* 1990, Holland 1992).

In particular, there is a tendency, at least amongst certain segments of the society, to draw upon repertoires of common sense, lay notions of 'everything in moderation', and 'fatalistic discourses' in which 'fickleness', 'luck' and 'chance' are dominant themes (Davison *et al.* 1992, 1991). This does not, however, mean that individuals are 'victims of their own ignorance'. Rather, people's views are based upon what, for them, is a realistic assessment of personal risk given the uncertainties and contradictions of current epidemiological reasoning. From this viewpoint, health promotion advice is likely to be counter-productive as it does not readily fit with beliefs found in popular culture that, 'a healthy lifestyle might be the death of you' (Lupton and Chapman 1995). Here we glimpse again, the dialectical relationship between reflexivity and risk, trust and doubt, expertise and counter-expertise at the turn of the century.

What then, does all this suggest? More precisely, how are we to reconcile the proliferation of (manufactured) risks and uncertainties in late modernity with the growth of ever tighter mechanisms of (bodily) surveillance and control? One possible solution is to argue that as the macro-social, economic and global environment becomes ever more unstable and uncertain, then new systems of surveillance and government are put into place in order to regulate and control the social and natural environment, including the body itself (Turner 1995). Seen in these terms, the discipline, surveillance and control of bodies may effect an albeit precarious 'resolution' of the more global threats and dangers we face at the turn of the century – one in which the current bodily preoccupation with health and fitness in consumer culture play no small part.

'Consumer bodies'/'performing' selves?

If reflexivity and risk bring bodies and selves into a new alignment, then these processes are consolidated and extended through the commodifying pressures of consumer culture. Within consumer culture our relationship to commodities is predicated less upon real need than their inexhaustible ability to 'incite desire'. 'I consume therefore I am' becomes a dominant cultural motif, as representations (of the 'good' life) are substituted for reality, and settled convictions are overturned in favour of flexibility, mobility and an incessant search for the new (Falk 1994; Featherstone 1991). It is against this backdrop that the project of the self becomes translated, to a greater or lesser degree, into the possession of 'desired goods' and the pursuit of 'artificially framed lifestyles'. As Giddens states:

> The consumption of ever-novel goods becomes in some part a substitute for the genuine development of self; appearance replaces essence as the visible signs of successful consumption come actually to out-weigh the use-values of the goods and services in question.
>
> (Giddens 1991: 198)

Given these commodifying pressures, there is a tendency for individuals to place ever more importance upon the appearance and presentation of the body as constitutive of self-identity. Here, in a seemingly 'narcissistic age' (Lasch 1979), a premium is placed upon corporeal images of youth, beauty, health and fitness. The closer the body approximates to these idealised images, the higher its 'exchange-value' (Featherstone 1991: 177).[4] This, together with the 'sexualisation of wants and desires' (Seidman 1991, 1989), means that the body itself becomes something of a 'fetishised' commodity,[5] one that has to be attractively 'packaged', 'marketed' and 'sold'. Indeed, it would not be too much of an exaggeration to say that the balance within consumer culture has tilted from bodies producing commodities (i.e. 'externalising objects of labour'), to commodities producing bodies (i.e. 'internalising objects of consumption') (Faurschou 1988).

Despite these commodifying pressures, the body and self are clearly not passive entities. Rather, as we have seen, the relationship between the body and self-identity becomes increasingly dynamic as a consequence of the growth of social reflexivity and the salience of risk. Viewed in these terms, lifestyle and body planning are not, as Lasch (1979) claims, wholly 'narcissistic' enter-prises. Instead, as Giddens (1991: 178) argues, they form a normal part of life in post-traditional, reflexive, social environments. What might at first appear to be a wholesale movement towards the cultivation of bodily appear-ance is, therefore, on closer inspection, an expression of a much deeper underlying concern to actively control and 'construct' the body through a pluralisation of lifestyle options and choices that reflexive modernity makes possible.

It is within this context that body maintenance comes to the fore. Whilst in pre-modern times, bodily discipline/asceticism was sought to serve higher spiritual ends and repress the 'temptations' of the flesh, today it is instead concerned with the (aesthetic) cultivation of outer appearance and the (hedo-nistic) expression of desire. Here, 'inner' concerns with health and the optimal functioning of the body merge imperceptibly with 'outer' concerns with appearance (i.e. 'the look'), movement and control of the body across social time and space (Featherstone 1991). Today, the firm, well-toned and muscled body has become a symbol of 'correct *attitude*'; 'it means that one "cares" about oneself and how one appears to others, suggesting willpower, energy, control over infantile impulse, the ability to "make something" of oneself' (Bordo 1990: 94–5).

If the mind is willing but the body weak, then biomedical technology, alongside the beauty and dieting industries, can always be called upon to help reconstruct bodies or 'turn the biological clock back'. There is now, for example, a 'booming market' in cosmetic surgery, with some 600,000 opera-tions performed annually in the US – what Wolf (1990) refers to as a kind of 'surgical age'.[6] Not only does plastic surgery throw into critical relief the commodified nature of the body in consumer culture, it also indicates the extreme lengths to which individuals will go in order to mould and shape their bodies in line with prevailing cultural mandates of youth and beauty. As Glassner notes, professional body remakers function like 'surrogate psychiatrists' – we literally imagine them capable of making us into 'some body new' (Glassner 1995: 175). Bodies, in other words, become objects to be bought and sold according to the latest corporeal fads and fashions. Viewed in this context, cosmetic surgery is at best 'dilemmatic', both a symptom and a solution, liberation and oppression, all at once – something that, paradoxically, enables women to feel 'embodied subjects' rather than 'objectified bodies' (Davis 1994: 161).

These processes are further enhanced by the fitness industry in which equip-ment such as running shoes, exercise bikes, weights and rowing machines, not to mention videos and stylish forms of sports clothing, are heavily marketed and sold. More broadly, the fitness 'craze' displays certain aesthetic and ideological similarities with other activities that have elsewhere been charac-terised as 'postmodern' (Glassner 1989). Exercise bikes, for example, together with rowing, walking and running machines are 'simulations' of the 'real' thing, whilst home videos comprise pastiches of dance, music and nostalgic/

futuristic images. It also blurs a number of other modernist dualisms such as body and self, inside and outside, male and female, work and leisure. Getting your body in shape, for instance, is said to promote a sense of wellbeing, an 'efficient mind' and an enhancement of the self. Similarly, leisure and fitness activities are now increasingly encouraged within the workplace: the tightly controlled body being a corporate emblem of the tightly run firm (Glassner 1989). Within this context, a 'transvaluation' of use values takes place: 'everything has to be good for something else and the range of alleged benefits multiplies endlessly' (Featherstone 1991: 185).

This focus on 'fitness', in turn, feeds into broader discourses on health within consumer culture. Health, as Crawford (1984) notes, is one of Western culture's supreme metaphors – a code for signifying personal qualities, moral capacities, and situations. More generally, these discourses, as he convincingly demonstrates, provide potent metaphors for the cultural values, symbols and ideologies that structure contemporary social and economic life. On the one hand, late capitalist imperatives of a disciplined, productive workforce are reflected and reinforced through the notion of health as 'control'. On the other hand, health as 'release', the alternative modality, serves as a potent metaphor for the imperative to consume.[7] Indeed, in consumer culture, a symbolic order based upon self-denial would be ruinous. The mandate for discipline therefore clashes with the mandate for pleasure, and our bodies serve as the 'ultimate metaphor' reflecting the general mood and cultural contradictions of late capitalist society. Seen in these terms, the pursuit of health becomes something of a popular 'ritual', one which provides a repertoire for making sense of and morally managing 'matter out of place' – i.e. a displacement onto the medicalised body and the language of somatic and psychic wellbeing, of the contradictory demands and internalised mandates of control and release as they are meaningfully experienced in the current era (Crawford 1998).

It is within this context that eating disorders loom large as potent metaphors of our times. Whilst bulimia expresses the unstable double-bind of consumer capitalism, anorexia (i.e. the work ethic in absolute control) and obesity (i.e. consumerism in control), embody an attempted 'resolution' of these cultural contradictions.[8] In each particular case, however, the production/consumption axis is gender-overlaid by a hierarchical dualism, one in which women's bodies pay the greatest material and symbolic toll, particularly in periods when traditional forms of gender organisation are being challenged (Bordo 1990, 1993). More generally, in keeping with the themes and existential parameters of this chapter, these eating disorders of late modernity can be seen to express a 'pathology of reflexive self-control', operating around a central axis of self-identity and bodily appearance (Giddens 1991). From this perspective, anorexia represents a striving for security and control in a world of pluralised, yet ambiguous options, set against the backdrop of the continuing exclusion of women from full participation in the universe of social activity that these options generate. The body, in short, becomes an emblem of safe existence in a reflexively 'open' social environment (Giddens 1991: 103–8).

Despite this 'tyranny of slenderness' (Chernin 1981), bulky bodies are none the less acceptable as long as they are 'tightly controlled' and managed. In this respect, body building, for men and women alike, has become an increasingly popular form of body transformation in recent years, allowing people to make strong public and personal statements about who and what they are (Shilling 1993). This 'quest for muscles' has been interpreted in a variety of ways, ranging from an 'archetypal expression' of male insecurity and vulnerability (Pleck 1982; Fussell 1991), to an attempt to 'reassert the validity of brawn' in an age of 'intelligent machines' (Dery 1996). The promise here seems to be that you can 'defy both nature and culture and transform yourself into that potent self-assured manly being that you've always dreamed of being' (Wacquant 1995: 164).

For women, in contrast, one of the main attractions of body building is that it holds out the possibility of challenging conventional notions of the 'weak feminine body': a challenge that, ironically, is hampered by the fact that in adding muscular bulk, women body builders run the risk of being denigrated for going 'too far' and looking 'too masculine'. As such, body building 'pumps the ironies' of gender relations in a particularly acute form (Mansfield and McGinn 1993). There are also more general risks and dangers involved in body building, not least of which is the emergence of 'megarexia', a new condition in which the individual becomes obsessed with increasing the sheer muscular bulk of the body – the very antithesis of the anorexic body discussed above.

If anorexic and megarexic bodies are extreme, yet symptomatic, expressions of life in consumer culture, then the anxiety, stigma and shame which ageing, sick and disabled bodies engender is another stunning indictment of an era premised on *doing* rather than *being*, and the virtues of the youthful, sexually attractive body. In such a culture, bodies which do not function 'normally' or meet 'acceptable' standards of appearance are regarded, both visually and conceptually, as 'matter-out-of-place'. Indeed, it becomes increasingly difficult to 'grow old gracefully' in an era where ageing itself assumes a negative cultural value. Even in the latter stages of life, therefore, body maintenance is encouraged, not so much because of the risks to health but the distorting 'mask of ageing' (i.e. the external signs of sagging flesh, wrinkles, loss of muscle tone, hair loss and overweight), which obscures the essentially 'youthful' self (Featherstone and Hepworth 1991). Ageing, in short, like death itself, comes to be seen as a 'disease' in need of cure.

'Capitalising' on the body: class, lifestyles and the search for social distinction

Until now, a strong emphasis has been placed on the *reflexive* nature of contemporary social life and the pluralisation of lifestyle options and choices in conditions of late modernity. Whilst lifestyles, from this perspective, are in an important sense 'routinised', the routines followed are none the less reflexively open to change in the light of the 'mobile' nature of self-identity (Giddens 1991). The logic of this argument would seem to suggest that 'discipline' in the sphere of consumption has recently declined, and that patterns of uniformity, especially class-based patterns of consumption, have weakened as a consequence.

Against this view, however, it can be argued that there is still a considerable degree of systematicity and constraint in consumption behaviour, both within and between social groups, and that these mechanisms help avoid or assuage some of the more 'anxiety-provoking' elements of consumer 'choice' (Warde 1994). In this regard, Bourdieu's work is especially relevant, not only as a counter-weight to Giddens, Beck and Bauman's emphasis upon the fluidity and dynamism of lifestyle (re-)construction, but also in terms of what it has to say about the body as a form of 'physical capital' and its symbolic role in the search for social distinction.

For Bourdieu, lifestyle variations between social groups are also elementary 'structuring features of stratification'. More precisely, it is in the interaction between social location, habitus and taste that distinct, class-related bodily forms and orientations are forged. Class culture, in other words, is literally *embodied* through the habitus (i.e. the 'structuring structure' and 'unchosen principle of all choice') and expressed through bodily hexis (see Chapter 3). As he states:

> *Taste, a class culture turned into nature, that is embodied, helps to shape the class body . . . the body is the most indisputable materialization of class taste*, which it manifests in several ways. It does this first in the seemingly most natural features of the body, the dimensions (volume, height, weight) and shapes (round or square, stiff or supple, straight or curved) of its visible forms, which express in countless ways a whole relation to the body, i.e. a way of treating it, caring for it, feeding it, maintaining it, *which reveals the deepest dispositions of the habitus. It is in fact through preferences with regard to food* which may be perpetuated beyond their social conditions of production (as, in other areas, an accent, a walk etc.), and also, of course, through the uses of the body in work and leisure which are bound up with them, *that the class distribution of bodily properties is determined.*
>
> (Bourdieu 1984: 190, our emphasis)

The physical body does not therefore simply reflect but actively contributes to social inequalities. Through the struggles that characterise the search for social distinction, bodies and lifestyles of the differing classes are accorded varying degrees of social and symbolic weight. These struggles are wide-ranging, and include the attempts of differing social groups to define and appropriate as 'their own' exclusive property, particular styles of dress, sports and many other forms of cultural consumption (Shilling 1993). In this respect, working classes are at a distinct disadvantage. The bodily forms they produce through the habitus constitute a form of physical capital which has less 'exchange value' than that developed by the dominant classes. The various social 'fields' that together constitute the 'space of lifestyles' (e.g. eating, exercise, health, sport, fashion, sexuality, etc.) and society more generally (e.g. art, economics, education), are structured in such a way that opportunities for the bestowing of value on working-class bodies are few and far between (ibid.). In contrast, the dominant classes tend to enjoy more valuable opportunities to *convert* their physical capital into other forms of capital (i.e. economic, cultural, social or symbolic), and are more likely to be in those social fields invested with the power of bestowing value on particular bodily forms and practices (Shilling 1993).

Herein lie the dynamics of the search for social distinction which, of necessity, involves regular struggles over the definition and control of those fields in which distinctive bodily forms are constituted and evaluated. Once acquired, however, these exchange values are unlikely to remain static. Rather, as Bourdieu emphasises, they tend to alter over the course of time as a consequence of the changing dynamics of the social fields and the degree to which these particular bodily forms, attributes and activities have been appropriated by those lower down the social hierarchy. The search for social distinction, in short, is a continual, dynamic process of claims and counterclaims.

These issues are usefully illustrated through the example of sport. As Bourdieu (1978) suggests, one only needs to be aware that class variations in sporting activities are due as much to variations in perception and appreciation of the immediate or deferred profits they are supposed to bring, as to variations in costs, both economic, cultural and bodily (i.e. degree of risk and physical effort involved), in order to understand in its broadest outlines, the social distribution of these activities amongst the various classes and class fractions. Even when different classes and class fractions pursue similar sporting activities – a trend that looks set to increase in contemporary society – the meaning and function of these activities is likely to differ considerably:

> It would not be difficult to show that the different social classes do not agree as to the effects expected from bodily exercise, whether on the outside of the body [bodily hexis], such as the visible strength of prominent muscles which some prefer, or the elegance, ease and beauty favoured by others, or inside the body, health, mental equilibrium etc. . . . [For example] . . . gymnastics may be asked to produce either a strong body, bearing outward signs of strength – this is the working class demand, which is satisfied by body-building – or a healthy body – this is the bourgeois demand, which is satisfied by gymnastics or other sports whose function is essentially hygienic. . . . Class habitus defines the meaning conferred on sporting activity, the profits expected from it; and

not the least of these profits is the social value accruing from the pursuit of certain sports by virtue of the distinctive rarity they derive from their class distribution. In short, to the 'intrinsic' profits . . . which are expected from sport for the body itself, one must add the social profits, those accruing from any distinctive practice, which are very unequally perceived and appreciated by the different classes.

(Bourdieu 1978: 835–6)

Extending these insights to the problem of 'ageing bodies', it can be argued that whilst the working classes may more readily come to accept the inevitability of bodily decline, it is in fact the 'new' middle classes who tend to be most anxious about the ageing process, engaging in a variety of body-maintenance techniques to combat the 'natural' ravages of time.[9] In contrast, the upper classes tend to have acquired orientations and dispositions towards their bodies, through the habitus and bodily hexis, which can overlay and disguise many of the negative effects of ageing – choosing instead to 'wear' their age unselfconsciously as a mark of social distinction rather than decline (Featherstone 1987a, 1991). In this respect, whilst certain struggles between working-class males may be resolved in terms of physical strength, age-group conflicts within the middle and upper classes may involve struggles over the very definition of *when* old age begins and what value it should be accorded (Shilling 1993).

Class, body and lifestyles are therefore intimately related in Bourdieu's analysis of consumption and the search for social distinction. As such, he offers an important counterweight to overly reflexive notions of lifestyle choice and the mobile nature of the body and self-identity. Critics may object, however, that in doing so, Bourdieu, through his stress on the habitus, simply moves too far in the opposite direction, stressing fixity at the expense of fluidity, stability at the expense of reflexivity. The habitus in other words, despite Bourdieu's claims to have transcended the structure/agency, subject/object divide, appears to operate, in large part, behind the actor's back (Jenkins 1992). Here we return to the sociological problem identified in Chapter 3 of the 'over-socialised' concept of (wo)man and the minimisation of embodied creativity and social change (Shilling 1997b). In this respect, what is really needed is an approach that recognises the dialectical interplay of freedom and constraint in contemporary society and accords equal weight to both in the constitution of the body, self and lifestyles (Williams 1995a).

'Cyberbodies/digital minds': Life in the 'posthuman' bodyshop?

As alluded to earlier, a fundamental issue underpinning many of the themes considered so far is, of course, the role of technology in late modern society, undermining still further our already precarious sense of what the body 'is', who 'owns' it, and what it might 'become'. More broadly, it is clear that technology is beginning to 'mediate' our social relationships, our self-identities and our wider sense of 'community' to an extent we are only now just beginning to grapple with.

Some writers have taken these arguments even further, claiming that we live in the age of the 'cyborg' – a 'posthuman' world involving the growing imbrication of humans and machines. As Haraway (1991) argues, hypothetically and materially, the cyborg is a 'hybrid' of cybernetic device and organism – a 'scientific chimera', but also a social and scientific reality, a 'myth and a tool', a 'representation and an instrument'. Cyborgs exist when two types of boundaries are simultaneously rendered 'problematic': that between animals (or other organisms) and humans, and that between self-governing machines (automatons) and organisms, especially humans as models of autonomy. Born of the 'interface' between 'automaton' and 'autonomy', nature and culture, masculinity and femininity, Self and Other, the 'leaky' cyborg renders these divisions indeterminate, thus offering the potential to escape from their oppressive confines (Haraway 1991).

Whilst this may sound wild and fanciful, the cyborg is clearly not just a creature born of science fiction. Rather, there are, it is claimed, already many cyborgs among us, from our grandmother with a cardiac pacemaker, to the state-of-the-art fighter-bomber pilot and the billions of potential still yet unborn humans who will be the products of genetic engineering (Gray 1995: 2–3). Indeed, the potential range of human machine couplings is 'mind blowing'.[10] Within all this, it is clear that developments in biomedical science, from the mainstreaming of cosmetic surgery to genetic engineering and nanotechnology, have played a central role, leading some to contemplate that the next generation may well be the last of 'pure' humans (Featherstone and Burrows 1995: 11–12; Deitch 1992). Even the quickest of tours of the human body, from head to toe reveals the great variety of ways that medicine can, potentially at least, turn humans into cyborgs – from *restorative* or *normalising*, to *reconfiguring* or *enhancing* technologies (Gray 1995: 3). More specifically, we can see these processes occurring on a number of different levels within the technological 'clinic' or 'posthuman' bodyshop of late modern medicine.

First, as mentioned earlier, recent advances in medical science and technology have meant that the body is becoming increasingly *plastic* (i.e. able to be moulded at will). In particular, technologies such as cosmetic surgery assume the constant honing and crafting of the human body according to the latest aesthetic trends and corporeal fashions. As such, they greatly expand the limits of how the body may be restyled, reshaped and rebuilt. Amongst the rapidly growing array of technologies on offer are facelifts, rhinoplasties (nose contouring), otoplasty (ear surgery), eyelid corrections, lip enlargements, chemical peeling and dermabrasion, breast correction (mastopexy, reduction, augmentation), the stripping of varicose veins, fat removal, body contouring (liposuction or suction lipectomy) and penile enlargement. In these 'body sculpting clinics' flesh is either added or taken away, wrinkles disappear, breasts become inflated or deflated and body shape is transformed (Davis 1994). As such, notwithstanding frequent complications – from scarring, bleeding, secondary infections and skin discolouration to nerve damage, loss of sensation and impaired motor ability – the 'makeability' of the human body and the power of medical technology are visually sustained in each 'exhibit' (Balsamo 1992, 1995a,b).

Not only are bodies becoming increasingly plastic, recent advances in medical technology are also now busy 'spinning plastic into tissue' (Langer and Vacanti 1995). Using biodegradable plastic seeded with cells, computer-aided 'scaffolding' has been constructed to provide a template for the formation of new tissue. As the cells divide, this plastic structure is covered and eventually degrades, leaving only tissue ready for implantation in the patient. Eventually, complex body parts, such as hands and arms will be produced through these forms of tissue engineering (Langer and Vacanti 1995). Indeed, the structure of these parts can already be duplicated in polymer scaffolds using computer-aided contouring, and most of the relevant tissue types (e.g. muscle, bone, cartilage, tendons, ligaments and skin) can now readily grow in culture. Seen in these terms, whilst the engineering of artificial tissue and organs is a logical next step in the treatment of injury and disease, 'this time the engineers will be the body's own cells' (Langer and Vacanti 1995: 100–2).

Second, bodies have become increasingly *bionic* with cardiac pacemakers, valves, titanium hips, polymer blood vessels, electronic eye and ear implants and even polyurethane hearts (Synnott 1993; O'Neill 1985). Here the human/machine interface is clearly evident as the cyborg moves out of the world of science fiction and into the realms of everyday life. Third, and closely related to this point, bodies are also becoming communal or *interchangeable* through developments such as organ donation and transplantation surgery (Synnott 1993). As Hogle (1995) notes, body parts are becoming increasingly 'widget'-like (i.e. standardised items to be replaced as needed on demand), and the organisation, procurement and delivery of human organs is shifting from an altruistic patient-centred enterprise to an increasingly international 'for-profit' market-based industry – one involving 'product-specific handling', marketing and even accounting systems. Indeed, whilst 'presentation', in the past, referred to the storage of materials *after* explantation and during transplant to the end user, now it begins much earlier within the human body itself:

> Recognising the considerable market potential of the human materials industry, pharmaceutical and medical supply companies have developed new products and entire new industries designed specifically for use in donor cadavers. These include free-oxygen scavengers, 'hibernation hormones', new perfusion and preservation fluids, and other chemicals to preserve tissue integrity before being removed, and to make the materials more 'immunologically silent' to prevent problems later when they are replaced inside another body. In essence, the human materials are

> being structurally, chemically and functionally transformed to make
> them more universal. In this way, they become not only substitutable
> mechanical parts, but more like off-the-shelf reagents, available for use
> in a variety of end-users.
>
> (Hogle, 1995: 208)

Through these 'core technologies', cadavers are being transformed into 'donor
cyborgs' as the physical body is 'reprogrammed' and 'retooled' for new uses.
When the donor cyborg reaches its 'almost-total-technology state', its parts
are dispersed and distributed throughout the 'communal body' to innumer-
able others. In this way, transplanted human body parts become the 'seeds'
that reproduce and replicate other new cyborgs (Hogle 1995: 207).

Not only are bodily organs interchangeable at the human-to-human level,
they also now *cross* species boundaries, as in xenotransplantation (i.e. the use
of animal organs for transplant surgery). To be sure this raises a number of
ethical dilemmas, issues made all the more pressing with the announcement
in late 1995 of a new development enabling scientists to produce a
customised pig whose organs would be less likely to induce fatal rejection in
the human recipient. The company involved, Imutran, reported the creation
of 'Astrid', the first of these pigs, which was duly given much media attention. Such developments, along with the creation of other 'transgenic'
animals (i.e. animals carrying genes from another species), and the use of
animals in tissue engineering (e.g. the 'mouse with the human ear'), pose
many moral, social and cultural questions about individual and species
bodies, and the constitution of the 'natural'.

This again raises, in acute form, thorny questions about the meaning(s)
of corporeality and the nature of death itself. If the pig, for example, is seen
as a ritually 'unclean' animal, one involving 'matter out of place' and the
'transgression' of cultural boundaries (Douglas 1966), then how do we see
ourselves with an animal heart inside us, and how does this square with, say,
orthodox Jewish beliefs, or those of a vegetarian or anti-vivisectionist? Does
the body become degraded, defiled or debased in some way as a consequence,
and if so, what implications does this 'grotesque' body have for our sense of
who and what we are? As Joralemon (1995) notes, transplantation challenges
traditional views of body/self integrity by distinguishing between the brain
and other, more replaceable, body parts, thereby reinforcing a traditional
Cartesian mind/body split. Sharp (1995) raises similar issues, stressing the
disjunction between the need to *personalise* and the need to *objectify* bodies and
organs. Whilst medical personnel put great stress on objectification (e.g. the
heart is 'only a "pump"'), transplant recipients experience conflict between
this mechanistic/reductionist view of the body and their wider cultural
beliefs about embodied selfhood – the 'sacred' heart, for instance, as the very
'core' of the person.

One of the greatest problems with transplant surgery to date has been the
issue of 'rejection'. Certainly, immunology can be seen as an important

'barrier' which is 'limiting' many of these technologies at present, and it is in this area that advances can be expected over the next few decades – a development that, in turn, links up with the advent of 'psychoneuroimmunology' as a new model within medical science and technology (Levin and Solomon 1990). More generally, as Langer and Vacanti (1995: 100) suggest, medical science, over the next few decades, will move beyond the practice of transplantation surgery altogether and into a new era of fabrication, the ultimate goal being to *manufacture* organs rather than simply move them, and to produce, through genetic engineering, universal donor cells (i.e. cells that do not provoke rejection by the immune system) for use in these engineered tissues.

Fourth, developments in modern medical technology mean that the body becomes increasingly *engineered* through new forms of gene therapy, and even chosen or *selected* from a growing number of ovum and sperm banks (Synnott 1993: 34–5). Over the course of medical history there have, as Anderson (1995) notes, been three great leaps in our ability to treat and prevent disease. First, the implementation of public health measures; second, the introduction of surgery with anaesthesia; and third, the use of vaccines and antibiotics. The introduction of gene therapy, at the turn of the twenty-first century, constitutes the 'fourth great leap'. Whilst today's understanding of the precise genetic bases for many diseases is sketchy, knowledge will increase enormously in the next few decades. By the year 2000, for example, scientists working on the Human Genome project should have determined the chromosomal location of, and deciphered parts of the DNA code in, more than 99 per cent of active human genes. Similarly, research aimed at uncovering the function of each gene is progressing rapidly. Such information should make it possible to identify the genes which malfunction in various diseases.

These new forms of gene therapy, in turn, key into broader debates concerning the new reproductive technologies. On the one hand, these new technologies – from artificial insemination to gamete intra-fallopian transfer (GIFT) and a host of hormonal and other infertility treatments – appear to offer a range of possibilities for extending the pleasures of parenthood to those who, for whatever reasons, have hitherto been unable to have a child. This, coupled with the ability to detect, before birth, any genetic defects or chromosomal abnormalities, and eventually to eliminate any problems before conception takes place, make them powerful tools in medicine's technological armoury at the turn of the twenty-first century (Stanworth 1987: 1).[11]

On the other hand, however, they also extend the boundaries and possibilities of medical and scientific practice in ways that threaten to outstrip public understanding, morality and control. Not only do they bring new dangers and unknown risks to parents and children alike who undergo them, they also allow greater scope for the re-emergence of eugenic policies, which place a higher premium on some lives rather than others and interfere with the so-called 'naturalness' of reproduction.[12] In addition, they also threaten to turn babies into 'commodities' that can be bought and sold. In this respect, the 'Frankensteinian nightmare' of 'science run wild' is readily conjured up in the public mind, as scientists start 'manipulating the very foundations of life itself', as well as potential problems across the life course (Stanworth 1987:1).

These new technologies, in other words, open up to sociopolitical and moral debate issues that formerly belonged to the realm of biological 'givens'.[13] Key issues here include the ethical and practical problems surrounding the manipulation of eggs, sperm and embryos outside the human body, the problems of 'parenthood', especially 'motherhood', and the 'threats' to identity which these technologies pose for the 'products' they create (Stanworth 1987: 2). Should these new reproductive techniques (NRTs) be used 'eugenically', for example, in order to produce 'brighter', more 'attractive', or more 'artistic' offspring, and should (donor) children have a right, when reaching maturity, to know who their 'real' genetic parents are? In short, what, potentially at least, is being transformed here is our conceptualisation of what it is to be 'human, male, female, reproductive, parent, child, fetus, family, "race" and even population' (Clarke 1995: 149). All must now be put in brackets and renegotiated as a consequence of these technological developments.

These issues have been hotly debated within feminist circles. For some, the creation of NRTs is seen as the end-stage of men's desire to control women and appropriate reproductive power. From this perspective the danger lurks that biological mothers will eventually be reduced to 'mother machines' (Corea 1985, Corea *et al.* 1985) or 'living laboratories' (Rowland 1992, 1985). Steinberg (1990), for example, argues that these procedures, notwithstanding their potentially harmful side-effects, involve the erosion of women's bodily and metaphysical privacy. Physiologically, women's bodies are 'opened, scrutinised, manipulated, parts extracted and then reintroduced'. This enables practitioners to unselfconsciously '*speak* of disembodied parts of women – "the ovaries", "ripe eggs", and of "recovering" these parts even as they *materially*, scrutinise, alter or remove these parts of women's bodies' (Steinberg 1990: 86). As a consequence, women not only become erased but also alienated and depersonalised in the process.

Others, however, have argued that it is not so much the technologies themselves that are problematic, but the context in which they are developed and applied, including the thorny issue of 'access' (i.e. '*who*' is allowed to conceive). Indeed, as Denny (1996) has convincingly shown, many women undergoing these forms of treatment view them positively as a 'resource' rather than a mechanism of (patriarchal) 'control' or 'oppression'. In this sense, the call for a return to so-called 'natural motherhood' is resisted, and it is argued instead that women must themselves participate in both the development and evaluation of these technologies, rather than leaving them in the hands of 'malestream' science and medicine (Stanworth 1987; McNeill *et al.* 1990).

More broadly, poststructuralist feminists have rejected the notion that the 'real' female body is passively 'acted upon', instead preferring to view it as both inscribed and (re)constituted through discursive practices and processes (Lupton 1994a). From this perspective these new technologies are themselves viewed as producing subjectivity rather than 'false consciousness'. As such, there is a focus on the struggles and resistances between men and women and the shifting configurations of knowledge/power that this involves (Sawicki 1991). Here the ultimate goal is to produce a feminist body/politics that allows women to speak about their bodies in their own chosen ways and thereby to resist dominant scientific and technological discourses (Jacobus *et al*. 1990). (See Chapter 6, this volume.)

To these four developments in biotechnology, we may also add a fifth, namely the advent of *virtual* medicine and the *hyperreal body*. Whilst many of these 'cutting-edge' technologies, including keyhole surgery, microengineering and nanotechnology, are still in their infancy or at the prototype stage, they none the less promise a radical transformation of existing surgical procedures. Developments such as graphic workstation computers and specialised tracking devices, for instance, have made it possible to build an advanced prototype simulator for minimally invasive surgery called the 'virtual clinic' (McGovern 1994, McGovern and McGovern 1994). The system uses tracking devices attached to actual surgical instruments that are then inserted into a fibreglass body mould. Graphic representations of the body change as the instruments are moved, whilst interaction is visibly displayed on a high resolution computer monitor located at the head of the 'virtual' patient. Data produced by computer tomography (CT) and magnetic resonance imaging (MRI) are used to supply a visual *re*presentation of the patient's actual anatomy. Computer manipulation allows the 'virtual surgical instruments' to interact with the 'virtual tissues' in a way that resembles what happens in 'real life', with new images automatically created as these 'virtual' tissues are probed and dissected (McGovern 1994: 1054).

Another interesting line of development here is 'tele-presence' surgery, performed on a patient in an operating theatre containing a stereoscopic camera and a robot. At a separate location the surgical control workstation has a three-dimensional monitor with surgical input–output devices that closely resemble actual instruments used in an operation (McGovern 1994). The advantage of this system, which has been developed for use in battle-fields, is that it allows surgeons to operate on patients at a distance. The issue of what happens to actual patients when things go wrong and communication lines break down, however, renders these 'virtual' forms of surgery, at present, highly problematic.

More generally, as Frank (1992a) observes, a panoply of 'screens' now pervade the modern technological hospital. First, there are those screens which, as discussed earlier, exteriorise direct images of the body's interior (e.g. ultrasound screens/fetal visualisation and diagnostic technologies); second, there are screens that display on-line digital images, coded into graphs and pictorial displays, of bodily processes and functioning (e.g. ECG monitors); third, there are screens that display symbolic images such as patient charts, schedules and other secondary data; finally, there are commercial television screens found in ever increasing numbers in hospital waiting rooms, lounges, wards and patient rooms (Frank 1992a). The upshot of this is that bodies become ever more elusive: instead of the patient's body being at the centre of contemporary medical practice and discourse, we find instead 'multiple images and codings' whereby the body is endlessly 'doubled and redoubled' through a self-referential chain of simulacra (ibid.; see also Waldby 1997). According to this scenario, the modernist concern with corporeality is slowly but surely giving way to the postmodernist concern with hyperreality (Williams 1997).

These issues of virtual medicine and the hyperreal body, in turn, key into broader debates concerning the advent of so-called cyberspace and the 'information superhighway' – trends that, as we have seen, carry profound implications for contemporary forms of (posthuman) embodiment, subjectivity and identity. As a number of writers have commented, computer technology at the turn of the century has become inextricably intertwined with the identities and destinies of human beings: a process by which computers have been thoroughly 'anthropomorphised', whilst humans have been portrayed as 'organic computers' (Berman 1989; Lupton 1994b; Williams 1995b). Certainly part of the seductive pleasure/terror of entering cyberspace and the simulated world of virtual reality – the latter involving a whole range of high-technology hardware including head-mounted display units, data gloves, whole-body data suits and laser-based retinal scanners – seems to be that it holds out the possibility of 'transcending' existing bodily boundaries. In this context, it is argued that minds can float 'free' of bodies, and computers can merge with human consciousness in a 'parallel' digital world of glittering sights and sounds (Gibson 1984).

Here, in this new social 'space' of electronic bulletin boards (BBS), virtual conferences, virtual communities and virtual experiences, issues of social reflexivity take on critical new dimensions as new forms of social interaction, emotions, trust and sexual intimacy begin to open up – the harbinger of Giddens's 'pure relationship' perhaps? The range of ways in which one can represent one's subjectivity also becomes far more varied and flexible. Here, one's digital on-line gender identity is free to take on a virtual life of its own, separate from and independent of the person's embodied life in the 'real' world – what Stenger (1991: 53) succinctly refers to as 'spring time for schizophrenia'. Seen in this light, the absurdity of the statement 'I am here but I've left my body behind', becomes a chilling reality in cyberspace.

The desire to enter cyberspace, to cross the human/machine boundary, to penetrate and merge, has also been described as a quasi-sexual experience – what Heim (1991) refers to as the 'erotic ontology of cyberspace' – involving a change in human embodiment and a loss of self similar to orgasmic ecstasy. Perhaps the most direct expression of these erotic possibilities comes in the shape of so-called 'cybersex' – i.e. the 'hot chat' between virtual strangers who simultaneously log on to various systems, as an autoerotic representation of a sexual experience – itself a 'core' feature of the BBS social world (Wiley 1995). Indeed, in the shadow of AIDS, this 'micro-processing of desire' (Baudrillard 1990) may be 'safest' sex of all, devoid of potentially dangerous and contaminating body fluids – although computers too, of course, are prone to 'viruses' through 'unsafe' or 'unprotected' disk swapping! (Williams 1995b). In this sense, computer technologies occupy a contradictory position involving both an 'escape' from the physical body and a 'fulfilment of erotic desire' through digital simulations, voyeurism and 'sex without a body' (Lupton 1994b, 1995b; Wiley 1995: 159).

Yet these so-called 'attractions' of cyberspace may be more apparent than real. On the one hand, as we have seen, the advent of cyberspace carries with it a range of potential benefits, including new (digital) forms of emotional trust, intimacy and sharing. Certainly for many groups, particularly the chronically sick and the physically disabled, computer networks and the BBS provide a potential antidote to the contemporary decline of our sense of 'publicness' and the nature of life in an increasingly 'atomistic' age. In particular, a number of 'virtual' support groups are beginning to emerge – from sex offenders to sufferers of eating disorders and a range of other personal and health-related problems – a development succinctly captured by the term 'cyber-recovery' (Denzin 1997).

On the other hand, however, the arrival of cyberspace also brings with it new risks and dangers. As Slouka (1995: 9) argues, within cyberspace, all the worst in human nature can quickly 'set up shop': a 'hybrid' world in which freedom becomes the 'freedom to abuse and torment'; anonymity, the 'anonymity of the obscene phone call'; and liberation from the constraints of the physical body, just an 'invitation to torture someone's virtual one'. Not only do cyberist visions downgrade or deny the very conditions that make us human (our mortal, flesh and blood, links with others, our bodily being/dwelling in the world, our *praxical* relationship to technology, etc.), they are also in danger of 'limiting' the imagination, 'forcing it to walk down certain paths rather than others', and distracting us from our responsibilities in the real world: famine and starvation, the devastation of nature, the unravelling of the social fabric, and the widening gap between a technocratic elite of *digerati* and the minimum-wage masses (Slouka 1995; Dery 1996). To put it quite bluntly, cyberspace, although still in its infancy, does not stand a chance of capturing the complexities of the human imagination, the subtleties and richness of our sentient, embodied relationship with the world, and our responsibilities to those within it. Nor indeed should it (Williams 1998a).

Forgetting about the body, as Stone (1991) rightly argues, is an 'old Cartesian trick' – one to which cyberspace has added a new technological twist – and it is important to remember that these technologies, no matter how 'virtual' they may seem, none the less originate in, and ultimately must return us to, the physical body. Indeed, far from slipping the problems of sex and gender, cyberbodies appear masculine or feminine to an exaggerated degree (Springer 1991), a situation in which technology itself is eroticised as feminine and the woman seen as the model of the perfect machine (Doane 1990). Seen in these terms, Haraway's (1991) optimistic vision of the 'leaky' cyborg in a postgender world appears little more than a postmodern pipe dream.

The upshot of this is that cyberspace resurrects rather than transcends the dualist legacies of the past. Indeed, as we edge ever closer to the twenty-first century, we would do well to remember that we are, for the foreseeable future, 'here to stay' in these bodies, on this planet, and that our responsibilities are located precisely here, not in some parallel digital universe (Dery 1996; Slouka 1995; Williams 1998a). Real bodies, real lives, real responsibilities.[14] It is to these mortal dilemmas of the fleshy body incarnate that we now turn in the concluding part of the chapter.

'Mortal' bodies and the 'sequestration' of experience: the 'extradition' of the dead?

It is perhaps a myth to suppose that death, or knowledge of death, has ever been greeted with total equanimity. Human beings, as Elias (1985) notes, are the only animals who know they are going to die and know that they know. Death, as both the 'possibility of impossibility' and the impossibility of possibility, cannot be 'believed', 'magicked' or 'scienced' away (Lofland 1978). Rather, every society is ultimately a collection of 'men [*sic*] banded together in the face of death' (Berger 1967), and it is culture that transforms this condition from the impossibility of a meaningful life into the very condition of life's meaning (Bauman 1992a,b).

The growth of social reflexivity, the relationship between the body and self-identity, and the shrinkage in scope of the 'sacred', mean that these mortal dilemmas become particularly acute in the late modern era (Mellor and Shilling 1993). As the 'scandal of reason', death throws into critical relief the human inability to reconcile the transcending power of 'time-binding mind' with the 'time-bound' transcience of our 'fleshy casing' (Bauman 1992a: 1). In the absence of overarching metaphysical systems of 'containment', individuals in late modernity find themselves increasingly 'naked' and 'exposed' before 'death's obscenity'. The more people prioritise issues relating to the self, and the more they invest in their bodies, the more difficult it becomes for them to face up to and cope with their own demise. Death, in short, becomes increasingly *individualised* and *privatised* in reflexive modernity.

This gradual privatisation and shrinkage of public space accorded death has been carefully mapped by Aries (1976, 1981). According to Aries, a major change in the social response to death and dying occurred in the middle of the nineteenth century – one involving a 'complete reversal of customs' and a loss of collective rituals. Death at this time, was 'driven into secrecy', made 'invisible' and shrouded in a 'veil of silence'. As a consequence, death has grown fearful again, imbued with its 'old savagery': 'we ignore the existence of a scandal that we have been unable to prevent; we act as if it did not exist, and thus mercilessly force the bereaved to say nothing' (Aries 1981: 562). Not only did this mark the 'beginning of the lie' for Aries, one in which dying patients were not told the prognosis, it also involved the 'medicalisation of death' as the dying were removed from their homes and the community and placed in the 'sanitised space' of the hospital in order to conceal its new 'indecency'.

Gradually, the nineteenth-century fight against plagues of consumption and pestilence, coupled with the twentieth-century image of medicine battling specific diseases suggested a war against mortality itself and a denial of what Illich (1976) terms the 'good death'. In a 'good death' (wo)man's fear and image of death was 'tamed' by a series of preparations and rituals designed to give the dying control over their death. The individual, in other words, presided over his or her own death. Today, in contrast, this 'good death' has been supplanted by the concept of the 'natural death' – a death that 'comes under medical care and finds us in good health and old age' (ibid.: 180). In the 'natural death', the individual power of decision making and control are ceded to the medical and hospital staff who, in effect, become the 'new masters of death'. Health, in other words, has been 'expropriated down to the last breath. Technological death has won its victory over dying' (ibid.: 207–8). Elias echoes these sentiments, noting how the modern individual in intensive care can be cared for according to the latest biomedical knowledge and techniques, but often neutrally as regards feeling: 'Never before', he remarks, 'have people died so noiselessly and hygienically as today . . . in social conditions fostering so much solitude' (Elias 1985: 85).

These processes, in turn, connect up with broader trends towards the 'sequestration of experience' in late modernity (Giddens 1991) – a process involving the separation from routine day-to-day life of potentially disturbing existential crises and moral dilemmas including sickness, madness, criminality and death. The organisation of life in late modernity therefore serves to strengthen the physical and symbolic boundaries between life and death, and accentuates the individualisation of selves and bodies. Little by little the dead cease to exist: a situation which Baudrillard (1976) has appositely termed the 'extradition' of the dead in Western society.

The very exclusion of death from everyday life and 'normality' means, however, that it haunts us all the more powerfully. Death, as Bauman (1992a,b) argues, spurs life efforts, 'saturating' the struggle for 'survival'. In particular, a new 'survival strategy' has, he suggests, come to the fore in late modernity – one focused on the 'deconstruction of mortality' itself through a variety of self-care measures. Individuals, in other words, are exhorted to do something about death in the here and now. No one dies a 'general' death anymore. Rather, in rationalist modernity, mortality itself is split into a 'multitude of individual occurrences', each possessing its own principally defeatable and hence 'preventable' cause. Body regimes and individual lifestyle choices are therefore proposed in order to reduce our chances of dying from coronary heart disease, stroke, cancer and so on, thus diverting attention away from these mortal dilemmas through the sheer investment of time, effort and money this strategy involves. Within this policy, immortality can effectively be 'deferred' or 'forgotten' through the endless battle for health and fitness. Here we return full circle to some of the themes identified earlier concerning the body as a 'project'. The paradox of this strategy, of course, as Bauman notes, is that:

> the ultimate meaning of staving off the danger of dying of cause A is the increase in probability that my death, when it comes, will be described by cause B, C . . . Z. 'I do not want to die' always translates, in its prag- matic conclusions, into 'I would rather die of that rather than this'. As the 'that' cannot be exhausted, the truth of this translation must not be admitted into consciousness, and this requires that survival effort scores ever new successes. Survival needs constant reassurance; and the only convincing reassurance is the death of others: *not me*.
>
> (Bauman 1992a: 10)

In short, the battle over death can never be won. The price for exchanging immortality for the constant vigil of health is 'life lived in the shadows of death' (ibid.: 20).

Against this dominant sociological view of death banished to the 'margins' of contemporary social life (i.e. 'publicly absent'/'privately present'), is an alternative view, one in which death is seen to be very much 'alive and kicking' in the public realm. Armstrong (1987), for example, challenges Aries's inter- pretation that a 'veil of silence' descended over the subject of death between 1850 and 1950. Certainly a change occurred in the way death was spoken about, but Aries is mistaken, he suggests, to assume that this involved the replacement of speech by silence. Rather, from a Foucauldian perspective, silence itself functions as an element alongside the things that are said. Between the mid-nineteenth century and its close there was an increasingly 'vocal discourse' on the certification, management and disposal of the dead. Medicine, in particular, ushered in a 'new regime' of investigation and analysis concerning the body, one that no longer examined the 'familial bonds of the dead for the mirror to the truth of life', but instead sought to scrutinise the internal organs of the physical body itself where the core of life and death was now thought to be located. More generally, rules, at this time, were laid down regarding the maximum time the body could be kept in the home, the location of cemeteries, the height of their walls, the distance between plots, and the length of time before a plot could be disturbed (Armstrong 1987).[15]

In contrast to this nineteenth-century medical interrogation of the corpse, Armstrong suggests that a 'new regime of truth' began to emerge in the late 1950s and early 1960s, one that Aries himself correctly identifies as a 'complete reversal of attitudes'. Within this new 'psychosocial' paradigm, death was seen to be surrounded by a 'conspiracy of silence' and a concomitant shift occurred from the 'interrogation of the corpse' to that of the 'dying patient'. From this point on, the truth of death ceased to be located in dark recesses of the silent *Korper* (objective body), and instead became embodied in the words and deeds of the dying patient.[16] As a consequence, the 'secret became broken', silence was allowed a new place in discourse, and the 'confession' was enacted. The dying, *qua* subjects, were therefore encouraged to speak (Armstrong 1987: 656). Gradually, as the focus of interest shifted to the analysis of bereavement, meaning and 'awareness of death', a new series of practices and organisations arose in order to accommodate and express this 're-assessment of human sensibility', the most prominent of which is, perhaps, the modern hospice, founded in 1976, and directed towards 'managing the anguish of the dying patient' (Prior 1989: 12).

Contrary to prevailing sociological views, it is therefore possible to argue that death, as in the past, continues to be a very public affair. Critics may none the less object that actuarial, demographic and medical discourses are not exactly 'public', and that death is still largely hidden behind the walls of the hospital and, more recently, the hospice. There is, however, one very public arena in which death makes a more than daily appearance, namely, the mass media. Indeed, as Walter *et al.* (1995) rightly argue, it is the mass media that really challenge the 'public absence of death' thesis. From westerns and thrillers, to other more recent fashions for ghost movies (e.g. *Truly, Madly, Deeply* and *Ghost*); cyborgs programmed to kill (e.g. the *Terminator* movies); near-death experiences (*Flatliners*); and the problems of corpse 'disposal' (e.g. *Cement Garden* and *Shallow Grave*), death makes a regular appearance on our cinema screens and home videos. Similarly, in TV dramas such as *Casualty*, death or its imminent possibilities is a central feature of the storyline, whilst part of the popular appeal of series such as *Prime Suspect* and *Cracker* has, no doubt, been their vivid portrayal of dead, assaulted and violated bodies – corpses that are prodded and poked, photographed and dissected for 'clues' to the identity of their assailants.

Death is also well covered in media reportage of personal tragedies (e.g. motorway disasters, airplane crashes, the abduction and murder of children) involving private citizens (Walter *et al.* 1995). Indeed, far from being averse to portraying the humanity of those killed and the emotions of those who grieve – as Gorer (1955, 1965) claimed in his classic 'pornography of death' thesis – reporters actually home in on these issues like 'flies to a glowing light'. A 'public invigilation of private emotion' is therefore effected, involving the simultaneous arousal and regulatory 'keeping watch over' the affective dispositions and responses associated with death (Walter *et al.* 1995: 584).

Underpinning these issues are a more general set of arguments concerning the 'revival' of death in contemporary western societies (Walter 1995). With more people than ever before having to live for an extended period of time with life-threatening conditions (e.g. cancer, heart disease, stroke, HIV) – what Lofland (1978) refers to as the transition from 'quick' to 'slow' dying – the modern pretence that death does not exist becomes less and less viable.

Instead, a variety of strategies for dealing with death now exist in the complex 'death culture' of our times. This 'revival', as Walter (1995) suggests, particularly its 'postmodern' strand, takes individualism to its logical conclusion, and asserts the authority of the individual not only over religion, but also over medicine – a situation in which people themselves can determine how they want to die or grieve. Indeed, *contra* Giddens, meaningful narratives of self in the face of death are in fact possible in the late modern age. Given the reflexive nature of self-identity, 'heroic self-affirmation', particularly in cases of cancer and AIDS, is a cultural 'script' available for many people in late modernity (Seale 1995). Death, in short, is far from the meaningless event and bleak arena for maintaining the integrity of the self that conventional sociological accounts imply.

This 'revival' of death is also echoed in Bauman's (1992a,b) deliberations on the 'postmodern' deconstruction of 'immortality' itself. For Bauman, life within consumer culture becomes transformed into an endless circulation of commodities and a constant series of rehearsals of 'reversible death'. Here, the irrevocable termination of life is substituted for 'temporary disappearance' as consumer bliss reaches its final stage of secularisation. In this way, 'transience and ephemerality become reforged into daily practice', glorified and ritualistically celebrated. Deconstructed in this way, immortality reveals mortality as its 'only secret'. Mortality, in short, need 'not be deconstructed but lived' (Bauman 1992b: 191–2).

'Public' or 'private', 'absent' or 'present': what are we to make of these differing views of death and dying in Western society? Is it possible to 'reconcile' them or are they inherently contradictory? One way out of this (im)mortal dilemma is to suggest that, at an institutional level, all societies past, present and future, have to organise for death. Indeed, death, as we have seen, is the mainspring of life's meaning and opportunities – the foundation upon which the whole edifice of Western culture is built. Whilst the social organisation of death and dying has undoubtedly shifted across the centuries – from a communal event surrounded by local rituals, to one of increasing secularisation, rationalisation and medicalisation – a number of 'revivalist' trends have emerged that are beginning to 'challenge' these dominant modernist responses – responses that have never really been about 'denial' as much as 'deferral' and sequestration. These span a diverse array of issues, from the 'public invigilation of private grief' to the so-called 'postmodern' deconstruction of immortality itself, and the 'celebration' of '(reversible) death'. Here, the 'vanguards of change' appear not only to be the so-called 'experts in the field' – in medicine, psychiatry, the social sciences, the hospice movement and also bereavement counsellors – but also the dying and bereaved themselves – people who are increasingly joining together in a common call for 'open awareness contexts' and a 'dignified', if not 'heroic', end to life (Walter 1995). Modernist 'life' strategies, therefore, increasingly rub shoulders with postmodern ones in the complex death culture of our times.

Conclusions

In this chapter we have considered a number of pertinent themes pertaining to the 'fate' of the body in late modernity. Key issues here include the reflexive nature of the body and self-identity, the changing parameters of risk, the pressures of commodification, and the dilemmas of technology and mortality at the turn of the century. Alongside other major developments such as the transformation of intimacy and the salience of emotions in a 'therapeutic' age (see Chapter 7, this volume), this points to a profound undermining of what bodies are and what they might become. Nowhere is this more so than in the technological clinic of late modern medicine and the 'disembodied' ether of cyberspace. Yet these developments, as we have argued, no matter how complex, are ultimately grounded and return us to the inescapable fact of our human *embodiment*. Only on this basis can a truly 'human ethics of existence' emerge – one that is not only capable of mounting an effective 'challenge' to the manufacturers of risk and uncertainty in a new technological age, but also of dispelling some of the over-inflated claims and disembodied myths of cyberspace. In short, real, material bodies are at stake in these struggles, and we would do well to hold on to this fundamentally embodied, fleshy fact, as we edge ever closer towards the twenty-first century.

5 The 'libidinal' body
Psychoanalysis, critical theory and the 'problem' of human desire

In contrast to the 'secret history' of the body in much classical and contemporary sociology, the relationship between the biological, psychological and social realms of bodily being has been of abiding importance to psychoanalysis since its inception. Indeed, as Bocock (1976) notes, the human body is central to Freud's work in a way that so much sociology, both before and since his time, seems to have missed or neglected. Here the general view seems to have been that, because Freud's work is built upon his analysis of 'instincts', it is at best 'un-sociological' and at worst 'biologically reductionist'.

Against these views, the position taken in this chapter, following the lead of Grosz (1994) and others, is that reductionist readings of Freud are largely mistaken. To be sure psychoanalysis lays great stress upon the 'biological body', yet this is perhaps best understood in terms of the various ways in which our bodies and their functions serve as models or metaphors for our relationships and actions in the world (Craib 1988). This, coupled with the essential humanism of Freud's work and his critique of civilised sexual morality, makes him a central figure in mind/body, biology/society debates. As we shall see, a line of theoretical continuity can be traced here, from Freud's account of the bodily ego and Lacan's discussion of imaginary anatomy, to Schilder's notion of body-image and Merleau-Ponty's phenomenological analysis of the sentient body-subject (Grosz 1994). This focus on the 'libidinal' body is also, of course, central to the work of 'sexual revolutionaries' such as Reich and Marcuse, and the 'schizoanalysis' of Deleuze and Guattari – one that not only challenges the oedipalising tendencies of Freudian psychoanalysis, but the whole edifice of Western binarised thought itself and the conceptualisation of desire as 'lack'.

Taken together, these perspectives offer the basis for a profound critique of Western dualism and civilised sexual morality, grounded as they are in the 'libidinal' flows and productive relations of corporeal desire. It is to these 'libidinal' issues that this chapter is devoted, providing as they do, a clue to the 'anti-Cartesian' path that follows.

Bodily 'tracings' and corporeal 'mappings'

Perhaps one of Freud's greatest, most original, achievements was the way in which he problematised, in a manner so few of his predecessors had done, the relationship between the mental and the physical, showing how each, in its very existence and operations, implies the other. From this perspective, as Grosz argues, human biology is not only 'psychologically pliable', but the ego itself is dependent on a 'psychical map' or 'cartographic tracing' of the libidinal body – a body that, through its orifices, 'erotogenic rims' and so on, becomes the 'loci of exchange between inside and outside, exhibiting active and passive sensations, subject and object relations, mind and body' (Grosz 1994: 36). The ego, in other words: 'is ultimately derived from bodily sensations, chiefly from those springing from the surface of the body. It may thus be regarded as a mental projection of the surface of the body, besides . . . representing the superficies of the mental apparatus' (Freud 1984 [1923]: 364fn).

Perhaps more significantly from a social viewpoint, the ego is not simply a reflection or representation of one's own body, but also the image of the other's body. This adds a significant sociocultural dimension to Freud's work. Bodies, are 'made' or 'completed' through psychic processes with sociosexual implications (Grosz 1994), and the corporeal ego is continually added to and augmented by the products of history and culture, including new instrumental capacities and technological supplements:

> With every tool [Man] is perfecting his [*sic*] own organs, whether motor or sensory, or is removing the limits of their functioning. Motor power places gigantic forces at his disposal, which like his muscles, he can employ in any direction; thanks to ships and aircraft neither water nor air can hinder his movements; by means of spectacles he corrects defects in the lens of his own eyes; by means of the telescope he sees into the distance; by means of the microscope he overcomes the limits of visibility set by the structure of his own retina . . . Man has, as it were, become a kind of prosthetic God. When he pulls on all his auxiliary organs he is truly magnificent, but these organs have not grown onto him and they still give him much trouble at times.
>
> (Freud 1982 [1930]: 90–2)[1]

Perhaps Freud's most radical assault on dualism, however, concerns his treatment of instincts and drives. As with much of Freud's work, his use of these terms is perhaps best seen in metaphorical terms. Thus, whilst 'instinct' is more closely allied to the biological aspects of human nature, 'drive', in contrast, is a more useful concept, combining as it does the idea of both instinctual energy and psychic representation (Craib 1988). Seen in these terms, (biological) instincts are amenable to 'psycho-symbolic takeover' as (sexualised) drives, whilst drives themselves, as ambiguous states, befuddle traditional mind/body, psyche/soma divides, being irreducible to either (Grosz 1994). Drive, in other words, transforms and transcends the instinct. In doing so, the body is quite literally 're-written' or 'traced over' by desire (ibid). The unconscious, too, is composed not of raw biological instincts, but of mental representations we attach to instincts. Again this suggests a far greater degree of 'openness' and 'plasticity' than Freud's critics have allowed, one in which the body and its drives are caught up in a complex web of psychosexual, cultural and symbolic processes that quite literally 're-write' and 're-inscribe' the physical body in social terms (Grosz 1994).

These Freudian themes and corporeal mappings have, in turn, been taken much further by poststructuralist writers such as the French psychoanalyst Lacan (1977, 1953), who argues that biology is always interpreted by human subjects and refracted through language. Indeed, there is no 'body', subject or unconscious for Lacan before language. In making these claims, Lacan is able to show in a far more radical and direct manner than Freud, how culture imposes meaning on anatomical parts of the 'real' body (Grosz 1994).

Central to these arguments are the distinctions Lacan makes between three separate realms of being and experience. First, the 'real', which is unknowable since it exists beyond language; second, the 'symbolic', which constitutes the spheres of language, discourse and culture; finally, the 'imaginary' world of idealised pre-verbal images and fantasies, whose logic is essentially visual, originating in the pre-oedipal, 'mirror stage' of the child's psychic development (Craib 1988). Whilst the mirror stage begins a fundamental process of alienation for Lacan – based as it is on the fantasy attempt to identify with the image and be perfectly together and in control of oneself – it is the oedipal crisis, interpreted linguistically, that marks the child's point of entry into the realm of the symbolic, involving an acceptance of the 'Name-of-the-Father' and the rule of the 'Phallus' (Craib 1988). The upshot of this, as Grosz notes, is to view the Freudian ego not simply as a projection of the 'real' physiological body, but as an 'imaginary' outline of its anatomy.[2] 'Imaginary anatomy', in other words, is primarily symbolic; 'something which the child acquires first of all in the mirror stage of its development and later through a resolution of the Oedipal complex' (Grosz 1994: 41).

In contrast to Freud, Lacan therefore writes primarily at the level of the symbolic, focusing on the phallus instead of the penis, 'imaginary anatomy' rather than the 'real' (biological/pre-social) body, and desire instead of drives and instincts (Sarup 1993). Language and desire, in other words, are intimately related in Lacan's work. Desire itself, predicated as it is on a fundamental lack, becomes the ultimate metonymy of the 'desire to want to be'. Indeed all our fantasies, according to Lacan, are symbolic representations of this desire for wholeness – something to which we are all condemned from birth. In this respect, as Sarup (1993) argues, Lacan's symbolic order can fruitfully be seen as an attempt to create *mediations* between libidinal analysis and linguistic categories.

Lacan's work has been particularly useful to poststructuralist feminists in 'problematising' sexual identity as a stable, fixed or given entity. From this 'de-centred' stance, 'normal' sexuality is simply a construction or 'ordering' of desire by language (i.e. the rule of the 'phallus'), not the result of the biological possession of a penis (Sarup 1993). Anatomy, in other words, is not seen to be the cause of 'differences' between men and women; rather what counts are the social differences between men and women that are 'imposed' on anatomy (Craib 1988). Critics may reasonably object, however, that Lacan, like other poststructuralist thinkers, has in fact gone too far in stressing the power of the 'social' (i.e. the symbolic). As a consequence, he has lost many important insights stemming from Freud's original analysis of the *interrelationship* between the biological and psychological realms of bodily being.

Here we return full circle to problems discussed in previous chapters, particularly the thorny issue of 'discursive essentialism' and an overprivileging of the 'social'. There is, as Craib rightly argues, no *a priori* reason why sexuality should not be natural and in some sense constructed: 'It is not, after all, a result of social definition that I have a flabby piece of flesh hanging between my legs, any more than my possession of a liver or lungs, or absence of wings sprouting from my shoulders' (Craib 1988: 126). Questions concerning the ontological status of the body as a pre-social entity are therefore obscured rather than resolved through a social constructionist epistemology in which the 'symbolic' is prioritised over the 'real'.

To summarise, both Freud and Lacan, in their different ways, point to the interrelationship between the biological, psychological and social realms of being and to the body's location and 'completion' at the intersection of these domains. What this implies is that the body, both literally and metaphorically, is written on, inscribed or 'traced over' by desire and psychosymbolic significations, at the anatomical, physiological and neurological levels (Grosz 1990, 1994). This in turn opens up the possibility of (radically) re-writing and re-inscribing the body in terms 'quite different' from those which currently 'mark' it, including the forms of 'sexed identity' and 'psychical subjectivity' at work today (Grosz 1994: 60–1). Building on these psychoanalytic themes and insights, it is to a fuller consideration of 'body-image', an implicit term in much of the discussion so far, that we now turn.

Body-image: bringing the biological, psychological and social together?

Implicitly or explicitly, 'body-image', as Grosz (1994) observes, has figured strongly in psychoanalytic conceptions of subjectivity, intervening, as a 'third term', between mind and body, psyche and soma. Despite a long tradition of (medical) research and writing on this topic – including Sir Henry Head's work on aphasia and his 'postural model' of the body – it is Schilder (1950) who stands out most clearly in the history of the term, drawing the physiological, psychological and social realms of bodily being together through a single, unified concept. Here the lines of theoretical continuity are easily traced. Certainly Freud's work forms a major part of Schilder's understanding of body-image, including the psychical processes of transcription and 'completion' it involves, and the libidinal structures it embodies (Grosz 1994). Schilder also echoes Max Scheler (1961 [1912]) when he claims that we should not treat the objective body (*Korper*) as a separate entity from the lived inner sensations of the subjective body (*Lieb*), including its feeling tone and emotional significance.

Most importantly for our purposes, the term body-image signals the impossibility of treating mind and body as separate entities, and the need to work at the interface between the physical, psychological and sociological realms of bodily being. Body-image, in other words, implies the fundamental 'inseparability' of mind and body, and the mutual interdependence of the social, psychical and biological in the genesis of this corporeal schema. As Schilder puts it:

> The image of the human body means the picture of our own body that we form in our mind, that is to say, the way in which the body appears to ourselves. These are sensations given to us. We see parts of the body-surface. We have tactile, thermal, pain impressions. There are sensations which come from the muscles and their sheaths . . . sensations coming from innervation of the muscles . . . and sensations coming from the viscera. Beyond that there is the immediate experience that there is a unity of the body. This unity is perceived, yet it is more than a perception. We call it a schema of our body or bodily schema, or, following Head, who emphasises the importance of knowledge of the position of the body, a postural model of the body. The body schema is the tri-dimensional image everybody has about himself [*sic*]. We may call it 'body-image'. The term indicates that we are not dealing with a mere sensation or imagination. There is a self-appearance of the body. It indicates also that, although it has come through the senses, it is not mere perception. There are mental pictures and representations involved in it but it is not mere representation.
>
> (Schilder 1950: 11)

Body-image unifies and co-ordinates postural, tactile, kinaesthetic and visual sensations of a subject located in a single space – sensations that can only be artificially separated (Grosz 1994). More precisely, it is through the ever changing libidinal intensities and meanings the subject invests in his or her bodily zones, organs and functions that body-image is generated and takes on its particular significance and form. The value of this is that it accords emotions a central role in the genesis of body-image – something that changes the relative value and clearness of the different parts of body-image according to 'libidinous tendencies'. More broadly, body-image, as Schilder remarks, is likely to vary according to the 'psychosexual tendencies' of the individual: 'full genital sexuality' being 'indispensible' for the 'full appreciation' of our own body-image (Schilder 1950: 170, 173).

The experience of unity, co-ordination and a single identity that body-image engenders in turn forms the basis for the undertaking of (meaningful) voluntary action in the world. All forms of willful action, Schilder suggests, necessarily involve the co-ordination of this underlying bodily schema:

> In this plan [of action] the knowledge of one's own body is an absolute necessity. There must always be a knowledge that I am acting with my body, that I have to use a particular part of my body. But in the plan there must also be the aim of my actions. There is always an object towards which the action is directed. The aim may be one's own body or it may be an object in the outside world. In order to act, we must know something about the quality of the object or our intention. And finally, we must know in what way we want to approach the object. The formula therefore contains the image of the limb or part of the body which is performing the movement.
>
> (Schilder 1950: 52)

Perhaps most importantly for our purposes, Schilder stresses that body-image is necessarily social as well as physical and psychological, in that *all aspects of body-image are developed and constructed in and through social relations*. Always accompanied by the image of others, body-image involves relations between the body and its surrounding spaces, including other objects and other bodies, organised according to such fundamental bodily co-ordinates as 'vertical' and 'horizontal', 'left' and 'right', 'backwards' and 'forwards' (Grosz 1994). More generally, it stems from shared sociocultural conceptions of bodies, as well as shared familial and interpersonal fantasies about particular bodies, thus lending itself to a variety of social, cultural and historical studies.

Schilder illustrates these ideas through a wide range of examples, from pathological findings concerning aphasia and brain lesions, to the social extension and relationships formed with the outside world and external environment.[3] In considering the case of phantom limb disturbance, for example, Schilder suggests that it represents a sometimes cumbersome 'narcissistic compensation' for the loss of the limb or bodily unity, a 'psychical attempt to reactivate a past body-image' in place of the present reality (Schilder 1950: 73). Similarly, regarding its incorporative capacities and social extensions with the outside world, Schilder notes how body-image can:

> shrink or extend; it can give parts to the outside world and can take other parts into itself. When we take a stick in our hands and touch an object with the end of it, we feel a sensation at the end of the stick. The stick has, in fact, become a part of the body-image.
>
> (ibid.: 202)

Perhaps more profoundly:

> objects which were once connected with the body always retain something of the quality of the body-image in them . . . whatever originates

or emanates out of our body will still remain a part of the body-image. The voice, the breath, the odour, the faeces, menstrual blood, urine, semen, are still parts of the body-image even when separated in space from the body.

(ibid.: 213)

In contrast, other parts can become 'loose' in their connection with the body. Fingers, for example, may become 'personified' in their own right. Indeed: 'all protruding parts can gain this relative independence in the postural model of the body' (ibid.: 188–89).[4]

To summarise, the notion of body-image serves as an important 'third term' linking body to mind and mind to body without serving to reduce one to the other. As a gestalt structure, body-image serves to unify the diverse sensations that flow through the body and to co-ordinate the individual subject's voluntary actions in social space and time (Grosz 1994). In this sense, a unified, co-ordinated body-image serves as the necessary basis for distinctions such as 'figure and ground', 'centre and periphery', as well as movement of various parts of the body instead of others, and notions of 'inside and outside', 'organ and processes', 'active and passive', 'subject and object' (ibid.: 84). Moreover, it also points to the social dimensions and extensions of body-image and its extreme 'pliability' in the face of biological, psychological and social upheavals. Any discussion of body-image as an isolated entity is therefore necessarily incomplete. Indeed, even a 'preliminary answer' to the problem of the body cannot, as Schilder remarks, 'be given unless we attempt a preliminary answer about personality and world' (Schilder 1950: 304). The elusive marriage of mind and body is thus well and truly consummated through psychoanalytic and phenomenologically informed terms such as body-image and the sentient body-subject (see Chapter 3, this volume).[5]

Critical theory and the sexually 'liberated' body

One of the central themes underlying much of the discussion so far has, of course, been the relationship between sexuality and society. Freud's (1963) theory of civilised sexual morality, for example, as Bocock argues, highlights the way in which social institutions such as the family, religion, education and the law, together with the political organisation of society, repress instinctual bodily impulses so that human beings, as a community, can co-operate with one another, work together, protect themselves from the worst effects of nature, and therefore obtain a greater sense of ontological security than would otherwise be possible (Bocock 1976: 12).[6] Civilisation, in other words:

aims at binding members of the community together in a libidinal way . . . and employs every means to that end. . . . It summons up aim-inhibited libido on the largest scale so as to strengthen the communal bond by relations of friendship. In order for these aims to be fulfilled, a restriction on sexual life is unavoidable.

(Freud 1982 [1930]: 48)

Freud's conclusions regarding the fate of human happiness were essentially pessimistic. Instinctual renunciation is not enough, for the wish persists and cannot be concealed from the (harsh) super-ego.[7,8] In spite of the renunciation that has been made, an inescapable sense of guilt therefore comes about: one in which a threatened 'external unhappiness' has been exchanged for a permanent 'internal unhappiness' (Bocock 1976). As to the future, Freud predicted that the eternal struggle between love and death would, in all probability, 'reach heights the individual finds hard to tolerate' (ibid.: 70).[9]

Others, however, have sought to challenge these pessimistic conclusions, using Freud against himself, so to speak, as the basis for a radical critique of modern capitalism and its libidinally repressive economies of desire. Perhaps the first and most famous of these 'sexual revolutionaries' was Reich, whose radical political views eventually led to his expulsion from the International Psychoanalytic Movement (Bocock 1976). In contrast to Freud, Reich saw no need to posit death instincts. Rather, antisocial, unconscious feelings were, he thought, simply the result of people being unable to enjoy 'full genital orgiastic potency'. Once 'compulsory' and 'compulsive' forms of sexual morality had been abandoned, and individuals learnt to enjoy full 'genital sexuality', hostile behaviour would simply disappear. Psychic health, in other words, depends upon:

> the degree to which one can surrender to and experience the climax of excitation in the natural sexual act. It is founded upon the healthy character attitude of the individual's capacity for love. Psychic illnesses are the result of a disturbance of the natural ability to love. In the case of orgiastic impotence, [*sic*] from which the overwhelming majority of people suffer, damming-up of biological energy occurs and becomes the source of irrational actions. The essential requirement to cure psychic disturbances is the re-establishment of the natural capacity for love. It is dependent upon social as well as psychic conditions.
>
> (Reich 1983 [1942]: 6)

Essentially, as Rycroft (1971: 42–3) argues, Reich's theory of 'sex-economy' boils down to seven key propositions. First, mental health is dependent on the capacity to experience 'orgasm' (i.e. full 'orgiastic potency' and an 'un-neurotic capacity for love'). Second, mental illness is the result of inhibition of the capacity to experience orgasm. Third, this inhibition of orgiastic capacity is both instituted and maintained by a psychological structure called 'character armour' which forms the basis of 'loneliness', 'helplessness', a 'craving for authority', the 'fear of responsibility', 'mystical longing', 'sexual misery', 'impotent rebelliousness' and 'resignation' of an 'unnatural, pathological type'

(Reich 1983 [1942]: 7). Fourth, and perhaps most importantly for our purposes, this character armour is expressed physiologically through the body, via muscular tension and disturbances of body posture. Fifth, this character armour develops in response to external pressures that are antagonistic to direct sexual expression. Sixth, these antisocial pressures arise within a specific family form, namely the 'authoritarian family' – one that is held together not by parental love so much as the oppressive and repressive use of power by the father. Finally, this form of family only occurs in patriarchal societies and is one of the techniques devised by such societies to produce a submissive population who are incapable of rebelling against its rulers.

Alienation and aggression, misery and suffering, were not therefore (biologically) inevitable. Rather, they were simply an artefact of socio-economic restrictions and patriarchal taboos imposed on the 'wisdom of the body': freedom and sexual health, in short, were one and the same thing (Giddens 1992). As Reich states:

> The unity and congruity of culture and nature, work and love, morality and sexuality, longed for from since time immemorial, will remain a dream as long as man [*sic*] continues to condemn the biological demand for natural (orgiastic) sexual gratification. Genuine democracy and freedom founded on consciousness and responsibility are also doomed to remain an illusion until this demand is fulfilled.
>
> (Reich 1983 [1942]: 8)

To this end, Reich wrote a series of books – including *The Function of the Orgasm* (1983 [1942]), *Character Analysis* (1949) and *The Sexual Revolution* (1969 [1951]) – which contain specific recommendations for reforms based on his theory of sex-economy – reforms designed to increase the experience and expression of sexual happiness and reduce the incidence of neurosis. Whilst equality of sexual expression between the sexes was seen as important, Reich was particularly interested in the sexual rights and play of children and adolescents as the future agents of social transformation and revolutionary change (Rycroft 1971). Children, he argued, should be granted the freedom to explore their own bodies, and adolescents the privacy to establish sexually gratifying pre-marital relationships. Perhaps most controversially of all, homosexuality, Reich thought, was simply the result of 'thwarted libido', something that, alongside pornography, would simply disappear with the progressive liberation of sexuality and the release of full genital orgiastic potency (Rycroft 1971).

In seeking to alleviate these 'ailments of modernity' at a practical level, Reich replaced the Freudian couch and Foucauldian confessional with a direct programme of physical therapy – what he termed 'character-analytic vegetotherapy' – based on relaxation, massage and the dissipation of bodily tension (Giddens 1992). Through the appropriate manipulation of the body and the re-establishment of 'biopsychical motility', the patient's defences against the spontaneous expression of emotions would, he believed, be weakened, thereby restoring full orgiastic potency and promoting sexual health.

Reich therefore provides some useful insights into mind/body, self/society relations through his focus on sexual freedom and psychic health. In particular, as Giddens (1992) notes, his views on the 'reflexive control' of the sexual body as central to the psychological difficulties of the modern individual not only echo nineteenth-century theories of hysteria, they also anticipate the arrival of stress as physical pathology later in the twentieth century. Ultimately, however, his sociopolitical/sexual stance – one that he himself came to denounce towards the end of his life – constitutes little more than a Panglossian view of the powers of the genital orgasm and a massive dismissal of the problems of dominance in human relationships (Rycroft 1971).

Similar attempts to recover the 'radical potential' of Freud's work can be found in the writings of the Frankfurt School – critical social theorists who, from the 1930s onwards, sought to reconcile Freudian psychoanalysis with humanist Marxism and a neo-Weberian emphasis on processes of rationalisation, domination and control. Freudian theory, it was thought, held out the possibility of overcoming many of the problems in Marxist thought itself, including the failure of Marx's predictions concerning the revolutionary overthrow of capitalism by the proletariat, the rise of Fascism, the problem of the authoritarian personality, the mass extermination of millions of Jews in the Nazi Holocaust, the growth of consumer culture and the failure of Russian communism.

Fromm, for example, an early exponent of these Freudo-Marxist views, saw the solution to these social ills in the 'art of loving':

> Society must be organised in such a way that man's [*sic*] loving nature is not separated from this social existence, but becomes one with it. If . . . love is the only sane and satisfactory answer to the problem of human existence . . . then any society which excludes, relatively, the development of love, must in the long run perish of its own contradiction with the basic necessities of human nature.
>
> (Fromm 1957: 129, 133)[10]

In contrast, recourse to Freudian instinct theory and the power of the unconscious was the means, Marcuse thought, by which the mechanisms of social repression could be exposed, thus giving substance to the emancipatory promise and critical potential of modernity (Giddens 1992). In fleshing these ideas out more fully in *Eros and Civilisation* (1969 [1955]), sub-titled *A Philosophical Inquiry into Freud*, Marcuse makes a fundamental distinction between 'basic' and 'surplus' repression. He also supplements Freud's reality principle with the notion of the 'performance' principle. Far from being universal, 'surplus repression' was, Marcuse thought, the product of specific socio-historical circumstances and economic conditions – a situation that could, in principle, be abolished if the division of labour were 're-oriented' on the basis of the gratification of 'freely developed individual needs'. Indeed, the very achievements of repressive civilisation seemed to create the preconditions for the gradual abolition of surplus repression. As a specific socio-historical configuration of political and economic power, the 'performance principle' was therefore capable of being transformed (Kellner 1984).

Emancipation, Marcuse argued, was very much tied to the primacy of pleasure and the liberation of Eros. Modern work disciplines and de-eroticises the body as an instrument of labour. Once surplus repression was abolished, however, leaving only 'basic' repression, a 're-sexualisation' of the body would occur – one that 'challenged' the prevailing libidinal economy of advanced capitalist societies. In particular, the liberation of Eros would, he thought, first manifest itself in a:

> resurgence of pre-genital polymorphous sexuality and in a decline of genital supremacy. The body in its entirety would become an object of cathexis, a thing to be enjoyed – an instrument of pleasure. This change in the value and scope of the libidinal would lead to a disintegration of the institutions in which private interpersonal relations have been organised, particularly the monogamic and patriarchal family.
>
> (Marcuse 1969 [1955]: 201)

In effect, what Marcuse is advocating here is a 'transformation of the libido' from a sexuality that is constrained under 'genital supremacy' to an 'eroticisation of the entire personality'. In a non-repressive society, sexual energy would tend towards its own sublimation, channelling itself into a multiplicity of different aspects of life, including social relations, work, art and the creation of culture itself (Kellner 1984). In Marcuse's vision, repressive reason would therefore give way to a new form of rationality based on libidinal 'gratification'; one in which 'reason and happiness converge'. Eros, in other words, 'redefines reason in his own terms. Reason is what sustains the order of gratification' (Marcuse 1969 [1955]: 224).

Marcuse, therefore, champions the life instincts (Eros) against the death instincts (Thanatos). The release and enhancement of the life instincts would, he thought, 'tame' and 'control' the destructive instincts – a struggle that parallels the Marxian class war (Kellner 1984). In non-repressive civilisation:

> Death would cease to be an instinctual goal. It remains a fact, perhaps even an ultimate necessity – but a necessity against which the unrepressed energy of mankind [*sic*] will protest, against which it will wage its greatest struggle. . . . In this struggle reason and instinct could unite. Under conditions of truly human existence, the difference between succumbing to disease at the age of ten, thirty, fifty or seventy, and dying a 'natural' death after a fulfilled life, may well be a difference worth fighting for with all instinctual energy. Not those who die, but those who die before they

must and want to die, those who die in agony and pain, are the greatest indictment against civilization.

(Marcuse 1969 [1955]: 235)

The full potential of Eros could, however, only truly be realised through radical social transformation: a situation in which the orgasm was no longer an 'instrument of alienated labour' and socially useful work was, at one and the same time, the 'transparent satisfaction of an individual need' (ibid.: 209–10). Marcuse, therefore, counters Freud's pessimism by arguing that a non-repressive civilisation is indeed possible. In doing so, he fleshes out and historicises the sociopolitical substance of Freud's work in a manner that counterposes rather than abandons the death instinct to the true 'liberatory potential of Eros'. The ultimate call here is for a re-eroticisation of the de-eroticised capitalist body, and the binding together of individuals through work, play, art and culture, in a sensuous, libidinally gratifying, new order; one in which reason and happiness converge (Kellner 1984).

Despite their inspiring potential, many have criticised the work of these 'sexual radicals' as little more than utopian dreams. Not only do they paint an overly optimistic picture of pleasurable co-operation in a non-repressive society – one based less on passionate love than the overflowing of Eros – but the political and institutional details necessary for these social transformations are nowhere adequately worked out (Kellner 1984). Marcuse, for example, exaggerates the role of play and underestimates the importance of the liberation of labour in his vision of a non-repressive civilisation. He also fails to analyse the specificity of women's oppression, and overestimates the power of Eros to tame aggressive destructive instincts and unify the personality in a higher mode of being (Kellner 1984). Ultimately, what this boils down to is a form of:

> utopian word magic – 'if only the world could be like this' – whether it be Fromm's world filled with loving persons or Marcuse's world after the abolition of surplus repression and the performance principle.
>
> (Bocock 1976: 158)

Anti-Oedipus: desiring-machines, schizoanalysis and the 'body without organs'

In contrast to these Freudo-Marxist visions of a new libidinally sensuous order, an alternative anti-Freudian/neo-Nietzschean account of the relationship between capitalism and desire can be found in the work of the philosopher Gilles Deleuze and the psychiatrist Felix Guattari. In two central texts, *Anti-Oedipus* (1984 [1972]) and *A Thousand Plateaus* (1988 [1980]) – volumes I and II, respectively of *Capitalism and Schizophrenia* – Deleuze and Guattari not only challenge Freudian notions of desire (as lack) and the unconscious, but also mount a critical attack on capitalism and the oedipal territorialisation of the subject through a radical form of what they term 'schizoanalysis'.

Contra Freud, Deleuze and Guattari claim that the oedipal structure (holy trinity of daddy–mummy–me) and its associated terms of reference (e.g. 'incest', 'parricidal desire', 'castration' etc.) originate not in desire or the unconscious, but in society itself. Oedipus, in other words, is a predominantly European (bourgeois) phenomenon that distorts and represses the productive nature of desire, inducing shame and guilt in the individual, thus giving rise to a variety of 'neurotic modes of living'. The unconscious therefore, through Freudian psychoanalysis, takes on a *post-facto* structure it does not possess: one that is ultimately built upon the desire to be 'led' – Nietzsche's despised 'herd' instinct – epitomised in Europe by the rise of fascism. Against these negative oedipal territorialisations (i.e. law, limit, castration, lack, lacuna, neurosis), *Anti-Oedipus* seeks to (re)discover the 'deterritorialised' flows of desire, the flows that have not been reduced to oedipal codes and the neuroticised territorialities, the *desiring-machines* that escape such codes leading elsewhere. A form of psychopolitical analysis in which the relationship between desire, reality and the capitalist 'machine' is seen to yield answers to concrete questions: '*Ars erotica, ars theoretica, ars politica*' (Foucault 1984b [1972]: xii).

Recast in these terms desire is a productive, actualising force of nomadic flows and revolutionary linkages that threatens to 'smother' the body politic: ' . . . desire is revolutionary in its essence . . . no society can tolerate a position of real desire without its structures of exploitation, servitude and hierarchy being compromised' (Deleuze and Guattari 1984 [1972]: 116). From this viewpoint, there is no separation between the personal and the social, the individual and the collective. Rather, both the political and the psychological field are invested by one and the same form of libidinal energy. Desire, in short, is 'everywhere': 'desiring-production' is one and the same thing as social production.

This general order or principle of desiring-production, the 'production of production', is not, however, the concrete existence or manifestation of desire. Rather, desire only ever exists in and through what Deleuze and Guattari variously refer to as 'desiring-machines' or 'assemblages' (i.e. 'passional' compositions of desire). As they state on the opening page of *Anti-Oedipus*: 'Everywhere *it* [desiring-production] is machines – real ones, not figurative ones: machines driving other machines, machines being driven by other machines, with all the necessary couplings and connections' (ibid.: 1). In stressing this notion of 'assemblages', the important question for Deleuze and Guattari is not what this sort of machine *means*, but rather how it *works*. Assemblages, in other words, are conceptualised in Spinozian terms of 'use' rather than 'meaning', thus introducing a 'functional' element to their work.[11] Use, function and production, in short, become one and the same thing for a Deleuzo-Guattarian assemblage.

Perhaps most importantly for our purposes, Deleuze and Guattari introduce a novel third term, borrowed from Artaud (1988), in order to 'complete' their theory of desire, namely; the 'Body without Organs' (BwO). In simple terms, the BwO, as a 'non-productive surface', is what connects assemblages or desiring-machines (the product) with desiring-production (the principle of desire) (Jordan 1995). The BwO is the place where an unlimited and unblocked productivity of desire occurs, and so stands opposed to any organisation involving blockages and interrupted flows. This is most apparent in Deleuze and Guattari's discussion of the relationship between the BwO, the organs and their organisation into the 'organism'. As they explain:

> Desiring-machines make us an organism; but at the very heart of this production, within the very production of this production, the body suffers from being organised in this way, from not having some other sort of organisation or no organisation at all. . . . Every coupling of machines, every production of a machine, every sound of a machine running, becomes unbearable to the body without organs. . . . In order to resist organ-machines, the body without organs presents its smooth, slippery, opaque, taut surface as a barrier. In order to resist linked, connected, and interrupted flows, it sets up a counterflow of amorphous, undifferentiated fluid.
>
> (ibid.: 9)

Desire, in short, passes through the body, and through the organs, but not through the organism: 'organisms', as Artaud (1988) puts it, are the 'enemies of the body'. From this we arrive at what is perhaps Deleuze and Guattari's most general statement of the BwO:

> The body without organs is the matter that always fills space to given degrees of intensity, and the partial objects are these degrees, these intensive parts that produce the real in space starting from matter as intensity=0. The body without organs is the immanent substance, in the most Spinozist sense of the word; and the partial objects are like its ultimate attributes, which belong to it precisely insofar as they are really distinct and cannot on this account exclude or oppose one another. The partial objects and the body without organs are the two material elements of the schizophrenic desiring-machine . . . the two together in a relationship of continuity from one end to the other of the molecular chain of desire.
>
> (ibid.: 327)

Again, the reference to Spinoza is significant here. Effectively, what Deleuze and Guattari are attempting to develop is a non-dualist ontology of the body – one that is understood more in terms of what it can do (i.e. its potentialities) than what it means. No longer 'centred' biologically or psychically as a unified 'organism' or the locus of an overarching metaphysical consciousness, the body is instead 'radically reconfigured' in terms of 'fragments and flows', 'intensities and multiplicities', linkages and connections of the desiring-machines or assemblages that compose it: a body without 'internal cohesion' and 'latent significance' (Grosz 1994: 169).[12]

Underlying these issues is a broader commitment to what Deleuze and Guattari refer to as 'rhizomatics' and 'schizoanalysis'. In contrast to centred or polycentric systems, the rhizome is an 'anti-genealogy' which operates by variation, expansion, capture, offshoots. Hierarchical modes and pre-established paths of communication are therefore abandoned in favour of the a-centred, non-hierarchical, non-signifying system of the rhizome – one that provides a 'model' for schizoanalysis as an 'anti-genealogy'. In adopting this position, Deleuze and Guattari distinguish between two particular manifes-tations of desire – the neurotic and the schizophrenic. These, in turn, relate to two main forms of society, the fascist/authoritarian and the revolutionary/libertarian. Instead of participating in a process of liberation, psychoanalysis, through its oedipal concern with issues of symbolic (i.e. 'transcendent' versus 'immanent') representation has taken part in the work of 'bourgeois repression'. Seen in these terms, a 'schizophrenic out for a walk' is, Deleuze and Guattari claim, a 'better model' than a 'neurotic lying on the analyst's couch' (Deleuze and Guattari 1984: 2). The neurotic, in other words, is:

> trapped within the residual or artificial territorialities of our society, and reduces all of them ... to Oedipus as the ultimate territoriality – as reconstructed in the analyst's office and projected upon the full body of the psychoanalyst (yes, my boss is my father, and so is the Chief of State, and so are you, Doctor). ... As for the schizo, continually wandering about, migrating here, there, and everywhere as best he [*sic*] can, he plunges further and further into the realm of deterritorialisation, reaching the furthest limits of the decomposition of the socius on the surface of his own body without organs. ... *The schizophrenic deliberately seeks out the very limits of capitalism*: he is its inherent tendency brought to fulfilment, its surplus product, its proletariat, its exterminating angel. *He scrambles the codes and is the transmitter of decoded flows of desire*. ... *Schizophrenia is desiring-production as the limit of social production.*
>
> (ibid.: 35, our emphasis)

In taking this most radical of stances, Deleuze and Guattari emphasise the need to distinguish the schizophrenic as an *entity* from the *process* of schizophrenia itself, and to avoid as much as possible the confusion of the former with the latter. As they explain, their concern is with the schizophrenic process (i.e. the schizoid pole), which they see as being truly revolutionary in the very sense that the paranoiac is reactionary and fascist. Given the oedipalising tendencies of psychoanalysis, the 'watchdog' of the capitalist state, the nega-tive task of schizoanalysis must therefore be 'violent, brutal: defamiliarizing, de-oedipalizing, decastrating; undoing, theatre, drama, and fantasy; decoding, deterritorializing' (ibid.: 381). More generally, it involves discovering the entire play of the desiring-machines and the repression of desire, through a Nietzschean celebration of the 'will to power', and a championing of pre-symbolic fusional relationships: a realm in which both body and 'self' dissolve through a poststructuralist metaphysics of fragmentation and flux, fluidity and flow (see Chapter 6, this volume).

Underpinning this radically reconfigured ontology lies Deleuze and Guattari's 'theory of lines', one that takes us from the molar to the molecular, and from there on to liberatory 'lines of flight' and the nomadic process of 'becoming-imperceptible'. Molar lines – that relate, they claim, to the *'macro-physics' of the paranoiac* – are the most general, rigid segmentary categories, defined in terms of prevailing power relations (e.g. male and female) and states of domination. As such they create blockages to the smooth, creative flows of desire through the construction of striated space and hierarchical modes of categorisation. Molecular lines, in contrast, although still following a determinate path through particular 'connections', are less rigid, less striated, less segmentary, referring instead to 'minoritarian', 'subordinated' microscopic processes, 'particles' and 'emissions', which 'scatter' the aggregations of molar, binarised, segmented lines. Finally, 'lines of flight' – the abstract assemblage of which Deleuze and Guattari term 'war-machines' – constitute the 'blowing apart' of segmentarity, the pure creative flow of productive desire, the full realisation of *desire* as a liberatory deterritorialising force (Grosz 1994; Jordan 1995). Lines of flight emerge precisely where molar and molecular lines 'break down', and something 'new' emerges. This shift from the molar to the molecular, together with the emphasis on lines of flight is encapsulated, Deleuze and Guattari suggest, in the *'microphysics' of the schizophrenic process*, one involving: 'waves and corpuscles, flows and partial objects . . . infinitesimal lines of escape, instead of the perspective of large aggregates' (Deleuze and Guattari 1984 [1972]: 280). Paranoiac macrophysics and schizophrenic microphysics are, in short, two 'radically different forms of investment': the first a *subjugated group* investment which socially and psychically represses the desire of persons, the second a revolutionary *subject-group* investment in the 'transverse multiplicities' which convey desire as a molecular phenomenon, subordinating the socius to 'desiring-production' (ibid.: 348).

These moves from the molar to the molecular, coupled with the seemingly abstract notion of 'war-machines' and 'lines of flight', in turn relate to Deleuze and Guattari's emphasis on the process of *'becoming'*. The only way to get outside the dualisms, they suggest, is 'to be-between, to pass between, the intermezzo' (Deleuze and Guattari 1988: 277). As 'transgressive movements', all becomings involve specific forms of 'motion and rest', 'speed and slowness', flows of intensity and multiplicity, thus rendering former binarised modes of Western thought obsolete (Grosz 1994). All becomings, for Deleuze and Guattari, are 'minoritarian', and must necessarily pass through the process of what they term 'becoming-woman' as an abstract line of flight.

As they state:

> What we term a molar entity is, for example, the woman as defined by her form, endowed with organs and functions, and assigned as a subject. Becoming woman is not imitating this entity or even transforming oneself into it. . . . All we are saying is that these indissociable aspects of becoming-woman must first be understood as a function of something else: not imitating or assuming the female form, but *emitting particles that enter the relation of movement and rest, or the zone of proximity, of a micro-femininity, in other words, that produce in us a molecular woman, create the molecular woman.* We do not mean to say that a creation of this kind is the prerogative of the man, but on the contrary that the woman as a molar entity *has to become-woman* in order that the man also becomes – or can become-woman.
>
> (ibid.: 275–6, our emphasis)

Becoming-woman, in other words, involves a process of 'going beyond' identity and subjectivity, the breaking down of all molar and molecular identities, the nomadic 'freeing up' of lines of flight. Alongside other modes of 'becoming' – 'becoming-child' as the desedimentation of adult modes of cohesion and control, 'becoming-animal' as a challenge to the anthropocentrism of Western philosophical thought, etc. – this is a process that eventually ends in complete 'dissolution': an immanent process of 'becoming-imperceptible' that problematises and replaces our most elementary notions of materiality and 'thingness' (Grosz 1994). In short, indiscernibility, imperceptibility and impersonality remain the end-points of Deleuze and Guattari's process of becoming. If it remains materialist at this level, then as Grosz rightly comments, it is a materialism that is 'far beyond or different from the body or bodies': ultimately their work is like an *'acidic dissolution of the body, and the subject along with it'* (Grosz 1994: 179, our emphasis).

Here we return again to some of the problems inherent in poststructuralist approaches to the body. On the one hand, Deleuze and Guattari provide us with a radically new way of thinking about desire and the body – one that goes far beyond the Foucauldian project and his critical ontology of the self. Not only do they celebrate the production of difference, they also disaggregate or 'de-massify' the objects of binary thought, breaking them down into micro-processes, intensities, multiplicities and flows of desire: a process of 'becoming', which 'flattens out' former hierarchical modes of organisation and dualistic ways of thinking. Within this radically reconfigured ontology, bodies themselves become Nietzschean sites for a multiplicity of intensities, (micro-) struggles and unexpected linkages.

On the other hand, however, this 'Deleuzo-Guattarian' approach to the body and desire is not without its problems. First, despite its appeals to a non-dualist ontology, Deleuze and Guattari's analysis none the less proceeds through a series of conceptual oppositions such as the hierarchical state and the nomadic tribe, territorialisation versus deterritorialisation, the paranoid and the schizophrenic, transcendent versus immanent interpretation, smooth versus striated space, and so on (Grosz 1994). There also remains a problematic element of 'functionalism' in their work which, despite claims to the contrary, remains unresolved (Jordan 1995).

Second, and perhaps most importantly for our purposes, we must also confront the problems involved in the abandonment of the modernist body, and their championing instead of a poststructuralist metaphysics that prioritises contingency, fluidity and flow, and the (endless) process of 'becoming'. To be sure this may seem an attractive option, particularly after centuries of rigid dualistic thought, but how exactly does it translate in practice and what is lost in the process? Ultimately, as we have seen, Deleuze's and Guattari's position results in a radical reconfiguration of materiality and an 'acidic dissolution' of the body and the subject (i.e. the process of 'becoming-imperceptible); a position that, quite simply, loses too much in the 'process'. In short, a similar fate befalls the Deleuzo–Guattarian and Foucauldian body: first it becomes elusive and eventually it 'disappears' altogether.

Third, Deleuze's and Guattari's emphasis on the process of 'becoming-woman' may be read, from a feminist viewpoint, as a male appropriation of women's politics, struggles and knowledges, implying the dissolution of women's claims to (sexual) specificity through a false universalism that masks men's specificities, desires and interests (Grosz 1994). This concern is reinforced through Deleuze's and Guattari's rather unfortunate use of masculine, 'machinic' terms and 'technocratic' tropes throughout their work. Seen in this light, whilst the notion of 'becoming' may indeed offer feminists an important 'way out' of the strait-jacket of former phallocentric, binarised systems of Western thought, the 'dissolution' that this implies may be 'too great a cost for the furtherance of women's specific interests' (Grosz 1994: 163).

Fourth, Deleuze and Guattari are also guilty of 'romanticising' the schizophrenic process of 'becoming' (imperceptible). To put it quite bluntly, whilst both options have their drawbacks, it is seriously open to question whether a 'schizophrenic out for a stroll' is a 'better model' than a 'neurotic on the analyst's couch'. This in turn connects up with another 'latent' problem regarding Deleuze's and Guattari's notion of 'becoming'. Despite being shrouded in notions of contingency, unpredictability and abstract lines of flight, their discussion of this process none the less suggests an underlying telos or determinate end-point: a direction in which, judgementally, they suggest we should all be moving. There may also be an 'implicit' hierarchy lurking within Deleuze's and Guattari's discussion of becoming-woman, child, animal, imperceptible.

Finally, on a broader political note, not only is the role of class and class struggle reduced to an 'index in the infrastructure of a libidinal investment of another nature' (Deleuze and Guattari 1984 [1972]: 379), but their emphasis on the production of 'difference' may ultimately translate into a form of 'political indifference'. Deleuze and Guattari, in other words, develop a poststructuralist politics that, paradoxically, is unconcerned with the differences between political movements, except in relation to their ability to produce difference (Jordan 1995). Creativity and the endless production of the 'new', therefore, overtake all other political considerations – something that, qualifications apart, includes capitalism itself, as an inherently creative (de/re)territorialising force.

Conclusions

Building on the notion of 'alternative' (anti-Cartesian) traditions with which to analyse the human body, this chapter has been centrally concerned with the dualist legacies of the past. As we have seen, a line of theoretical continuity can be traced here, stretching from Freud's account of the bodily ego and Lacan's notion of 'imaginary anatomy', through Schilder's analysis of body-image to Merleau-Ponty's concept of the sentient body-subject (discussed in Chapter 3, this volume). What these analyses share in common is a refusal to leave the body out of consideration, and an emphasis on the need to work at the interface between the biological, psychological and social realms of human embodiment. Seen in these terms, it is not simply a case of 'mapping' a biological body onto a psychosocial domain, but the 'interconstituency of each to the other', and the 'uncontainability' of human corporeality in any one domain or discourse (Grosz 1994).

However, it has been left to 'sexual radicals' such as Reich and Marcuse to fully flesh out the carnal implications and libidinal possibilities of this project, through a fusion of Freudo-Marxist and neo-Weberian themes. In doing so, they have provided a profound critique of the 'ailments' of modernity, countering Freud's pessimism through the free play of Eros. To this we may also add Deleuze's and Guattari's radical, albeit problematic, poststructuralist 'reading' of the body (without organs) and the oedipalising tendencies of Freudian psychoanalysis: the 'watch-dog' of the capitalist state. Utopian, to be sure, but taken together these critical 'libidinally-informed' perspectives none the less point towards a radically reconfigured ontology of the body and desire, reason and emotion as a challenge to former binarised modes of Western thought: issues we further explore in the following two chapters.

6 'Uncontainable' bodies?
Feminisms, boundaries and reconfigured identities

In the lifecycle, as in the Garden of Eden, the woman has been the deviant.
(Gilligan 1982)

One is not born, but becomes a woman.
(de Beauvoir 1972 [1959])

The starting point of this chapter concerns Spelman's (1988) contentious claim that Western feminism has been infected by a form of 'somatophobia': something contracted from centuries of Western fears associated with women's bodies and 'voracious' sexual appetites. Feminisms have tended to be somatophobic, Spelman suggests, because all too often the link made between women and their bodies has been used against them as a means of curtailing their own as well as 'others' (i.e. blacks, lesbians, children, the disabled, etc.) freedoms. As a consequence, in arguing against such biological determinism, the body has remained under-theorised, pointing instead towards the broader social, cultural and political determinants of women's oppression in Western patriarchal society (Birke 1995).

In this chapter we take a closer look at these issues through a consideration of how feminists, over the past few decades, have conceptualised the body. In doing so, we examine a range of key issues which are central to the book as a whole, from the problem of dualism to the critique of bodily 'containment', and from a reconstructed (feminine) metaphysics of fluidity and flow, to the links between materialism and constructionism in a corporeal feminism. As we shall see, recent attempts by feminist writers to reconcile the materiality and social construction of 'sexed' bodies represent a significant step forward in transcending the false dualisms of the past and moving towards a more inte-grated social theory of embodiment – one that links (lived) *experience* to (cultural) *representation*. It is to a preliminary discussion of these dualistic lega-cies and the problem of biology in feminist thought that we now turn.

Women as 'Other': biology as destiny?

From the language used to describe female organs to the social and political theories of Western society, women have been conceptualised as 'other'. Aristotle, for example, declared that women were constitutionally unfit for public life, whilst Rousseau stated 'It is of men that I am to speak'. Human nature as described by these and other thinkers (e.g. Aquinas, Machiavelli, Locke, Hegel), was intended to refer to male human nature. Indeed, misogyny is reflected in the very roots of words used to describe women's physiology. Pudenda, for instance, comes from the Latin word *pudere* meaning 'to be ashamed of'; oestrogen from the Greek work *oistros* meaning 'insane desire'; and hysteria, from Ancient Greek meaning 'wandering womb'.

Underpinning this, as previous chapters have suggested, is a rationalist division of the world into nature/culture, body/mind, emotion/reason, private/public. These dualisms, in turn, translate into other divisions such as reproduction and production, the family and the state, the individual and the social: women associated with the former, men with the latter. As Gatens states:

> Only culture, the mind and reason, social production, the state and society are understood as having a dynamic and developmental character. The body and its passions, reproduction, the family, and the individual are often conceived as timeless and unvarying aspects of nature. This way of conceptualizing human existence is deeply complicit in claims such as 'women have no history' and 'reproduction involves the mere repetition of life'.
>
> (Gatens 1992: 122)

Historically, this patriarchal ideology has permeated all social institutions, including science and medicine, where all stages of women's reproductive lives are defined as potentially 'pathological' and thus in need of 'expert' (i.e. male) control. Throughout the scientific biological literature, the male body is seen as the 'norm' against which female bodies are measured and judged (Martin 1987). The socially constructed nature of these differences is powerfully illustrated by Laqueur (1987, 1990) in his historical study of the 'making' of 'sex', from the Greeks to Freud. For several thousand years before the Enlightenment, female and male bodies were not in fact conceptualised in terms of 'difference'. Rather, in this 'one sex' model, women's genitals were simply lesser, inverted homologies of men's: women were simply men turned inside out and the lack of specific terms for women's organs (e.g. vagina, ovaries, clitoris) reflected not a disregard for their importance, but an assumption that in this men and women were equal.

By the 1800s, however, writers were beginning to stress that the sexes were opposite, both physically and morally. In particular, the existing model of social difference based on 'inverted homologies' gave way to an anatomy and physiology of 'incommensurability' as science began to 'flesh out' the categories of 'male' and 'female' based on 'biological differences'. Closely allied to these developments was the emergence of 'sexuality' as an essential human attribute linked to self-identity and firmly contrasted with the opposite sex. As a result social and cultural differences in terms of the sexes became grounded in what Laqueur terms a 'biology of incommensurability'. The ovaries in particular, came to be identified as the 'control centres' of reproduction and the 'essence of femininity itself'. These views were later reinforced in the nineteenth and early twentieth centuries when menstruation and pregnancy were treated as 'abnormal' and as a 'sickness' rather than normal bodily functions. Within patriarchal medicine, women were seen as being 'controlled' by their uterus and ovaries, and doctors found reproductive 'disorders' behind almost every female complaint from headache to sore throats and indigestion (Ehrenreich and English 1974: 29). Middle-class women, in Victorian writing, were portrayed as 'delicate', 'irresponsible', 'hysterical creatures', in need of men's protection and guardianship. Indeed, too much development of a woman's brain was, at this time, thought to 'atrophy the uterus', hindering the reproductive function which women were, by their very 'nature', designed to fulfil (Ehrenreich and English 1974; Lupton 1994a).

Even to the present day, contemporary medical textbooks continue to portray the male body as the standard against which the female body is judged, and comparative references to female anatomy continue to employ terms such as 'smaller', 'feebler', 'weaker', 'less well developed', to demonstrate how women differ from men (Scully and Bart 1978; Lawrence and Bendixen 1992). This, in turn, has paved the way for the increasing 'medicalisation' of women's bodies and lives from menstruation to childbirth and pre-menstrual tension to the menopause (Bleier 1984; Oakley 1980, 1984; Riessman 1989; Todd 1989; Lupton 1994a).

In challenging these patriarchal views, feminists have experienced a somewhat ambivalent relationship to their 'biological' bodies. One response to this corporeal dilemma has been to claim that women are 'biologically disadvantaged' relative to men. From this perspective, social reform can only achieve so much, leaving the rectification of remaining inequalities to increases in control over nature (i.e. biology). Whilst de Beauvoir (1972 [1959]) stands out as perhaps the clearest exponent of this position, Firestone's *The Dialectic of Sex* (1970) was also influential in perpetuating the view that science could fulfil a liberatory role for women. Pregnancy, for Firestone, was 'barbaric' – 'childbirth *hurts*' she proclaimed – and the answer to women's subordination lay in future technological control over the 'tyranny' of their 'reproductive biology'. The 'specificity' of the reproductive body, in other words, had to be overcome if sexual equality were to be achieved (Gatens 1992; Birke 1995).

In contrast, an alternative position has been to suggest that women should not aspire to be 'like men' at all. Rather, women should celebrate and affirm their bodies, including the capacity to recreate and nurture. In its strongest form, women are presented as essentially peace loving, caring or 'biophilic' whilst men are seen to be selfish, 'necrophilic' and gynophobic (Daly 1978). For these theorists, essential sexual difference should be retained, rather than overcome, by scientific intervention (Gatens 1992; Birke 1995). Hovering somewhere in between these two strands of essentialism lies the work of feminist writers who, in their differing ways, speak about how women, as potential or actual reproducers, experience oppression. O'Brien (1981, 1989), for example, sees women's oppression as originating in the 'male discovery of their role in paternity' (Birke 1995). For men, she suggests, physiology is 'fate', and paternity an 'alienated' experience:

> For women, giving birth is a unity of knowing doing, of consciousness and creative activity, of temporality and continuity. Paternity is quite a different phenomenon. The essential moment of paternity . . . is abstract and involuntary, it must be given meaning by abstract knowledge rather than by experience.
>
> (O'Brien 1989: 14)

Whilst this statement implies biological determinism, O'Brien stresses that reproduction is, in fact, deeply rooted in material and cultural processes of patriarchal oppression. As such, she sees unity with 'nature' – itself a problematic term – as a desirable future state of affairs.

In a similar, albeit more radical vein, Rich (1976) asks women to reconsider their relationships to their bodies and female biology (Birke 1995). 'I know of no woman' she proclaims, 'for whom her body is not a fundamental problem'. Rather than simply perpetuate these (masculinist) views, women must learn, Rich argues, to 'repossess' their bodies:

> In arguing that we have by no means yet explored or understood our biological grounding, the miracle and paradox of the female body and its spiritual and political meanings, I am really asking whether women cannot begin, at last, to *think through the body*, to connect what has been so cruelly disorganised – our great mental capacities, hardly used; our highly developed tactile sense; our genius for close observation; our complicated, pain-enduring, multi-pleasured physicality.
>
> (Rich 1976: 284)

Whilst these responses to women's corporeal specificity are often taken to exhaust the 'sexual equality versus sexual difference debate', they are ultimately, as Gatens (1992) notes, caught up in one and the same paradigm, one that understands the body as a biologically 'given' entity and assumes rather than transcends a mind/body, nature/culture dualism. In particular, the sex/gender distinction, so central to feminism in the 1970s and early 1980s, failed to question how society constructs the 'natural body' itself.[1] Ultimately, as we have already seen, sex is no more natural than gender, given that speaking of both is mediated by our existence as *social* beings and *historical* agents.

It is the recognition of this fact that has led recent feminist scholarship to an alternative view of the body and power – one that points to the discursive constitution of 'sex' itself and therefore challenges the dualistic manner in which sexual difference has been articulated. Instead of seeing 'sex' as a biological phenomenon and gender as a cultural category, these thinkers, from Irigaray to

Butler, are concerned to undermine the dichotomy altogether. The pre-social body is therefore rejected in favour of a discursive body, a body that is bound up in the 'order' of desire, power and signification. Related to this is a fundamental acknowledgement/celebration of 'difference', one in which culture rather than biology 'marks' bodies and creates the specific conditions in which they live and recreate themselves (Grosz 1994). Broadly speaking, the emphasis here is 'deconstructive' – a position that seeks to 'destabilise', 'challenge', 'subvert', 'reverse', 'overturn' ossified conceptual forms in favour of more plural, fluid positions (Barrett and Phillips 1992).

As this preliminary discussion suggests, no question is more vexed in feminist thought than the relationship between biology and culture, essentialism and constructionism. These are issues to which we shall constantly return throughout this chapter. For the moment, however, it is to a more explicit focus on the nature of bodily boundaries and the problem of 'containment' that we turn in the next section. Exploration of these issues, as we shall see, leads us directly into poststructuralist calls for a more 'fluid' position regarding female embodiment and the nature of feminine desire.

Gender, the lived body, and the problem of 'containment'

As the foregoing discussion suggests, it is male minds, bodies and life experiences that, implicitly or explicitly, have been taken as the 'norm' against which 'all else' is judged. Modern social theory, in this respect, is no exception in its treatment of the seemingly neutral (i.e. male) human subject and the false universalism it presupposes. Once we begin to climb down from these seemingly 'lofty pretensions', however, to 'immerse ourselves in the ambiguities of the lived body', it would appear natural to describe the specificities of 'sexed bodies' (Young 1990). Exploration of the lived body, in other words, needs to take account of the particular *gendered* modalities, structures and conditions of our embodied being-in-the-world.

This challenge is taken up by Young (1990), for instance, in her classic phenomenological study 'Throwing like a Girl'. In doing so, she provides not only an important critique of Merleau-Ponty's seemingly neutral body-subject, but also extends and develops the Maussian notion of body-techniques in important, gender-related, ways. Feminine movement, Young suggests, exhibits an *'ambiguous transcendence'*, an *'inhibited intentionality'* and a *'discontinuous unity'* with its surroundings. More precisely, this gendered use of the body manifests itself in at least three particular ways. First, in a hesitance and caution that precedes action; second, in a reactive rather than proactive engagement with objects; and third, in a tendency to use only certain 'parts' of the body rather than putting the whole of the body behind an action. These issues, she suggests, are perfectly illustrated in relation to throwing and catching:

Men more often move out towards a ball in flight and confront it with their own countermotion. Women tend to wait and then *react* to its approach, rather than going forth to meet it. We frequently respond to the motion of a ball coming *at* us, and our immediate bodily impulse is to flee, duck, or otherwise protect ourselves from its flight. Less often than men, moreover, do women give self-conscious direction and placement to their motion in sport. Rather than aiming at a certain place where we wish to hit a ball, for example, we tend to hit it in a 'general' direction.

(Young 1990: 146)

In thinking these corporeal issues through, Young considers two possible explanations: first, that women's social *'training'* makes them less equipped to act in space, and; second, echoing de Beauvoir's (1972 [1959]) analysis of femininity, that women are more aware of themselves as *'objects'* (i.e. through the objectifying male gaze). Taken together, training and objectification constitute, she argues, an inhibition in female embodiment and the use of space – one that obviates trust in the pre-reflective capabilities of the body. As lived bodies, women are not 'open' and 'unambiguous transcendences', that move out to 'master a world that belongs to us, a world constituted by our own intentions and projects'. Rather, they are 'physically handicapped' in a 'sexist society' (Young 1990: 153).[2]

The problem with such an analysis, however, as Young herself readily admits, is that femininity itself is constructed simply as 'liability'. From this perspective, female experience is seen in terms of victimisation, and masculine styles of bodily comportment implicitly assumed as the norm (Young 1990: 6). In contrast, some of Young's other essays have a more 'gynocentric' cast; one in which the physical and emotional harms that women suffer in masculinist institutions are counterbalanced by an exploration of some positive experiences and pleasures of the female body such as being breasted and the embodiment of pregnancy. In doing so, she adopts an explicitly feminine process metaphysic which, as Irigaray suggests, might conceptualise women's bodily being as fluid rather than solid:

Fluids, unlike objects, have no definite border; they are unstable . . . fluids surge and move, and a metaphysic that thinks being as fluid would tend to privilege the living, moving, pulsing, over the inert dead matter of the Cartesian world view. This is, simply, a process metaphysics, in which movement and energy is ontologically prior to thingness and the nature of things takes its being from the organic contexts in which they are embedded. . . . A process metaphysics, a metaphysics of fluids . . . where we cannot delineate clearly what is inside and outside, is a better way to think about the world from an ecological point of view. Inasmuch as women's oppression derives to a significant degree from literal and figurative objectification, I am suggesting, subverting the metaphysics of objects can also be liberating for women.

(Young 1990: 1993)

This reconstructed (feminine) metaphysics of fluidity and flow, and the problems of corporeal 'containment' it raises, are also taken up by Battersby (1993) in her critique of Johnson's (1987) *The Body in the Mind*. According to Johnson, our encounter with 'containment' and 'boundedness' is one of the most 'pervasive features' of our bodily experience, serving as one of a number of underlying structures of embodiment that shape and constrain the imagination via gestalt-type patterns or schemata at the pre-conceptual level (see Chapter 3).[3] Why then, given Johnson's assumptions of 'intuitive assent', does Battersby feel so alienated and estranged on reading this account of embodied experience: 'How is it that . . . [it] . . . makes me feel so singular: odd; a freak; outside the norm?' (Battersby 1993: 31). In seeking an answer to this question, Battersby considers a number of possible explanations, including the suggestion that she is somehow idiosyncratic or peculiar, that there is something the matter with her image schemata, perhaps in the manner of Sacks's (1985) freakish case studies of neurological disorders in which patients mistake their wives for 'hats', or feel peculiarly 'disembodied'.

Battersby readily discounts these explanations, drawing upon Martin's (1987) classic study, *The Woman in the Body*, in support of her claim.[4] As Martin's study shows, whilst different models are prevalent in the language of middle-class and working-class women (including black working-class women), women of all classes quite frequently talk about their bodies in ways that suggest extreme fragmentation, with the self located 'outside' the body. This central image of self 'separate' from the body, in turn, has a number of corollaries in women's minds, including notions such as the following: 'Your body needs to be controlled by your self'; 'Menstruation, menopause and birth contractions are separate from the self.' They are 'the contractions' , 'the hot flushes (not mine)'; they 'come on'; women 'get them' (Martin 1987: 77–8). In contrast to their working-class counterparts, middle-class women typically accepted dominant spatialised models of the body as a 'container' (of eggs, blood, womb, etc.), but often went on to state that this 'internal model' was not in fact relevant to them. Martin's analysis therefore interprets the 'containment' imagery as the educated middle-class subjects' (unsuccessful) attempts to make their body-image coincide with the medical or scientific rendition of female reproductive processes. In doing so, she implicitly undermines any simplistic understanding of bodily containment as a universal schema, as well as any attempt to restrict the containment schema to a 'homogenised Western self' (Battersby 1993):

> Because their bodily processes go with them everywhere, forcing them to juxtapose biology and culture, women glimpse every day a conception of another sort of social order. At the very least, since they do not fit into the ideal division of things (private, bodily processes belong to home), they are likely to see that the dominant ideology is partial: it does not capture their experience. It is also likely that they will see the inextricable way our cultural categories are related and so see the falseness of the

dichotomies. When women derive their view of experience from their bodily processes as they occur in society, they are not saying 'back to nature' in any way. They are saying onto another kind of culture, one in which our rigid separations and oppositions is not present.

(Martin 1987: 200)

It is this 'non-rigid' view that Battersby endorses in seeking to explain her difficulties with spatialised (masculine) models of corporeal 'containment'. Women have, she suggests, echoing Young (1990), a different relationship to their bodies than men. Recognition of this fact necessitates a more 'fluid' notion of female embodiment, one modelled on Irigaray's conceptualisation of feminine desire, and a self that exists not by repulsion/exclusion, but via interpenetration of self with otherness:

What I have been wanting to stress . . . is that not all talk of identity involves thinking of the self as unitary or contained; nor need boundaries be conceived in ways that make identity closed, autonomous or impermeable. We need to think individuality differently; allowing the potentiality for otherness to exist within it, as well as alongside it; we need to theorise agency in terms of patterns of potentiality and flow. Our body-boundaries do not *contain* the self; they *are* the embodied self.

(Battersby 1993: 38)[5]

Boundaries, in other words, are 'essentially' masculine products that seek to 'contain' women's corporeal 'flows' and the amorphous nature of feminine desire. It is to a fuller discussion of this more 'fluid' position, one central to (French) poststructuralist feminism, that we now turn.

Feminism, psychoanalysis and the 'specular' politics of *'différence'*

the role of 'femininity' is prescribed by a masculine specula(risa)tion and corresponds scarcely at all to women's desire.

(Irigaray 1991)

In contrast to earlier forms of feminism, recent (French) writers have drawn on certain currents within poststructuralist thought in order to understand women's physical and social existence, and the symbolic constitution of the subject in and through language. Central figures here include Cixous, Irigaray and Kristeva who, despite many differences, share a critical appropriation of Lacanian psychoanalysis (see Chapter 5, this volume)[6] and Derridean 'difference', a rejection of individual subjectivity as a unified and stable set of characteristics, and a deep-seated concern with (the repressed aspects of) language, texts, writing and justice (Sarup 1993). The word 'critical' needs to be emphasised here because, whilst Lacan, to paraphrase Gallop (1988: 125), has 'produced a Freud' that might be of use to feminists, his phallocentrism is 'particularly hard to swallow'.

Cixous, for example, rejects the negativity and lack inherent in the Freudian and Lacanian privileging of the phallus: one in which women become represented as the 'other', simultaneously signifying both the completion of (male) subjectivity and a threat to it. For Cixous, female sexuality is rich and plural – the word '*jouissance*', for instance, infers that rapturous and intense pleasure, which women know and men fear – and it is on this libidinal basis that she is able to explore the parallel between feminine desire and writing. In doing so, Cixous argues for the possibility of a 'bisexuality' rather than a denial of sexual difference, one that involves a lived recognition of plurality and the simultaneous presence of masculinity and femininity within an individual subject (Sarup 1993).

Although impossible to define, a feminist writing practice will, Cixous argues, always 'surpass the discourse that regulates the phallocentric system' (Cixous 1991: 226). Feminine writing comes from 'deep within': a 'place' that precedes 'prohibition', taking the individual through various 'doors', 'walls', 'obstacles' and 'distances' forged within the course of life. Women must, therefore:

> *write through their bodies*, they must invent the impregnable language that will wreak partitions, classes and rhetorics, regulations and codes, they must submerge, *cut through*, get beyond the ultimate reserve – discourse. . . . If woman has always functioned 'within' the discourse of man . . . it is time for her to dislocate this 'within', to explode it, turn it around, and seize it; to make it hers, containing it, taking it in her own mouth, biting that tongue with her very own teeth to invent for herself a language to get inside of.
>
> (ibid.: 229)

Closely allied to these ideas is Cixous's notion of '*the gift*'. In contrast to masculine notions of exchange based on economic principles of giving and receiving, Cixous proposes instead an alternative feminine economy of giving, which derives from Bataille's solar principles of a giving sun – one that dispenses energy (wealth) without any expectation of return. Like female sexuality itself, the emphasis here is on a feminine relationship of giving based on spontaneity, generosity and trust as opposed to masculine forms of repetitive/possessive desire and control (what Cixous terms '*the proper*'). This stress on the 'transformative potential' of language and the gift has, however, been sharply criticised by those feminists who argue that its revolutionary potential ultimately translates into the 'literary pretensions' of an intellectual elite, one that not only denies illiterate (Third-World) women a legitimate voice, but requires excellent writing skills from Cixous's own students (Hughes 1996).

This more fluid position on writing and feminine desire is also echoed in the work of Irigaray. Like Cixous, one of Irigaray's main aims is to lay bare the foundations of patriarchy, particularly in the work of philosophers, and in doing so, to define female identity in a way that avoids becoming ensnared in the patriarchal frameworks from which she is trying to escape. Western culture, she suggests, is 'monosexual', characterised by the principles of identity and non-contradiction in which ambiguity/ambivalence is minimised and everything is either one thing or another: a refusal, in other words, to think of a self that is permeated by 'otherness' (Battersby 1993). From this viewpoint, women are simply seen as 'lesser', 'inferior' or 'defective' men, who lack an identity of their own.

Returning to the earlier critique of 'containment', what Irigaray is suggesting here is that identities based on ideas such as spatial containment, substances and atoms belong to masculinist imagery – one that privileges 'optics', 'straight lines', 'self-contained unity' and 'solids' – and that what is missing from our culture is an alternative tradition with which to think identity – one that prioritises notions of fluidity and flow, and feminine touch over the masculine aesthetic of looking (the most distant of the senses).[7] As she states:

> Within Western phallocentric logic, the 'visual' is predominant. In contrast, woman takes pleasure more from touching than from looking, and that entry into a dominant scopic economy signifies, again, her consignment to passivity: she is to be the beautiful object of contemplation. . . . If woman takes pleasure precisely from [her] incompleteness of form . . . that pleasure is denied by a civilization that privileges phallomorphism. . . . The *one* of form, of the individual, of the (male) sexual organ, of the proper name, of the proper meaning.
>
> (Irigaray 1991: 206)

In making these claims, Irigaray is highly critical of the way in which the complexity and multiplicity of female logic is misrepresented in phallomorphic terms.[8] In contrast to the unitary penis, woman does not have 'one sex'. Rather, her sexuality is always double or plural, involving a spontaneous autoeroticism centred particularly on the labia (i.e. 'the lips'):

> Woman's autoeroticism is very different from man's. In order to touch himself, man needs an instrument: his hand, a woman's body, language. . . . And this self-caressing requires at least a minimum of activity. As for woman, she touches herself in and of herself without any need for mediation, and before there is any way to distinguish activity from passivity. Woman 'touches herself' all the time, and moreover, no one can forbid her to do so, for her genitals are formed of two lips in continuous contact. Thus, *within herself, she is already two – but not divisible into one(s)* – that caress each other.
>
> (ibid.: 204–5)

The fact that this continuous state of self-arousal is not necessarily conscious enhances the subtlety of female sexuality for Irigaray. Woman, as Irigaray argues, has 'sex organs' more or less everywhere: 'the geography of her plea-sure is far more diversified, more multiple in its differences, more complex, more subtle, than is commonly imagined – in an imaginary rather too narrow focus on sameness' (ibid.: 207–8).

Echoing Cixous, Irigaray therefore suggests that women need a language of their own (an *écriture féminin* or a *parleur féminin*), one modelled on this plurality, fluidity and flow that does not imprison, but instead enables women to grow. For woman to '(re)discover herself involves her 'never simply being one'. Rather, woman always remains 'several'. Whilst the models of feminine writing that Cixous and Irigaray endorse are those of male authors (e.g. Nietzsche, Hegel, Joyce, Levinas, Derrida), the dangers of 'colonising' this feminine space are explicitly addressed by Irigaray through an emphasis on the notion of 'woman-as-subject'; a position in which women themselves must be involved in the making of cultural and political reality (Sarup 1993). Seen in these terms, Irigaray's emphasis on the 'lips speaking together can be read fruitfully, both literally and metaphorically, as a means of discovery, recovery and invention of women's culture: a 'challenge' to the false univer-sality of Kantian transcendental subjectivity.

Moving from Cixous and Irigaray, to Kristeva, her work is somewhat more difficult to characterise in purely feminist terms. Certainly Kristeva's views lead her to a rejection of any notion of an inherently feminine or female *écriture féminin*. In keeping with these other two thinkers, however, she none the less believes in the revolutionary potential of the marginal and repressed aspects of language (Sarup 1993). Moreover, like Cixous, she also claims that there are specifically 'feminine forms' of meaning and signification that cannot be contained in the rational structures of the symbolic order (Sarup 1993) and therefore, despite being marginalised, constitute challenges to its sovereignty (Sarup 1993).

For Kristeva (1986), there is a basic problem in the argument for a femi-nism of equality as it is unable to theorise sexual and reproductive equality and is subsequently unable to deal adequately with the position of women in the social and symbolic order (Sarup 1993). Kristeva clarifies this link between sexual and symbolic functioning in the following way:

> Sexual difference – which is at once biological, physical, and relative to reproduction – is translated and translates a difference in the relation of subjects to the symbolic contract which is the social contract: a differ-ence, then, in the relationship to power, language and meaning. The sharpest and most subtle point of feminist subversion brought about by the new generation will henceforth be situated on the terrain of the inseparable conjunction of the sexual and the symbolic, in order to try and discover, first, the specificity of the female, and then, in the end, that of each individual.
>
> (Kristeva 1982: 21)

In the *Powers of Horror: An Essay on Abjection* (1982), Kristeva ascribes a constitutive role to mechanisms of disgust in the formation of identity during the process of weaning. According to Kristeva, the boundary of the body and the distinction between self and not-self is established through a process of repulsion that occurs at a pre-conceptual/pre-oedipal (*féminin*) stage, before the child's entry into language (i.e. the symbolic and the realm of the father) and before the child has clearly demarcated the boundaries between self and (m)other (Grosz 1994). 'Nausea', as she states; 'makes me balk at that mild cream, separates me from the mother and father who proffer it. . . . I expel myself, I spit myself out, I abject myself within the same motion through which "I" claim to establish myself' (Kristeva 1982: 3).

Drawing heavily on Douglas's (1966) 'seminal' work in *Purity and Danger*, Kristeva discusses three broad categories of abjection, namely: abjection towards food and thus bodily incorporation; abjection towards bodily waste and the extreme horror of the corpse; and finally, abjection towards signs of sexual difference. In each particular case, as Grosz (1994: 193) rightly observes, Kristeva is, in effect, discussing the social constitution of the body; the process of 'sorting', 'segregating', and 'demarcating' the body so as to conform with but not to exceed cultural expectations. The abject, for Kristeva, is 'dirty', 'filthy', 'contaminating', 'waste': a liminal category, which is neither 'self' nor 'other', 'inside' nor 'outside'. Transgressive in nature, it respects no borders, rules or positions. Rather, its boundaries continually threaten to merge with our own: 'it is something rejected from which one does not part . . . it beckons to us and ends up engulfing us' (Kristeva 1982: 4).

Perhaps most controversially of all, Kristeva links menstrual fluids with dirt and creates a dualism between 'non-polluting' body fluids (i.e. tears and, significantly, semen), and those that 'pollute' and 'defile' (i.e. excrement and menstrual blood). Kristeva therefore associates menstrual blood with excrement. In doing so, consciously or otherwise, she reinforces a dominant masculine notion of feminine sexuality as inherently 'dangerous'. To be sure, as Grosz (1994) notes, this is a puzzling equation, and it is difficult to understand how Kristeva is able to claim that menstrual blood poses a danger (to both sexes) in a way that semen does not. Here we confront some of the tensions concerning Kristeva's status as a 'feminist' thinker. The representation of female sexuality as a 'dangerous' uncontainable flow, as seepage associated with the 'unclean', perpetuates the very assumptions about women's bodies from which feminists have been trying to escape (Grosz 1994).

What Kristeva does offer, however, is a means of linking the notion of 'abjection' to the 'lived experience of the body, the social and culturally specific meanings of the body . . . the privileging of some parts and functions while resolutely minimising or leaving un- or underrepresented other parts and functions' (Grosz 1994: 192). Moreover, like Cixous and Irigaray, Kristeva believes that there are feminine modes of signification that, whilst not specifically linked to feminine libido, cannot be contained within the rational structures of the Western symbolic order. In this respect, she contrasts a pre-oedipal 'feminine' semiotic, dominated by primary processes and the space of the mother's body – one modelled on the *chora* in Plato's *Timaeus* – with the symbolic, oedipalised system – an order imposed on the semiotic, which is regulated by secondary process and the Law of the Father (Sarup 1993). For Kristeva (1986), the semiotic, with its rhythmic proliferation of pleasures, colours and sounds, can return, like the repressed, to haunt, disturb and disrupt the symbolic. The symbolic, with its stress on unity, is therefore dialectically related to the semiotic, which underlies, subverts and 'cuts through' this linguistic realm, breaking down traditional unities and gender divisions. Particularly in times of crisis, revolution and rupture, its subversive, dispersive energies lead to a transgression of the boundaries or tolerable limits of the symbolic order – an order in which men, too, can be constructed as 'marginal' (Sarup 1993).

To summarise, despite their many differences, these French poststructuralist feminist thinkers unite in seeking to challenge former dichotomised modes of (male-stream) Western thought in which women have been conceptualised as 'Other'. In doing so, they point to an alternative process metaphysics of feminine desire, one in which the masculine privileging of optics, straight lines, solids and self-contained unities, gives way to more pluralised (pre-oedipal) notions of fluidity and flow, generosity and trust.[9] Kristeva's work, in particular, provides a way of exploring the relationship between the lived experience of the (sexed) body and the socially and culturally specific meanings through which it is symbolically marked and inscribed (Grosz 1994). Underlying these issues, of course, are deep ontological and epistemological questions concerning how, precisely, we are to theorise 'sexed' bodies in a way that acknowledges both their materiality and their cultural construction. It is to a further consideration of this dilemmatic corporeal question that we now turn in the next section.

'Sexed' bodies: beyond materialism and constructionism?

Throughout this chapter so far, the tensions in feminist thought between biology and culture, essentialism and constructionism, experience and representation, equality and difference, have proved abiding themes. Is there, however, a way out of this dilemma, one that holds to a view of the 'sexed' body as simultaneously biology and culture, materiality and inscription? To be sure, work such as Kristeva's goes some way towards meeting this goal, but much still remains to be done in order to adequately theorise these links, and to do so in ways that do not 'dematerialise' sexual difference in the process.

A bold, albeit problematic, attempt to do so can be found in the work of Judith Butler (1990, 1993a) on the discursive limits of 'sex'. In reconceptualising the Lacanian notion of 'sex' as a quasi-permanent 'linguistic norm' or 'regulatory ideal', Butler is able to challenge the 'structural stasis of the heterosexualising norm' without dispensing with what is clearly valuable in psychoanalytic perspectives. In doing so, she is also able to address the materiality of bodies as 'sexed', through a notion of 'performativity' as 'citationality'. 'Sex', in other words, is an 'ideal construct' that is forcibly 'materialised' through time: 'It is not a simple fact or static condition of the body, but a process whereby regulatory norms materialize sex . . . through a forcible reiteration of those norms' (Butler 1993a: 1–2).

This represents a deft move on Butler's part. What she is arguing for here is not a denial of the materiality of the body, including its fixity, its contours and its movements. Rather, materiality itself needs to be fundamentally rethought as an effect of power, indeed as power's most productive effect: 'once "sex" itself is understood in its normativity, the materiality of the body will not be thinkable apart from the materialization of that regulatory norm' (Butler 1993a: 2). Seen in these terms 'sex' is not simply what one has, or what one is, rather it is one of the regulatory and reiterative norms by which one becomes 'viable' at all.

At stake in such a reformulation are five key propositions. First, in Foucauldian terms, a recasting of body matters and the matter of bodies as a dynamic effect of power, and the regulatory norms that govern their materialisation and signification. Second, the understanding of 'performativity' as a reiterative power of discourse to (re-)produce the very phenomena that it regulates and constrains. Third, the construal of 'sex' as no longer a 'bodily given' upon which gender constructs are artificially imposed, but instead a 'cultural norm' that governs the materialisation of bodies. Fourth, a rethinking of the process by which a bodily norm is assumed, appropriated or adopted as one in which the very subject, the 'speaking I', is constituted by virtue of having gone through the process of assuming a 'sex'. Finally, a linking of the assumption of 'sex' with the question of *identification*, and the discursive means by which the 'heterosexual imperative' enables certain 'sexed' identification whilst foreclosing and/or disavowing others (Butler 1993a: 2–3).

Echoing Kristeva, Butler notes how this 'exclusionary matrix' by which 'sexed' subjects are formed, simultaneously requires the production of a domain of 'abject beings' – those who are not yet 'subjects', but who form the constitutive outside to the domain of the subject – an abject outside, which is, after all, 'inside' the subject as its own 'founding repudiation' (Butler 1993a: 3). It is this 'uninhabitable' zone that Butler sees as constituting the discursive 'limits' of 'sex'. The task she therefore sets herself is to use these transgressive forms of 'abjection' as a critical resource in the struggle to rearticulate the very terms of 'symbolic legitimacy' and 'illegitimacy'. It is in this context, Butler suggests, that the contentious practices of 'queerness' can be understood, not simply as an example of 'citational politics', but also as a specific 'reworking of abjection into political agency'. From this viewpoint, the public assertion of 'queerness' enacts performativity as citationality for the purposes of resignifying the 'abjection' of homosexuality into defiance and legitimacy (ibid.: 223–42).[10]

Butler's work is therefore informed by a commitment to a radical resignification of the symbolic domain; 'deviating the citational chain towards a more possible future to expand what counts as a valued and valuable body in the world' (ibid.: 22). In doing so, not only are Lacanian notions of the 'fixity' of the subject in the symbolic order of language counterposed to a more dynamic or contested notion of discourse in the work of Foucault, but Foucault too is used against himself, so to speak, in a way which takes the materiality of 'sexed' bodies seriously. In this way, Butler is able to reconceptualise the question of the materiality of sexed bodies, not as a site or surface, but rather as *a process of materialisation which stabilises over time to produce the effect of boundary, fixity, and surface we call matter*' (ibid.: 9).

To be sure this is a powerful achievement, one in which questions of 'sexual' and 'racial' difference are taken seriously. Moreover it also, as alluded to above, keys into broader developments in 'queer theory', including the decentring of sexual identities, the greater appreciation of sexual fluidity, the emphasis on knowledge as a social force, and the claim that the categories of hetero-/homosexuality shape the broader cultural and institutional order of society. In this respect, queer theory is not the study of a minority group (e.g. the 'making' of the lesbian/gay/bisexual subject), rather it constitutes a study of:

> those knowledges and social practices that organise 'society' as a whole by sexualising – bodies, desires, acts, identities, social relations, knowledges, culture and social institutions. Queer theory aspires to transform homosexual theory into a general social theory or one standpoint from which to analyse social dynamics.
>
> (Seidman 1996: 13)

Yet, for all its complexity, we still return to the same underlying problem that haunts all poststructuralist approaches to the body and identity. Butler's analysis, in short, is still largely driven by a 'discourse determinism', albeit one that, this time, is yoked to a reconceptualisation of the 'material' and the power of discourse to constitute that very materiality. Indeed, when pushed into a corner by her imaginary interlocutors – critics who seek assurances that there are, at least minimally, sexually differentiated parts, activities, capacities, hormonal and chromosomal differences that can be conceded without reference to 'construction' – Butler's reply is both yes and no. As she states:

> To 'concede' the undeniability of 'sex' or its 'materiality' is always to concede some version of 'sex', some formation of 'materiality'. Is the discourse in and through which that concession occurs – and, yes, that concession invariably does occur – not itself formative of the very phenomenon that it concedes? To claim that discourse is formative is not to claim that it originates, causes or exhaustively composes that which it concedes; rather, it is to claim that there is no reference to a pure body

which is not at the same time a further formation of that body. In this respect, the linguistic capacity to refer to sexed bodies is not denied, but the very meaning of 'referentiality' is altered. In philosophical terms, the constative claim is always to some degree performative.

(Butler 1993a: 10–11)

Here we return, full circle, to the Lacanian notion of the 'real' as an unknowable domain except through the symbolic realm of language. Ultimately, therefore, what we end up with is a form of analysis in which the social shapes the material to a far greater degree than the material shapes the social. The body that performs, however much Butler insists it is produced by performance itself, must nevertheless 'abide between performances, existing over and above the sum total of its performances' (Grosz 1995: 212). Sexuality is more than simply a position in social space, yet there is little attempt here, on Butler's part, to understand the physicality of the phenomenal body, or its material decline and decay across the life course (Turner 1995: 233). As Birke succinctly puts it: 'Like many women I have trouble thinking about theories of social construction that ignore or play down my bodily pain and bleeding, or that ignore the way that desire (however constructed) finds expression through my material body' (Birke 1995: 2). This, coupled with an overly decentred position on questions of sexual identity – which is itself a form of essentialism, albeit a non-essentialist one – means that Butler's discursive (i.e. performative and citational) approach to the body is both promising and problematic.

Perhaps a more fruitful way out of this dilemma is provided by Grosz (1994) in her account of 'sexed' bodies. As she argues, a truly informed corporeal feminism should embrace the following six factors. First, it must avoid the impasse involved in dividing the subject into the mutually exclusive categories of mind and body: resolving this in favour of some kind of *embodied subjectivity* or 'psychical corporeality'. Second, corporeality itself must no longer be associated with only one sex (or race). Third, a corporeal feminism must refuse singular models, based on one type of body as the norm by which all other bodies are judged. Fourth, whilst dualism must be avoided, so too, where possible, must biologistic or essentialist accounts. The body must, instead, be regarded as 'a site of social, political, cultural, and geographical inscriptions, production, or constitution' (Grosz 1994: 23). Fifth, whatever models are developed, they must demonstrate some sort of internal or 'constitutive articulation' or 'disarticulation' between the biological and the psychological, the inside and the outside of the body, whilst avoiding a reduction of the mind to the brain. Finally, and perhaps most importantly for our purposes, instead of participating in and adhering to one side or other of a binary pair, these pairs can more readily be problematised by regarding the body as:

the threshold or borderline concept that hovers perilously and undecidably

at the pivotal point of binary pairs. . . . In the face of social constructionism, the body's tangibility, its matter, its (quasi) nature may be
invoked; but, in opposition to essentialism, biologism, and naturalism,
it is the body as cultural product that must be stressed.

(Grosz 1994: 23–4)

In seeking to develop this framework further, Grosz borrows a useful model
from Lacan, in which he likens the subject to a Möbius strip (i.e. an inverted
three-dimensional figure eight). Seen in these terms, bodies and minds are
not in fact two distinct substances, or indeed two attributes of a single
substance, but somewhere in between. The Möbius strip points to the inflection of mind into body and body into mind, and the ways in which, through
a kind of 'twisting' or 'inversion', one side becomes the other. It also enables
us to rethink the relation between the 'inside' and 'outside' of the subject (i.e.
the relationship between the 'psychical interior' and 'corporeal exterior'), by
showing not their fundamental identity or reducibility, but the 'torsion' of
one into the other, the 'passage, vector, or uncontrollable drift of the inside
into the outside and the outside into the inside' (ibid.: xii).

It is on this basis that Grosz is able to consider the vexed question of the
'sexed' body (i.e. sexual *specificity*). Do inscriptions, for instance, 'produce'
sexual differentiation? Or does sexual difference imply a differential mode of
inscription? The answer to such questions, as Grosz rightly argues, involves
an examination of the complex intertwining and interchanging between
writing and bodies, 'bodies as blank or already encoded surfaces of inscription' (ibid.: 189–90). The 'sexed' body, in other words, cannot be understood
in terms of a fixed, ahistorical biology, although it must clearly contain a
biological dimension. Biology, in short, needs to be reconceptualised as an:

> open materiality, a set of (possibly infinite) tendencies and potentialities
> which may be developed, yet whose development will necessarily hinder
> or induce other developments and trajectories. . . . The kind of model I
> have in mind here is not simply then a model of an imposition of inscrip-
> tion on a blank slate, a page with no 'texture' and no resistance of its
> own. As any calligrapher knows, the kind of texts produced depends not
> only on the message to be inscribed, not only the inscriptive tools –
> stylus, ink – used, but also on the quality and distinctiveness of the
> paper written upon. Perhaps then, a more appropriate model for this
> kind of body writing is not the writing of the blank page – a model
> which minimizes the impact and effects of the paper itself – but a model
> of etching, a model which needs to take into account the specificities of
> the materials being thus inscribed and their concrete effects in the kind
> of text produced.

(Grosz 1994: 191)

It is dialectical models such as these that free us from the straitjacket of former either/or debates. In doing so, they not only provide important insights into how bodies come to be 'sexed' but also, more generally, how we can move towards a position in which the dualist legacies of the past can effectively be transcended through notions such as the 'cultural materiality of embodiment' (Prendergast 1995). Biology, in other words, does not have to be 'written out' (as it is by social constructionists), but neither does it have to be seen as determinative (Birke 1995).[11]

The upshot of this is clear, not only must the relationship between nature and culture, biology and society, mind and body, be fundamentally rethought, the 'interior' as well as the 'exterior' structures and process of the 'sexed' body need opening up for critical scrutiny, interrogation and debate.[12] The body, in short, both inside and out, is far too important to leave to the natural sciences.

Conclusions

As this chapter so clearly demonstrates, feminist thought is itself located at the intersection of a number of classical dualisms in Western thought such as body/mind, nature/culture, biology/society, sex/gender, male/female, self/other, reason/emotion, public/private. In this respect feminism raises, in acute form, the problems and dilemmas of embodiment in social theory today. Not only has recent feminist scholarship treated embodiment as a central topic of investigation, thereby countering the charge of 'somatophobia', but writers such as Grosz, in their call for a corporeal feminism, have made significant steps forward in reconciling materialist and constructionist views of the 'sexed' body. As a consequence, not only have the dualist legacies of the past been effectively challenged, but the 'cutting edge' of contemporary social theorising around the body may in fact be located within feminism itself: the ultimate challenge of a feminist body/politics?

7 The emotionally 'expressive' body

Despite their obvious importance to a range of issues within the social sciences, emotions, like the body to which they are so closely tied, have tended to enjoy a rather 'ethereal' existence within sociology, lurking in the shadows or banished to the margins of sociological thought and practice. Certainly, it is possible to point towards implicit if not explicit emotional themes in classical sociological writing. Marx's emotions, for example, were grounded in the social, historical and material conditions of existence; conditions which led to feelings of alienation and estrangement from our species being under the capitalist mode of production. Durkheim, in contrast, in keeping with his claim that social facts are things in themselves, chose to emphasise the collective, moral nature of human feelings and sentiments, solidified into rituals, both sacred and profane. To this we may also add Weber's work on Western processes of rationalisation, asceticism, and the emotional significance of the charismatic leader, together with Simmel's analysis of the sociological significance of the senses and the vicissitudes of mental life in the metropolis. None the less, it is really only within the last decade or so that a distinct 'corpus' of work, mostly American in origin, has begun to emerge in the sociology of emotions.

The roots of this neglect lie deeply buried in Western thought – a tradition that ever since the time of Plato has sought to divorce body from mind, nature from culture, reason from emotion, and public from private. As a consequence, emotions have tended to be dismissed as private, 'irrational', inner sensations that have been tied, historically, to women's 'dangerous desires' and 'hysterical bodies'. Here, the dominant view seems to have been that emotions need to be 'tamed', 'harnessed' or 'driven out' by the steady hand of (male) reason.

Historically, we should have learnt the important lessons that stem from the unbridled use of instrumental rationality, devoid of human feeling, empathy and compassion: a legacy chillingly demonstrated by atrocities like the Holocaust (Bauman 1989, Lynch 1985). Even to the present day, emotions are seen to be the very antithesis of the detached scientific mind and its quest for 'objectivity', 'truth' and 'wisdom'. Reason, in short, is regarded as the 'indispensable faculty' for the acquisition of human knowledge (Jaggar 1989). Yet, as a variety of critiques have demonstrated, such a view neglects the fact that rationality, even at its most positivistic, involves the incorporation of human values and emotions.[1] The effective use of thought and decision making, for example, must rely on emotionally embodied and corporeally informed readings and reactions as criteria for deciding between alternatives. Reflective thought and the deployment of reason, in other words, requires the 'tagging' of cognition with emotions (Damasio 1994). Seen in this light, (male) Western culture displays an 'irrational passion for dispassionate rationality' (Rieff 1979) – one that is, at root, wholly 'unreasonable', serving certain sociopolitical ends. As Seidler states:

> We have learned, especially as men, to identify with our minds and to segregate and disdain our bodily experience. We have learned to value reason in a way that has estranged us from our emotional and spiritual lives. We have learned to identify progress with the domination of nature that we can no longer feel at home in. As we no longer feel at home in our bodies, so we no longer feel at home with our 'natural selves'.
>
> (Seidler 1994: 84)

This, in turn, suggests that it is necessary to fundamentally rethink Western (rationalist) epistemology, and to construct alternative models of being and knowing which demonstrate the 'mutually constitutive, rather than oppositional, relations between reason and emotion' (Jaggar 1989: 156–7; see also Bordo 1986; Rose 1994).

A major strength of the study of emotions lies in its ability to transcend many of these former dichotomous ways of thinking that serve to limit social thought and scientific investigation in unnecessary, self-perpetuating ways. In particular, the sociology of emotions sheds important new light on biology/society, structure/agency, micro/macro debates, together with other salient methodological issues such as the relationship between positivism and naturalism, prediction and description, the quantitative and the qualitative (Kemper 1990a). Again, this forces us to confront deep underlying questions about the nature of human embodiment and the need for alternative ways of being and knowing. Key questions here include: whether emotions are culturally specific or universal in nature; whether or not we can circumscribe a distinct, autonomous realm of emotions as 'measurable' phenomena (McCarthy 1989); and how, at a broader level, we relate the lived experience and management of emotions as embodied modes of being in the world to macro-structural issues of power, domination and control.

It is to debates such as these that this chapter is devoted. In particular, in considering the relevance of emotions to the body, we shall focus on five pertinent sociological themes: first, the biosocial versus social constructionist debate; second, the problem of micro–macro linkages; third, issues of gender, sexuality and the transformation of intimacy; fourth, the fate of emotions in a 'therapeutic' age; and finally, at the broadest possible level, tensions between 'postemotionalism' and the 're-sensualisation' of society. Underpinning these five issues, of course, lies a sixth implicit theme, one that threads throughout the book as a whole, namely; the 'Cartesian masculinisation of thought' and the vicissitudes of mind/body dualism. It is to the first of these issues, the biology/society debate, that we now turn.

Biological versus social explanations?

Within the sociology of emotions, debates continue to rage over what, precisely, emotions are, and how we should study them. In this respect, as Kemper (1990a) observes, the confrontation between the biological and the social is both more focused and more heated than in many other sub-fields of sociology. Whilst few sociologists would deny or dispute the physiological substrate of emotions, the central question concerns just *how* important this is. Broadly speaking, approaches to emotions can be conceptualised along a continuum ranging from the 'organismic' at one end to the 'social constructionist' at the other, with 'interactionist' approaches, as the term implies, somewhere in between.

Darwin (1955 [1895]), for example, in the organismic tradition, chose to focus on emotional expression (i.e. physical *gestures* and displays) rather than the subjective *meanings* associated with them. In keeping with his general theory of evolution, these gestures, he argued, were acquired during a prehistoric period and have survived as 'residues' or 'serviceable associated habits' (Hochschild 1983). Love, for instance, is seen as a vestige of what was once the direct act of copulation, whilst the expression of disgust is the archaic relic of what was once the direct act of regurgitating a noxious thing. As to the question of whether or not these gestures were universal or culturally specific, Darwin's own general conclusion was to emphasise that they were indeed innate – as have other writers since his time (e.g. Ekman 1977, 1982, 1984; Ekman *et al.* 1983). What is missing from these accounts, as Hochschild (1983) rightly notes, is any conception of emotion as subjective and a more subtle and sophisticated notion of how social and cultural factors impinge on emotional experience and expression.

Freud's approach, in contrast, is somewhat more difficult to characterise, moving as it did through various different stages (Hochschild 1983). In his early writing, Freud viewed affect as dammed-up libido (i.e. a manifestation of repressed instinct), emphasising tension and anxiety. At the turn of the century, however, he came to view 'affect' as a concomitant of drive whilst, by 1923 in *The Ego and the Id*, he stressed instead the mediatory role of the ego between id (drive) and conscious expression: affects were now seen as 'signals of impending danger' (from inside or outside) and an impetus for action (Freud 1984 [1923]). Unlike Darwin, Freud singled out one particular emotion – anxiety, as the model for all others. The meaning of a feeling (i.e. the ideational representation of affect) was, however, crucial for Freud, albeit often at an unconscious level, leaving his status as a truly 'organismic theorist' ambiguous (see Chapter 5, this volume). Like Darwin, however, Freud had little to say about 'how cultural rules might (through the superego) apply to the ego's operations (emotion work) on id (feelings)' (Hochschild 1983: 210).

If emotion, for Darwin, is an instinctual gesture with an archaic evolutionary heritage, and if, at least for early Freud, it is the manifestation of dammed-up libido, then for James in contrast, emotion is the brain's conscious reaction to instinctual bodily change and visceral feeling. On this there seemed to be some slight disagreement between James – for whom emotion is conscious feeling and bodily change together – and Lange – for whom emotion is bodily change and feeling secondary – but not enough to prevent the two being referred to together as the James–Lange theory of emotion (James and Lange 1922).[2]

Given these limitations, and the absence of any noteworthy differences in the visceral accompaniments of feelings such as fear and anger, psychologists sought to differentiate between emotions according to *cognitive* factors, therefore laying the basis for the development of social psychology. More generally, it suggests the need for a more 'intricate' model than organismic theorists propose of how social and cognitive factors join physiological ones in the genesis of that complex human compound, the emotions (Hochschild 1983; Gerth and Mills 1964).

Moving to the opposite end of the spectrum, social constructionist approaches, as the name implies, stress the primarily social as opposed to the biological nature of human emotions. As a general rubric, the term 'social constructionist' houses a variety of differing theoretical perspectives. None the less, what they share in common is an emphasis on the socially and culturally faceted nature of emotions as 'emergent' cognitive and interpretive phenomena. In doing so, they too, like organismic theorists, fall foul of the temptation to overstretch their explanatory frames of reference (i.e. to explain everything in terms of the 'social').

For social constructionists, emotions cannot be studied mechanistically, as in specificity theory. Whilst emotions may be *accompanied* by physiological changes, their existence is not explained in these terms. Indeed, some emotions such as pride and jealousy, it is argued, seem to have no specific biochemical 'substrate' at all. Emotions in other words, with the possible exception of so-called 'primary emotions' such as anger and fear, are socially, culturally and historically variable in terms of their meaning, experience and expression. According to this line of reasoning, sociologists should not focus on 'physiological details' until the varieties of emotions, their meaning, functions and relationship to the broader sociocultural, moral and ritual order, have been thoroughly investigated (Harré 1986). In taking this line, social constructionists echo Durkheim's classic sociological dictum concerning the non-reducibility of social facts to biological or psychological levels of explanation.

A good example of this perspective is provided by McCarthy (1989), who develops what she terms an autonomous (Meadian) sociological perspective on mind, self and emotion as 'emergent' social properties: one that will not concede to the psychologist or physiologist exclusive or even primary rights to the domain of emotions. Whilst functionally related to the organism, emotions can neither be reduced to nor explained by the organism. Rather, geared as they are to the ebbs and flows of everyday life, emotions are part of the conscious relations, actions and experiences of selves. Seen in these terms: 'Emotions are not "inside" bodies, but rather actions we place in our world . . . feelings are *social* . . . constituted and sustained by group processes . . . *irreducible to the bodily organism* and to the particular individual who feels them' (McCarthy 1989: 57, our emphasis).

In a more Wittgensteinian vein, Harré (1986, 1991) argues that the study of human emotion involves a focus on a certain kind of social or public act within a broader moral and cultural order. From this viewpoint, there is no such thing as 'an emotion', only various ways of acting and feeling emotionally, of displaying one's judgements, attitudes and opinions 'dramatistically' in certain appropriate bodily ways. Anger, for example, refers not to what someone is, but rather what someone *does*. By reifying anger, we can be:

> tempted into the mistake of thinking that anger is something inside a person exercising its invisible and inaudible influence on what we do. But *to be angry is to have taken on the angry role on a particular occasion as the expression of a moral position.* This role may involve the feeling of appropriate feelings as well as indulging in suitable public conduct. *The bodily feeling is often the somatic expression to oneself of the taking of a moral standpoint.*
>
> (Harré 1991: 142–3, our emphasis)

According to this line of reasoning, emotions are, and indeed always have been, the bodily enactments of mainly *moral* judgements and attitudes, judgements devoid, in large part, of conscious ratiocination. This, in turn, suggests that the methodological strategy for a social constructionist approach to emotions should focus on: (i) the repertoire of public *'language games'* available in any given culture (i.e. what are the emotional vocabularies and under what conditions are they used?); (ii) the *moral order* within which the moral appraisals that control both the meaning and use of emotional terminologies are themselves meaningful; (iii) the *social function* (i.e 'acts') that particular emotions display; (iv) the *narrative* forms that the unfolding of the situations revealed in (i), (ii) and (iii) realise; and finally (v) the system of *rules* by which these complex forms of social/emotional action are maintained, accounted for, taught and changed (Harré 1986: 13). Then, and only then, according to Harré, are we likely to engage profitably in tracking the physiological details which the above five points enable us to understand.[3]

This emphasis on the 'social construction' of emotions, in turn, keys into broader poststructuralist and postmodernist critiques of the Cartesian rationalist project (and subject) – positions that abandon any notion of a core-abiding subjectivity and instead seek to celebrate the corporeal intimacies and affective dimensions of social life through productive notions of desire.

The problem with these perspectives, as we have already suggested, is that emotion, like the body, is more than simply a matter of social or cultural construction. A 'purely' constructionist perspective, in other words, ignores biological processes and presents a largely 'disembodied' view of human emotions (Freund 1990: 455). Here we return to the point that 'going beyond' the organic does not mean leaving it out altogether. An expanded understanding of the social *and* biological ontology of human emotion is therefore required if we are to move beyond the 'limits' of constructionism.[4]

It is here, at this embodied nexus, that 'interactionist' theories, broadly defined,[5] offer most promise in capturing the complexities of human emotional experience and expression, sitting as they do in the analytical space between organismic and social constructionist accounts. As with the previous two approaches, a variety of theoretical perspectives can be housed under this general rubric. None the less, what they all share in common is an approach to emotions that seeks to interlock biological and social factors in a dynamic rather than reductionist, monocausal way. Seen in these terms, ontological questions concerning the nature of human emotions can no longer be framed in *either/or* terms. Instead, the reality of emotions lies in the *interaction* of the biophysical, personal and social, and the complex affective compounds that are thereby formed in the process. Whilst the biophysical, personal and social realms of emotions form a synthesis, the particular influence of each on the resultant synthesis (and therefore on experienced and expressed emotions) is a variable product of biographical, situational and cultural contingencies (Wentworth and Ryan 1994: 4).

Emotions, as Wentworth and Yardley (1994) note, display a 'deep sociality' (i.e. the capacity to make emotionally founded, self-to-self relationships and, in turn, a profound dependence on them). Through the medium of emotions, evolution has yielded a 'powerful means of ensuring intersubjectivity' and a 'potent sense that it is imperative to do so'. The greater the sociality of the species, the more emotionality moves to the very centre of information processing and communication. As such, they provide a powerful means of intersubjectivity – one that possesses the capacity to bind individuals into a social entity and motivate them to perform certain tasks and avoid others (Wentworth and Yardley 1994: 45).[6]

To these 'evolutionary' approaches – approaches that accord the biological due weight and recognition in social explanation without slipping into former reductionist traps – we may also add what is, perhaps, the best known 'interactionist' account of emotions in contemporary sociology, namely, Hochschild's (1979, 1983, 1990, 1998) 'emotion management' perspective. Emotion, as Hochschild, stresses, is unique among the bodily senses, being related to *cognition* as well as *action*. In doing so, it provides a central means through which we know the (social) world and our relation to it. In this sense, emotion may be defined as 'bodily co-operation with an image, a thought, a memory – a co-operation of which the individual is aware' (Hochschild 1979: 551). As such, emotion is crucial for the survival of human beings in group life, signifying 'danger' on the template of prior expectations. In adopting this stance, Hochschild joins three theoretical currents in order to theorise emotions. First, drawing on Dewey (1922), Gerth and Mills (1964) and Goffman (1959) within the interactionist tradition, she explores what gets 'done' to emotions and how feelings are 'permeable' to what gets done to them. Second, from Darwin (1955 [1895]) in the organismic tradition, she is able to posit a sense of what is there, impermeable, to be 'done to' (i.e. a biologically given sense, which in turn, is related to an orientation to action). Finally, through Freud's (1984 [1923]) work on the 'signal' function of feelings, Hochschild is able to 'circle back' from the organismic to the interactionist tradition, by tracing the way in which social factors influence what we expect and thus what these feelings actually 'signify'.

From this theoretical starting point, Hochschild is able to delineate her own 'emotion management' perspective which, as we shall see below, enables her to span the micro–macro divide in a subtle and sophisticated way through the 'commoditisation' of human feeling and the loss of authenticity in late capitalist society.

So what, then, given these differing perspectives, are emotions, and how, sociologically speaking, should they be approached and studied? These questions become all the more pressing in the light of the fact that, despite a recent upsurge of interest in 'the emotions', the object under study is rarely defined – a key rule of sociological method. Against this trend, the position taken in this particular chapter is that emotions are complex, multifaceted phenomena that are irreducible to any one domain or discourse. Emotions, in other words, are thinking, moving, feeling 'complexes' that, sociologically speaking, are relational in nature and linked to 'circuits of selfhood' (Denzin 1984); comprising both corporeal, embodied aspects, as well as sociocultural ones. Whilst basic emotions – rooted in our biological make-up and shared amongst all human beings as embodied agents – are involved, they are endlessly elaborated, like colours on a painter's palette, through time and culture. As Burkitt states:

> Emotions . . . are multidimensional and cannot be reduced to biology, relations, or discourse alone, but belong to all these dimensions as they are constituted in ongoing relational practices. As such, the objects of our study in the sociology of emotions cannot be understood as 'things', but are complexes composed of different dimensions of embodied, interdependent human existence.
>
> (Burkitt 1997: 42)

Seen in this way, emotions are essentially communicative, intercorporeal and intersubjective, constituted as physical and cultural dispositions through techniques of the body, forged within a social habitus.[7] These body techniques, in turn, can only properly be understood within the context of the power relations of particular social and cultural groups, located in historical space and time (ibid.).[8]

Emotions, in short, are most fruitfully seen as *embodied* existential modes of being – ones that centrally involve self-feelings as the 'inner-core' of human emotionality (Denzin 1984) and an active engagement with the world.[9] Not only do emotions underpin the phenomenological experience of our bodies in sickness and health (Williams and Bendelow 1996), they also provide the basis for social reciprocity and exchange (i.e. the 'deep sociality' of emotions (Wentworth and Yardley 1994)), and the 'link' between personal problems and broader public issues of social structure (Mills 1959). The interactive, relational character of embodied emotional experience, in other words, offers us a way of moving 'beyond' micro-analytic, subjective, internal or individu-alistic analyses, towards more 'open-ended horizons' in which embodied agency can be understood not merely as individual but also 'institution making' (Csordas, 1994a: 14; Lyon and Barbalet 1994). Indeed, to para-phrase Giddens (1984), structure may fruitfully be seen as both the *medium* and *outcome* of the *emotionally embodied practices* it recursively organises. The emphasis here, is on the active, emotionally expressive body as the basis of self, sociality, meaning, and order set within the broader sociocultural realms of everyday life and the 'ritualised' forms of interaction and exchange they involve. Here we confront the central issue of micro–macro linkages in the sociology of emotions. Hence, it is to this thorny sociological problem that we next turn.

The micro–macro divide: emotions as the 'missing link'?

Whilst a variety of supposed 'resolutions' to the structure/agency debate have been suggested in mainstream sociological theory over the years – from the 'structuration theory' of Giddens (1984) and Bourdieu (1990), to the 'morphogenetic' approach of Archer (1995) – none of these theorists have rigorously addressed the 'reconciliatory' power or potential of emotions. In contrast, as a number of writers within the sociology of emotions have argued, many of the central processes of macro-sociology (i.e. social order, solidarity, stratification, conflict) ultimately rest on the much neglected micro-foundation of emotions.

Collins (1975, 1981, 1990), for example, in a fusion of Durkheimian and Goffmanesque themes, argues that social order and solidarity ultimately rest on collective moral sentiments and commitments that emerge in the course of 'interaction ritual chains' and emotional exchanges at the micro-level. Conflict, too, rests on an emotional foundation, involving as it does the mobilisation of sentiments of anger towards carriers of opposing social values and interests (Kemper 1990a, b). 'Power rituals', for instance, which mainly occur in large-scale organisations, involve interactions structured in terms of 'order-givers' and 'order-takers'. Whilst order-givers derive positive 'emotional energy' from these interactional exchanges, order-takers, on the other hand, frequently experience a loss of emotional interest as a consequence of being neglected and their wishes ignored. 'Status rituals', in contrast – which are somewhat independent of power-based rituals – involve interactions structured along the lines of membership 'inclusion and exclusion', 'centrality or periphery' of location, and the 'localism or cosmopolitanism' of one's network of interactional associates: divisions that, like power-based rituals, increase or decrease emotional energy, respectively (Collins 1990; Kemper 1990a).

Underpinning these ideas is Collins's suggestion that interaction patterns, and the 'transient emotions' they involve, provide a micro-foundation of long-term emotional resources or energies, which in turn serve as the basis for further interactions. It is these 'interaction ritual chains' – chains that accumulate across time and space – that provide the macro-structures of social stratification. As Collins states:

> The IR [interaction ritual] chain model . . . proposes that individuals acquire or lose emotional energy in both power and status interactions. Order givers gain EE [emotional energy], order-takers lose it; successful enactment of group membership raises EE, experiencing marginality or exclusion lowers it. . . . Interaction rituals are connected in chains over time, with the results of the last interactions (in emotions and symbols) becoming inputs for the next interaction. Thus, EE tends to cumulate (either positively or negatively) over time.
>
> (Collins 1990: 39)

It is in this way that society 'gets inside' the individual's mind. Emotional energy ebbs and flows across a chain of interaction rituals depending on the ups and downs of the individual's experiences of power and status, operating both to 'stably reproduce social structure', and to 'energize the dynamics of conflict and change' (ibid.: 52).

To be sure, Collins's analysis has a number of merits, linking as it does micro- and macro-social processes through a focus on emotions and the ritualistic encounters of everyday life. Nevertheless, it leaves out what is perhaps most important for our purposes, namely, a critical exploration of the *embodied* nature of emotions as an ongoing structure of lived experience. Despite all its references to interactional issues, Collins's model also ultimately ends up with an overly deterministic view of the individual who is likely to respond with emotion X, Y or Z, given factors A, B or C. In doing so, the Durkheimian (positivistic) overtones of Collins's project ultimately win out over his more interactional, Goffmanesque, concerns. More generally, the interactional ebbs and flows of emotional energy may, perhaps, more fruitfully be reconceptualised through the Bourdieuesque notion of 'capital'. 'Emotional capital' is a concept that readily translates Collins's 'emotional energy' into a more thorough-going socioeconomic frame of reference. From this viewpoint, patterns of emotional exchange – involving as they do an intricate 'balance sheet' of profits and losses, investments and debts, including 'economies' of gratitude and feelings of resentment, pride and shame – mesh more or less closely with broader structures of power, prestige and social (dis)advantage in society. In addition, returning to our earlier embodied definition of emotions, the notion of 'capital' also captures the underlying link between body techniques, the social habitus and broader struggles for power and prestige (i.e. distinction) in the criss-crossing fields that together constitute society (Williams 1998b).

Another promising line of research into these micro–macro links is provided by Hochschild's emotion management perspective – one that enables her to move from the private realm of personal troubles to broader public issues of feeling rules, ideology and social structure – itself the defining hallmark of the 'sociological imagination' (Mills 1959). Feeling rules, as she explains, are the public side of ideology that deal with the affective dimensions of social life. Emotion management, in contrast, is the type of work it takes to cope with these feeling rules. In this respect, in Goffmanesque fashion, Hochschild distinguishes between what she terms 'surface acting' and 'deep acting'. Surface acting involves a strategy of pretence (i.e. *pretending* to feel what we do not) – the hackneyed American phrase 'Have a nice day', for instance, connotes 'a genuine effort to be agreeably disposed but not deeply emotionally involved while expecting pleasant predictability from others' (Stearns 1994: 292). In contrast, deep acting requires a taking over of the 'levers of feeling production' in order to actually alter what we feel (e.g. the suppression of anger and its replacement with sympathy): to 'work on' a feeling or emotion is the same as to 'manage' an emotion or to do deep acting. It is this latter strategy of deep acting that concerns Hochschild most. Emotion work, as she explains, can be done by the 'self upon the self', 'by the self upon others' or 'by others upon oneself'. Whatever the result, it is the *effort* rather than the *outcome* that is important here (Hochschild 1979: 561–2).

The dilemmas of emotion management are classically illustrated by Hochschild in her study of flight attendants, a job that points to the 'dramaturgical stress' involved in deep acting, and the commercialisation of human feeling in late twentieth-century capitalist society. Not only do flight attendants have to pay particular attention to their physical appearance, they are also faced with the dilemma of how to feel identified with their role, the company and their passengers whilst maintaining something of themselves (i.e. the problem of 'authenticity'). One possible response to this dilemma is to engage in surface acting, something that Hochschild suggests is unlikely to be successful due to the 'phony' element and loss of self-esteem involved its performance. Instead, many experienced flight attendants opt for deep acting, thereby allowing them to escape the feelings of insincerity associated with surface acting. Reasons for rude or aggressive passengers, for instance, were often sought by these women, thereby enabling them to feel sorry or sympathetic instead of angry.

Whilst promoting a 'smooth' and 'uneventful' passage, these strategies are not, however, without their physical and emotional costs. Certainly the physical consequences of such work are now well recognised. For instance, the face work required by flight attendants (e.g. frequent smiling), leaves permanent marks in the form of lines and wrinkles, a process exacerbated by problems of dehydration in planes and the lack of time to drink water whilst flying (Shilling 1993). To this we may also add a catalogue of other physical symptoms and complaints, including varicose veins, bunions, low backache, hearing loss, diminished pulmonary function and early menopause (Lessor 1984). This, coupled with the difficulties of establishing regular sleep patterns, the use of stimulants and depressants to manage these disruptions, and the common problem of eating disorders, suggest that a flight attendant's 'lot', despite (managed) appearances to the contrary, is not necessarily a happy one!

Underpinning this analysis lies a deeper set of concerns regarding the increasing 'commoditisation' of human feeling and the 'loss of authenticity' in late capitalist society – processes that, given the fact that these 'meaning-making' jobs are more common in the middle class, may not have equal salience for all social classes. As Hochschild states:

> Conventionalised feeling may come to assume the properties of a commodity. When deep gestures of exchange enter the market sector and are bought and sold as an aspect of labour power, feelings are commoditised. When the manager gives the company his [*sic*] enthusiastic faith, when the airline stewardess gives her passengers her psyched-up but quasi-genuine reassuring warmth, what is sold as an aspect of labour power is deep acting.
>
> (Hochschild 1979: 569)

In requiring employees to manage and manipulate their feelings, emotion work, in short, can be seen as a central component of the social relations of inequality at work (Shilling 1993). Indeed, *The Managed Heart* (1983) is replete with references to the 'human costs' of emotional labour, from 'burnout' to feeling 'phony', 'cynicism' to 'emotional deadness', 'guilt' to 'self-blame', costs that could, Hochschild suggests, be reduced if workers felt a greater sense of control over the conditions of their working lives.

The more our activities as individual emotion managers are managed by organisations, the more we tend to celebrate the life of 'unmanaged feeling' (Hochschild 1983: 190). In this way, Hochschild, in true Goffmanesque style, champions the little ways in which we resist the institutional pull of commoditised emotional exchange, from the circumvention of feeling rules to the wider cultural concern with so-called 'spontaneous', 'natural' or 'authentic' feeling. It is precisely here, at this nexus, that a central paradox emerges: the more we attempt to 'get in touch with' or 'recover' our 'true feelings', the more we make feeling itself subject to command, manipulation and various forms of management (Hochschild 1983: 193). In this respect, Hochschild's concern with issues of authenticity – including the inauthenticity of the search for authenticity itself – ultimately translates into a profound Rousseauesque critique of the human condition in late twentieth-century capitalist society – one that calls not simply for a practical politics of worker control, but an existential reclaiming of authentic self-feeling and a championing of the 'unmanaged heart'.

Despite the widespread appeal of this emotion management perspective – from organisational theory (Fineman 1993) to the trials and tribulations of heterosexual coupledom (Duncombe and Marsden 1993, 1997) – it is also open to criticism on a number of counts. Not only is Hochschild's analysis disappointing from a comparative, historical perspective – one that reveals that 'emotion management' has, in fact, been going on for millennia – it is also limited in focusing simply on contemporary commercial constraints and operating with a problematic private/public distinction. As Wouters states:

> Developments in standards of behaviour and feeling do not stop at the borders of either public or private life; to live up to them signifies overall demands on emotion economy, an overall pattern of self-regulation, a sort of 'overall design of emotion management'. Hochschild only deals with the process of commercialisation in this century. In the more remote past she apparently visualises a more ideal society. . . . But such an ideal society never existed. Emotion management was never a private act, nor were rules for feeling ever only privately negotiated.
>
> (Wouters 1989a: 104–5)

Over the last hundred years, emotional exchange has become more varied, more escapable, and hence more open to idiosyncratic nuances. What Wouters refers to as a process of long-term *'informalization'* can, therefore, be interpreted as a 'reversal' of a long-term trend, whilst at the same time being a 'continuation' as far as demands on affect economy and the management of drives and emotions are concerned.[10] From this viewpoint, only stronger, more even, all-rounded self restraints allow for a greater sensitivity and flexibility of social conduct (Wouters 1989a: 105–6). This, coupled with the underlying problem of tapping truly 'authentic' feelings (Duncombe and Marsden 1997), means that Hochschild's legacy is ambiguous: on the one hand, opening up a whole new way of seeing the world, on the other hand, operating with some problematic concepts and historically contested distinctions.[11]

Perhaps the area where Hochschild's emotional insights have been most recently applied, to good effect, has been in relation to health. To the extent that Hochschild's emotion management perspective has been readily translated into studies of the emotional division of labour in health care, including the sentimental order of the technological hospital/detechnologised hospice (James 1989, 1992; James and Gabe 1996; Lawler 1991; Smith 1992), it has constituted a rich new seam of research within the sociology of health and illness. In addition, it has also opened up a whole new way of seeing and theorising the social inequalities in health debate – one that, alongside such concepts as emotional capital, provides important new insights into the psychosocial causes of disease and the link which emotions provide between the micro- and macro-levels of sociological analysis (Williams 1998b).

As Freund (1982, 1988, 1990, 1997) argues, differing modes of emotional being are, in effect, different felt ways of feeling *empowered* or *disempowered*, feelings that, in turn, are very much linked to people's material and social conditions of existence.[12] Having one's feelings ignored or termed irrational – what Hochschild (1983) terms the absence of 'status-shields' to protect the self – is analogous to having one's perceptions invalidated. Less powerful people, in other words, face a 'structurally in-built handicap' in managing social and emotional information and this handicap may, in turn, contribute to 'dramaturgical stress' (i.e. the dilemmas of role playing (Goffman 1959)), existential fear (i.e 'ontological insecurity' (Laing 1965)) and neuro-physiological perturbation of many different sorts (e.g. endocrinological disorder). Emotional being, social agency and structural context, are therefore inextricably related, and it is this relationship that, Freund suggests, comes to be physically as well as emotionally embodied in many different ways.

In particular, Freund (1990) argues that social relationships may engender a form of 'schizokinesis' in which a split arises between what is consciously shown and experienced, as opposed to what occurs somatically. As continued emotional and other kinds of distress alter physiological reactivity, neurohor-monally related functions such as blood pressure may markedly increase in response to a stressor, but not be consciously experienced.[13] Here Freund poses two extremely pertinent sociological questions: first, just how 'deep' can the social construction of feelings go? And second, can emotion work eliminate the responses of an 'unconsciously knowing body'? The implications of his argument seems to suggest that the answer is 'very deep indeed': society affects physiological reactivity deep within the recesses of the human body although, as the concept of schizokinesis implies, the 'mind' may, consciously at least, be unaware of the body's response. As Freund states:

> One's positions, and the roles that accompany them in various systems of social hierarchy, shape the conditions in which one lives. This position influences access to resources. It may also determine the forms of emotional–social control to which one is subject as well as the severity of the impact these controls have on the person. . . . Such a process may mean internalising the emotional definitions that others impose on what we are or 'should' be. The physiological aspects of such processes are of interest to those studying emotions. However, these physical aspects may also be seen as examples of ways in which controls are sedimented and fixed in the psycho-soma of the person. Physiological aspects of social activity can also act as a form of feedback that colours the tone of existence. This feedback can *indirectly* serve social control functions. For

instance, conditions that create depression . . . construct an emotional mode of being where the motivation to resist is blunted.

(Freund 1990: 470)

The argument here is for a subtle and sophisticated form of 'socialised' (i.e. externally 'pliable') biology rather than a reductionist sociobiology, one that accords emotional modes of being a central role in linking the health and illness of the embodied social agent with wider structures of power and domination, civilisation and control in society. The fact that socioeconomic factors now primarily affect health through indirect psychosocial pathways rather than direct material routes (Wilkinson 1996), adds further weight to these arguments. This, in turn, raises broader questions concerning the relationship between emotions, health and 'distributive justice', including problems of emotional capital and democracy, income distribution and social cohesion – issues that need to be at the forefront of future policy initiatives in this area (Williams 1998b).

Gender, sexuality and the 'transformation of intimacy'

As a number of recent writers have observed, we are currently witnessing a profound transformation in the spheres of sexuality and interpersonal intimacy – one in which new, more 'androgynous' images of love and self-development are coming to the fore (Cancian 1987).[14] As Weeks comments:

> The majestic edifice of 'sexuality' was constructed in a long history, by many hands, and refracted through many minds. Its 'laws', norms and proscriptions still organise and control the lives of millions of people. But its unquestioned reign is approaching an end. Its intellectual incoherence has long been rumbled; its secular authority has been weakened by the practice and politics of those social-sexual movements produced by its own contradictions and excesses; now we have the opportunity to construct an alternative vision based on a realistic hope for the end of sexual domination and subordination, for new sexual and social relations, for new, and genuine, opportunities for pleasure and choice. We have the chance to regain control of our bodies, to recognise their potentialities to the full, to take ourselves beyond the boundaries of sexuality as we know it. All we need is the political commitment, imagination and vision. The future now, as ever, is in our hands.
>
> (Weeks 1991: 260)

Central to these developments has been the emergence of what Giddens (1992) terms 'plastic' sexuality; a 'decentred' form of sex, freed from the needs of reproduction and the rule of the phallus, which is moulded as a trait of personality and intrinsically bound up with the project of the self. The more self-identity is reflexively made, and the more the organisation of the life span becomes internally referential, the more sexuality becomes the property of the individual. Sexuality, in other words, has been 'opened up' and made accessible to the development of varying lifestyles. As a malleable feature of self, it functions as a 'prime connecting point between body, self-identity and social norms' (Giddens 1992: 15).

This growth of social reflexivity and the emergence of 'plastic' sexuality is, in turn, tied up with profound changes in the emotional order. Today, for the first time, women claim equality with men, and it is women, Giddens claims, who have paved the way for these transformations in intimacy as the 'emotional revolutionaries' of late modernity. It is within this context that that notions of the 'pure' or 'ideal' relationship come to the fore. 'Pure' relationships, as Giddens explains, have nothing to do with sexual purity. Rather, their roots lie in the late eighteenth-century emergence of romantic love, which was built around the assumption that a durable emotional tie could be established with others on the basis of qualities intrinsic to the tie itself.

The pure relationship, according to Giddens, involves an opening out of oneself to another, which is built around a form of what he terms 'confluent' love – one that is contingent rather than forever. Unlike the romantic love complex of the past, confluent love is not necessarily monogamous in the sense of sexual exclusiveness. Rather, what holds the pure relationship together is the acceptance by each partner, 'until further notice', that each gains sufficient benefits from the relationship to make it worthwhile and keep it going. Sexual exclusivity, therefore, has a role to play, but only to the extent that it is deemed mutually desirable by both partners. Like the pure relationship to which it is so closely tied, confluent love has no specific connection to heterosexuality. In particular, it is gay men and women who, in operating without traditionally established frameworks of marriage, have preceded most heterosexuals in developing these new forms of relationship based on relative equality between partners (see Gidden 1992; also Chapter 6, this volume). These transformations can, in turn, be seen as part and parcel of what Giddens claims to be a 'generic restructuring of intimacy' in late modernity – one that is 'potentially explosive' in terms of its connotations for pre-existing forms of gender power.

Slowly but surely, love becomes a 'blank' that lovers must 'fill in themselves'. Individuals who wish to live together are therefore becoming the 'legislators of their own way of life', the 'judges of their own transgressions', the 'priests who absolve their own sins' and the 'therapists who loosen the bonds of their own past' (Beck and Beck-Gernsheim 1995: 5). In this respect, the struggles to reconcile family and career, love and marriage, 'new' motherhood and fatherhood have increasingly, it is claimed, come to replace the class struggle. Indeed, in a 'runaway world', love becomes ever more important as a kind of 'rebellion' – a way of getting in touch with forces to 'counteract the intangible and unintelligible existence' we now find ourselves in. Love, in short, becomes a latter-day 'secular religion' (Beck and Beck-Gernsheim 1995: 178).

These trends hold out both positive and negative possibilities. On the one hand, as Giddens claims, there stands the very real possibility of creating new forms of emotional democracy and intimacy that parallel those forged in the public sphere. Seen in these terms, the changes affecting sexuality are truly 'revolutionary' in their consequences (Giddens 1992: 3). On the other hand, however, an 'emotional abyss' has, at present, clearly opened up between the sexes. As such, the 'normal chaos of love' still remains (Beck and Beck-Gernsheim 1995). On a darker note, we also need to question whether love, our latter-day 'secular religion', can indeed help us confront the ultimate contradiction of human embodiment, namely that sexuality, in the shadow of AIDS, may be the 'death of us' (see Chapter 4, this volume).

This, in turn, raises a number of other more specific problems with these types of social commentary and analysis. First, as we saw earlier, in Chapter 4, despite Giddens' emphasis on the body and self-identity, his commitment to issues of social reflexivity ultimately translates into a peculiarly 'disembodied' approach to the 'pure relationship' and 'confluent love', one that contrasts markedly with such writers as Bataille (1987/[1962]), whose work on eroticism is *sensually* rather than cognitively based (Shilling and Mellor 1996). For Bataille, eroticism is 'assenting to life up to the point of death' (1987 [1962]: 11) – something that involves a partial dissolution of the individual as a separate being and a temporary fusion, dissolution or intermingling of selves. Seen in this light, the whole business of eroticism is, at heart, to:

> destroy the self-contained character of the participants as they are in their normal lives. . . . Through the activity of organs in a flow of coalescence and renewal, like the ebb and flow of waves, surging into one another, the self is dispossessed.
>
> (Bataille 1987 [1962]: 17–18)

Eroticism, in short, always entails the breaking down of established patterns of the regulated moral order, through a somatic sense of transcendence and a total blending or fusion of two discontinuous beings. Here we return to our earlier discussion, in previous chapters, of desire, excess and the transgression of corporeal boundaries, issues that strike at the heart of late modernity as a reflexive (i.e. cognitively based) social order.

Second, both Giddens and Beck tend to paint these transformations in broad brush strokes with little attention to empirical detail. How, for example, do these arguments mesh with particular social groups, and are they more or less advanced in certain segments of society than others? Seen in these terms, not only is the pure relationship best seen as an 'ideological ideal' of late modernity (Craib 1995), but recognition of the impact of differential power on actual relationships seriously undermines many of its 'core' features. What, in short, is missing from these accounts is any formulation of *who* precisely is doing the transformation and *how* they are doing it: questions that rest on issues of power, inequality and stratification (Hey *et al.* 1993/4: 72). Equally, it is important to emphasise more fully variations *amongst* as well as *between* men and women. Here, we return again to problems identified earlier concerning the 'overly reflexive' nature of social reflexivity and the prioritisation of individual over structural issues (see Chapter 4, this volume).

Ultimately, exploration of socially regulated or 'managed' gender divisions in intimate emotional behaviour entail two interrelated, yet distinct, questions. First, are men and women equally 'susceptible' to emotions or discourse of love and intimacy? And second, do they handle such emotions in similar ways in the context of these close personal relationships (Duncombe and Marsden 1998)? As Duncombe and Marsden (1993) show in a recent empirical study of love and intimacy in heterosexual coupledom,[15] women experience considerable unhappiness at men's unwillingness or incapacity to 'do' the emotional intimacy they feel is necessary to sustain a close heterosexual relationship. Overwhelmingly, women reported that their male partners had 'psychically deserted' them, prioritising paid work over emotion work and 'coupledom'. Men were also accused of 'intellectualising' or speaking without experiencing emotion and deploying a cool, calculated, verbally articulate logic focused tightly on immediate issues.[16] From men's perspective, women's dissatisfaction over intimacy was apt to express itself in the form of 'sexual difficulties', whilst they themselves felt 'pulled apart by the contradictory demands of coupledom and work' (Duncombe and Marsden 1993: 226–8). Extrapolating these trends into the future, Duncombe and Marsden suggest that:

> gender differences in emotional behaviour seem likely to become a *greater source of friction and unhappiness* among heterosexual couples as the 'institution' of marriage is transformed by ideologies of the personal 'relationship' which call for greater emotional communication. Men's difficulties in expressing intimate emotions will emerge as a *major source of the 'private troubles' underlying the 'public issues' of rising divorce and family breakdown*, or the instability of cohabitation among couples who may often be parents.
>
> (Duncombe and Marsden 1993: 233, our emphasis)

Tensions between the ideological ideal of 'emotional democracy' and the 'normal chaos of love' therefore look set to continue well into the twenty-first century, as women claim equality in the personal as well as public spheres of their lives, and men struggle to 'get in touch' with their feelings in a seemingly 'runaway' world. It is within this context that a burgeoning therapeutic industry has grown up in order to 'manage' and help 'put us in touch' with our emotions.

Emotions in a 'therapeutic' age: 'liberation' or 'oppression'?

As notions of 'social reflexivity' and 'lay re-skilling' suggest, ours is an age characterised not simply by the significance we invest in emotions (i.e. *what* we feel, *how* we feel, *why* we feel the way we do), but also by the way in which we seek *advice* for our 'emotional problems'. Today, as McCarthy observes, we've given up the idea of 'cures' and replaced it instead by a growing number of therapies in which the emphasis is placed upon voluntary relationships and lengthy conversations about the self in order to get us 'in touch' with our feelings through the emotional content of the therapeutic encounter. Seen in these terms, therapy is 'emotion work' *par excellence* (McCarthy 1989: 64).

Not only have the number of so-called 'experts' in the field of emotional health and illness mushroomed in recent years – from psychiatrists and clinical psychologists, to psychotherapists, relationship counsellors, art therapists and 'agony aunts' – but lay people themselves have increasingly come to 'frame' their problems in professional terms: what de Swaan (1990) refers to as a process of 'proto-professionalization'.[17] This, in turn, suggests important new elements of surveillance and control centred around what has come to be known, in poststructuralist parlance, as the 'psy' complex. From this perspective, intervention is designed to 'normalise' rather than simply to treat, to 'fabricate' rather than to disclose, whilst the power to regulate emotional life and norms of conduct becomes ever more intangible and diffuse, dispersed as it is through a rapidly expanding network of professional 'experts' and 'proto-professional' clients: what Rose (1990) has referred to, in Foucauldian terms, as *'Governing the Soul'*. The upshot of these processes is clear, what we now call emotions – whatever they were in other periods – are now:

> constructs of an age of psychology and therapeutic knowledge and practice ... they are inconceivable apart from those institutions, social relations and forms of thought ... one of the distinguishing features of this psychological age is that emotions acquire a meaning previously absent: feelings of anger, sexual longing, guilt, anxiety, and so on, become significant objects of one's attention and action; emotions are 'worked at' and 'worked on', one has an 'emotional life' ... in which its protagonist, the self, discloses and creates it authenticity at the same time.
>
> (McCarthy 1989: 66)[18]

This growing preoccupation with emotions is also evident, of course, in broader trends towards the cultivation of the body and mind through appeals to 'holistic health'. To be sure, as a variety of commentators have suggested, recent years have witnessed a radical change in what is meant by 'health', 'illness' and 'disease'. Previously regarded simply as the absence of illness, we are now encouraged to set our sights much 'higher' on a notion of health as true 'wellbeing': one involving the integration of body and soul, mind and emotions, and the development of mutually satisfying relationships with others (Coward 1989). Within this context, health becomes an endlessly pursued but rarely achieved goal – one that is inextricably linked to individual attitudes, personal commitment, and individual responsibility (Crawford 1980, 1984; see also Chapter 4, this volume).

These beliefs have received an enormous boost in recent years with the steady growth of complementary therapies such as homeopathy, acupuncture, herbalism, reflexology and Shiatsu. Central to many of these therapies is the idea that the body can 'heal itself' (i.e. the *vis mediacatrix naturae*) and that we can only truly be well if we achieve a state of 'whole person' health based on 'natural balance' and 'harmony' (Coward 1989). Underpinning these views, is a focus on the 'vital energies' of the body – one that links the more 'accepted' therapies such as acupuncture, homeopathy and naturopathy to other more 'marginal' or 'fringe' forms of medicine (Coward 1989). Here the proposition is a simple and straightforward one, namely, that 'blockages' or 'imbalances' in the life forces that flow through the body result in (a susceptibility to) illness. In acupuncture, for example, an 'imbalance' in the (vigorous) *yin* or the (restraining) *yang* elements is thought to throw the body's life force (*chi*) out of kilter, thus resulting in illness or a deterioration in general wellbeing. Treatment, therefore, involves the insertion of needles into various energy meridians running through the body in order to rectify such 'imbalances' and restore 'health' and 'wellbeing'. It is in this context that emotions come to the fore. Indeed, it is attention to emotional states and personality predispositions that, perhaps more than anything else, informs the idea of 'whole person' treatment (Coward 1989: 71).

At one level this suggests a somewhat rosy picture – an image of ideal health to which we are all supposed to be striving and that, in contrast to orthodox medicine with its aggressive militaristic imagery and 'war' against disease, seeks to integrate not just our bodies and our minds, but also our emotions through a warm embrace with 'mother nature'. What more could one ask for: total health, total wellbeing, all within our own grasp and under our own personal (i.e. emotional) control? At another level, however, this utopian vision of heaven on earth may be more apparent than real. Whatever the therapy, *personal* responsibility is invariably placed high on the agenda, thereby tending to deflect attention away from the wider political economy of health and illness (Crawford 1980; Berliner and Salmon 1980). Following directly on from this first point, there also appears to be something of a paradox here surrounding the notion of 'personality types'. On the one hand, a supposedly 'whole-person' approach to healing prioritises individual control and the ability to 'change'. On the other hand, however, a belief in personality types often carries with it associations of 'fatalism', implying a:

> static and limited model of a world of fixed emotions and personalities into which human behaviour, characteristics and illness can be fitted . . . the unresolved tension between calls for change and beliefs in fixed personality types has tended to be the way in which guilt-provoking and moralistic notions of illness have been able to grow.
>
> (Coward 1989: 73–4)

To this we might also add the problematic use of the term 'natural' and the fact that, despite an emphasis on the unity of mind and body, an underlying hierarchical form of dualism none the less remains as mind is accorded primacy over body in the 'healing' process.

At a broader level, 'holistic health', whatever its claims, contains important elements both of 'de-medicalisation' and 're-medicalisation'. Whilst the locus of causality is firmly restored to the individual and status differentials between providers and clients are seemingly minimised, thereby suggesting a process of de-medicalisation, the exponential expansion of the 'pathogenic sphere' and remit of the holistic health movement (i.e. lifestyle modification, mind–body continuity), simultaneously suggests a drastic increase in medicalisation in late Western society (Lowenberg and Davis 1994; Armstrong 1986). Seen in this light, the 'liberatory' potential of 'complementary' therapies and 'holistic' health takes on a more troubling hue, as important elements of 'continuity' with biomedicine and consumer culture are instead thrown into critical relief (Sharma 1996). Even the notion of 'energy' conforms to late capitalist ideologies and imperatives of 'production' and 'control' (Coward 1989: 57). 'Liberation' or 'oppression'? The tensions of a 'therapeutic' age are therefore thrown into critical relief through a focus on the emotionally reflexive body in late modernity.

Postemotionalism and the re-sensualisation of society

Talk of the tensions between reflexivity and sensuality, the cognitive and the emotional, the authentic and the inauthentic, raises a broader set of sociological reflections as to whether or not we are living in what has recently been termed a 'postemotional' age.

According to Mestrovic (1997), Western consumer-oriented, media-scape societies are entering a new-era phase of development – one involving a new form of 'bondage' to carefully crafted, managed and manipulated emotions. Postemotionalism, as he explains, is a neo-Orwellian system designed to avoid emotional disorder, to prevent loose ends and to civilise 'wild' arenas of emotional life, so that the social world 'hums as smoothly as a well maintained machine' (ibid.: 150). Emotions, in other words, to borrow Ritzer's (1993) well-worn phrase, have become truly McDonaldised by the culture industry – carved up into handy bite-sized, pre-packaged, rationally manufactured products that are then consumed by the masses like fast-food in a burger bar.

Within a postemotional order, feelings become increasingly separated from action, social solidarity breaks down and 'quasi-emotions' become the basis for widespread manipulation. This transition to a postemotional order is made possible, Mestrovic argues, by a social character that has succeeded Riesman's (1969 [1950]) 'other-directedness' in that the bulk of people's emotional reactions have been reduced to being 'nice' versus indignant. These issues are clearly illustrated through the postemotional packaging of the Balkan war and the O. J. Simpson trial – events in which, Mestrovic claims, 'curdled indignation' and 'compassion fatigue' loom large as 'live' emotional responses are substituted for 'dead' ones (i.e. recycled feelings stretching far back into the distant past). The power of the mind, enshrined in the Enlightenment has, in short, given way to an 'indolent mindlessness' and 'kitsch emotional reactions' to serious world events.[19]

The 'ways of escape' have also been rationalised, according to Mestrovic, from leisure to pseudo-therapy. Indeed, a whole new 'authenticity industry' has grown up, leaving little room for a truly authentic emotional response. Set against the troubling backdrop of widespread processes of social fission and Balkanisation – not simply along ethnic lines, but also in terms of gender, sexual preference, lifestyle and a myriad of other group identifications – post-emotionalism holds the potential to degenerate further into an entirely new form of totalitarianism – one that is so 'nice' and charming that it cannot lead to indignation or rebellion of any sort (Mestrovic 1997: 146). Seen in these terms, the postemotional packaging of the Balkan war may indeed, as Mestrovic suggests, provide the 'crystal ball' into a disturbing social future.

Moving to the opposite end of the spectrum, writers such as Michel Maffesoli (1995, 1996), for instance, celebrate what is claimed to be the contemporary shift from Promethean to the Dionysian values in Western culture. A shift, that is, from the Weberian Protestant Ethic (i.e. productivist modernity) towards a society, or more precisely a form of sociality, governed by the empathetic logic of emotional renewal and the (non-productivist) expressivity of collective effervescence.

We are, Maffesoli claims, living at a decisive moment in the history of modernity, one in which the 'rationalization of the world' is being displaced if not replaced by a parallel 're-enchantment of the world': a process in which 'emotional renewal' comes to the fore. In contrast to writers such as Giddens and Beck, this is an age, Maffesoli claims, characterised by the 'decline of individualism' and a 'return of the tribes': a form of 'sociality' based on a new 'culture of sentiment' and multiple forms of 'being together' (what he terms '*proxemics*'). The 'sacred canopy' has indeed all but collapsed, only to be replaced by a looser, more shifting or fluid series of alliances and sensual solidarities – points of communication and connection that, taken together, spell a resurgence of the 'sacred' in a multitude of disparate, vibrant, effervescent ways. Signs of this, Maffesoli claims, are all around us:

> even in the most aseptic places, and in the gregarious solitude that the contemporary techno-structure has contrived to construct, we already see a collective reappropriation of space that ploughs its furrows deep. Sporting events, musical or political gatherings, the sounds and hubbub of the streets of our towns, and festive occasions of all kinds forcefully underline the pre-eminence of the whole. What is more, its pre-eminence increasingly tends to result in a fusional reality, or in what is termed 'the return of Dionysiac values', with individual characteristics

being replaced by organicity or what Fourier called the *'architectonic* of the whole'.

(Maffesoli 1996: 72)

For Maffesoli this 'underground centrality' of sociality – one that bubbles up in resistance to stifling Promethean instrumental rationality – bestows strength, vitality and effervescence to social life: an emotional rejuvenation of social life and an antidote to cultural life, and the 'crisis' of individualism (Evans 1997). From New Age movements and alternative therapies, to the 'relativization of the work ethic', and from networks of 'amorous camaraderie' to the importance of dress and cosmetics, the emblematic figure of Dionysus is giving rise, he claims, to what Weber termed ' "emotional cults" as opposed to the atomization characteristic of bourgeois or aristocratic dominance' (Maffesoli 1995: 156).[20]

Sociality, in other words, a 'fusion realm' or 'communalised empathy', constitutes all those forms of 'being together' that, for the past few decades, have been transforming society. As Maffesoli comments, 'Losing one's body, either metaphorically or literally, within the collective body, seems to be a characteristic feature of the emotional or affective *community* that is beginning to replace our utilitarian "society"' (Maffesoli 1996: 154). This, in turn, as Evans notes, marks a shift from morality as an overarching, universal system of duties and obligations, to a more protean, ambivalent, fractal and relativistic emphasis on local ethics and a stylisation of life more in keeping with Foucault's deliberations on the 'care of the self' in Ancient Greek culture (i.e. an *'ethics of aesthetics'*) than with the Kantian tradition of 'legislative' reason (Evans 1997: 231).

Certainly, in taking this stance, Maffesoli paints a very positive picture of contemporary social and emotional life: one that champions the Dionysian over the Promethean, the polymorphously perverse over the orderly and rational, the fusional over the individualistic, and so forth. We are not, in short, to answer Agnes Heller's (1989) question, 'living in a world of emotional impoverishment': quite the reverse. In this respect Maffesoli, like Latour (1993), forces us to confront the intriguing question of whether or not we have ever truly been 'moderns', stressing instead important elements of cultural continuity with the past, including the 'traditional world' of clans, bands and 'tribes' (Evans 1997).

Seen in this light, Giddens's emphasis on late modernity as a 'de-traditional' order, organised around the reflexively mobilised self, again appears, at the very least, problematic. Maffesoli's own position, however, is equally open to criticism. Perhaps the main problem concerns the fact that, in adopting this largely one-sided Dionysian stance he not only underestimates the dangers of 'neo-tribalism', but also underplays the contradictory features of modernity itself as *both* 'order' and 'chaos', 'rationalisation' and 'subjectification' – i.e. the dialectic between the instrumentalisation of the world as embodied in science and technology, and the growth of individualism, expressivity, freedom and democratic rights (Evans 1997; Touraine 1995). Modernity, as Evans rightly states: 'is not simply identified with a reified totalised system of rationalised oppression and disenchantment, but rather, is a complex network of *mixed possibilities* involving a constant *dialectic* between the subject and reason' (Evans 1997: 240).

In this respect, Mellor and Shilling (1997) present what is perhaps a more promising or 'balanced' line of development in their account of ambivalent bodies and the Janus-faced nature of modernity. Drawing upon the 'extra-rational' dimensions of Durkheim's work, they point towards the emergence of a moral order shaped less by cognitive control than the sensual impulses and possibilities of 'effervescent bodies'. For Durkheim, as Mellor and Shilling explain, the rational demands of society are intimately related to the 'irrational "fires" of effervescent sociality': forms of sociality that, through the immanence of powerful passions and emotions associated with the 'sacred', sensually transform people's experiences of their fleshy selves and the world around them.[21]

On the one hand, early forms of Protestant modernity (e.g. the disciplined and individualistic) are, they suggest, being extended through banal forms of sociality and the individualisation of *contracts*. On the other hand, however, these 'disciplined bodies' are slowly but surely giving way to more sensual forms of *sociality* – forms that echo the seductive sacred corporeality of counter-Reformation baroque cultures, substituting 'tribal fealties' (i.e. 'blood commitments' that reject rationality as a basis for sociality) for individual contracts.[22] In this respect, information-based society may indeed have become banal, but it has not yet, as Mellor and Shilling rightly observe, (fully) absorbed 'people's sensualities into its circuitry' (1997: 173).

Seen in these terms, the Janus-faced nature of modernity as both order and chaos, discipline and liberty, is at last fully evident. The return of the sacred and the resurgence of more sensual, carnal forms of knowledge and experience is not simply the return to prominence, in time-honoured Durkheimian tradition or Maffesolian postmodern theorising, of effervescent forms of *solidarity*, but also the opportunity for new conflicts, dangers and fears to emerge (Mellor and Shilling 1997). Indeed, from the bloodshed of the Balkan war to the resurgence of neo-fundamentalism, feelings and passions can run high in ways that prove both troubling and difficult to 'contain' or 'manage' rationally. The sacred, in short, can be virulent, violent, and unpredictable. As Mellor and Shilling state:

> The emotions that emerge from social relationships and solidarities may enable people to 'keep warm together' in a world which too often appears out of control and morally bankrupt [cf. Maffesoli], but they can also prompt a passionate intensity, hatred and blood revenge.
>
> (ibid.: 201)

Whatever the outcome, one thing remains clear, namely the 'resilience of human bodies to cognitive control' and the enduring significance of more sensual (i.e. emotional and 'sacred') forms of solidarity and carnal forms of knowledge – good or bad, bloody or harmonious, binding or destructive (Mellor and Shilling 1997). Postemotional control, in short, can never be absolute. Herein, as ever, lie the corporeal dynamics and emotional underpinnings of modernity as *both* order and chaos, liberty and discipline, transgression and taboo.

Conclusions

Previously banished to the margins of sociological thought and practice, emotions are now firmly on the research agenda. Whilst debates continue to rage over what, precisely, emotions are and how they should be studied, the position taken in this chapter has been to suggest that, far from being 'irrational', they are most fruitfully viewed as *embodied* existential modes of being, which involve an *active* engagement with the world and an intimate connection with both culture and self. As complex physical, cultural and relational compounds, emotions underpin the sensual experience of our bodies and selves, providing the existential basis of social reciprocity and exchange, and the missing link between personal problems and broader public issues of social structure. Emotions exert a powerful influence over whether social structures are faithfully reproduced or experienced as alienating and therefore in need of transformation. Indeed, as we have argued, structure may fruitfully be reconceptualised in these terms as both the *medium* and the *outcome* of the *emotionally embodied practices* and *body techniques* it recursively organises.

The study of emotions, therefore, provides an expanded understanding of the place of bodily agency in society, linking as it does the somatic and communicative aspects of being in the world, and thus the bodily, social and cultural domains (Lyon 1998). More broadly, emotions throw into critical relief what Mellor and Shilling (1997) appositely term the Janus-faced nature of modernity: from the tensions and dilemmas of 'love' and 'sex', 'liberation' and 'oppression' in an increasingly reflexive, 'therapeutic' age, to the problems of postemotionalism and the resurgence of more sensual solidarities and collective forms of effervescence at the turn of the century. Underpinning these issues, as we have seen, lie deeper existential questions and Rousseauesque concerns regarding the fate of 'authenticity' in an 'inauthentic' age. Emotions, and the triumph of will over form, lie at the heart of these dilemmas.

Despite this promising start, much still remains to be done, particularly if we are to move beyond the current proliferation of competing perspectives and alternative research agendas, towards a more integrated phase of sociological theorising on emotions in social life. Whilst this suggests constraints as well as opportunities, it none the less points to the fact that a sociology of the emotionally 'expressive', 'sensual' or 'mindful' body, could potentially become a 'leading edge' of contemporary social theory. Emotions, in short, have truly come of age!

8 Pain and the '*dys*-appearing' body

Illness is the doctor to whom we pay most heed; to kindness, to knowledge, we make promises only; pain we obey.

(Proust)

the way in which we gain knowledge of organs during painful illness is perhaps a model of the way we in general arrive at the idea of the body.

(Freud 1984 [1923]: 363)

Pain and the dominant voice of medicine

Pain is never the sole creation of anatomy and physiology. Rather, as Morris (1991) states, it emerges only at the 'intersection of bodies, minds and cultures'. In any language there may be wide variations in the interpretation and meaning of pain. According to the *Oxford Reference Dictionary* (1986), for example, pain refers to any or all of the following:

PAIN [from the Latin *poena*, meaning penalty or punishment]

1 An unpleasant feeling caused by injury or disease of the body.
2 Mental suffering.
3 [Old use] punishment (e.g. on pain of death).

In Greek, the word used most often for physical pain is αλγος (*algos*), which derives from roots indicating neglect of love (Procacci and Maresca 1985). Another Greek word is αχος (*akos*), meaning 'psychic pain', from which we derive the English word 'ache'. Implicit in these meanings is a broader definition of pain than the narrowly defined Cartesian proposition, which inevitably acts to divorce mental from physical states and tends to attribute single symptoms to single causes. Indeed, the notion of pain having a substantial emotional component, literally the obverse of pleasure, is much older than that of pain being a physiological sensation, and can be traced back to Plato's deliberations on extremes and opposites in the *World of Forms*. Pleasure and pain, Plato declares, are twin passions of the soul, the results of interaction between earth, air, fire and water. Aristotle developed this pain/pleasure principle further, describing them as basic moral drives guiding human action. Pain, he believed, was negative passion – conveyed by the blood to the heart – which had to be conquered by reason. As such, Aristotle excluded it from his classification of the five senses, instead preferring to describe it as a 'quale' or 'emotional quality' of the soul; 'a state of feeling and the epitome of unpleasantness'. Literature, theology and philosophy abound with considerations of the nature and purpose of pain. Within these diverse traditions – from Kierkegaard's *Works of Love* (1962 [1847]) to C. S. Lewis's *The Problem of Pain* (1977 [1940]) and Tillich's (1968) *Systematic Theology* – the pleasure/pain dichotomy is constantly evoked and reinforced.[1] De Montaigne, for example, wrote:

> Our well being is only freedom from pain. That is why the philosophical school which has given the greatest importance to pleasure has also reduced it to mere absence of pain. Not to suffer is the greatest good man can hope for . . .
>
> (de Montaigne 1959/[1592]: 44)

The dominance of the scientific medical paradigm in which the sensory aspects of pain are the primary focus (i.e. *specificity theory*) coincided with the emergence of physiology as an experimental science. Here, the proposition is a straightforward one, namely that a *specific* pain system carries messages from pain receptors in the skin to a pain centre in the brain – a theory first classically described by Descartes in 1664.

In Descartes' model, pain works by means of a simple mechanism. Fast-moving particles in the fire disturb filaments in the nerves of the foot. These pass along nerve fibres until they reach the brain, activating the so-called 'animal spirits', which, in turn, travel down through the nerves to the muscles, thus producing the movement that removes the foot from the flames. The key concept here for Descartes was the idea of 'mechanism', whereby impulses travelling from the foot produce pain, just as 'pulling on one end of a cord, one simultaneously rings a bell which hangs at the opposite end' (Descartes 1972: 34). This simple 'rope-pulling' model, however primitive it may seem to us now, is a direct precursor of the standard medical model that developed along Cartesian principles in the mid-nineteenth century and is still, in many quarters, in existence today. To be sure the terms may have changed (e.g. nociception and endorphins rather than filaments and animal spirits), but the basic idea underpinning these views is unchanging (Morris 1994, 1991).

Whilst medical concern in the nineteenth century centred around the exact location of the pain centre (Melzack and Wall 1988, 1965), it was the philosopher Marshall (1894) who, amidst these anatomical debates, emphasised the strong negative *affective* quality associated with pain – one that drives us into activity. We are compelled to do something about pain and to

Figure 8.1 Descartes's illustration of the specificity theory of pain. If for example, fire (A) comes near the foot (B), the minute particles of this fire, which as you know move with great velocity, have the power to set in motion the spot of the skin of the foot which they touch, and by this means pulling upon the delicate thread (cc) which is attached to the spot of the skin, they open up at the same instant the pore (d e) against which the delicate thread ends, just as by pulling at one end of a rope one makes to strike at the same instant a bell which hangs at the other end.

Source: Reprinted from Descartes (1972: 35)

act effectively in order to relieve it, a response that goes far beyond any simple reflex action. This places affective processes parallel with sensory processes, yet, as the Cartesian model suggests, the emotional aspects of pain are less likely to be acknowledged. 'Real' pain, in other words, means physical pain, anchored in visible tissue damage. Ultimately, what this amounts to is a view of 'pain in a vacuum', one that accords meaning and context a minimal role:

> Detached from meaning and social context, reinvented as mere agonized entrapment, pain stretches before us as a potentially endless shuttle of electrochemical impulses. It threatens not only health but also any prospect of inner coherence.
>
> (Morris 1994: 13)

Pain did not, however, die with the advances in medical science and effective surgical anaesthesia. Rather, in a 'greying' population, it has multiplied alarmingly. Indeed, as Morris rightly comments, perhaps one of our greatest forms of 'illiteracy' in the Western world, despite a 'veritable cornucopia' of biomedical publications and 'overflowing' medicine cabinets, is ignorance about pain: *'what* it is, what causes it, *how* to deal with it without panic' (ibid.: 15). Seen in these broader sociocultural terms, the biomedical model of pain, built as it is on Cartesian mind–body principles and elaborated over the last few centuries through research in anatomy and physiology, is fundamentally inadequate. Even the 'placebo', normally dismissed as an 'irritating' or 'confounding' variable in (medical) science, offers doctors a powerful illustration of how minds and cultures, emotions and beliefs, shape the meaning and experience of pain, as well as responses to treatment (ibid.: 22).[2]

In arguing against this 'medicalised' view of pain, it is of course important to emphasise the critique that has already begun to develop within medicine itself. In particular, the widespread acceptance of Melzack and Wall's (1965, 1988) 'Gate-Control Theory' of pain,[3] and the influence of the hospice movement have shifted the pain paradigm in significant new ways, increasing the emphasis upon cultural and psychological components and the need for a multidisciplinary approach. As Vrancken (1989) shows, a variety of different approaches to treatment now exist within academic pain centres: treatments that range from somatico-technical and dualistic body-oriented perspectives, through to behavioural, phenomenological and consciousness approaches, the latter incorporating existential, as well as physical and emotional aspects of pain.[4] More generally, Foucauldian perspectives on issues such as childbirth and dental pain have emphasised how medical approaches have shifted over time from a one-dimensional corporeal space based on physiology, to the two-dimensional psychosocial space that encompasses patient subjectivity (Nettleton 1992; Arney and Neill 1982).[5]

None the less, despite these important shifts in medicine, much still remains to be done in order to re-establish the historically severed ties between 'pain and meaning' (Morris 1991). Not only would a more sophisticated sociological approach allow for the inclusion of feelings and emotions, it would also serve to (re)locate the *embodied* individual within the broader sociocultural contexts of meaning and action, thereby freeing pain from exclusive biomedical jurisdiction. In taking up this challenge, the remainder of the chapter is therefore devoted to this critical enterprise at two closely interrelated levels. First, in keeping with the general aims of the book, we seek to explore the embodied nature of pain as an ongoing structure of *lived experience*, one that incorporates the affective as well as sensory dimensions of human suffering and the circuits of selfhood they involve. Second, in moving outwards from experience to *representation*, we also draw attention to the social and symbolic nature of pain – particularly the role of narrative and the cultural shaping of pain. In doing so, we show how existing medico-psychological approaches to pain – ones that stress sensation over emotion – can be seen as unnecessarily limiting and reductionist.

From embodiment to dys-embodiment: pain and the vicissitudes of dualism

The starting point of our analysis concerns the phenomenologically absent nature of the body in everyday life (Leder 1990). That is to say, our relationship to our bodies, in the normal course of events, remains largely unproblematic and taken-for-granted; bodies are only marginally present, giving us the freedom to be and to act.[6] 'It is through the body that I view the world and act within, yet in doing so', as Sartre would say, 'it passes me by in silence'. Our bodies, in short, are both highly articulated and yet in a state of (continual) disappearance. As Leder explains:

> Whilst in one sense the body is the most abiding and inescapable presence in our lives, it is also characterized by absence. That is, one's own body is rarely the thematic object of experience . . . the body, as a ground of experience . . . tends to recede from direct experience.
>
> (Leder 1990: 1)

This in turn suggests that bodies, at the most general level, become most conscious of themselves when they encounter 'resistance' or 'difficulties' of various kinds – from the physical accompaniments of overexertion to the corporeal consequences of social embarrassment. If this is true of bodies in general, then it is particularly true of sick and painful bodies. Here the scale, intensity and duration of such experience takes on new meaning and significance through a profound disruption of our biographies, selves and the taken-for-granted structures of the world upon which they rest. Suddenly, the body becomes a central aspect of experience, albeit in an alien, dysfunctional sense. The normal modes of 'disappearance' that characterise ordinary, everyday functioning are therefore substituted for a heightened sense of bodily '*dys*appearance' and corporeal 'betrayal' (Leder 1990). (Severe) pain produces:

> alienation, an existential vacuum; being cut off from the outer world, thrown back upon the body in itself, is isolation, disintegration, pain. . . . Immediately a dichotomy is brought about . . . through the unpleasantness of pain, the body and 'I' instantly seem to have parted company. For the sake of the integrity of our personality we make an 'it' of the body and an abstraction of pain. . . . Pain makes us believe that we can cut our*self* off from the body. Through rationalizing pain . . . 'I' and my body become two separate entities. Thus *pain can be depicted as the experience of psychophysical dualism.*
>
> (Vrancken 1989: 442)

[handwritten margin note: AND I WOULD ADD 'ABNORMAL' BODIES]

More precisely, pain's intensity results in an *intentional disruption* (i.e. a rendering unimportant of previously central projects) and a *spatiotemporal constriction* (i.e. self-reflection and isolation) of our lives (Leder 1990). The painful body emerges as an estranged, alien 'thing-like' presence, separate from the self, which exerts a *telic demand* upon us. This telic demand can, in turn, be further sub-divided into a *hermeneutical* and a *pragmatic* component. At the hermeneutical level pain and suffering give rise to the quest for meaning, legitimacy and understanding (see below), whilst at a pragmatic level, the telic demand is to 'get rid of it' or to master one's suffering; instead of just acting *from* the body, I act *toward* it in the hope of finding relief (ibid.).

The upshot of these arguments is clear. Whilst at an *analytical* level the study of pain and human suffering demands the dissolution of former dualistic modes of thinking in drawing attention to the relatedness of self and world, mind and body, inside and outside, it must also confront and account for the 'enduring power and qualities of these dichotomies at the *experiential* level of suffering' (ibid.).

These issues are well illustrated in Good's case-study of Brian, a chronic pain sufferer. Rather than simply 'live through' his body in the 'world of everyday life', Brian has instead been 'taken over' by pain. In effect, Brian 'objectifies' both his body and his pain as 'thing-like', a 'demon', a 'monster', an 'it': 'when I think . . . I'm outside myself . . . as if my mind were separated from myself' (Good 1992: 39). Alternatively, people in pain may seek relief by moving in the opposite direction towards an increased *subjectification* of their suffering; one that is less concerned to reduce the power of pain by claiming its non-existence, than with attempting to (re-)integrate the pain more closely with the self. In this sense, as Jackson (1994) notes, pain confounds any simple subject–object dichotomy: 'objectification' and 'subjectification' instead stand in a *dialectical* relationship to one another. For the most part, however, people in pain see their problem as one of 'matter over mind'. The intractable nature of their condition makes them feel that their lives, 'their emotions, their spirituality, their personalities, their destinies are dominated by their painful bodies' (ibid.: 207). The sick body, in other words:

> menaces. It erupts. It is out of control. One damned thing follows another. . . . The fidelity of our bodies is so basic that we never think of it – it is the grounds of our daily experience. Chronic illness is a betrayal of that fundamental trust. We feel under siege: untrusting, resentful of uncertainty, lost. Life becomes a working out of sentiments that follow closely from this corporeal betrayal: confusion, shock, anger, jealousy, despair.
>
> (Kleinman 1988: 44–5)

Loss of confidence in the body is quickly followed by a loss of confidence in the self (Bury 1982).[7] The alienating, privatised, nature of pain seems to shatter the self into a series of 'lived oppositions' (Leder 1990). Not only do individuals have to suffer the physically debilitating effects of their condition, but also the profound sense of loneliness, isolation, stigmatisation and dependence that frequently follows in its wake. Loss of self, therefore, becomes a fundamental form of suffering in (chronic) pain and illness (Charmaz 1983). Murphy (1987) for example, in a moving account of his gradual transition from 'normal' to quadriplegic, describes his new and permanently altered feelings of 'who and what I was', including the unwillingness of other people to 'audit' his experience 'empathically'. In contrast, Zola (1982, 1991), having spent most of his life forcing his 'disabled' body to be 'disciplined' and 'productive', learns in his week-long stay in Het Dorp – a Dutch village designed as a permanent residential facility for the disabled – to question the very identity norms that, hitherto, he had unthinkingly internalised and accepted (Frank 1990). In doing so, Zola seeks to recover alternative possibilities of both living in and with our bodies – possibilities that 'able-bodied' society denies or impedes (Frank 1990).[8]

The fact that mind, body and self are thoroughly interfused in pain, albeit in a problematic way, also points to another fundamental issue raised earlier, namely, that physical experience is inseparable from its cognitive and emotional significance. As argued in the previous chapter, the study of emotions requires a conception of the human body as a structure of ongoing lived experience. If we recognise pain as an emotional experience, then, as Turner comments, we immediately begin considering the idea of the person as 'an embodied agent with strong affective, emotional and social responses to the state of being in pain'. A theory of embodiment is therefore an 'essential prerequisite for understanding pain as an emotion within a social context' (Turner 1992: 169).

Explorations of pain, madness, disability and death are human events literally 'seething with emotion' (Scheper-Hughes and Lock 1987). The emotional pain of grief, for example, is inseparable from its 'gut churning, nauseating experience', whilst physical pain bears within it a 'component of displeasure, and often of anxiety, sadness, anger that are fully emotional' (Leder 1984–5: 261). The study of pain, therefore, requires a conception of the 'mindful', emotionally 'expressive' body – one that oscillates precariously between unity and dissolution (Scheper-Hughes and Lock 1987; Freund 1990; Williams 1996b).

Unfortunately, however, the problems of dualism do not end here. Rather, the individual's contact with and experience of medicine may reinforce rather than heal this split. First, through their contact with doctors and the use of their prescribed medical regimens, the chronically sick may come to describe their bodies through highly technical medical language and vocabulary. As a consequence, the body and disease become reified products of the biomedical gaze and its prioritisation of 'disease' over 'illness' (Taussig 1980). Second, medical regimens may themselves serve to reinforce an already heightened sense of corporeal awareness (i.e. a 'somatic preoccupation') amongst the chronically ill. These regimens can include anything from diet and drugs, to the use of advanced medical technology such as renal dialysis. Indeed, in some cases the treatment can be as bad as the illness, consuming valuable time, energy and money and requiring hard work on the part of the individual and their families (Strauss and Glaser 1975). Underpinning both these issues, of course, is the way in which current biotechnology is rendering the body increasingly 'uncertain', an issue succinctly captured in the hybrid, machine-like figure of the (medical) 'cyborg' (see Chapter 4, this volume). All in all, this suggests that a reified sense of the body and disease may be the unhappy consequence of people's dealings with modern medicine at times that are already highly charged with physical suffering and emotional distress. Medicine, in short, is both a fountain of hope and a font of despair, one that, rather like Humpty Dumpty, offers the chronically sick and ill little hope of putting themselves 'back together again'.

Yet, to leave things here would, of course, be misleading. For out of this dualism and sense of bodily betrayal, like a phoenix rising from the ashes, individuals do none the less struggle, sometimes heroically and against all odds, to effect something of a re-alignment between mind and body, self and society. Here a sort of 'negotiated settlement' occurs – one that, although never quite able to return the individual to their former embodied state, none the less attempts an approximation to it (Williams 1993, Williams 1996b). It is to this practical and symbolic 'struggle against dissolution' (Murphy 1987) that we now turn in the next section of the chapter. In doing so, we again draw attention to the way in which human embodiment provides the existential basis of both culture and self (Csordas 1994a).

The cultural meaning and shaping of pain: 'realigning' body, self and society

Human beings are simultaneously part of nature and culture: culture shapes 'nature', whilst nature constitutes a 'limit' as well as an 'opportunity' for human agency (Turner 1984). The natural and cultural realms are therefore interlocked and interwoven in complex, multifaceted ways that defy easy answers or simple resolutions. Explorations of pain, suffering and the human condition lie at the heart of these issues, serving yet again to highlight the 'uncontainability' of the body within any one domain or discourse.

As we have argued, a medicalised view neglects the important insights on pain that can be gained through an appreciation of art, literature and culture. In this respect, pain can be said to have enjoyed something of a 'dual history' (Morris 1991). In traditional cultures, as Illich (1976) notes, pain was regarded as an inevitable part of the 'subjective reality of one's own body', a fact made 'tolerable' by integrating it into a *meaningful* setting. It is culture, in other words, that fills the 'existential space' between the immediate embodiment of disease as a physiological process and its 'meaning-laden character as experience' (Kleinman 1988). The central task therefore becomes how to integrate these medical and cultural discourses on pain without allowing the former the dominance it has hitherto enjoyed over the latter. Narrative, we suggest, is central to this enterprise. It is here, on this uncertain biographical terrain, that the dialectical relationship between nature and culture, meaning and significance is played out and the disrupted relationship between the body, self and society symbolically 'repaired'.

Narratives of pain

People in pain, as we have suggested, need to find *meaning* for their suffering, even if it is 'dysfunctional' from an orthodox scientific viewpoint. Without such meaning feelings of loneliness, isolation and despair may develop. On the one hand, pain may be experienced as a constriction of our essential possibilities and a poignant reminder of human contingency and finitude. In this respect, as Turner (1992) notes, theodicies of pain and idioms of distress address fundamental aspects of human experience that point to a 'shared ontology of the body'. Within these narratives, explanations of suffering may be linked to deeply entrenched religious or spiritual beliefs (i.e. the problem of explaining a just God in an unjust world), even if an individual does not follow any particular faith, and notions of punishment and self-blame are common themes.

On a darker note, it is also possible that the very meaning of pain may be the negation of all meaning; a 'soundless scream', a 'solipsistic inwardness' (Morris 1994). Pain, in other words, may serve to 'deconstruct' or 'unmake' our habitual world, a problem compounded by its sheer invisibility (Scarry 1985). Indeed, perhaps the main problem for those with chronic pain is that they are bereft of adequate cultural resources for organising their experience.[9] Here, in this 'meaningless world of torment', sufferers frequently report that it is only fellow sufferers who can really understand their pain (i.e. audit their experience empathically). This understanding is not, however, achieved through the normal medium of communication (i.e. spoken language), but rather through intuitive, pre-linguistic forms of communication based on a *'communitas'* of mutual recognition and shared understanding (Jackson 1994). The language of pain becomes therefore, paradoxically, an anti-language – 'antithetical to ordinary everyday understanding, but a code nonetheless' (ibid. 213–14). Again we return here to the 'discursive limits' of social constructionism.

Pain may also, however, signal something positive or creative, not only in the sense of childbirth but also in terms of physical, emotional, artistic and spiritual achievements, or it may serve as a much needed 'catalyst' for important changes in our lives (Leder 1984–5). In this respect, Carmichael advocates *using* pain rather than becoming a passive victim of it:

> Constructive use of pain can only be achieved if we can see the pain as an ally – if we confront it. The natural response is to express; the social

response is to suppress. Fearing it, distancing it, protecting ourselves from it, makes it stronger. The more you push it away the more it pushes its hooks into you . . . you need to confront it, enter into a dialogue with it, asking it what it is saying to you . . . anger can provide a substitute for pain, but may be used destructively rather than constructively . . . permanent anger is a stuck form of pain. What is useless is denial or avoidance of pain; we need, as Camus advised in *The Plague*, to root ourselves in our distress.

(Carmichael 1988: 9)

As this variety of meanings suggests, pain poignantly thrusts questions upon us such as 'why me?' and 'why now?'. Through a process of social 'narratisation', the individual is encouraged to turn the alien 'it' of illness, one that imposes itself so unwelcomingly upon their life, into a meaningful story that she or he tells (Frank 1995). The recurrent effect of narrative on physiology, and of pathology on narrative constitutes the 'shape and weight of lived experience'; a 'felt world' that combines feelings, thoughts and bodily processes into 'a single vital structure' underlying continuity and change (Kleinman 1988: 55). Seen in these terms, narratives are fundamentally embodied and are central to the coherence of our lives. As such, they help bridge the gap between the clinical reductions of biomedicine and a lost metaphysics, serving as biographical reference points between individual and society in an unfolding process that has become profoundly disrupted (G. H. Williams 1984). When illness is told, its 'lack' becomes 'producing' (Frank 1991a). By focusing on narrative one is, therefore, able to shift the dominant cultural conception of illness away from passivity (i.e. the sick person as 'helpless victim') to activity, thus transforming 'fate' into 'experience' and reclaiming pain and human suffering from exclusive biomedical jurisdiction (Frank 1995). Stories, in short, as well as physicians can 'heal', and it is through narrative that bodies are 'joined together' in a 'shared sense of vulnerability' and a search for a lost 'ethics of existence' (ibid.).

Cultural 'responses' to pain

Culture, of course, not only shapes the meaning of pain, but also the responses we fashion to it. Beecher (1959), a physician by training, was one of the first to stress these social and cultural influences on pain perception and response in injured combat soldiers during the Second World War. These soldiers, he observed, reported little or no pain associated with their wounds, despite serious tissue trauma. Having established they were actually capable of feeling pain and that they did not appear to be in shock, Beecher concluded that their perception of pain had been altered by the motivation of being able to return home.

Medical anthropologists since this time, have emphasised the cultural dimensions of pain behaviour, thus extending the analysis of pain in important ways. Helman, for example, puts forward the following anthropological propositions:

1   Not all social or cultural groups respond to pain in the same way;
2   How people perceive and respond to pain, both in themselves and others, can be largely influenced by their cultural background;
3   How, and whether, people communicate their pain to health professionals and to others, can be influenced by cultural factors.

(Helman 1990: 158)

A useful distinction can be drawn here between 'private' and 'public' pain.[10] Reactions to pain are not simply instinctual, but take place within a social context and contain a voluntary component in that action to relieve pain may or may not be sought, and the help of others enlisted or not as the case may be. Cultural beliefs and values may also serve to 'normalise' experiences of pain in ways which for others appear problematic. Keeping pain private or expressing it publicly, therefore depends, in large part, on the context, beliefs and values of particular social and cultural groups (Helman 1990). Zborowski (1952), for example, in a classic study, found significant variations in cultural responses to pain amongst Italian-Americans, Jewish-Americans and largely Protestant 'Old Americans'. The Italians were described as laying great emphasis on the immediacy and actual sensation of pain, but quickly forgot their suffering once it had gone. The Jewish group, in contrast, were mainly concerned with the meaning and significance of the pain in relation to their health and welfare – their anxieties were focused on the future implications of the current pain experience. Finally, the 'Old Americans' were described as 'much less emotional' and more 'detached' in reporting pain, often having an idealised picture of how to react so as to avoid 'being a nuisance'.[11]

Building on this earlier work, Kotarba (1983) has more recently situated pain through a contextual analysis of how it is managed in occupational life. In doing so, he contrasts two key occupational roles – the professional athlete and the manual worker – where physical capabilities are paramount and pain a perennial threat. In athletics, for example, an 'average' level of pain can be expected through the rigours of training and competition. Recourse to the 'athletic sub-culture' serves, therefore, as an important framework and point of reference for the individual in knowing whether to disclose pain, and if so, to whom, or to conceal it, and if so, how (e.g. through pharmacological drugs, interactional strategies, etc.). A manual worker, in contrast, may at first sight have less reason to conceal pain. However, the rewards for disclosure may be less relevant than the symbolic costs involved (e.g. threats to one's self-image and identity, one's 'fitness' for work, and one's capabilities as a 'bread-winner'). Here, in contrast to athletes, manual workers find the resources for handling such situations – which include the circulation of information about treatments, the folk prescription of alcoholic beverages as painkillers, etc. – in what Kotarba terms the 'tavern culture'.

For athletes and manual workers, therefore, pain is a familiar feature of their *normal* everyday lives: something that gives rise to a 'chronic pain sub-culture'. Athletes risk injury in training or competition, whilst manual workers risk the perennial threat of job-related accidents or back-ache. In both cases, however, the social costs and benefits of pain disclosure need to be carefully weighed before any subsequent action is taken:

> The pain-afflicted person may decide to conceal the experience of pain from potentially critical audiences if the social and emotional costs resulting from disclosure outweigh the perceived benefits. The benefits of pain disclosure include access to health care, sympathy for one's suffering and help in adjusting to the contingencies affected by the pain. But the costs of pain disclosure, as learned through experience, can be perceived as overwhelming. Certain reactions of critical audiences may elicit feelings of shame and guilt.
>
> (Kotarba 1983: 134–5)

Important though these studies are in drawing attention to the social dimensions and cultural shaping of pain, many have been criticised for crudely reinforcing ethnic and occupational stereotypes. Perhaps most importantly, they have tended to be rather collectivistic and deterministic in orientation, portraying the individual as someone who passively responds to sociocultural forces. In contrast, there is a need for a far more interpretive approach to these issues, one which, whilst recognising the crucially important role that social and cultural factors play, accords a far more active, critical and reflective role to the individual who draws upon their own lay knowledge and beliefs in shaping their interpretations and responses to pain. In this respect, more recent interpretive approaches that stress illness 'action' rather than 'behaviour' (Dingwall 1976; Calnan 1987; Williams and Calnan 1996), may represent the most fruitful way forward in the sociological study of pain as a sociocultural phenomenon.

Like age, class and ethnicity, gender is also, of course, central to the meaning and experience of pain. Since antiquity, women's pain has been interpreted within patriarchal cultures built upon myths of male power and female fragility and weakness (Morris 1991). In the medico-psychological literature on pain perception, for example, either gender is not seen as a variable of any significance, or females are thought to have 'lower pain thresholds' than males. Indeed, beyond the general construction of women as biologically 'vulnerable', the focus on sex differences in 'thresholds' and 'tolerance levels' to experimentally induced noxious stimuli, appears to be the *only* issue regarding gender and pain perception to have received any systematic attention. A typical experiment in America, for example, inflicted a noxious heat stimulus on a 'normal' sample of undergraduate men and women, concluding that there was in fact a 'biological basis' for the lower pain thresholds of the women (Feine *et al.* 1990). Whilst asserting this finding as the most 'logical' explanation, the authors none the less conceded that another possible interpretation could be that men delay responses more than women. However, this minimal attempt to theorise 'other' possible explanations is rarely demonstrated in 'scientific' studies of this type.

In contrast, using in-depth interviews and visual imagery techniques in order to explore the meaning and experience of pain, Bendelow (1993) found that both men and women credited females with a 'natural' ability to cope with pain lacking in men, and explained this in terms of their 'biological' and 'reproductive' functioning. For example, a woman stated:

> Women are made to suffer pain because we have periods and childbirth. Whatever social climate, women end up child-rearing, therefore, they don't have the 'privilege' of giving in to pain and sickness.

Similarly, a man succinctly remarked:

> Women have more physical awareness – a more intimate and responsible instinct to their biology – all we do is shave!

Whilst all respondents acknowledged or made reference to the existence of emotional pain as a concept, men were more likely to operate with mind/body splits in conceptualising pain. Women, in contrast, tended to have a more holistic or integrated approach to pain, one that acknowledged a sense of 'emotional vulnerability'. For example, a woman stated:

> Emotions are definitely crucial to physical sensations of pain – when I can step back from what's going on and detach myself – when I can recognise that I'm more than this body that's going through its process in its own way. The body has a strong self-righting mechanism that when I can detach from it, I can let it work itself out, it can balance itself. I don't need pain-killers but then also if you are in extreme pain and you don't have a strong enough sense of your own being as apart from your body then it can just compound it. I have become interested in consciousness through this and I practice meditation – I think that an awareness is essential, not only for the health of the body but of the mind and emotions.

In contrast, a man commented:

> Of course there is mental pain as well, but in its true sense pain is phys-ical – I mean they're not the same thing . . . the pain that I've known has been purely physical sort of thing . . . the other sort of pain comes through problems but it's not related to the physical part. I suppose the few times I've been in jail I would say it's painful, but not physically so.

Underpinning these issues are differing 'styles' of adjustment to (chronic) pain and illness. Radley and Green (1987), for example, have usefully identified four different styles of adjustment in chronic illness, namely: 'accommodation', 'active-denial', 'secondary gain' and 'resignation'. These are conceptualised in terms of their location on a cross-cutting grid in which the self is either opposed or complementary to the illness and social participation is either retained or lost. Thus, whilst the self may be complementary to the illness and social participation retained in 'accommodative' styles of illness adjustment, it remains fundamentally opposed to illness in the 'resignatory' modality as social participation is lost. The bodily constraints that are resolved in the course of these adjustments need locating, as Radley argues, in the 'practices and discourse of the people concerned' (Radley 1989: 237). 'Accommodation', for example, tends to occur when roles are more flexible and where choices about how symptoms are to be presented can be developed through more 'elaborate' (middle-class) forms of communication. In contrast, 'active-denial' involves the adoption of a style whereby the illness is opposed through increasing engagement in everyday activities and where communication is of a more 'restricted' nature. Here we return to the deeper dispositions of the habitus at work and the underlying styles of bodily hexis they invoke (see Chapter 4, this volume).

Additionally, of course, any investigation into the nature of pain must also confront the capacity of humans to inflict pain on their own and other species. The need to understand how it is possible for one human being to stand beside another, and to disregard the fact that s/he may be inflicting agonising pain, is evoked as a central issue in Scarry's powerful linguistic analysis of *The Body in Pain*. Torture, she suggests, is an extreme event parallel to war: 'a sensory equivalent, substituting prolonged mock execution for execution', which is made all the more frightening by its 'acting out' properties (Scarry 1985: 27). By inflicting bodily pain, torture destroys and replaces personal language with the objectification and 'deconstruction' of the body and the person. Arguing polemically, both torture and war may be regarded as essentially *masculine* phenomena (cf. Frank's 'dominating' body), counterposed to *feminine* ways of thinking, knowing, feeling and acting (cf. Frank's 'communicative' body). Again, this highlights the importance of an approach to pain that is sensitive to the social construction and influence of gender (see also Belenky 1986; Ruddick 1990; Heritier-Auge 1989).[12]

Conclusions

A central aim of this chapter has been to argue for an embodied approach to pain, one that combines the physical, affective and cultural dimensions of human suffering in a seamless web of lived experience. Pain, in other words, is located at the intersection of mind, body and culture. As such, it demands the dissolution of former dualistic modes of Western thought that have sought to divorce mind from body, biology from culture, reason from emotion. However, as we have

seen, we must also confront the enduring power of these divisions at the experiential level – one in which a sense of alienation and bodily betrayal are
all-too-common themes (Leder 1990). As both a language and an anti-
language, pain befuddles conventional notions of discourse, speaking, at one
and the same time, to a pre-social body and body that is thoroughly permeated
by culture.

Following directly on from this first point, people in pain need to find
meaning for their suffering, however 'unscientific' this may seem, and to
have their experiences 'audited empathically' by others, both professional and
lay alike. In an 'anaesthetised', 'pain-killing' culture such as ours, this search
for meaning and a lost metaphysics of existence becomes increasingly difficult. It is here, we have argued, that narratives of pain and idioms of distress
come to the fore as a symbolic means of realigning body, self and society in an
unfolding biographical process that has become profoundly disrupted. This
focus on narrative in turn serves to highlight possibly the most neglected
voice of all within the medical encounter – the subjective voice of the
patient.

This brings us to the third main point we wish to emphasise, namely that
the dominant medico-scientific discourse on pain represents only part of a
broader sociocultural canvas upon which the true nature and reality of pain
needs to be painted. Certainly, cultural and historical studies have served to
question the homogeneity of the very word pain: from 'medieval Christian
pain' to 'Victorian hysterical pain', and from 'pagan Stoic pain' to 'Nazi
Holocaust' pain (Morris 1994). Pain may also, as we have seen, take on more
positive qualities, linked to physical, emotional, moral or spiritual achievement or atonement. Again this returns us to the need to champion other
voices on pain; voices currently 'silenced', 'subjugated' or 'forced to the
margins' of public discussion and biomedical debate.

Whilst a more holistic understanding of pain is clearly relevant to medical
practice on a number of different levels, there are also much broader implications to these arguments. Historically, we should have learnt the lesson that
potentially serious implications stem from the separation of reason and feeling.
Instead of the blind hopes of a new and better world based upon reason that
Descartes envisaged – one that signified an end to ignorance and superstition –
the ultimate implications of rationality can be seen in a far more chilling and
sinister light: the sheer 'rationality' of Auschwitz, where the mathematical
idea of a 'final solution' bore witness to a 'fatal flaw' in the philosophical foundations of modern Western civilisation (Lynch 1985: 309).[13]

To conclude, exploration of pain demands the dissolution of former
dichotomous ways of thinking that have hitherto impeded a more unified
understanding of its social, cultural and biological elements. The medical
discourse of pain is just one amongst many other voices. By integrating the
medical and cultural discourse of pain, we can transcend the false dualisms
into which it has been forced, thus 'reclaiming' pain from the exclusive
biomedical jurisdiction (Morris 1991). In doing so, we would not only

increase our understanding of pain but, perhaps more importantly, help release medicine from the impossible task of a 'pain-free' existence. In this respect, a thought-provoking quote to end on comes from Huxley. When offered the choice of a *Brave New World* totally devoid of pain and discomfort, Huxley's savage rejects it thus:

> 'But I don't want comfort. I want God, I want poetry, I want real danger, I want freedom, I want goodness. I want sin'.
>
> 'In fact', said Mustapha Mond, 'You're claiming the right to be unhappy'.
>
> 'All right then', said the Savage defiantly, 'I'm claiming the right to be unhappy'.
>
> 'Not to mention the right to grow old and ugly and impotent; the right to have syphilis and cancer; the right to have too little to eat; the right to be lousy; the right to live in constant apprehension of what may happen tomorrow; the right to catch typhoid; the right to be tortured by unspeakable pains of every kind'.
>
> There was a long silence.
>
> 'I claim them all', the Savage said at last.
>
> (Huxley 1982 [1932]: 197)

9   The 'dormant' body
Sleep, night-time and dreams

> The bed, you must remember, is the symbol of life. . . . There is nothing
> good except the bed, and are not some of our best moments spent in sleep?
> (Guy de Maupassant, nd: 682)

> The sleeper is never completely isolated within himself [sic], never totally a
> sleeper . . . never totally cut off from the intersubjective world. . . . Sleep and
> waking, illness and health are not modalities of consciousness or will, but
> presuppose an 'existential step'.
> (Merleau-Ponty 1962: 162)

> The notion that going to sleep is something natural is totally inaccurate.
> (Mauss 1973 [1934]: 80)

Introduction

Building on the bodily themes of previous chapters, particularly pain and
emotions, this chapter focuses on another strangely neglected topic of central
significance to an 'embodied' sociology. We are, of course, talking about
sleep. Like death, sleep is an inescapable fact of human embodiment and a
central feature of all societies, yet its sociological import, by and large, has
been neglected. Even the most cursory scan of the literature reveals a dearth
of work on the sociological aspects of sleep. Instead, the field is dominated by
medical and psychological studies of the problems and sequelae of sleep
disturbance, and psychoanalytic and phenomenological literature on the
process and meaning of dreams and dreaming. Literature, too, abounds with
references to sleep and dreaming, from Shakespeare to Montaigne, Shelley to
de la Mare, Milton to Cervantes, Coleridge to Dickens, yet its sociological
significance has yet to be recognised.[1]

Reasons for this sociological neglect are manifold, but three in particular
warrant further discussion. First and foremost, we have the general argument
that sociology, as the study of society and the geometry of social forms, is
primarily concerned with waking rather than sleeping life. To investigate the
latter, according to this line of reasoning, is at best a marginal and at worst a

futile sociological exercise. At first glance this seems a reasonable enough assertion. Sleep, after all, is a highly personal, privatised experience in contemporary Western society – a liminal, unconscious, aspect of bodily being and an 'a-social', 'in-active' form of corporeal 'activity'. Even on its own terms of reference, however, a moment's thought reveals the limitations of this position as sociologically untenable.

Sleep is fundamental to any given society or group (i.e. a 'functional' prerequisite), permeating its institutions as well as its embodied agents, its beliefs as well as its practices, its rituals as well as its mythologies, its spatio-temporal arrangements as well as its discursive and culturally constituted boundaries. The fact that sleep, as a temporal, embodied state, is 'lived through' and presupposes an 'existential step' (cf. the Merleau-Ponty quote above), further underlines its sociological relevance. Even if sleep itself is not an entirely social practice, the language within which it is discussed and the cultural constraints on its meanings, motives and methods are indeed genuine sociological concerns (Taylor 1993: 464).

A second possible reason for this neglect is that the study of sleep is best suited to the disciplines of biology, psychology or, in the case of dreams and dreaming, psychoanalysis. Certainly sleep, as discussed below, involves a biological process of replenishment, rejuvenation and repair. Psychoanalytic perspectives on dreams and dreaming – what Freud saw as the 'royal road to the unconscious' – are equally entrenched features, for better or worse, of Western culture and contemporary society (see, for example, Freud 1976 [1953]; Murray 1965). Seen in this light, the 'what' and 'why' questions of sleep and dreaming, as unconscious mental and physical processes, are perhaps best left to such disciplines. This does not, however, as Taylor rightly argues, rule out the possibility of other more interesting sociological questions to do with the '*how*', '*when*' and '*where*' of sleep – i.e. its connection with the broader sociocultural and historical order, including disciplinary technologies and strategic configurations of power/knowledge – from being posed. In this respect, the key sociological problematic becomes one focused on the '*doing*' of sleep rather than 'being asleep' (Taylor 1993: 464).

Dreams also, however, are sociologically significant, not simply in terms of the archetypal imagery and symbolic associations that ritualistically unite and divide us – cf. Durkheim's notion of 'collective effervescence' in *Elementary Forms of Religious Life* (1961 [1912]) (see also Chapter 8, this volume) – but also through the (proto)professionalisation of our innermost thoughts and desires in the (post-) therapeutic climate and narcissistic culture of our times – what Rose (1990) appositely refers to as 'governing the soul'. In this particular case, the sociological focus is more upon the *use* of dreams, both individually and collectively, socially and culturally, politically and therapeutically, than the psychological process of dreaming as such.

Closely connected to these first two points, a third possible reason for this neglect concerns the problem of 'sociological imperialism': a professionalising process in which sociologists seek to extend their empire still further, arrogating power and transgressing disciplinary boundaries under the all encompassing banner of 'the social' (Strong 1979): a problem compounded when having *something* to say is confused with having *everything* to say (Craib 1995).

To be sure these are important points to bear in mind. Yet in no way do they preclude the possibility of a sociology of sleep from flourishing. Like emotions, sleep is a multifaceted phenomenon, providing a 'litmus paper test' and fascinating case-study of the relationship between the mind and the body, the biological and the social, the body and society. A proper grasp of this most complex of topics, therefore, demands just such an interdisciplinary effort: to claim otherwise, quite simply, is disciplinary hubris. Seen in this light, territorial battles and disciplinary border skirmishes merely serve to distract us still further from the real (sociological) task in hand. Whilst, as we shall see below, the sociological aspects of sleep have not totally escaped the notice of its embodied practitioners, there are certainly many advantages to be had in bringing these scattered insights together in a new, more integrated, way. Indeed, whilst possible objections of the kind mentioned above may doubtless be raised, it would be hard to find a sociologist who did not see sleep as a socially significant topic, worthy of further investigation and debate.

Sleep, as we shall argue, is a prime example of the 'socially pliable' body, one that displays a high degree of malleability in relation to changing sociocultural and historical forms. More generally, sleep, an inescapable fact of human embodiment, constitutes a central social resource, linked as it is to issues of time and space, agency and identity, and providing, in the process, a key sociological indicator of societal development, from incest taboos to the 'civilising of bodies', and from power relations to the institutionalised division of labour and the rationalisation of work and leisure in late capitalist societies (Aubert and White 1959a,b). Key questions to be addressed here include the following. What is the sociological significance of sleep and how should it be studied? What light can a sociology of sleep shed on mind/body, biology/society, structure/agency divides? How are we to conceive of temporality, spatiality and intentionality in this context? To what extent can the sociological study of sleep furnish us with new insights into more macro-oriented processes of power and surveillance, discipline and control? It is to issues such as these that we now turn in the hope of 'fleshing out' more fully the contours of this hitherto largely 'dormant' sociological enterprise – one that provides yet another example of the insights that can emerge from a truly 'embodied' sociology.

The sociological significance of sleep

1 *Biology/society*

Without sleep, waking life – the staple diet of sociology to date – would be impossible. Indeed, as we have argued, the very notion of waking life assumes a vast area of uncharted sociological terrain (i.e. sleep and embodiment, energy and rest), that informs and underpins even the most mundane of tasks. Our embodied actions in the world, in other words, including our skills as competent social agents, are crucially dependent on the sleep, energy and rest that our non-waking life provides as a biologically imperative means of rejuvenation, replenishment and repair. As a physiological function, sleep results either when neuromuscular fatigue cuts down cortical excitation, or when for physiological reasons still not fully understood, both the cortex and the 'wakefulness centre' of the brain become inactive after a few days (Aubert and White 1959b: 5). This is not, of course, to suggest that sociologists focus their attention on these biological processes and imperatives *per se*. Rather, what is most important here, sociologically speaking, is the affordances they afford, the accordances they accord, for the conduct of everyday social life. Seen in these terms, these physiological substrates, and their relationship to everyday waking life, constitute necessary components of a broader sociological analysis of the social significance of sleep, energy and rest.

This, in turn points us, yet again, to the socially pliable nature of human biology (i.e. its 'completion' by culture), and the tilting of the balance from unlearned to learned forms of behaviour. There is, apparently, no specific physiological mechanism linking human sleep with darkness or the astronomical cycle of day and night (Aubert and White 1959a,b). The pattern of human sleep cannot, therefore, be explained in primarily physiological terms. Indeed, a wide range of sleep behaviour is physiologically possible: something that indicates very directly that many of the taken-for-granted features of sleep have less to do with physiological necessity than with sociocultural determination. Sleep, in short, is more than a straightforward biological activity, it is also, in large part, a 'motivated act', bestowed with symbolic value and moral significance, and necessitating, like all other activities, the adoption of a prescribed sociocultural role (ibid.).

As Mauss's (1973 [1934]) discussion of body-techniques and the habitus suggests (see Chapter 3, this volume), there is no 'natural way' for the adult, to claim otherwise is 'totally inaccurate' (cf. the quote at the beginning of this chapter). If this is true of body techniques in general, then it is particularly true of sleep and sleeping. Mauss himself, for example, recounts how the war taught him to 'sleep anywhere' – on horseback, standing up in the mountains, on heaps of stones – yet never was he able to 'change bed without a moment of insomnia': only on the second night could he quickly get off to sleep (Mauss 1973 [1934]: 80). Indeed, all sorts of different ways of sleeping are practised throughout the world. Members of some societies, for instance, have nothing to sleep on except the floor, whilst others have 'instrumental assistance'. There are also people with pillows and those without; people with mats and those without; populations who lie very close together in a ring, with or without a fire, in order to sleep; and those, such as the Masai, who can sleep on their feet (ibid.).[2]

These arguments and insights extend to other techniques of the body, such as rest. Members of certain societies, for example, take their rest in what, through Western eyes, seem very 'peculiar positions'. The whole of Nilotic Africa and part of the Chad region all the way to Tanzania (formerly Tanganyika), for instance, is populated by men who 'rest in fields like storks. Some manage to rest on one foot without a pole, others lean on a stick' (ibid.: 81).

All in all, this suggests a view of sleep and rest as what, for want of a better term, may be referred to, in embodied terms, as a socioculturally shaped (i.e. 'active') form of corporeal 'inactivity'. Far from belonging to the realm of biological 'givens', sleep, in other words, bears the imprint of time and the marks of culture. Here we return to the distinction, introduced earlier, between being asleep and 'doing sleep' (Taylor 1993). Sleep, as we have suggested, is a *social role*, displaying a high degree of plasticity in relation to changing sociocultural and historical forms. It is here, at the intersection of physiological *need*, environmental *constraint* and sociocultural *elaboration* that the *emergent* nature of sleep as a sociological process is most readily apparent. This, in turn, raises other important questions concerning the relationship between sleep, temporality and intentionality, issues to which we now turn in the next section of this chapter.

2 Night-time/day-time: temporality, intentionality and dreams

Sleep, as alluded to above, is a temporally bounded activity – one that displays considerable sociocultural variability. Whilst the minimum amount of sleep which is physiologically needed cannot be specified – the best estimate being approximately seven hours, age variations notwithstanding – it is generally the case that in most societies our physiological need for sleep is less than the social time accorded it (Aubert and White 1959a). There also appears to be no physiological reason why sleep should occur at night-time, and whilst other environmental factors such as temperature and relative humidity are important constraints,[3] a wide range of adjustment to these factors is indeed possible. A considerable amount of training, for example, is involved in getting children to sleep at night-time and to fit into 'appropriate' (i.e. adult-set) sleeping patterns. That sleep tends to occur most commonly at night-time, therefore, represents a complex mixture of social and environmental factors: a time when, traditionally at least, isolation and quiet are more easily obtainable, and when a diminution in vision and temperature induces a need to be indoors (Aubert and White 1959a) – factors that become increasingly redundant due to technological developments that do away with these environmental and physical constraints on our ancestors.

An encounter with sleep, as Aubert and White note, represents a qualitative break in time concepts between night and day, placing a formidable social barrier between two successive days and the social activities they encompass. As such, it opens up the opportunity for a 'fresh start': 'a communion rite in which minor sins and cares are washed away' (ibid.: 53). Sleeping also provides what they appositely refer to as a 'temporal resource', enabling us to get more or less out of the day, depending on our particular circumstances. Thus, whilst I may decide to forgo sleep and 'burn the midnight oil' for a week in order to finish this chapter, others, through boredom or involuntary detention (e.g. the prisoner) may choose instead to 'sleep the time away' in order to hasten its passage. In a different vein, caregivers frequently complain about their loss of sleep when those, such as old people with dementia, turn 'night into day'.

Night-time is also, of course, a time for 'surreptitious' activities of various kinds, from crime to sex, cultural innovation to black magic, werewolves to vampires. Always a time of fear: 'Predators move unseen under the cover of darkness and all animals, man [*sic*] included, are most vulnerable to their enemies when they sleep' (Alvarez 1995: 22). If, as Goffman (1971) argued, normal appearances are the most troubling of all, then this is particularly true of the people one encounters and the places one inhabits late at night. Night-time, in short, constitutes a time of danger and vulnerability, feeding on our poor visibility and transforming even the most innocent of day-time gestures (i.e. a stranger asking us the way) into suspicious, potentially menacing acts (e.g. a possible mugger, killer, rapist, etc.). On the other hand, it can also be a time of great festivity and celebration, from the spectacular illumination of the night sky by fireworks to Midnight Mass, and from New Year's eve to the Midsummer Solstice (Alvarez 1995: 14).

If night-time constitutes one key temporal dimension of sleep, then dreams and dreaming constitute another. Like night-time itself, dreams leave us similarly vulnerable: 'those otherworldly visitations when secret fears and desires come drifting to the surface' (ibid: 22). In this respect, the physical conquest of 'outer darkness' (e.g. the advent of electricity, street lighting etc.),[4] has now been replaced by the gradual illumination of 'inner darkness' (i.e. the 'darkness inside the head') through disciplines such as psychoanalysis (ibid.).

In dreams, the conscious sequencing of time, common to waking life, is suspended if not reversed – condensed, displaced and overdetermined by unconscious mental processes that defy rational ordering or logical temporal form. Whether or not dreams become viewed as evil and irrational expressions of human nature, or are valued as intrinsically 'good' – furnishing insights into past, present and future events – is a socioculturally defined matter (Aubert and White 1959b). In some cultures, as Aubert and White note, they are connected up with supernatural and spiritual dimensions of social life, or are used, through the invocation of sleep spirits, to induce sickness and nightmares in others (ibid.). Stories of medieval legends abound concerning those who have gone to sleep and been – or are to be – awakened many years later: often with new insights and wisdom. Epimenides, the Greek poet, for example, is said to have fallen asleep in a cave when a boy, and not to have awoken for 57 years, when he found himself possessed of all wisdom. Similarly, legends associated with King Arthur, Charlemagne and

Barbarossa, and stories such as the Seven Sleepers of Ephesus, Tannhäuser, Ogier the Dane, and Rip Van Winkle, not to mention Sleeping Beauty, attest to the temporal dimensions of sleep, the symbolic significance of the sleeper and the magical properties of dreaming. In our own times, however, psycho-analytic interpretations notwithstanding, the validity, reliability and responsibility of dream life have tended to be downplayed if not denied (i.e. accorded little legitimacy). The dreams of people in the Western world are, in other words, 'relatively unsocialised events in contrast to the heavy sociali-sation of primate man [*sic*] in his role as sleeper' (Aubert and White 1959b: 4; see also Woods 1947).

Here, questions concerning the temporality of sleep merge imperceptibly with other more general issues of intentionality regarding the roles of sleeper and dreamer, and the social functions that these activities perform both within and between societies. Unlike death, sleep is a 'temporally bounded' activity that is 'lived through', so to speak. Consequently, there are many ways in which it can be talked about and used (both appropriately and inap-propriately) in the contexts of everyday waking life (Taylor 1993). On the one hand, for example, lack of sleep or tiredness may be used as an excuse (legitimate or otherwise) for dereliction of interactional duty, the 'incompe-tent' performance of practical tasks, or to politely bring a tedious evening to a premature close – 'Sorry, I have to get up early in the morning'. It may even, as is common these days, provide the basis for a social event itself – as in children's so-called 'sleep-over' parties. On the other hand, we may choose, consciously or otherwise, to avoid, ignore or insult somebody through sleep or tiredness – the unsuppressed yawn, for instance, or the feigning of sleep in a boring lecture. Fellow travellers may also become rather too intimate when sleep renders their normal modes of corporeal propriety problematic (e.g. drowsy, rocking heads that come to rest, innocently or otherwise, on other passengers' shoulders). Here, we have a primal sociological scene and unfolding drama of which Goffman himself would have been proud: one where sleeping in public places is acceptable, if not condoned, but where certain standards of bodily decorum, deference and demeanour still apply, even with one's eyes closed!

3 The public and the private

Returning to some of the corporeal themes raised earlier in Chapter 2, insights into the historical aspects of sleep across the public/private divide have, perhaps, most successfully been achieved, albeit indirectly, through the sociological work of Elias (1978 [1939], 1982 [1939]) on the 'civilising process'; particularly his analysis of manners in the bedroom (see also Mennell 1989, Gleichmann 1980). In the Middle Ages, for example, the sleeping/waking cycle of the individual was relatively undisciplined and unruly. People often slept in the daytime, and in any place that was conve-nient. Sleeping, in other words, at this time, was a relatively 'public', undifferentiated, matter and the physical space within which it occurred was shared, not infrequently, with (many) others: in the upper classes, the master with his servants, or in the other classes, men and women in the same room, often with guests staying overnight (Mennell 1989). Erasmus, for example, in *De Civilitate Morum Puerilium* (1530), instructed his readers: 'If you share a bed with a comrade, lie quietly; do not toss with your body, for this can lay yourself bare or inconvenience your companion by pulling away the blankets' (cited in Elias 1978 [1939]: 161).

People, we are told, slept naked and the sight of the fleshy human body was a common occurrence, especially in bath-houses. This 'unconcern' for nakedness, as we have seen, slowly disappeared in the sixteenth century, progressing more rapidly in the seventeenth, eighteenth and nineteenth centuries – first in the upper classes and much more slowly in the lower classes. Garments to be worn in bed, for example, were gradually introduced from the Renaissance onwards (Mennell 1989). To have to share a bed was also, by the eighteenth century, quite exceptional (for the upper classes) and consequently details of how to behave if the need arose, were largely left unspoken. La Selle, for instance, in *Les Règles de la Bienséance et de la Civilité Chrétienne* (1729) writes: 'You ought neither to undress nor go to bed in the presence of another person' – the tone becoming appreciably stronger in the later 1774 edition.

The upshot of these developments, as Elias (1978 [1939]: 163) observes, is that the bedroom has become one of the most 'private' and 'intimate' areas of human life, and sleeping, like most other bodily functions, has been increasingly shifted 'behind the scenes' of social life (cf. Giddens' (1991) notion of the 'sequestration of experience' discussed in Chapter 4, this volume). Here too, in much the same way as with eating:

> the wall between people, the reserve, the emotional barrier erected by conditioning between one body and another, grows continuously. To share a bed with people outside the family circle, with strangers, is made more and more embarrassing. Unless necessity dictates otherwise, it becomes usual even within the family for each person to have his [*sic*] own bed and finally – in the middle and upper classes – his own bedroom. . . . *Only if we see how natural it seemed in the Middle Ages for strangers and for children and adults to share a bed can we appreciate what a fundamental change in interpersonal relationships and behaviour is expressed in our manner of living.* And we recognise how far from self-evident it is that *bed and body should form such psychological danger zones as they do in the most recent phase of civilization.*
>
> (Elias 1978 [1939]: 168, our emphasis)[5]

If sleep, historically speaking, has been privatised, it has also, as Taylor (1993) notes, become something of a 'leisure pursuit' in late Western society. Asked what they intend to do with their weekends, vacations or retirement, many people cite sleeping as both an 'acceptable' and 'desirable' pastime.

This, in turn, is linked to the attainment of a certain level of socioeconomic development: members of a hard-working subsistence economy, for example, are more likely to define sleep as necessary respite from exhausting physical labour than a leisure pursuit (Taylor 1993: 468). Perspectives on, and commonsensical definitions of sleep, in other words, are likely to differ according to social location, context and function. Plenty of sleep before an important job interview, exam or strenuous bout of physical exercise may, for instance, be considered a vital necessity.

It is also worth reflecting, at this point, on the intriguing cultural overtones and symbolic associations between sleep, sexuality and death in contemporary Western culture. It is now commonplace, for example, to describe (illicit) sexual liaisons through the 'discourse of dormancy' (e.g. 'She's sleeping with him', 'He's sleeping with her', 'They're sleeping together') – which, of course, in most cases, is a fairly inaccurate description of what actually occurs! (Taylor 1993). Carnal activity, in other words, is dressed up as corporeal inactivity, naked desire as mortal slumber. Discussion of death is also often expressed through the language of sleep (e.g. the 'big sleep', 'rest in peace') (ibid.), in a way that transforms its finality into something altogether more liminal and less threatening – a discursive twist that both resonates with and reinforces the notion that the dead are merely slumbering passengers on the way to 'another' or 'better' place, the status of which remains uncertain to us earthly mortals. As Shelley so poetically put it:

The Daemon of the World

How wonderful is Death
Death and his brother Sleep!
One pale as yonder wan and horned moon,
With lips of lurid blue,
The other glowing like the vital morn,
When throned on ocean's wave
It breathes over the world:
Yet both so passing strange and wonderful!
(Percy Bysshe Shelley 1792–1822)

Death, in short, is not so much denied as deferred: a 'life-strategy' in which mortality itself is 'deconstructed', 'tamed' or romanticised through the idiom of sleep and the discourse of dormancy (Bauman 1992b,c; Aries 1976; Illich 1976).

These symbolic associations, in turn, have been seized upon, marketed and sold by the leisure and entertainment industries. Indeed, from Walt Disney's production of *Sleeping Beauty* to Oliver Sacks's *Awakenings*, and from *Sleepless in Seattle* to *Nightmare on Elm Street*, dormancy has become a media spectacle and a box office hit: an 'obscenity', in Baudrillard's (1988) terms, in which 'all becomes transparence and immediate visibility' and everything is exposed to the 'harsh and inexorable light of information and communication'. Here we glimpse the complexity of contemporary society, on the one hand, continuing trends towards the privatisation or sequestration of all 'natural' bodily functions, on the other hand, pushing towards their 'all-too-visible' (i.e. obscene) public exposure as the latest form of media hype. Viewed within this context, modernist concerns with corporeality are slowly but surely giving way to postmodern concerns with hyperreality (i.e. images without grounding) (Williams 1997).

Discussion of these corporeal issues, in turn, leads us to what is perhaps the fourth and final way in which a sociology of sleep can most profitably develop.

4 From sick role to sleep role: the 'institutionalisation' and 'social patterning' of slumber

As recent research on the body and emotions demonstrates, attention to corporeal issues can shed important new light on sociological topics such as the nature of 'work', the public and the private, and the institutional dynamics of transition and change in late capitalist society (Hochschild 1983; Bendelow and Williams 1998; Fineman 1993). Similar claims, we venture, can be made for a sociology of sleep as another prime facet of embodied social life across the micro–macro divide.

A key feature of work and institutional social life concerns the spatio-temporal ordering of the sleeping/waking cycle and the disciplining of 'docile' (i.e. productive) bodies – from the prison to the factory, the military barracks to the (boarding) school, the hospital to the hotel (cf. Foucault 1979; Goffman 1961). In this respect, the socially prescribed and culturally variable role of the sleeper (of which more below), is a central one in any given society. Indeed, without these 'institutional arrangements' society would, quite simply – given an ever more complex division of labour and specialisation of functions – be impossible. Sleep, in other words, and its social organisation through the sleep role, is a functional prerequisite. Some cultures, for example, as we have seen, have elaborate collective rituals and symbolic practices surrounding the symbolic significance of dreams and the portents they provide, others do not. Some, partly for climatic/environmental reasons, have institutionalised the Siesta – thereby allowing people to rest during the hottest part of the day – others have not. At a more 'concrete' level, buildings themselves are often described and evaluated, in their very architecture if not their function, in units of measurement predicated on sleep and rest. When searching for a house, for instance, one of the first things one stipulates is that it has to be one, two or three bedroom. Hospital capacity and 'through-put' is also measured in terms of beds and bed-days, and hotel rates are calculated on a bed and breakfast basis (i.e. number of nights stayed). Even on the roads, motorists are told to 'take a break – tiredness kills'!

Meanwhile, a whole sleep and rest 'industry' has grown up, supplying us with everything from (sexy) nightwear and pharmacological aides, to the ultimate bed where a 'silent night' is more or less guaranteed. In Greater London, for example, the number of beds purchased in any one year is estimated to be around 321,000, whilst the total time spent in bed in a week by Greater Londoners amounts to a staggering 371,200,000 minutes (J. Hind 'London Index: Beds', *London Evening Standard*, 3 October 1997). There is also the intriguing question as to whether or not we are actually sleeping less these days. It is certainly true that there are more all-night facilities and services, from nightlines to nightclubs and from 24-hour supermarkets to around-the-clock television – something that is, in large part, due to market pressures for ever more consumption. Increasing urbanisation and noise pollution, not to mention the problems of caffeine, add to these dilemmas, with knock-on consequences for sleep, health, neighbourly relations and efficiency both at work and elsewhere.

These issues are particularly well illustrated in relation to the modern hospital. Indeed, the modern hospital is, *par excellence*, a microcosm of the 'dormant' or 'sleeping society'. Even the quickest of strolls though its wards and corridors, its theatres and pharmacies, its staff quarters and laundry rooms, reveals the sociological significance of sleep. First, we have the role of sleep itself as a 'therapeutic tool': a 'natural' cure or healing process, whereby we sleep our way through illness (i.e. 'sleep it off'). Second, we have the spatial organisation of sleep, embodied through the physical regimentation of beds, linen and other accessories on the wards. Next, closely allied to issues of space, we have the temporal ordering of the sleeping–waking cycle, including infamous early morning starts and 'lights out' orders in this most 'total' of total institutions (Goffman 1961).[6] Fourth, we have the public monitoring and surveillance of sleep on the wards and intensive care units, together with the problems of sleep that hospitalisation itself bring for patients themselves. Next, we have what may be termed the 'pharmacology of sleep' in the shape of anaesthetics, sleeping tablets and a variety of other sleep-inducing drugs and therapeutic aides – factors that may not simply 'ease' the problems of 'sleeping sickness', but also serve as powerful disciplinary means to render bodies truly docile and passive.[7] Closely allied to this, we have the 'instrumentation' of sleep, including sleep clinics/laboratories with multidisciplinary personnel and a panoply of electrical equipment, graphs and digital images designed to 'measure' things such as REM and brain activity whilst asleep – i.e. electrophysiological monitoring techniques, clinical observations, etc. (see Alvarez 1995: Chapter 3). Sixth, we have, of course, the problems of long hours and shiftwork for hospital staff themselves, including medical mistakes and their iatrogenic consequences. Next, we return to the links, common in popular culture, between sleep and death: from patients dying in their sleep to the ethical dilemmas that the medical imperative to sustain life at all costs creates for patients in comatose or (near) vegetative states. Finally, at the broadest most general level, we have here a clear expression of the 'professionalisation' or 'medicalisation' of sleep – one that, like all professionalising strategies, may or may not be in our own best interests.

Underpinning these institutional issues, are broader questions of power, surveillance and control. Sleep, as we have suggested, particularly through its (cultural and symbolic) associations with night-time, leaves us vulnerable. In this respect, the balance of power tips firmly in favour of those who remain awake *vis à vis* those who sleep. Whilst the general thrust of the civilising process may indeed be towards increasing thresholds of shame and embarrassment towards the 'natural' body, and the removal behind the scenes of carnal activities and experiences such as sex, sleep and death, it is none the less the case that certain groups of people, such as children, the hospital patient, the prisoner, the homeless, have their sleeping as well as waking life monitored far more closely than others, at times and in circumstances far from their own choosing (cf. Foucault 1979 and Elias 1978 [1939] above). Indeed, from the nightwatchman to the hospital nurse, the monitoring of sleep and the 'policing' of the times within which it occurs is a central or 'core' feature of society. Sleep may also be 'withheld' in various ways, as a form of punishment, torture or interrogation – a process likely to wear down even the most recalcitrant and resistant of individuals. In short, sleep can be profitably analysed in terms of the observer/observed relationships, together with the broader power/knowledge dynamics and webs of surveillance and control it raises across the social spectrum (Taylor 1993): factors that, adapting Jamous and Pellioule's (1970) use of the term in a different context, are succinctly captured by the determinacy/indeterminacy ratio (i.e. a measure of the degree to which sleep patterns are set by self or others).

The fact that none of us are immune from the need to sleep, however, and that sleep, like illness and death, is no respecter of status or hierarchy – what Philip Sydney appositely referred to as the 'indifferent judge' between the 'high' and 'low'; the 'poor man's wealth, the prisoner's release' – means that today, in Western society, the institutionalised role of sleeper ensures, in most cases, at the very least the following duties, rights and obligations – ones that resonate with certain 'core features' and defining characteristics of the Parsonian 'sick role' (Parsons 1951).

Duties/obligations:

1 To sleep at night and therefore to conform to the general pattern of sleep time, unless legitimate social circumstances, such as work arrangements, dictate otherwise.

2 To sleep in a bed, or similar device, in a private place, away from public view, in proper attire (i.e. pyjamas, nightdress etc.) – the latter is not an absolute requirement and indeed, is increasingly being circumvented if not flouted.

Rights:

3 Freedom from noise and interference from others, except in times of emergency.

4   Exemption from normal role obligations.
5   No loss of waking role status whilst asleep.

(Parsons 1951)

Certainly some of these obligations and privileges can be found in cultures very different from our own. The Navaho, for example, believe that evil is brought by even stepping over a sleeping person, whilst amongst the Bedouin Rwala, a 'culprit' cannot be killed whilst sleeping by an avenger, lest it bring similar vengeance on the latter's own head! (Aubert and White 1959a: 54).

Beyond these general, if not universal features of the sleep role, it is equally clear that sleep is 'socially patterned' in various ways according to a broader range of socio-structural and demographic factors. Age is an obvious example – babies, for instance, spend more time sleeping than adults. The amount of sleep required across the life course, however, varies considerably due to the complex interaction of biological and social factors. Adults in the Health and Lifestyles Survey (HALS) – a study involving a sample of some 9,000 women and men aged over 18 (Cox *et al.* 1987; Blaxter 1990) – were almost evenly divided between those who claimed to sleep for 7–8 hours, those who 'usually' slept for less and those who 'usually' had longer. Younger men and women were more likely to quote more than 8 hours, with the proportions sleeping under 7 hours rising steeply with age – a factor confounded by health status.[8]

Gender is also important here. While tiredness and fatigue, as Ridsdale (1989: 486) comments, are part and parcel of the 'normal chaff' of daily life, studies suggest that females show an excess of tiredness over their male counterparts. Again, findings from the HALS are instructive here: 20 per cent of men and 30 per cent of women reported 'always feeling tired' in the month before interview (Cox *et al.* 1987). Experiences of tiredness were also found to vary in interesting ways *amongst* as well as between men and women themselves. Those aged under 39, for example, those without children, and those with children aged between 6 and 16, were less likely to report 'always feeling tired' than those with younger children. Likewise, as the number of children increased, so did the proportion reporting tiredness (Cox *et al.* 1987). Echoing these gender-related patterns, Popay (1992) found that tiredness, particularly severe or chronic tiredness, featured as one of the most frequent symptoms or conditions referred to spontaneously by women in her study. As Brannen and Moss (1988) show, women's tiredness varies in both type as well as quantity: young babies and broken nights bringing one sort of tiredness; being at home full-time another centred on boredom and lethargy; trying to combine domestic and paid work a third type derived from physical and mental fatigue.

Similar points can be made in relation to class. Not only is the 'epidemiology' of sleep, energy and rest likely to vary, in more or less predictable ways, according to socioeconomic factors, but so, too, is its very definition. Hunt *et al.* (1986), for example, in a large community survey, found a greater prevalence of sleeping problems – as measured on the Nottingham Health Profile (NHP) – amongst those from traditional manual working-class backgrounds. It may also be suggested, on the basis of these and other findings, that those in upper social-class circles are more likely, on average, both to retire to bed and rise later than their working-class counterparts: itself another key index of social power, status and privilege (i.e. the freedom or flexibility, expressed through the determinacy/indeterminacy ratio, to set one's own sleep pattern) (Aubert and White 1959a). Overcrowded housing conditions, and problems of shiftwork – the likelihood of which increases as one descends the social scale – underline these class-related issues, having a profound effect both on sleep patterns and sleeping arrangements. On the other hand, lack of sleep may also serve as a mark of social distinction, as when the hurried business executive or the harassed politician complains of 'feeling tired' or 'not needing much sleep', snatching a few hours here or there (i.e. 'power napping'), in a whirlwind life of international meetings and impossible deadlines.

The interaction between socioeconomic status and factors such as age and gender, serves to further reinforce these points, highlighting the rich and varied picture that the social patterning of sleep, energy and rest provides – one that may serve, in an analogous fashion to Durkheim's concept of anomie or Marx's notion of alienation, as a key contemporary indicator of social malaise and societal 'unrest'. Seen in this light, debates over social structure, including the inequalities (Townsend *et al.* 1988; Wilkinson 1996) and lay concepts (Cornwell 1984; Calnan 1987; Stainton-Rogers 1991; Radley 1993) literature on class and health, could usefully be extended through a sociological focus on sleep, energy and rest.

Little work has been done, to date, on the ethnic patterning of sleep, yet many of the above points apply equally well. Not only is the value, practice and significance of sleep likely to vary according to cultural group membership, but distinctive patterns of work and employment, together with problematic housing conditions suggest a complex picture – one that may be less about ethnic patterning *per se*, than the underlying socioeconomic and material circumstances in which these minority groups live, and their implications for health (Smaje 1995). In the early post-war years of migration (i.e. the 1950s and 1960s), for example, many South Asian men, employed on a shiftwork basis, shared beds on a 12-hour rotating cycle (Ratcliffe 1980). Similarly, in the current economic period, shiftwork, especially in the manufacturing industry (e.g. textiles), is particularly prevalent amongst the Muslim community. Overcrowding (i.e. over two people per room) is another striking feature of the Pakistani and Bangladeshi communities – suggesting that, civilising processes notwithstanding, the sharing of bedrooms, if not beds, is still commonplace in certain segments of contemporary Western society (Ratcliffe 1996a,b). These and many other issues raise significant sociological questions about sleep and rest, yet to date, as I have argued, we have little direct empirical evidence upon which to base these contentions.

There is, in short, an urgent need for more empirical as well as theoretical work in this important and promising new area of research on the institutionalisation and social patterning of sleep.

Conclusions

As we have seen, the study of sleep meshes closely with 'core' sociological problematics – from the problem of social 'order' to the dilemmas of bodily 'control'. The fact that sleep, as a temporal resource, is 'lived through', so to speak, and that the sleeper is never entirely 'cut off' from the intersubjective and intercorporeal world of which s/he is a part, further underlines this sociological point. The argument here, in short, is for a sociological analysis of the material and sociocultural circumstances, contingencies and consequences of sleep as an embodied activity (i.e. the '*doing*' of sleep and the sociocultural significance (or otherwise) of dreams and dreaming), rather than the more medicocentric or psychoanalytic focus on its whys and wherefores. The very nature of sleep, we venture, can only fully be understood when placed within the sociological meanings and contexts, actions and purposes of embodied agents across the spatio-temporal zones and environmental boundaries separating day from night, the public from the private.

Like other aspects of our human embodiment (e.g. pain and emotions), sleep is an 'uncontainable' term in any one domain or discourse – something that lies ambiguously across the nature/culture, biology/society divide, transcending many former dichotomous modes of Western thought. This, in turn, suggests a (partially) 'socialised' view of biology itself (Shilling 1997a), one that challenges former reductionist thinking and the spectre of sociobiologism. Re-written and re-read in this new, more open way, the biology/society equation becomes, in fact, far more complex, subtle and sophisticated – a position that demands and necessitates a *dialectical* rather than a reductionist stance on sleep and sleeping. Sleep, in other words, as we have suggested, is an emergent property, the genesis of which lies at the intersection of physiological *need*, environmental *constraint*, and sociocultural *elaboration*.

A central issue here, as we have seen, is the notion of the 'sleep role'. To be sure, the norms and expectations surrounding this role are likely to vary considerably, both historically and cross-culturally, yet the need to sleep is a universal feature of human embodiment. In all societies, in short, the role of sleeper is central, latent or manifest, sacred or profane. This, coupled with the spatio-temporal organisation of sleep, its social patterning, together with the broader questions of power and surveillance, discipline and control it raises – of which the observer/observed, determinacy/interdeterminacy ratios are key indexes and cross-cutting axes – suggest a viable and indeed challenging new area of sociological research and investigation. Schematically, this may be mapped out as follows in Table 9.1.

More broadly, sleep, it can be suggested, provides a key indicator of soci-

Table 9.1 Schematic outline for a sociology of sleep

Level	Problem	Key concept(s)/divisions	Empirical question(s)/example(s)
1 Body	Biology—society links	Pliable biology Bodily techniques Habitus	Types and styles of sleep and sleeping
2 Time/space	Temporal/spatial aspect of sleep	Day/night Civilising process Sequestration Public/private	When and where does sleep occur?
3 Social/ symbolic/ interactional	Uses of sleep in waking life	'Doing' sleep Discourses of dormancy, socialised dreaming, sacred/profane	Relationship between sleep, sexuality and death, social significance of dreams
4 Social structure	Institutional/hierarchical organisation	Sleep role Power/surveillance Determinacy/indeterminacy ratio Work/leisure	Rights and duties of the sleeper Power naps

etal development, an index of social organisation, and a fruitful vantage point from which to revisit old sociological issues, as well as to develop new ones (Aubert and White 1959a, b). From the state of civilised bodies to the social organisation of time and space, and from the nature and status of incest taboos and family relations to the institutionalised division of labour, the sociological study of sleep furnishes us with invaluable insights into the contours and existential parameters of society, classical or medieval, feudal or industrial, (late) modern or postmodern.

What then of future research agendas in this important, yet embryonic, new area of sociological study? Certainly, as we have argued, there is a need to focus on the experience (i.e. phenomenological) as well as the representational (i.e. discursive/symbolic), the material as well as the cultural, the institutional (i.e. macro-) as well as the individual (i.e. micro-) aspects of sleep. Perhaps the most pressing issue, however, concerns the need to develop a coherent set of sociological concepts, adequate to the task in hand. In this respect, the analytical framework outlined above is merely the beginning of a much broader theoretical and empirical research enterprise, risks of 'sociological imperialism' notwithstanding.

To conclude, it is high time, in short, that somnolent sociologists, as embodied practitioners, stopped 'sleeping on the job' and fully 'woke up' to the significance of this most important of topics and neglected of domains. In this respect, Milton's provocative quote 'What hath night to do with sleep', may serve as a useful point of departure and a promising platform from which to fashion other similarly challenging sociological questions concerning the nature of sleep within dormant society. Perhaps the last word in this literary vein, however, should go to Cervantes who, in *Don Quixote*, expresses the matter in the following eloquently 'equalising' terms:

> Blessings on him [*sic*] who invented sleep, the mantle that covers all human thoughts, the food that satisfies hunger, the drink that slakes thirst, the fire that warms cold, the cold that moderates heat, and, lastly, the common currency that buys all things, the balance and weight that equalises the shepherd and the king, the simpleton and the sage.

An incontrovertible fact of embodied human nature, sleep's time it seems, sociologically speaking, has finally arrived!

10 'Artistic' bodies

*Re*presentation and resistance

the body is central to our imaginary and, so far as we can tell, has always been so. Representations of the body, then, constitute a wonderfully rich set of resources, useful for moral and intellectual ends as well as artistic ones.

(Jordanova 1997: 112–13)

Gray's Anatomy . . . legitimised notions of 'serious' science and powerful medicine unchallenged by the 'frivolity' of art. . . . Anatomical art for the millenium has already been hijacked by internet artists and the virtual images of the future are the anatomies of Cyborgs.

(Petherbridge 1997: 96)

Our starting point in this chapter concerns the sorely neglected topic of a sociology of the arts. At first glance, as Bourdieu remarks, sociology and art make an 'odd couple'. On the one hand, the artist holds total belief in the uniqueness of their 'gift' or talent, whilst the sociologist, on the other hand, aims to classify and explain, thereby fragmenting and disturbing the doctrinaire (Bourdieu 1980: 207).

Although the impact of social thought on art history is clearly evident, from Marxist and feminist analyses to more recent poststructuralist critiques, reciprocal attempts to use art itself to enhance our understanding of social processes are still relatively underdeveloped within British and American sociology. Indeed, despite recent challenges to the constitution of knowledge and the focus on issues of cultural representation, there still appears to be a remarkable reluctance to endorse anything but the written word as text.[1] Even when visual images are used, they are seldom displayed without captions or labels.

The roots of this (sociological) neglect can be traced back to the equation of science with progress and the subsequent dichotomisation of intuition and logic, subjectivity and objectivity (Zolberg 1990). Given the increasing 'destabilisation' of these categories in social theory today, a sociology of the arts would seem an obvious next step. Certainly the twentieth century has heralded enormous changes in the understanding of art, both historically and culturally. These developments have, in turn, resulted in an extension of definitions of 'the arts' and 'high culture' beyond the realm of fine art and painting, to include photography, 'performance art' and, perhaps more controversially, the media.

Like society, art is the creation of individual members who are themselves socially (trans)formed in the process. Similarly, the appreciation of art itself is not a natural 'God-given' gift, but a socially inculcated disposition – one that is unevenly distributed throughout society, predisposing some to define themselves as 'art lovers' whilst others are deprived of this privilege (Bourdieu et al. 1990). More generally, art provides a powerful medium through which dominant ideas and beliefs about the body and its relationship to the broader social, cultural and political order are reflected and reinforced (Adler and Pointon 1993).

In taking these issues forward, we return again to some central themes of the book, including the corporeal problems of power/knowledge, gender, emotions, sexuality, pain and sickness, sleep and death. Underpinning these issues – from Nazi imagery of the Aryan body to contemporary debates about the 'naked' and the 'nude' – are a broader set of arguments concerning the relationship between sociology and art. Far from being an 'odd couple', the 'marriage' between sociology and art, we suggest, provides a potentially very fruitful alliance, one of particular relevance to newly evolving debates on the relationship between body and society.

Ideological representations of the body politic: discipline, surveillance and control

From the beginning of this century, two distinct traditions have dominated art history and criticism: the first was preoccupied with definitions of the 'best' and 'highest' forms of art within modern Western culture (i.e. a focus on aesthetics and elitism (Frascina and Harris 1992)); the second was concerned with revealing the socially constructed nature of art forms and the dominant interests of elites (Becker 1982; Wolff 1993, 1981, 1975). Building on this second tradition, Zolberg (1990) maintains that it is from within sociology that the sharpest insights have arisen, producing the most profound observations on the deeply complex relationship between art, culture and society. As a consequence, historians, art historians, musicologists, aestheticians, critics and philosophers are, she claims, increasingly reorientating their disciplinary perspectives to the language and frameworks of sociology. In doing so, three basic assumptions about what art is have been challenged: first, that a piece of artwork is unique; second, that it is conceived and made by one creator; and third, that the piece of art is a spontaneous expression of genius (Zolberg 1990: 53).[2]

In particular, these 'new' sociologically informed approaches resist the tradition of highlighting the aesthetic and marginalising the structural dimensions of art. Berger's (1972) Ways of Seeing, for example, broke new ground, using a variety of visual images and materials to explore the social placing and positioning of bodies in relation to class, race and gender. In doing so, Berger and his followers not only provide us with a striking visual account of how power relations are expressed through the body,[3] they also serve to extend the very definition of what counts as 'art', from European oil paintings to advertisements in popular magazines.

Central to these developments has been the role of photography. As the most widespread means of visual communication over the past century and a half, photography has done more than any other artistic medium to shape our notion of the body in modern times. Whilst its overt function was to celebrate the individual, photography has always carried with it important elements of surveillance and control: from the facilitation of so-called 'scientific' developments such as physiognomy,[4] and the colonial stereotyping of 'others' in non-white cultures, to the visual recording of prolonged periods of social unrest and proletarian uprising across Europe and America (Tagg 1988). These overtly political functions of the camera were, however, masked by the march of 'scientific progress'. As Pultz observes:

> Photography seemed the perfect Enlightenment tool, functioning like human sight to offer empirical knowledge mechanically, objectively, without thought or emotion. The existence of photography also buttressed the Enlightenment account of the coherent individual, or subject. A whole series of relationships within the photographic process – camera to subject, lens to film, observer to photograph – reproduce the position of a privileged, unique Enlightenment subject: the observer apart, freely viewing some object or scene.
>
> (Pultz 1995: 9)

More generally, as Bourdieu (1996) shows, the norms that define the occasions and objects of photography as a 'middle-brow art' serve to display the socially differentiated functions of, and attitudes towards, the photographic images and act. For some groups, photography is primarily a means of preserving the present and reproducing the euphoric moments of collective celebration, for other groups, however, it is the occasion of an aesthetic judgement, in which the photos are endowed with the dignity of 'works of art'.

These issues of art/power are graphically illustrated through Nazi depictions of the Aryan body. In the 1920s and 30s the subject of the body (in relation to the decimation of war) became an obsessive focus for many painters, particularly with the rise of Expressionism and Dadaism. Like Dix and Grosz (himself a Dadaist), these artists sought to formulate another 'dirty Modernism' based on shit, provocations and sex – a response determined by a view of the body (politic) as inherently corrupt (Stonor Saunders 1995). In response to these chaotic, scatological movements, Bauhaus emerged as a form of design, painting and architecture that was completely 'stripped back', geometric and simple. Bauhaus was deeply influenced by Le Corbusier, a Swiss rationalist and puritan architect, who believed that the war had provided the impetus for a massive purging of the past into a new Age of Reason. Purism, as an aesthetic, laid great emphasis on cleanliness and hygiene as well as complete clarity of function and form. Le Corbusier echoed this puritan rhetoric in his call for 'order' and 'control' over the social body, something that found its ultimate architectural expression in the Weissenhof Siedlung exhibition of proposed new housing in Stuttgart in 1927, providing a 'Modernist solution' to dirt and overcrowding (Stonor Saunders 1995).[5]

The 'New Body' was, at this time, becoming a national obsession. Health spas, sanatoria and sports stadia mushroomed as images of young athletic Hitler Youth engaged in eurhythmics and callisthenics bombarded the public consciousness – Nazi propaganda, given an added twist by the sheer precision and timing of movement and formation. At the heart of these issues were intense nationalist ideologies of 'racial hygiene', coupled with Social Darwinist beliefs about the 'natural' superiority of the Aryan master race – views upheld by the linkage of physical appearance to personal qualities, and embodied in the stereotype of the tall blond, blue-eyed Nordic hero. In contrast, Jews were depicted as misshapen, dark-skinned, ugly, malevolent 'sub-humans': the source of all Germany's problems, portrayed through metaphors of 'pollution', 'dirt' and 'disease'. So strong were these beliefs, that a plan for state-controlled breeding – modelled on classically proportioned Polykleiton individuals – was said to have been proposed and partially implemented.[6] Himmler, for example, estimated that under a 'proper breeding programme', the German people could become 'fully Polykleiton within 120 years'. To this end, a magazine entitled *Rasse*, published tables of bodily proportions, with sub-sections devoted to faces, noses, ears and hands, which were to be accepted or rejected (Hersey 1996: 17).

These Nazi beliefs were powerfully expressed in a 1935 exhibition entitled: 'The Miracle of Life'. The posters for this exhibition were designed by Bauhaus teacher Herbert Bayer, with the Third Reich depicted as the Body and Hitler as the Brain. The 'Body of the People' was now a total organism, functioning with machine-like efficiency to overpower and overwhelm weaker specimens. Within such ideologies, birth itself becomes masculine: 'men create the future, the Fuhrer, power, and the *Reich* . . . totalities' (Theweleit 1989 [1978]: 88).[7] One of the main stands at this exhibition was organised by an architect-turned physician and cultural theorist Dr Paul Schultze-Naumburg, author of the influential *Kunst und Rasse* (1928), which attacked the 'excesses' of the modernist movement, linking them to Jewish influences. His *Entartete Kunst* (degenerate art) exhibition compared photographs of mentally and physically handicapped and deformed people with the subjects of avant-garde artists such as Picasso. In particular, the art of Rubens was singled out for praise as the best place to find the reproductive ideals of the German race. In contrast, Rembrandt and his physical types were seen as responsible for the 'rivers of pollution' that flowed through German art, continually propagating degenerate reproductive ideals (Hersey 1996: 17). In short, in keeping with the dominant spirit of the age, Schultze-Naumburg's message was clear, namely, that the disorder and subsequent insanity engendered by these degenerate art forms were a threat to the 'Body of the People' (Stonor Saunders 1995: 17).[8] As Nazism and Fascism gained momentum, the conservative gaze of these movements turned towards the more obvious statements of power and beauty in neo-classicist forms. Consequently, many of the architects of the Bauhaus movement went to the United States in search of work.

It is, however, the *realism* of photography that ultimately makes it such a powerful and emotive medium of communication. Although the notion that the 'camera captures the truth' is an uneasy one, the non-verbal language of photorealism is universally understood across cultures, capturing the carnage of war and the depths of human pain and suffering such atrocities evoke in an unprecedented manner. Once seen, visual images are often impossible to dismiss: the unimaginable, inadmissible nightmares of documentary photographic evidence testifying to piles of dead bodies overseen by nonchalant Nazis in the death camps of the Holocaust; the horror of the burning body of the little Vietnamese girl running down the road to escape napalm; and the newsreels showing the charred, blackened bodies of raped and mutilated women in Bosnia. These, and many other similarly chilling images, lie sedimented in our psyches, serving to remind us, if ever they needed to, of the crimes committed and the barbarism perpetrated on our bodies and minds in the name of 'hu*man*kind'. Some indeed, have gone further, claiming that if photographic evidence of the Holocaust had been available earlier, then the public response would have been greater. As Pultz states:

> the two World Wars of the twentieth century produced few photographs of the effect on the body of the cruelty of war . . . the greatest contemporary sacrilege to the human body was the Holocaust, the systematic extermination of the Jewish people in Europe carried out under the orders of Hitler and the National Socialist Party. When only the written word reported them, the atrocities of the Holocaust remained unfathomable. It was the publication of the first photographs from the liberated camps that made the unthinkable devastatingly real. Photographs such as those made by the British photojournalist Lee Miller at Buchenwald and Leipzig-Mochau in 1945 shaped both world opinion and world emotions.
>
> (Pultz 1995: 101)

Increasingly, at the turn of the twenty-first century, the artistic leanings of postmodernism reflect an overwhelming sense of dissolution, fragmentation and flux. Within this Baudrillardian scenario of dazzling lights and glittering impressions, life becomes an endless series of (fast-forward/rewind) images in which traditional distinctions between 'fact' and 'fiction', 'fantasy' and 'reality' become increasingly blurred – trends that have been exacerbated by the recent advent of cyberspace and virtual reality (see Chapter 4, this volume).

Panoptic systems of power/knowledge have also given way to more narcissistic forms of 'self-surveillance',[9] including the 'tyranny' of idealised images and a 'fragmentation' of the body into a series of specialised areas and inter-ests: a phenomenon succinctly captured in Mapplethorpe's controversial gay nudes and his 'egoistic obsession' with the 'perfect part' (Gill 1989). As a key art form in late twentieth-century Western society, photography provides a perfect vehicle for this *trans*formation of the (post-)modern body and cultiva-tion of the narcissistic self:

> not only because it provides the technical means of ceaseless self-scrutiny but because it renders the sense of selfhood dependent on the consump-tion of images of the self, at the same time calling into question the reality of the external world.
>
> (Lasch 1979: 48)

Art does not, however, simply reflect and reproduce the dominant struc-tures of society. Rather, it can also be used to challenge them through various 'resistant' forms of body/politics, including women's body art. Hence it is to these issues that we now turn in seeking to flesh out a more praxical relation-ship to the production and consumption of art.

Feminism, 'resistance' and women's body art: representation, performance and *praxis*

A central concern for feminists and non-European/American art historians alike has been the way in which white, male, middle-class heterosexual values are cultivated and reproduced within the discourses and practices of art. Almost without exception, female artists, until the twentieth century, have been daughters or lovers of famous male artists, and 'femininity' has repeatedly been dissociated from 'creativity' and 'high culture' (Nochlin 1973b). In this respect, art both reflects and reinforces the dualistic opposi-tions so prevalent in Western culture with its dominant masculine aesthetics (Chadwick 1990; Harper 1985; Tickner 1978; Lippard 1976).

The female body, as Pollock (1982) notes, has provided a privileged arena over which male artists could claim their modernity, develop their aestheti-cism and contest the leadership of the avant-garde. Central to these issues has been the manner in which women have been treated as mere objects and mere bodies.[10] From paintings in the 'Old Master' tradition to Playboy pinups and advertising of various sorts, women's bodies have been consciously posed to invite the objectificatory male gaze (Berger 1972).[11] (See Plate 10.1.)

Although the female nude is undoubtedly an icon of high culture, its representation acts to suppress and deny women's own experiences and sexu-ality, revealing instead an underlying *masculine* insistence on idealised exteriority and complete surfaces. In this respect, as Nead states:

> the female nude can almost be seen as a metaphor for the processes of separation and ordering, for the formation of the self and the spaces of

Plate 10.1 London 1982

Source: Photographed and permission to reproduce by Jill Posener, San Francisco

the other. If the female body is defined as lacking containment and issuing filth and pollution from its faltering outlines and broken surface, then the classical forms of art perform a kind of magical regulation of the female body, containing it and momentarily repairing the orifices and tears.

(Nead 1992: 7)

In contrast, feminist art, as a conscious act of 'resistance', has sought to challenge these dominant objectificatory positions. In particular, women's body art sought to reveal the 'repellent interior', developing throughout the 1970s as part of a backlash to overt male fears and misogyny directed at the 'mysterious' qualities and inner workings of female corporeality. Broadly speaking, the objective of this art was to transform women from passive objects of representation into *active*, speaking subjects (see Chapter 6, this volume). Feminist art of this period articulated the rights of women to re-present their bodies and sexual identities in their own terms through vaginal imagery, performance work, and the representation of previously taboo subjects like menstruation: facets of female corporeality that, hitherto, had been hidden from public view under a veil of 'shame' and 'indecency' (Nead 1992).

Judy Chicago's *Red Flag* (1971), for example, depicts the removal of a bloody tampon, whilst her *Dinner Party* (1975) – using vulvic and vaginal iconography, centred around thirty-nine place settings with individually designed crockery and cutlery, to celebrate notorious women in European and

American history – was banned in several art galleries. Although Chicago herself interpreted this criticism as merely reproducing the revulsion and shame women are made to feel about their bodies, it also raised outrage amongst some feminists, particularly socialist feminists, who were infuriated at the intellectual and cultural implications of these pioneering women's achievements being reduced to a unitary symbol of female genitalia. Michelle Barrett, for example, remarked:

> I was in fact horrified to see a 'Virginia Woolf' whose image to me represented a reading of her life and work which contradicted all she had ever stood for. There she sits: a genital sculpture in deep relief . . . resting on a runner of pale lemon gauze with the odd blue wave embroidered on it.
> (Barrett 1982: 45)

As well as the problem of universalistic assumptions, there was also criticism of these women artists' use of their own bodies in their works. Rather than challenge the status quo, they might, it was feared, be 'reappropriated' for male sexual arousal. 'It is', as Lippard warned, 'a subtle abyss that separates men's use of women for sexual titillation from women's use of women to expose that insult' (Lippard 1976: 125).

Another powerful illustration of this type of art is provided by Cindy Sherman who, particularly in her early work, used her own body to re-enact female social roles – evoking film imagery from the 1950s in which women were portrayed as 'vulnerable' and 'mentally unstable'. As with many feminist artists, however, the influence of postmodernism and poststructuralism meant that Sherman's early essentialism gradually gave way to a more 'fragmented' view of the female body, often through the parodying of soft pornography or the reduction to physical by-products such as viscera, vomit or menstrual blood. An untitled print in 1992, for example, portrays a grotesque female body in a centrefold pose composed of plastic body parts and prostheses with a heavily wrinkled, possibly male face. The legless plastic torso has pubic hair and some placenta-like material exuding from the bright red vaginal lips, set against a backdrop of what appears to be human-like hair. A body, in short, that 'morphs' into a sort of 'prosthetic idealised numbness' – one in which 'the self has all but disappeared' (Searle 1997).[12]

Whatever its aesthetic consequence, performance art suggests a form of embodied praxis, which not only challenges the distinction between experience and representation, but also blurs the boundary between art and social theory. Carol Schneemann's *Interior Scroll* (1975), for example, culminates in the artist reading a scroll unravelled from her vagina, symbolising the internal and matriarchal knowledge of the female body. Here, as Frank astutely observes, performance enacts power on the site of the body itself: 'By embodying her anger in her art and making it a performance, Schneemann keeps her praxis from becoming a will to domination. . . . Her performance *mediates* play and anger, the hurt and joy of her woman's body' (Frank 1991a: 85).

This, in turn, relates to more general issues concerning other participative modes of 'embodied art' such as dance and theatre. As an embodied, expressive, form of communication, dance engenders a sense of 'bodily appearance' in which corporeal 'limits', 'contingencies' and 'vulnerabilities' are (albeit temporarily) shared and transgressed (Hanna 1988). As such, dance becomes a paradigmatic example of Frank's (1991a) 'communicative' body – one that is producing in its expressiveness, communal in its associations, and continually *in the process* of creating itself (see Chapter 3).[13]

Here we return again to the feminist critique of corporeal 'containment' and the need for a more 'fluid' position concerning women's bodily boundaries and libidinal flows. Work such as Sue Arrowsmith's One, Two, Three, Nine, (1985), for example, provides an alternative visual representation based less upon the body as a 'hermetically sealed container', and more upon the permeability of corporeal boundaries, including the dynamics of a self moving in relationship to 'otherness' (Battersby 1993). In these and many other ways, women's body art is able to transcend the surface/interiority dichotomy, and move toward more 'ambiguous' representations of feminine desire (see Chapter 6, this volume).

Underpinning these issues are a broader set of tensions concerning the relationship between 'aestheticism' and 'eroticism' in art: a debate that, historically speaking, has centred on the 'naked' and the 'nude'. Hence, it is to this crucial, yet controversial, issue that we now turn.

The naked and the nude: aestheticism or obscenity?

> God created man in his own image, in the image of God created he him; male and female created he them . . . and they were both naked, the man and his wife, and were not ashamed.
>
> *(Book of Genesis)*

Within European culture, for more than two thousand years, the naked body has been regarded as the epitome of energy, power and beauty, and the source of profound emotions such as grief, love and anger. Study of the nude has always been a central tenet of an artist's training: itself a measure of 'ideal form', and the foundation of classical architecture. As Gill comments:

> The nude was a key symbol for the Renaissance and for the earlier pagan cultures whose standards helped to formulate our own. In ancient Greece it was the ultimate visual expression of the society's values. The austere frontality of the marble young men who walk toward us out of the archaic past reminds us of the rectilinear grandeur of the temples in which they worshipped. Columns, frieze and cornice echo the harmonies of thighs, torso and shoulders. Their confident grace survives the sophistication of decorated bronze, which the Greeks were to develop to a degree of realism which we would find disturbing if carried out in sculpture today.
>
> *(Gill 1989: 10)*

Despite this elevated status, the dualistic opposition between the naked body deprived of clothes, and the nude body 'reclothed' by art, has given rise to controversial debates concerning the distinction between the aesthetic and the pornographic. Griffiths (1996), for example, emphasises how the Hegelian view of aesthetic response leaves the object of its delight alone, for others to revel in. The point, he maintains, is not so much to deny that a work of art may be erotic, but rather to question the very nature of 'eroticism' itself, how it differs from sexual pleasure, and how it is possible to find such a piece erotic without being attracted to any of the figures or acts represented in it. From this viewpoint, art's pleasures are one step removed from consumption: 'Essentially sensuous though a work of art is, this sensuousness yields itself up over and again to many people, maintains itself in real independence of any individual's rapture or excitation' (Griffiths 1996: 21). These 'ambivalences of ocular introjection' (Brown 1966), in other words, involve the tensions between a distanced (aesthetic) reception of literary and iconic representations on the one hand, and an 'authentic' presencing ('realness') on the other (Falk 1994). Focusing specifically on the case of pornography, Falk suggests that the pursuit of 'evidential explicitness' in contemporary Western iconography promotes, paradoxically, its very opposite, namely, a Baudrillardian version of 'hyperreality' that cancels the difference between (authentic) presence and (fictional) representation, reducing it to mere '(special) effect or s(t)imulation' (Falk 1994: 213).

The classic text on these issues, however, was written by Lord Kenneth Clark, who held many influential public positions in art and culture in Britain throughout the 1960s and 1970s. First published in 1956 and still selling in its eighth edition, *The Nude* has been one of the few comprehensive accounts of this core aspect of the visual arts and traces the history of the nude from Greek antiquity to European modernism. In doing so, Clark appears, on the one hand, to endorse a loosely Kantian aesthetic of 'pure' form and disinterested appreciation. On the other hand, he elucidates a frankly erotic response, qualified only by an insistence on the contemplation of material that does not sink to the level of pornography but remains instead within the realms of 'high culture'. No nude, however abstract, Clark insists:

> should fail to arouse in the spectator some vestige of erotic feeling. If it does not do so, it is bad art and false morals. . . . The desire to grasp and be united with another human body is so fundamental a part of our nature that our judgement of what is 'pure form' is inevitably influenced by it; and one of the difficulties of the nude as a subject for art is that these instincts cannot lie hidden, as they do for example in our enjoyment of a piece of pottery, thereby gaining the force of sublimation, but are dragged into the foreground where they risk upsetting the unity of responses from which a work of art derives its independent life.
>
> (Clark 1956: 6)

Embedded within this account are tacit, gender-based assumptions about the naked and the nude. The naked body is equated with lowly passion, femininity and objectification. The nude, in contrast, has connotations of elevated 'masculine attributes' such as reason, culture and the subject (Nead 1992: 14). As Wolf comments:

> To live in a culture in which women are routinely naked where men aren't is to learn inequality in little ways all day long. So even if we agree sexual imagery is a language, it is clearly one that is heavily edited to protect men's sexual – and hence – social confidence, while undermining that of women.
>
> (Wolf 1990: 139)

The question as to why the nude male is so much more threatening than the female is, therefore, central to any critique of patriarchy. Although the male nude was a symbol of power and beauty in the statues and figures of classicism, its portrayals have been shrouded in controversy ever since the Council of Trent, in 1563, declared that 'lascivious portrayal of unashamed beauty is sacred and forbidden' (quoted in Cooper 1995: 8). The subsequent impact of this edict has lasted for well over four hundred years to the present day. Indeed, until very recently, the only acceptable themes in which the naked male body could be depicted were pain and suffering, and it is really within the last decade or so that the male nude has been 'fully exposed', so to speak, in the work of photographers like Robert Mapplethorpe.

Heterosexual men, in particular, appear to perceive the male nude as an alarming reminder of their own vulnerability. The 1978 'Male Nude' exhibition in New York, for example, gave rise to a variety of negative comments from largely male critics including: 'A man's body doesn't lend itself to abstraction like a woman's' and: 'Nude women seem to be in their natural state, for some reason men merely look undressed'. Another exhibition in London evoked an equally hostile response with comments in the visitor's book such as: 'Should please a few queers', 'a right poofter's show', and numerous letters of complaint about the 'blasphemous plagiarism from the Bible' that was indistinguishable from pornography (reported in Cooper 1995: 184). Whilst the rest of the body can be 'worked on' and 'built up', penis size, by and large, remains fixed, thus making it highly problematic to compete with potential media 'ideals' and popular myths surrounding the 'male member'. Deep-seated (male) anxieties about penis size and comparability may, therefore, form an unspoken rationale for the continuing ban on erections in photography and film (Cooper 1995).[14] Predictably, however, in a competitive, narcissistic age such as ours, plastic surgery techniques for penile enlargement are now being developed – techniques that, although not widely available, are potentially hazardous to health.

Despite these anxieties, fears and phobias, the unclothed male body is now becoming increasingly apparent in contemporary Western society. Whilst there are obvious benefits to raising men's consciousness about their bodies – an issue given much prominence in the current era of AIDS and the contemporary emphasis on men's health issues – there are also, as with women, potential hazards concerning the dividing line between representation and exploitation. Although ostensibly obeying the 'erection ban', overt political consciousness-raising magazines such as *Gay News*, for example, now carry semi-pornographic advertisements and homoerotic pinups in which images of well-developed muscular men with enormous half-erect penises 'sell' phone lines inviting the listener to 'sit on this' or 'suck it and see' (see Plate 10.2). In doing so, the male gaze is, paradoxically, turned back upon itself: a process in which objectification of the male body is promoted rather than challenged by men themselves. These advertisements are not, however, sold as pornography and they lie cheek-by-jowl with serious investigative journalism aimed at exposing injustice and discrimination.

Yet commercialisation and commodification of the male body is not confined to gay culture. Rather, it has been generalised throughout contemporary Western society with the growth of consumer culture, particularly advertising aimed at women – gaining cult status in the late 1980s with the notorious Levi jeans advert, which featured a famous male model stripping down to his underpants and washing his clothes publicly in a launderette – often under the guise of 'female liberation'. Magazines such as *For Women* and *British Playgirl*, feature erotica of various sorts (whilst still observing the 'no erection' rule), and the (idealised) male body is now used to sell everything from domestic cleaners to soft drinks.[15] More generally, it has become commonplace for groups of women workers to spend their evenings watching male strippers like the 'Chippendales' for a 'good night out with the girls'.

These, and many other examples of 'reverse sexism' could be used to support the popular media conception that the 'objectified' male body will redress the historical imbalance between genders. Women, as Wolf comments:

> could probably be trained quite easily to see men first as sexual things. If girls never experienced sexual violence; if a girl's only window on male sexuality were a stream of easily available, well-lit, cheap images of boys slightly older than herself, in their late teens, smiling encouragingly and revealing cuddly erect penises the colour of roses or mocha, she might well look at, masturbate to, and, as an adult, 'need' beauty pornography based on the bodies of men. And if these initiating penises were represented to the girl as pneumatically erectable, swerving neither to left nor right, tasting of cinnamon or forest berries, innocent of random hairs, and ever ready; if they were presented their measurements, length and circumference to the quarter inch; if they seemed to be available to her with no troublesome personality attached; if her sweet pleasure seemed to be the only reason for them to exist – then a real young man would

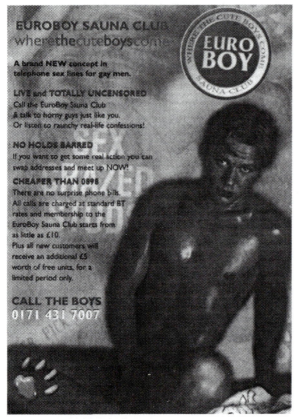

Plate 10.2 Advertisement for 'Euroboy Sauna Club'

Source: Reprinted from *Gay Times* (June 1996). Designed and photographed by Neal Cavalier-Smith of Prowler Press

probably approach the young woman's bed with, to say the least, a failing heart.

(Wolf 1990: 154)

Despite this recent upsurge of interest in male bodies, however, it is arguable whether it compares, in any real way, with the long history of objectification of the female body, particularly in consumer culture where 'idealised' body images appear to weigh most heavily on women's shoulders. For many years, as Cooper notes:

women have regularly had such comparisons forced upon them: beautiful slim figures . . . page three pinups invariably show models with large firm well-rounded breasts . . . women constantly have to compete with such models, and may very easily be made to feel inferior.

(Cooper 1995: 185)

There are also worrying health implications in these trends, as witnessed, for example, in the rapid rise of eating disorders amongst young women, and the steady increase in male anorexia (see Chapter 4, this volume). For some feminist critics, this depiction of the male body is yet another *man*ifestation of masculine strength – one that underlines rather than challenges male power. From this viewpoint, it is questionable whether the objectification of the male body for commercial, sexual or artistic purposes, really does represent a significant step forward in the continuing struggle for sexual equality. Perhaps more cynically, it may simply reflect the increased spending power of both women and gay men. At worst, it merely serves as a form of 'revenge', enabling women to reverse the discriminatory practices of thousands of years, acting towards men in ways that are undermining, degrading and humiliating.

Autobiographical art: pain, suffering and the human condition

As well as reflecting a core feature of society, challenging dominant beliefs and exposing underlying values, art provides a powerful medium for the expression of biographical themes concerning artists' own embodied lives and existential predicaments. Whilst a variety of artists could be used to illustrate these autobiographical themes and corporeal dilemmas, three in particular stand out in terms of their own personal depiction of pain, suffering and the human condition – including sickness, sleep and its symbolic associations with death.

The first of these is, of course, the expressionist painter Edvard Munch (1863–1944). The son of a doctor, raised in late nineteenth-century Norwegian middle-class society, Munch experienced a tragic life beset by illness and loss. His mother died of consumption when he was 5 years old, and his sister Sophie when he was 13. In his adult life, Munch's other sister, Laura, was institutionalised suffering from schizophrenia and his brother, Andreas, died after a brief and unhappy marriage. This, together with his own unhappy love affairs, alcoholism and an inability to settle in any one place, meant that Munch could not help but express his troubled life through his paintings.

The Dead Mother and Child, for example, depicts the death of his own mother. In an interesting temporal twist, the only family member portrayed in terms of their actual age at the time of bereavement is Sophie, a 6-year old child whose face is distorted in silent unspeakable horror with her hands over her ears.[16] The shrouded corpse of the mother is also presented at a flat foreshortened angle in *The Death Bed*, throwing into pale relief the hands and faces, but not the features, of the grieving adults, as death's dark shadow approaches. In this painting, as in *Death in the Sick Room*, which depicts Sophie's own death, the mourners are again portrayed, not in terms of their actual age, but the age they were at the time of the picture, as if to suggest they are forever frozen in the presence of death.[17] Sickness, as Munch tragically remarked, followed him throughout his entire childhood and youth: 'those I loved most died, one after the other' (quoted in Wood 1992: 3).

Following these tragic childhood events, Munch inextricably linked women and sexuality with fear and death. *Puberty*, for example, displays a young pubescent girl sitting naked on her narrow bed almost overwhelmed by the large menacing shadow of her own body, suggesting the perils of the future. In Munch's girl, as Bischoff remarks:

> we perceive both awakening sexuality and a sense of being at the mercy of the Unknown: we see this in her wide-open eyes, and in the crossing of her arms over the pubic region (in terms of body language, this position speaks volumes) . . . the conjunction of fear and sexuality which was to become central in *The Frieze of Life*.
>
> (Bischoff 1993: 34)

Building on these themes, paintings such as *The Sphinx* and *The Dance of Life* juxtapose symbolic representations of the 'ideal', submissive, virginal woman dressed in white, with an erotically threatening, oppressively sexual, woman in red. The consummation of love is depicted in *The Kiss*, whereby the couple merge into one another and lose their identities (cf. Bataille 1987 [1962] on eroticism). In *Vampire*, in contrast, originally entitled *Love and Pain*, Munch returns to the theme of predatory, sexually oppressive women. These troubling qualities are also conveyed in *Madonna*, but linked, this time, with the female capacity to generate new life. Again, the woman is portrayed as a classic combination of virgin and whore, wearing a saintly halo but smiling voluptuously at the climax of sexual love and at the moment of conception, whilst the border of the painting is symbolically decorated with sperm and foetuses. These and other paintings such as *Jealousy*, *Separation* and *Melancholy*, progressively depict love, undermined by infidelity, leading to anxiety, loss and despair – feelings symbolised through bowed heads and brooding dispositions. Woman, in short, for Munch, was 'a parasite on [Man's] spiritual existence' (Munch, quoted in Wood 1992).[18]

Uncontrollable anxiety and despair reach their peak in *The Scream*, a painting that, despite its mass production and commercialism, still remains an intensely powerful and evocative image of the human condition. As Munch himself described it, this was inspired during a bout of illness in 1892:

> I felt tired and ill. I stopped and looked out over the fjord – the sun was setting and the clouds turned blood-red. I paused, feeling exhausted and leaned on a fence – there was blood and tongues of fire above the blue-black fjord and the city – my friends walked on, and there I still stood, trembling with fear. I sensed a scream passing through nature; it seemed to me that I heard a scream. I painted this picture, painted the clouds as actual blood. The colour shrieked.
>
> (quoted in Bischoff 1993: 53)

If Munch provides one vivid illustration of the relationship between art and embodiment, then Frida Kahlo's (1907–54) life of personal tragedy provides another. Born into a bourgeois family in Mexico City, the third daughter of a Mexican mother and German father, Kahlo contracted polio at the age of 6, and sustained serious injuries to her spine in a bus crash aged 17 – afflictions that resulted in her undergoing numerous operations on her foot and spine throughout her life. At the age of 22, she married the famous revolutionary artist, Diego Rivera, and although they had a passionate relationship throughout their lives, one that combined intellectual and artistic creativity, Rivera's infidelities (including an affair with Frida's younger sister) caused her much pain and misery, as did her repeated miscarriages and inability to bear children. They divorced in 1939, only to be remarried a year later, yet despite her poor health, Kahlo continued to be politically and creatively active until her death from pneumonia at the age of 47.

Like Munch, many of the major events of Kahlo's life were documented in her paintings, often in extraordinary anatomical detail. *My Birth*, for example, depicts her own birth in the form of an adult woman's head emerging from the womb of a naked female, her legs splayed but her face covered by a sheet – an image referring both to a recent miscarriage and the death of her own mother whilst working on the picture. This theme of miscarriage is also graphically portrayed in *Henry Ford Hospital*, a painting that shows the artist lying naked on a massive hospital bed soaked in blood in the middle of a vast plain, with an industrial city in the background. Over her abdomen, still swollen from pregnancy, she holds several red strings resembling arteries which are connected to symbols of her female sexuality and failed pregnancy, such as the lost child, an anatomical model of the lower body showing her damaged backbone, a faulty piece of machinery, a snail and an orchid (Kettenman 1992). The vulnerability of the body in the huge bed conveys Kahlo's profound sense of loneliness, helplessness and despair in the face of her inescapable corporeal predicament.

This combination of physical and emotional suffering is also graphically conveyed in *The Broken Column* – painted when Kahlo's own health had deteriorated to the point where she had to wear a steel corset. The painting depicts her painful, 'nail-ridden body' encased in this steel corset, set against a barren, fissured plain and cloudless sky. A broken Ionic column has replaced her spine but her face, although covered in tears, is impassive and bleak. Similarly, in *The Heart*, emotional pain is conveyed through a portrayal in which disembodied arms and dresses use a sword to pierce a hole where her heart lies – a pictorial expression of the anguish Kahlo suffered during the affair between her husband and sister. Her broken heart lies bleeding by her disfigured foot, its disproportionate size communicating the scale and intensity of her pain, and her helplessness indicated through her lack of hands. In these and many other self portraits, Kahlo is able to express and impart a life of passion and pain lived through her own body.

In a more contemporary vein, Jo Spence (1934–92) has used photographic images of her body as a means of coming to terms with cancer and the imminent possibility of death. Beginning her career as a commercial portrait photographer, Spence's political convictions compelled her to abandon this in favour of more socially engaged documentary photography. Whilst Spence had already begun to challenge classical art forms, including the female nude, her important work on health dates from 1982, when she started to document and research her own recently diagnosed breast cancer. After insisting on having a lumpectomy rather than radical mastectomy, she stabilised her cancer for nine years through a rigorous naturopathic health diet only to find, in 1991, she had developed chronic lymphatic leukaemia – thought to be due to overwork and neglect of her diet – from which she died, aged 58.

Spence's (1986) frank photographs concerning her bold struggle with cancer, vividly illustrate the experience of 'fragmentation' and the battle against reification which encounters with biomedicine and the ravages of the 'diseased' body bring in their wake. The words *How Do I Begin to Take Responsibility for my Body?'*, for example, are featured on a montage of different parts of Spence's body centred around a mirror image of herself carrying out an exercise routine for her pectoral muscles (see Plate 10.3). Building on these themes, *Rite of Passage* shows Spence's 'pre-surgical' body wrapped in a sheet with an 'X' inscribed above the breast to be operated upon, whilst *Narratives of Disease* shows her faceless naked body with the damaged breast, first with a rosette marked 'Booby Prize', and second, with the word 'Monster' written across her thorax (see Plate 10.4).

Through this medium of 'visual narrative', Spence (1986) attempted to open up for critical discussion and debate the (medical) politics of women's bodies, extending private and personal images into the public domain, and challenging dominant images of disease, disfigurement and disability. This work continued until her death, including an extraordinary collaborative book with David Hevey (1992) on photography and disability imagery, entitled *The Creatures Time Forgot* – one that celebrates the struggle for alternative imagery surrounding the 'disabled body', and in doing so, questions our very assumptions about 'able' bodiedness itself (see Plate 10.5). Spence's work was also recently featured in '*Our Bodies, Ourselves*', a photographic exhibition on women's health in which other female artists also featured themselves in their pictures. Clare Park, for instance, staged scenes in which she re-enacted her response to anorexia, including a photograph of her naked self crouched under a table with her head and lower face bandaged as she holds a piece of fruit in her hands.[19]

Taken as a whole, what these artists exemplify, in the spirit and practice of their craft, are the outlines of a truly embodied sociology, one that, healthy or sick, happy or sad, epic or tragic, is never simply *about* bodies, but emerges instead *from* bodies and their praxical engagement with a social world of hope and despair.

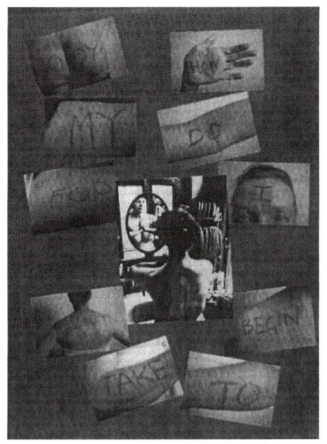

Plate 10.3 How Do I Begin to Take Responsibility for My Body?
Source: Reprinted from J. Spence (1986) *Putting Myself in the Picture*, London: Camden Press. Copyright permission from Terry Dennett, curator of Jo Spence Memorial Archive

Conclusions

Art, as we have seen, is central to an embodied sociology. Not only does art, in its manifold forms, reflect and reinforce dominant beliefs and ideologies within the broader body/politic, it also constitutes a key site of (embodied) 'resistance' to prevailing modes of discourse with their 'normalising' assumptions. In these and many other respects, the boundaries between art and social theory, science and morality, begin to blur if not collapse, thereby opening up new spaces and possibilities of 'becoming' (other). Indeed, it is this emphasis on 'embodied praxis' (i.e. performance art) and 'visual narratives' (i.e. autobiographical art) that, we have argued, provides an important counterweight to the predominantly textual forms of representation within sociology to-date. Perhaps most radically of all, art, in its manifold forms,

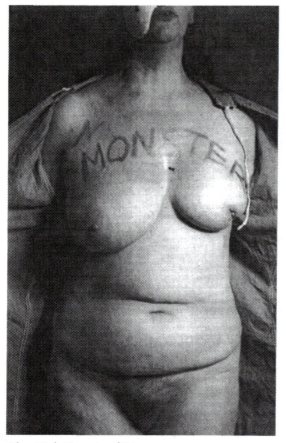

Plate 10.4 Narrative of Disease

opens up wider possibilities for a critical celebration of embodied *sensuality* –
one in which reason is no longer prioritised over emotion, and new ways of
'being', 'seeing' and 'relating' to the world – including those 'anatomies of
the cyborg' mentioned at the beginning of this chapter – can freely evolve.[20]

To return to the initial question posed at the beginning of this chapter, far
from being an 'odd couple', the 'marriage' of sociology and art provides,
therefore, some fertile new terrain upon which evolving debates concerning
the dilemmas of human embodiment – including the relationship between
'experience' and 'representation', 'reason' and 'emotion', 'aestheticism' and
'eroticism', 'reproduction' and 'resistance' and so on – can take root and
flourish.

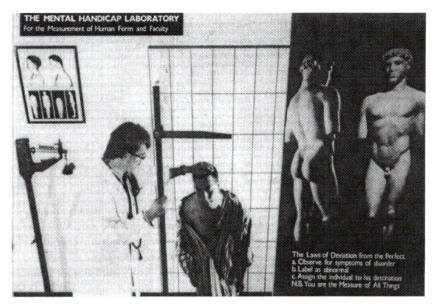

Plate 10.5 The Mental Handicap Laboratory

Source: Reprinted from D. Hevey (ed.) (1992) *The Creatures Time Forgot: Photography and Disability Imagery*, London: Routledge. Designed and photographed by Jessica Evans, Open University, Milton Keynes

Conclusions

A central argument running throughout this book has been that the dualist legacies of the past – legacies which have sought to divorce mind from body, nature from culture and reason from emotion – have proved unnecessarily limiting in approaching the question of human embodiment. In this respect, we have surveyed a variety of different theoretical perspectives on the body which have been evaluated in the light of these dichotomous modes of thought and the associated problems they raise for a more 'integrated' approach to human embodiment as both nature and culture.

Dual*ity*, we have suggested, is a stage, albeit an analytically important one, in the 'development' of human consciousness – one founded, despite its obvious appeal, on a problematic view of mind/body relations. More broadly, as we have seen, the transformation of this duality into an '*ism*' – one in which the mind/body divide appears somehow 'natural', rational and unconditional – sets in train a series of other unfortunate consequences, including the ideological separation of nature from culture, reason from emotion, public from private, and so on. Rather than dispense with these analytical categories altogether, however, they must be engaged with in order to move 'forward', so to speak, to a 'third' stage of development; one 'prepared for', as it were, by these previous stages of conceptual distinction and analytical elaboration.

In responding to this challenge, we have sought to reconcile these former divisions through the unifying notion of the *lived*, experiential, body – an active, expressive, 'mindful' form of *embodiment* that serves not only as the existential basis of culture and self, but also of social institutions and society more generally. To the extent that embodiment, as a praxical relationship to the world and the primordial basis of our being within it, may be thought of in this way, it provides an important source of challenge to 'representational' theories in which mind/subject/culture are prioritised over body/object/biology. Pushing these arguments further, it is mind that emerges from body, not vice versa. In this way, a certain bodily 'realism' is retained, thus puncturing the overinflated claims of constructionists and their privileging of the 'social'. The 'mindful' body, in other words, is no mere artefact of society, rather it provides the *active* sentient basis of agency and meaning creation in relational and social forms.

Embodiment – an 'uncontainable' term in one domain or discourse – captures the essential ambiguity of human being as both nature and culture, and the transcendence of duality at the pre-objective level of lived ongoing experience. Here, mind and body, reason and emotion, can only be arbitrarily separated by an act of conscious reflection and objectification (*Cogito ergo sum*). These processes, as we have seen, are well captured through Grosz's (1994) corporeal appropriation of the Möbius strip – a three-dimensional model that shows, through an inverted figure eight, a relation between two 'things' (e.g. mind and body) which presumes neither total identity nor a radical disjunction, but a capacity instead to 'twist' one into the other. In taking this position, however, we readily acknowledge the fact that no 'single', 'final', resolution to these problems is possible: even the idea of 'going beyond' dichotomies creates its own duality (i.e. dichotomous versus non-dichotomous modes of thought). None the less, what our approach does constitute, we believe, is a more satisfactory *approximation* to such a 'resolution', dispensing on the way, with the associated ideological baggage of past dualisms.

The argument here, is not simply for a 'sociology *of* the body' (in which the body is 'objectified' or 'subjectified' from 'outside', so to speak), rather that sociology should itself be fundamentally *embodied*; theorising not so much *about* bodies (in a largely disembodied male way) but *from* bodies as *lived* entities, including those of its practitioners as well as its subjects. Social institutions and discursive practices cannot be understood apart from the real lived experiences and actions of embodied human beings across time and space. Social theory must therefore be rooted in the problems of human embodiment. Only on this basis can we begin to put minds back in bodies, bodies back in society, and society back into bodies. Here we return to Frank's (1991a) typology of body use in action, and his reworking of Giddens' structuration theory in corporeal terms (see Chapter 3, this volume).

These arguments, as we have seen, are well illustrated through a focus on the 'emotionally expressive' body. To be sure, emotions involve a biological or physiological substrate, but they are also precisely the means whereby human bodies achieve a 'social ontology'. Emotions, in other words, play a fundamental role in embodied human agency and social praxis. Far from being individualistic in orientation, a focus on embodiment can, therefore, lead to a deeper awareness of the sociality of human being and emotion. Viewed from this perspective, it becomes quite possible to characterise social institutions in terms of the bodily forms which they necessitate and which make them possible. Social relations, in short, can be understood in terms of their characteristic bodily relations (Lyon and Barbalet 1994), and embodied agency can, in turn, as an emotional mode of being-in-the-world, be understood not merely in individual terms as 'meaning making', but also in social terms as 'institution-making' (Csordas 1994a).

As with emotions, so with pain. Pain, as we have argued, lies at the intersection of minds, bodies and cultures, challenging former dualistic modes of thought and the dominant voice of medicine which reduces it to a mere 'signal function'. As an emotional as well as physical experience, pain is rooted in the lived, expressive body, linked as it is to the wider sociocultural realms of meaning and significance through the narratives of suffering and idioms of distress it calls forth. Seen in these terms, pain provides a perfect example of how a foundationalist ontology of the body (as a material, pre-social entity) can profitably be combined with a social–constructionist epistemology – one in which culture and narrative fill the existential space between the 'immediate embodiment of disease as brute materiality' and its 'meaning-laden character as human experience' (Kleinman 1988). A truly satisfactory account of pain must also, however, confront the enduring power of these dichotomies at the experiential level. As an 'anti-language', pain, paradoxically, 'deconstructs our world', shattering the self into a 'series of lived oppositions' and rendering all meaning meaningless. Here we return to the 'discursive limits' of social constructionism and the need for more complex, foundational, approaches to the body, disease and illness.

Where then does all this leave us, and what future agendas does it suggest for a truly embodied sociology? It is to questions such as these that we now turn in closing. In addition to the need for a more sophisticated under-standing of human embodiment, including the embodiment of social action, the social reciprocity of bodies over time, and their sociocultural and histor-ical formation (Turner 1994), greater attention also needs to be paid, we believe, to the following key issues. First, as suggested above, there is a need for more integrated analytical frameworks and the development of 'link' concepts between the different levels of analysis pertaining to the body/self/society relationship. Certainly there are promising signs here – including Falk's (1994) recent theory of the 'consuming body' and Mellor's and Shilling's (1997) account of the interrelationship between human sociality, the sacred and embodied patterns of reality construction since the Middle Ages – as previously antagonistic positions are gradually 'reconciled' in the interests of a more coherent approach to the question of human embodiment. The conceptual means of achieving this, in our view, involve a move from phenomenologically embodied notions such as the *body-subject* and *body-image* (e.g. Merleau-Ponty and Schilder), through a focus on *body tech-niques* – including the socialised dispositions of the habitus – and *intercorporeality* (e.g. Mauss, Bourdieu and Goffman), to broader historical and institutional issues of *bio-power* and the *civilising process* in the work of writers such as Foucault and Elias. By bringing these approaches together in this way, we obtain a more sophisticated grasp of corporeal awareness and the practical modes of mastery and hermeneutic *techne* this involves, located as they are in broader historical webs of power/knowledge and 'resistance' (Crossley 1993, 1994, 1996). It is here, through an 'imperceptible twist' that the bodily 'inside' becomes the 'outside' and the corporeal 'outside', in turn, flips over to become the 'inside'.

This emphasis on integrated analytical frameworks also returns us to another central question concerning the relationship between art, the body and social theory. As we have argued, not only does art, in its manifold forms, reflect and reinforce dominant beliefs and ideologies about the body and society, it also throws into critical relief the relationship between *experience* and *representation, aestheticism* and *eroticism, regulation* and *resistance*. Performance art in particular, especially women's body art, enacts power and resistance on the *site of the body itself* as a mode of communicative praxis, thereby effacing the boundary between art and social theory. Here, the dilemmas of modernity and civilisation, power and ideology, emotions and rationality, pleasure and pain, life and death, are vividly brought to life, played out through the strokes of an artist's brush, the form and contours of classical sculpture, the realism captured through the photographer's lens, or the expressive performativity of the communicative body in dance. In these and many other ways, art challenges the dominance of the spoken and written text, so prevalent in social theory today, providing powerful visual narratives and embodied statements of the human condition, past, present and future.

Moving from the problem of integrated analytical frameworks, and the relationship between art and social theory, to a third key issue, there is clearly a need to rethink fundamentally the 'biological' in non-reductionist terms if it is to be satisfactorily incorporated into a truly embodied form of sociology. For far too long, the biological has been dismissed as 'irrelevant' to the sociological enterprise. To claim a biological foundation for the body does not necessarily imply reductionism if the very nature of biology itself is fundamentally rethought within the social sciences. Biology is not simply a 'limit' or 'constraint'. Rather, it provides the active basis and transformative potential of our embodied being-in-the-world. Without a certain level of evolutionary development, including a biological capacity for tool and language use, 'society' would not be possible. It is society, however, that 'completes' human beings as 'unfinished creatures', transforming the raw material of biological dispositions into socially valued skills and culturally defined attributes.

These issues are perfectly illustrated in relation to children's bodies, in which processes of biological development and social maturation intertwine in complex ways that mirror, within one lifetime, the long historical curve of the civilising process across numerous generations. Sleep, too, as we have seen, is an embodied activity and inescapable biological fact that spans a number of traditional divisions and divides, including the material and the social, time and space, the public and the private – located as it is at the intersection of physiological *need*, environmental *constraint*, and sociocultural *elaboration*. Indeed, sleep provides a particularly fascinating example of the 'socially pliable' nature of human biology. Seen in these terms, biology is not merely a 'constant', rather it is in a state of considerable flux and indeterminacy, influenced in no small part by the sociocultural and material environment.

This discussion of the 'biological' again returns us to the 'knot of natural difference'. As we have seen, the tensions between biology and society, essentialism and social constructionism have been hotly debated by feminists over the decades. Increasingly, however, in keeping with the broader move towards more integrated theoretical frameworks discussed above, a reconceptualisation of the 'sexed' body as both a material and social entity has taken place. In doing so, feminists have argued against the all too easy equation of biology with essentialism. Rather, whilst accepting the existence of a pre-social, material body – including corporeal experiences unique to women such as menstruation, pregnancy, childbirth, lactation and menopause – the central issue involves a 're-writing' of the female body as a 'positivity' rather than a 'lack'. Being the raw material of social and cultural organisation, the sexually specific body is subject to the endless rewriting and inscription that constitute all sign systems. It is social practice that distorts, transforms or negates our common biological heritage. Stripped of its ideological baggage, biology, therefore, provides a radical critique rather than justification of existing social arrangements. More generally, this corporeal unease at the tendency to 'write out' the raw biological material of the human body, so prevalent in social theory today, suggests the need to investigate the 'interior depths' as well as the exterior surfaces of the body, including current imaging of the immune system and the cultural encoding of the human genome (Birke 1995).

All in all, this suggests an exciting and indeed challenging future for an 'embodied sociology', spanning as it does a diverse array of issues, including pain and emotions, children and ageing, sleep and death, art and social theory. This, coupled with continuing debates over the (post)modern body, consumption and risk, gender and sexuality, and the implications of cyberspace, the cyborg and the new 'genetics', for traditional modes of embodied subjectivity, point to a thriving corporeal research agenda extending well into the twenty-first century.

As to the question of whether we should be pursuing an *embodied* sociology or a sociology *of* embodiment – an issue that mirrors the debate over a *postmodern* sociology or a sociology *of* postmodernity – the position adopted throughout this book has been to emphasise the former without wholly discarding the latter. Only on this basis, we have suggested, can sociologists – as embodied practitioners and living, thinking, feeling agents – put minds back into bodies, bodies back into society, and society back into the body. To adopt any other stance is, quite simply, to perpetuate the very sort of disembodied myths and dualistic positions from which we have been trying to escape.

Whatever its future direction, one thing remains clear, namely, that in this world of uncertain times and digitally mediated forms of communication, any truly human notion of ethics and trust must ultimately be grounded in and return us to our embodied being-in-the-world and the life–political agenda this raises. From this viewpoint, not only are the 'playful' deconstructions of postmodernism really only an option for the healthy rather than the sick (Charlton 1993; Williams and Bendelow 1998), but the 'disembodied

visions' of cyberspace and virtual reality constitute an 'evasion of our responsibilities in the real world', from global warming to the starving children of
Rwanda, and from the risks of the new genetics to the senseless torture and
killings of numerous wars both past and present (Slouka 1995). Embodiment,
in short, a common carnal bond, becomes both our hope and our salvation.

Notes

Introduction

1 With both Descartes and Kant, reason is defined as an 'independent faculty', set in opposition to our 'animal natures' (see Seidler 1994).
2 In stressing these issues, we are not, of course, denying the existence of alternative non-dualist traditions to draw upon – from Schopenhauer to Nietzsche, Spinoza to Merleau-Ponty – only the dominance of this particular rationalist view of the world in the history of Western thought.

1 Sociology and the 'problem' of the body

1 See, for example, Turner (1984/1996), Shilling (1993) and Frank (1990, 1991a).
2 Connell (1987) usefully distinguishes here between two main versions of the naturalistic doctrine of 'difference': the first taking society to be epiphenomenal to nature, the second seeing the two as somehow additive. See also Shilling for another interesting and informative account of 'naturalistic' bodies, including a useful critique of the dubious premises upon which they rest.
3 Husband (1982), Kiernan (1982), Jordan (1982, 1969) and Walvin (1982), for example, provide a series of fascinating accounts and critiques of the history of racism and slavery, including (pseudo-scientific) appeals to so-called 'natural difference'; beliefs and convictions which, implicitly or explicitly, evoke notions of 'purity' and 'danger', the 'civilised' and the 'barbaric', based on centuries of colonial rule. For a similar treatment of the 'making' of 'sex', from the Greeks to Freud, see Laqueur (1987).
4 Building on this notion of *homo duplex*, together with the views developed in *Primitive Classification* (Durkheim and Mauss 1975 [1902]) and *Elementary Forms of Religious Life* (Durkheim 1961 [1912]) concerning the *irrational* bases of human sociality, Mellor and Shilling (1997) have recently argued that Durkheim's work can be read as a 'direct, corporeally oriented challenge' to previous cognitive and rationalist readings of his work – i.e. the focus on an ordered realm of 'social facts' (see also Shilling 1997; Mestrovic 1997, 1991). This alternative, emotionally-informed/corporeally oriented reading is discussed more fully in Chapter 7, this volume.
5 For a fascinating study of the history and cultural significance of the bodily senses, see Classen (1993).
6 These issues are most clearly expressed in Simmel's classic sociological essay on 'The Metropolis and Mental Life': particularly his discussion of reserve and the blasé outlook. Instead of reacting emotionally to the fluctuations and discontinuities of the external milieux, the metropolitan type reacts primarily 'in a rational manner, thus creating a mental predominance through the intensification of

consciousness . . . which is furthest removed from the depths of personality'
(Simmel 1971: 326).

7 For an interesting recent attempt to reconstruct Parsons in a more postmodern
vein, see Frank (1991b).

8 In writing his book *Body and Society*, for example, Turner confesses to becoming
increasingly uncertain as to what precisely 'the body is' (1984: 7). Indeed, as
suggested earlier, a multitude of 'bodies' now litter the pages of academic books
and journals, the list growing longer everyday. In addition, of course, we also
now have the well-rehearsed German distinction between *Korper* (i.e. the fleshy
shell) and *Leib* (i.e. the 'lived' body), as well as the elaboration of this division
into the body *incarnate* (i.e. the living body), the *corporeal* (i.e. the fleshy shell)
and the *somatic* (i.e. the medicalised body) (Frankenberg 1990). Nowhere is this
uncertainty more clearly evident, however, than in postmodern writing, through
its abandonment of the modernist project of 'knowing' the body as an ontological essence. Instead, in its most extreme versions, the body is simply viewed as
a 'sign-receiving system' or worse still a 'body-without-organs'; one which is
endlessly elaborated through a processes of (re)inscription, (re/de)territorialisa-
tion and the endless play of intertextual effects (Kroker and Kroker 1988;
Deleuze and Guattari 1988, 1984; Fox 1993). Indeed, given the postmodern
'sign-fetishim' of writers such as Baudrillard (1983a,b, 1988), the body ultimately 'disappears' altogether through an endless chain of self-referential
images/simulacra without any 'external' referents (see also Radley (1995) for a
critique of this 'elusive' body).

9 See also D. Johnson's *Body* (1983); O'Neill's *Five Bodies* (1985) and *The
Communicative Body* (1989); M. Johnson's *The Body in the Mind* (1987); Martin's
The Woman in the Body (1987); Barker's *The Tremulous Body* (1989); and Feher's *et
al.* three-volume edited collection, *Fragments for a History of the Body* (1989a,b,c).
More recently, other key texts have appeared such as Leder's *The Absent Body*
(1990); Pouchelle's *The Body and Surgery in the Middle Ages* (1990); Turner's
Regulating Bodies (1992); Synnott's *The Body Social* (1993); Grosz's *Volatile Bodies*
(1994); Mellor and Shilling's *Re-forming the Body* (1997); and Shildrick's *Leaky
Bodies* (1997) .

10 Stripped to its bare essence, sociobiology – the leading exponent of whom is
E. O. Wilson (1975, 1994) – views individual behaviour, culture and social structure as the end products of processes of biological selection and genetic
transmission. Indeed, according to sociobiologists, everything from altruism to
the assumed greater promiscuity of males is capable of explanation in biological
evolutionary terms. In this respect, as Husband notes, sociobiology represents a
complex 'fusion of Darwinian evolutionary theory with modern population
genetics', combining principles of 'survival of the fittest' with sophisticated
models of genetic transmission (Husband 1982: 17). Perhaps the most successful
populariser of these views in Britain is Richard Dawkins, whose book *The Selfish
Gene* (1976) enjoyed widespread exposure. See also Morris (1967, 1969).
  On the one hand, as Connell (1987) notes, these biologically reductionist
arguments are too weak to account for the social phenomena they try to explain.
On the other hand, however, they appear far too strong, presupposing a mechanism of genetic or hormonal control far more powerful than physiological
research has actually found. The upshot of these arguments is clear: 'innate
differences' in human evolutionary development pale into insignificance when
compared to the 'common capacities', from bipedalism to tool and language use,
which serve to 'mark us off' from other species and constitute the 'evolutionary
jump' from pre-wired biological drives to human history. Seen in these terms,
biological reductionism is 'two or three million years out of date' (Connell

1987: 71–2). See also Shilling (1993) and Kaplan and Rogers (1990) for other useful critiques.

11 See also Barchas (1976) for an interesting account of 'physiological sociology'.

12 Landmark texts here include, in the US, Pleck and Sawyer's edited volume *Men and Masculinity* (1974), and in the UK, Tolson's *The Limits of Masculinity* (1977), which developed an economic class analysis of post-war masculinities. (See also Pleck and Pleck's *The American Man* (1980), Pleck's *The Myth of Masculinity* (1982) and Metcalf's and Humphries' *The Sexuality of Men* (1985).) More recently, other key texts have included: Kimmel's edited collection *Changing Men* (1987); Theweleit's two-volume study *Male Fantasies* (1987/[1977], 1989/[1978]); Jeffords' *The Re-Masculinization of America* (1989) and *Hard Bodies* (1994); Hearn and Morgan's edited volume *Men, Masculinity and Social Theory* (1990b); Morgan's *Discovering Men* (1992); Connell's work on *Masculinities* (1993, 1995); Seidler's analysis of *Unreasonable Men* (1994); and Cornwall and Lindisfarne's edited collection of comparative ethnographies entitled *Dislocating Masculinities* (1994). To this list we may also add Robert Bly's *Iron John* (1990), subtitled: *A Book About Men*, in which it is argued that men have 'lost touch' with their emotions and need to communicate with each other in order to find their 'inner', 'true' selves.

13 For an insightful discussion of the mutually informative relationship between queer theory and sociology, together with a more general account of the former's contextual emergence, see Seidman (1996).

14 See also Wacquant (1995a) for a recent extension of this approach to boxers as 'entrepreneurs of physical capital'.

15 For a poststructuralist Deleuzo-Guattarian analysis of similar issues in relation to youth/rave culture, see Jordan (1995).

16 See also Prendergast (1995) on adolescent menstruation.

17 Key texts here include: Armstrong on the *Political Anatomy of the Body* (1983); Sontag (1991) and Herzlich and Pierret (1988) on illness as metaphor; Townsend *et al.* (1988) and Wilkinson (1996) on social inequalities in health; Anderson and Bury (1988), Kleinman (1988) and Sacks (1985) on the experience of (chronic) illness; Bunton *et al.* (1995) on health/risk and consumption in the 'epidemiological clinic' of late modern medicine, and Lupton on the *Imperative of Health* (1995a); Zola (1972, 1991), Oakley (1984) and Martin (1987) on the 'medicalised' body; Robinson (1994) and Williams and Calnan (1996) on the problems and dilemmas of life and death under high-technology medicine; and Stacey (1988), James (1989, 1992), Smith (1992) and Lawlor (1991) on gender and the emotional division of labour in health care. See also, on this latter theme, recently edited collections by James and Gabe (1996) and Bendelow and Williams (1998).

2 Bodily 'order': cultural and historical perspectives on conformity and transgression

1 For a critical account of these similarities and differences, see Chapter 2 of Giddens (1992) *The Transformation of Intimacy*, Cambridge: Polity Press.

2 See also Connerton's (1989) *How Societies Remember*, for an excellent critique of the 'cognitive tilt' and discursive orientation of recent social theorising on the 'body'.

3 In this respect, Falk complements and extends Classen's (1993) analysis of the bodily senses: the configuration of which, both in terms of their number and relative order of importance, is open to significant sociocultural and historical variation. Sensory orders, in short, are not static entities, rather they emerge

over time, just like cultures and corporeal transgressions themselves (Classen 1993: 7).

3 Bodily 'control': body techniques, intercorporeality and the embodiment of social action

1 See also Connerton (1989) on how memory is sedimented or amassed within the body through incorporated practices and performances. 'Performativity', as he states, 'cannot be thought without a concept of habit; and habit cannot be thought without a notion of bodily automatisms' (Connerton 1989: 5).

2 Descartes sought to locate the source of this limited interaction between mind and body in the pineal gland, a small portion of the brain. Only here, he argued, does the mind directly exercise its power over the body, like a 'rider on horseback' (Wilson 1978).

3 Classen (1993) too explores broadly similar themes in her excellent book entitled *Worlds of Sense*. We know the world, as she rightly argues, both literally and metaphorically through our sensory and sensual bodies. The sensory foundations of many of the words we think with, for example, demonstrate not only that we 'think *about* our senses, but *through* them' (Classen 1993: 9, original emphasis).

4 The body in 'high' modernity and consumer culture

1 These points, in turn, feed into Shilling's (1997b) more general critique both of structuration theory and analytical dualism – Giddens's (1984) duality of structure thesis and Archer's (1995) morphogenetic approach – in which the weight of theoretical emphasis on consciousness (i.e. the creative powers of human reflexivity as a 'counter-weight' to the 'over-socialised' agent) neglects the 'socially shaped somatic bases of action and structure' – something that results, Shilling claims, in an 'undersocialised' view of the embodied agent.

2 Douglas and Calvez (1990), for example, have identified four popular types of attitude towards the risks of HIV infection within the lay populace – attitudes that are closely related to the physical and social body. First, a notion of the body as a *'porous'* thing that is completely open to every type of invasion; second, a view that emphasises the body's *strength*, including the possession of an effective immune system with the power to cope with infections and restore equilibrium; third, a view of the body that stresses its two *protective layers* – the physical skin with its own specific points of entry and egress, and the protective skin of the community, which classifies boundaries, controls points of entry and egress and codifies sexually acceptable and unacceptable behaviour; fourth, a view of the body as a *'machine'* – one that resonates with age-old images – whose own protective envelope, if pierced, admits invasive agents that interfere with its own internal functioning and expose it to infection. Given such a view, medical precautions are justified as part of the normal regulation of the body, alongside hygienic and prophylactic measures. Contamination by AIDS is therefore seen as a 'mistake', albeit a costly one, involving a moment's carelessness – if only a victim of AIDS had behaved properly then s/he would not have succumbed (Douglas and Calvez 1990: 453–4). See also Waldby (1996) on *AIDS and the Body Politic*.

3 The HIV test, for example, becomes a 'fetishised way of regulating bodies', invoking fears about bodily integrity, which lead to unconscious self-surveillance and the surveillance of 'others' – mandates that fit well with the 'new sobriety' discourse of late capitalism (Lupton *et al.* 1995: 105; Singer 1993, 1989).

4 The trick of consumer culture rests precisely on these unattainable ideals as the guarantee of ever renewed consumption.

5 Within consumer culture the public realm becomes infused with sexual images and enticements concerned with the 'hard sell', from car advertising to the seductive pleasures of chocolate, whilst sex aids and pornography are now marketed and sold almost as openly as other consumer products such as cosmetics, clothing and exercise products (Lupton 1994a).

6 Whilst women comprise the vast majority of those succumbing to 'the knife', there is now a steadily growing male market.

7 In the first discourse of 'control', health is seen as a moral duty that must be achieved through various 'health-promoting' behaviours. Within this discourse, weight becomes the 'metaphor within the metaphor' so to speak: to be 'thin' is not only to 'be in shape' but an unmistakable sign of self-control, discipline and will power (Crawford 1984). Here we return to Bordo's (1990) earlier point about the 'tightly controlled body' as a symbol of the 'correct attitude'. In contrast, the second discourse, health as 'release', suggests the very opposite view. Here the language of power, control and regulation is replaced by one of wellbeing, contentment and enjoyment, a view summed up in the motto: 'if it feels good, it can't be all bad' (Crawford 1984: 81).

8 For a more general discussion see Lupton's *Food, the Body and the Self* (1996).

9 Seen in these terms, it is Bourdieu's 'new petite bourgeoisie' who become the central carriers of these new trends toward the 'stylisation of life' and the cultivation of the body as a 'project' in consumer culture (Featherstone (1987b).

10 As such, cyborgs are perhaps best conceptualised on a continuum with the human organism at one end (i.e. the 'all too human pole') and the pure machine (automaton) or artificial intelligence (AI) device at the other (Featherstone and Burrows 1995: 11–12).

11 Clarke (1995) notes a difference here between 'modern' approaches to reproduction – techniques centred on achieving and/or enhancing *control* over bodies and reproductive processes for a variety of purposes via monitoring, planning, limiting, bounding and the setting up of boundaries – and so-called 'postmodern' strategies, centred around the new reproductive technologies, which concentrate instead upon the 're/de/sign' and *transformation* of reproductive bodies and processes to achieve a variety of goals, including future possibilities of ectogenesis (i.e. the creation of human life outside the womb) and cloning (i.e. the creation of genetically identical individuals).

These 'postmodern' views are also echoed by Casper (1995: 186–7), who notes how a range of contemporary technologies in science and medicine have made possible the emergence of what she terms 'fetal cyborgs' and 'techno' mothers. These include fetal visualisation technologies; fetal diagnostic technologies; technologies that enable a fetus to live inside a brain-dead woman's body; technologies that transform aborted fetuses into 'materials' for scientific research and new forms of biomedical therapy; technologies that produce physiological knowledge about fetuses; and finally, an array of fetal treatment technologies, including 'fetal surgery'.

12 As noted earlier, within late modernity, processes of social reflexive and internal referentiality have resulted in a thorough-going 'socialisation of biological mechanisms' (Giddens 1991).

13 What Giddens (1991) refers to, in more general terms, as the 'life-political' agenda of late modernity, including the politics of self-actualisation and the reconnection with potentially disturbing existential questions surrounding 'sequestrated experiences' such as sickness, madness, sexuality and death.

14 As Mellor and Shilling (1997) argue, the rational projects of modern embodiment have not 'died and gone to cyberspace'. Rather what we are witnessing is

the emergence of a 'baroque form of embodiment', marked by a sensualisation of experience, which is changing how people 'see' and 'experience' the world around them.

15 Prior (1989: 7) makes a similar set of points. To claim, as he argues, that death was hidden from the folds of everyday consciousness for most of the twentieth century is to ignore the fact that at least three disciplines – demography, as the scientific study of populations, pathology, as a science of disease, and sociology (with anthropology) as the science of society and culture – held such an object in their respective fields of vision for many decades. The latter, in particular, had discovered in death something that both reinforced and reflected the nature of the 'social'.

16 Sociologically, death was reconceptualised at this time in social terms as a 'non-scheduled' status passage, and the emphasis duly shifted to qualitative studies of dying trajectories, 'awareness contexts' and the social organisation of death and dying within the hospital (Glaser and Strauss 1965; Sudnow 1967).

5   The 'libidinal' body: psychoanalysis, critical theory and the 'problem' of human desire

1 These timely words become all the more prophetic in the light of recent developments in biotechnology such as plastic surgery, organ transplants, genetic engineering and the advent of so-called cyberspace – a situation in which the boundaries between nature, culture and technology are increasingly blurred through the 'leaky' figure of the 'cyborg' (see Chapter 4, this volume).

2 Lacan, as we shall see, derives many of his insights regarding imaginary anatomy from the work of writers such as Schilder (1950).

3 Laing's observations on the 'embodied' and 'unembodied' self are also instructive here. As he suggests, the ontologically insecure individual, particularly in times of existential crisis and schizophrenic breakdown, may come to experience themselves as primarily 'split' into mind and body: 'Instead of being the core of his [sic] true self, the body is felt as the core of a false self, which a detached, disembodied "inner", "true" self looks on at with tenderness, amusement or hatred as the case may be' (Laing 1965: 69).

4 These issues have recently been explored through the Wellcome Trust's first Sci-Art initiative, which aims to bring the techniques of science and art closer together, exploring in the process a range of corporeal themes, including body-image. Images of phantom-limbs, for example, are first generated by reversing an image of the surviving limb. Feelings of transparency, telescoping and distortion are then digitally represented in consultation with the descriptions of patients themselves. Issues such as whether amputees can 'see' as well as 'feel' a phantom-limb, and whether it 'belongs' to them, are therefore captured as the lived experience of body-image is digitally represented (Aldersey-Williams 1997: 44): a turning, in effect, of the body 'inside-out'.

5 For a general review of interdisciplinary work on body-image see Tiemersma (1989); for a recent debate on its respective merits in medical sociology see Williams (1996c) and Kelly and Field (1997).

6 This 'repressive hypothesis' has, of course, been attacked by writers such as Foucault (1979) in *The History of Sexuality* (vol. 1) (see Chapter 2).

7 Even as early as 1908 Freud, in his classic paper 'Civilised sexual morality and modern nervous illness', had suggested that the majority of the population were 'constitutionally unfit' for sexual abstinence.

8 For Freud, the super-ego, as an internal agency of civilised society, watches over the individual's aggressive desires 'like a garrison in a conquered city' (Freud 1982 [1930]: 61).

9 Elias (1978 [1939], 1982 [1939]) makes a similar point in his account of the 'civilising process' – one that always leaves 'scars' (see Chapter 2, this volume).

10 The death instincts, which Freud began to write about in the 1930s, were never accepted by Fromm. This, coupled with his abiding interest in matricentric societies, and spiritualisation of sexuality into 'loving relationships', proved to have fundamental consequences for his thinking – views that increasingly set him apart from other members of the Frankfurt school, particularly Horkheimer, Adorno and Marcuse, after the Second World War (Bocock 1976).

11 The breast, for example, is a 'machine that produces milk', and the mouth a 'machine coupled to it'. Similarly, the mouth of an anorexic wavers between several functions as an 'eating-machine, an anal machine, a talking machine or a breathing machine (asthma attacks)' (Deleuze and Guattari 1984 [1972]: 1).

12 These processes are admirably captured in the work of the artist Francis Bacon. Indeed, Bacon, for Deleuze, is *the* poststructuralist artist, painting in that indeterminate area and liminal space between life and death, human and animal, figuration and abstraction, and directing us to a 'pulpy deconstruction' of language, the body and desire (Boyne 1991).

6 'Uncontainable' bodies? Feminisms, boundaries and reconfigured identities

1 As Oakley notes, many classic feminist texts at this time were 'hard-hitting' elaborations on the basic theme of social construction: 'It is cultural prescription – gender, not sex – which explains why women fail to have proper orgasms, are ill-fitted to be brain surgeons, suffer from depressive illness, cannot reach the literary heights of Shakespeare and so on and so forth' (Oakley 1996: 5).

2 These issues are graphically portrayed in Wex's (1979) photographic study *Let's Take Back Our Space*, one which clearly illustrates 'typical' differences in the manner in which men and women perform basic mundane actions such as sitting, standing and walking. See also Goffman's (1979) classic analysis of *Gender Advertisements*, and Davis's (1997) edited volume on *Embodied Practices: Feminist Perspectives on the Body*.

3 From this perspective, bodies are seen to be 'three-dimensional containers' that protect against and resist external forces, whilst holding back internal forces from expansion and extrusion. As a consequence, all that is other is on the outside, whilst the inner self is 'shielded from the direct gaze of others by skin and other non-transparent features of the body-container' (Johnson 1987: 21–1).

4 Martin's study explores the different ways in which women's reproductive processes – menstruation, childbirth and menopause – are perceived, contrasting the views of medical science with those of ordinary women from diverse social and economic backgrounds. In doing so, she uncovers the metaphors of economy and alienation that pervade women's imaging of themselves and their bodies, applying to the women studied some of the techniques of metaphor analysis employed by writers such as Johnson (1987), Lakoff (1987), Lakoff and Johnson (1980), themselves.

5 These issues are more fully addressed in Battersby's recent book *The Phenomenal Woman: Feminist Metaphysics and the Patterns of Identity* (1998): a book that explores new ways of thinking about embodiment, sameness and difference – ways that take the woman as norm through a metaphysics of fluidity and flow.

6 See also Mitchell (1976), and Mitchell and Rose (1982).

7 This standard ranking of these senses, with sight occupying the prominent position, followed by hearing, smell, taste, then touch, was in fact, as Classen notes, first given its authority by Aristotle. In many other cultures, however, hearing is

more clearly associated with knowledge than sight – e.g. the Suya of the Brazilian Mato Grosso (Classen 1993: 9).

8 According to traditional psychoanalytic accounts, female sexuality is represented in either clitoral or vaginal terms.

9 Haraway, in her deliberations on 'cyborgs', seems to be embarking on much the same project as Irigaray, namely: a reconceptualisation of female identity in terms of a different understanding of boundaries and a notion of selves as 'dissipative systems'. As she states, 'Cyborgs might consider more seriously the partial, fluid, sometimes aspect of sex and embodiment' (Haraway 1991: 180). Seen in these terms it is not simply a question of abandoning identity altogether, rather identity has to be understood in terms of 'potentialities and flows'.

10 Whilst Butler lays great emphasis on this normative heterosexuality as a dominant regulatory ideal, she is also careful to stress that it is only partially responsible for the kind of form that contours the bodily matter of 'sex' and the setting of limits to bodily intelligibility. Other regulatory regimes are equally responsible for contouring the materiality of bodies. In this respect, she argues that it is crucial to rethink the scenes of reproduction not only through the dominant heterosexualising imperative, but also in terms of how the boundaries of 'racial' distinction are constructed and contested.

11 Connell (1983, 1987), too, seeks to unravel the 'knot of sexual difference' through a strong non-reductionist formulation of the connection between biology and the social – one that stresses the active role of social praxis in the *transcendence* and *negation* of our reproductive biology. Seen in these terms, reproductive biology is 'socially dealt with' in the historical process we call 'gender' – a history that 'negates' its biological materials as well as its social ones. We do not, therefore, have to fall back on biological essentialism in order to keep the body and its ways in view. Rather, 'In practical transcendence, the body is carried forward, so to speak, into the next transaction. It remains a presence, indeed a ferment, in the order of things constructed by more complex social processes' (Connell 1987: 82).

12 As writers such as Birke (1995) have argued, feminists need to go 'beyond' bodily surfaces to the interiority of the body. For recent examples, see Haraway (1991) and Martin (1994) on the cultural imaging of the immune system, and Oudshoorn (1994) on the 'archaeology of sex hormones'.

7 The emotionally 'expressive' body

1 See, for example, feminist epistemological critiques which have served to highlight the disembodied myths and patriarchal ideologies that underpin (masculine) claims to 'dispassionate' (scientific) inquiry – claims that, like all ideologies, serve certain social and political functions (Rose 1994; Bordo and Jaggar 1989; Jaggar 1989; Kirkup and Keller 1992; Smith 1988; Harding 1986; Belenky *et al.* 1986).

2 A theory subsequently discredited by Cannon's (1927) experimental work in which the total separation of the viscera and central nervous system was not found to alter emotional behaviour.

3 Stearns (1994) also takes a broadly constructionist line in his recent historical analysis of twentieth-century *American Cool*. As he shows, emotional culture underwent a major transformation between the 1920s and the 1950s, with subsequent implications for emotional expression in the latter half of this century: a transition succinctly captured through the juxtaposition of Victorian fervor and the new street-credible phrase 'Be cool. Chill out.' Underpinning Stearns' analysis is a view that emotional culture not only forms the basis for

constructing reactions to one's own emotions, but also in some respects the emotions themselves. Emotional experience, in other words, contains a strong cognitive and self-reflective element that is greatly affected by the cultural standards applied to that experience. (For other historical studies of a similar nature, see Stearns 1989; Stearns and Haggerty 1991; P. N. Stearns and C. Z. Stearns 1985, 1986, 1994; C. Z. Stearns and P. N. Stearns 1988.)

4 For other useful critiques of the constructionist case, both in relation to emotions and more generally, see Craib (1995, 1997) and Lyon (1998).

5 'Interaction' is being used here in special way – one that concerns the interdigitation or interlocking of biological and social factors in the genesis and management of emotions. In this respect, it may embrace elements of, but certainly is not synonymous with, symbolic interactionism.

6 For Elias's (1978 [1939], 1989a,b,c, 1991) evolutionary analysis of symbol emancipation and the tilting of the balance towards 'learned' rather than 'unlearned' forms of civilised behaviour and emotional response, see Chapter 2, this volume. See also J. H. Turner (1996) for an interesting Darwinian–Durkheimian analysis of the evolution of emotions in humans; Lyon (1994) on the complex interaction between biology, emotion and culture in human respiration; and Kemper (1990b) on the links between sociological and biological processes in the formation of emotion.

7 Burkitt draws mainly on Elias (1978 [1939]) for these insights, but see also Mauss (1973 [1934]) and Bourdieu (1984, 1990).

8 In pushing this sociological line on emotions as embodied and relational we do not, however, fully endorse Burkitt's (1997) claim, in a Wittgensteinian vein, that the traditional inner–outer distinctions should be abandoned – i.e. that emotions occur *between* people, not *inside* a single person, and that experience and bodily expression are, therefore, one and the same thing. Clearly this *is* often the case, but we also have feelings we find hard to communicate and express, or which seem to arise independently of our action and behaviour in the social world.

9 For other existentially inspired accounts of emotions see Sartre (1962 [1939]) *Sketch for a Theory of the Emotions* and, more recently, Crossley's (1997) fusion of phenomenological and Habermasian themes in relation to an emotionally informed theory of communicative action.

10 What Elias and Dunning refer to, in another context, as an 'enjoyable and controlled de-controlling of emotions' (1986: 44).

11 For an ongoing debate on the historical merits of the emotion management perspective see Hochschild's (1989) reply and Wouters' (1989b) further rejoinder. For a more general overview and evaluation of Hochschild's contribution to sociology, see Williams (1998c).

12 In this respect, Freund draws upon the work of Buytendijk (1950, 1962, 1974), who sees emotions as 'existential modes of being' involving a fusion of physical and psychic states.

13 Lynch reaches similar conclusions in his book *The Broken Heart: the Medical Consequences of Loneliness* (1977), where he presents compelling evidence of the links between cardiovascular disease and emotionally distressing life events. See also Brown and Harris (1978, 1989) on the relationship between life events, psychological distress, and physical illness.

14 For a recent discussion of the cultural meaning of love as a neglected emotion in sociological discourse, see Jackson (1993).

15 See also Mansfield and Collard (1988), Ingham (1984), and Brannen and Collard (1982) for earlier British studies, and Hochschild (1990) for a comparable American study of *The Second Shift*.

16 Rubin (1983) and Hite (1988) report similar findings.

17 A proto-professional lay person, according to De Swaan, is an expert in re-defining everyday troubles as problems amenable to treatment by this or that profession: 'he or she organizes the everyday world according to the existing division of labour among the professions' (1990: 14).

18 De Swaan makes a similar point, arguing that mental problems must, in an important sense, be 'articulated, told and "made" by the patient and [sic] his therapist' (1990: 15). In this respect they are 'social constructions'.

19 The wave of national sentiment and media hype surrounding Princess Diana's tragic death is, however, harder to categorise in these terms. On the one hand, it may be viewed, *par excellence*, as the latest chapter in the postemotional story: a media spectacle based on quasi-emotional responses and a viscerated, vicarious compassion dressed up as genuine concern. On the other hand, however, the sheer magnitude, scale and intensity of emotional feeling and action this evoked amongst the public, in contradistinction to the monarchy, suggests that this is something much more than curdled indignation or a bored and blasé response to a hyperreal event.

20 See also Melucci (1996) on person and meaning in the 'planetary society'.

21 These Durkheimian issues are further explored by Shilling (1997a) in his account of 'Emotions, embodiment and the sensation of society'. See also Connerton (1989) on how images and recollected knowledge of the past are conveyed and sustained through ritual performances of a bodily kind.

22 Examples include the proliferation of cults and gangs in modern America (Ruthven 1989).

8 Pain and the '*dys*-appearing' body

1 For a detailed history of pain, from Antiquity to the first half of the twentieth century, see Rey (1995) *The History of Pain*.

2 The ambiguous nature of pain is vividly illustrated by Wittgenstein during his deliberations on logical positivism in *Philosophical Investigations* (1968). Here Wittgenstein relates how he recorded the word *'Empfindung'* (sensation) continu-ously over several days in his diary, but questions whether the sensation of the pain can be considered to be of the same quality in each specific instance – a fundamental dilemma of any pain measurement.

3 The Gate Control theory, as developed by Melzack and Wall, hypothesises that psychological and cognitive variables (heavily influenced by sociocultural learning and experience) have an impact on the physiological processes involved in human pain. The basis of the theory is that a neural mechanism in the dorsal horns area of the spinal cord:

> acts like a gate which can increase or decrease the flow of nerve impulses from peripheral nerve fibres into the central nervous system. Somatic input is therefore subjected to the modulating influence of the gate before it evokes pain perception and response.
>
> (Melzack and Wall 1988: 222)

4 Vrancken's study was conducted in the Netherlands. For other comparative research see Csordas's and Clark's (1992) American survey, and Bendelow's and Williams's (1996) UK-based study of a pain relief clinic.

5 See also Fox (1993) for a Deleuzo-Guattarian inspired approach to these issues, including the biomedical 'territorialisation of the Body-without-Organs (BwO)', and Williams and Bendelow (1998) for a critique.

6 Perception of anything, for example, demands a kind of 'absence or transparency of the perceiving organ' – an organ that, as it were, opens out 'ecstatically' onto the world. Similarly, there are disappearances of a visceral kind; a 'recessive' mode of bodily being which, for obvious reasons, are 'wired' in to our neurological system (Leder 1990).

7 As Kelly and Field (1996) note, biological and physical facts are sociologically significant because they: (i) impinge directly on the self; (ii) provide signals for identity reconstruction; and (iii) act as 'limiting' factors on social (inter)action. See also Williams (1996c) on the relevance of body-image to these sociological debates.

8 For another autobiographically informed account of these processes see Frank's (1992b) *At the Will of the Body: Reflections on Illness*.

9 What Hilbert (1984) refers to as the 'acculturation' dimension of chronic pain. Bazanger (1989) also makes links here with Durkheim's sociological concept of anomie.

10 Cf. Wittgenstein's account of 'public' pain behaviour. For Wittgenstein, the word 'pain' is not a label for some private inner sensation. Rather, talk of pain becomes a learned substitute for the groaning and wincing that is the natural expression of pain. In other words, the linguistic devices or 'language games' we use to talk about pain, anger and so on, are publicly learned replacements for these more natural expressions of pain in behaviour.

11 See also Zola (1966, 1973) for studies of a similar nature on pain and ethnicity.

12 Heritier-Auge links these issues of gender, war and pain to men's and women's differential relationship to blood:

> What man values in man, then, is no doubt his ability to bleed, to risk his life, to take that of others, by his own free will; the woman 'sees' her blood flowing from her body . . . and she produces life without necessarily wanting to do so or being able to prevent it. . . . It is in this relation to blood that we may perhaps find the fundamental impetus for all the symbolic elaboration, at the outset, of the relations between the sexes.
>
> (Heritier-Auge 1989: 298, cited in Frank 1991a)

13 Bauman (1989) reaches similar conclusions in *Modernity and the Holocaust*.

9 The 'dormant' body: sleep, night-time and dreams

1 Perhaps the classic text in this respect is Walter de la Mare's (1939) *Behold, This Dreamer*, London: Faber and Faber, comprising a wonderful collection of poems and passages in prose of reveries, night, sleep, dream, love dreams, nightmare, death, the unconscious, the imagination, divination, the artist, and kindred subjects. See also Cosnett's (1997) intriguing exploration of 'Charles Dickens and sleep disorders'.

2 See also Johnson (1931) and Johnson *et al.* (1930) for other early work on bodily position in restful sleep.

3 Cf. the Spanish 'siesta' or Norway's proverbial 'long winter nights' and 'spring awakening' (Aubert and White 1959b: 13).

4 Street-lighting in London, for example, first began as a 'primitive enterprise' when, in 1694, Edward Heming obtained a licence to put lights outside every tenth house from 6 p.m. to midnight between Michaelmas and Lady Day, and to charge householders 6 shillings a year for the privilege of 'relative security'. Similar attempts began some thirty-two years earlier in France, instituted by a Parisian cleric, the Abbé Laudati (Alvarez 1995: 17–18).

5 For other interesting work on the history of the bed and the use of the bedroom see Wright (1962) and McIlvaine Parsons (1972), respectively.

6 As Goffman observes, the central feature of a 'total institution' can be described as the breakdown of the barriers ordinarily separating sleep, play and work – activities that normally occur in different places, with different co-participants, under different authorities. Within a total institution, all aspects of life are conducted in the same place, in the immediate company of a large batch of others, and in a tightly scheduled sequence – activities brought together into a single rational plan purportedly designed to fulfil the official aims of the institution (Goffman 1961: 17).

7 The number of sleeping pills swallowed per night in Greater London is estimated to be in the order of 522,250 plus (Hind 1997).

8 This strong association between current health and current sleeping habits led Blaxter to conclude that the use of sleeping habits as a 'voluntary' behaviour was unjustified (Blaxter 1990: 127).

10 'Artistic' bodies: representation and resistance

1 Notable exceptions here include Goffman's (1979) path-breaking *Gender Advertisement* and the subsequent wealth of feminist and cultural analyses of representation in the visual media (Williamson 1978; Fyfe and Law 1988; Bonner *et al.* 1992). See also Wex's (1979) photographic work on 'female' and 'male' body language in public space, and Theweleit's (1987 [1977], 1989 [1978]) use of visual imagery in his fascinating two-volume study *Male Fantasies*. More broadly, the recent *The Quick and the Dead: Artists and Anatomy* exhibition provides a particularly good example of the 'meeting of text and image' (Petherbridge 1997). (See also note 12 below.)

2 See, for example, Baxandall's (1972) analysis of the sociopolitical underpinnings of fifteenth-century Italian painting, and Alpers' (1983) account of seventeenth-century Dutch painting.

3 The body, as Butler notes, has the capacity to be represented as an 'ontologically transparent layer' through which art and science are mutually visible and can be reconciled (Butler 1993b: 81).

4 Cf. Galton's use of facial characteristics to categorise criminal and 'racial' groups.

5 Le Corbusier was himself heavily influenced by the French fascist physician Dr Pierre Winter. The links between this art form and the newly emerging dominant ideology were astutely observed in 1927 by the architectural historian, Franz Schule, who remarked that the Nazis wanted a world that was every bit as 'clean' in their terms as the Modernist architects did in theirs (Stonor Saunders 1995).

6 Polykleiton proportions are those that are supposedly sought to maximise physical beauty and sexual attractiveness, dating back to the Greek sculpture Polykleitos in the fifth-century BC.

7 Throughout the paintings, sculpture and photography of this time, in a 'Europe under the Dictators', the body was graphically portrayed as a source of power, including huge pavilion statues, the uniformed precision of military rallies and youth movements, and depictions of the violence and inhumanity of War (e.g. Picasso's *Guernica*). See Ardes *et al.* (1995).

8 Hans Prinzhorn's innovative work with psychotic patients, for example, was misappropriated by the Nazi propaganda machine as precisely the sort of art it wished to eradicate, founded as it was on 'madness' and 'unreason'. An exhibition of this work, entitled *Art and Psychosis*, was recently shown at London's Hayward Gallery, to great acclaim.

9 Cf. Foucault's (1988b) 'technologies of self'.

10 Anthea Callen (1995) has also shown how physiology, in the work of artists such as Degas, was used to denote 'inferiority' of class, race or gender.

11 Whilst, as Young notes, the source of this objectified bodily existence lies in the attitude of others, 'woman herself often actively takes up her body as a mere thing. She gazes at it in the mirror, worries about how it looks to others, prunes it, shapes it, molds and decorates it' (Young 1990: 155).

12 Other examples of this 'visceral' art include Jayne Parker's black and white images of her own naked body expelling animal organs and blood, 'knitted' into a dress, and Damien Hirst's exhibits of dead cows dripping in pools of blood, their entrails fully visible (see Betterton 1996). Francis Bacon's tortured 'carnalities' and butchery of the 'flesh' are also, of course, part of this genre, painting as he did between 'flesh and meat, human being and beast' (Boyne 1991: 290). See, for example, the 1998 Bacon Exhibition: 'The Human Body'. In a broadly similar vein, the recent 'The Quick and the Dead: Artists and Anatomy' – an exhibition that brings together a diverse array of artistic material on medicine and the body throughout the centuries, ranging from the macabre to the fantastical, and from exquisite fine drawings to extraordinary prints of self-flaying heads (Petherbridge and Jordanova 1997) – seeks to collapse the boundaries between art and science, the moral and the philosophical, the erotic and the rational. In doing so, it not only serves as a stark reminder of the brute materiality of the body as flesh and bone, meat and muscle, but also the chilling fact that, if anything, we are 'more estranged' from our bodies now than ever we were in the past. 'Who nowadays', as Searle rhetorically asks in response to prosthetic or grotesque work such as Cindy Sherman's and Robert Gober's, 'looks upon the body with the cool analytical eye of Leonardo da Vinci?' (A. Searle 'Corporeal entertainment', *The Guardian*, 4 November 1997 (Review), pp. 10–11).

13 Other examples of embodied art include the more 'touchy', 'feely', actively sensual work of Carl André. On a broader 'stage', Artaud sought to create, through the medium of embodied theatre, an 'alchemical arena' that operates on the flesh as much as the spirit. Theatre, he says, is the exercise of a 'terrible and dangerous act': 'THE REAL ORGANIC AND PHYSICAL TRANSFORMATION OF THE HUMAN BODY' (Artaud 1988).

14 Wolf (1990: 139) provides a classic example of these double male standards when she reports how hand-made AIDS education subway posters, showing illiterate people how to put a condom on an erect penis were confiscated by New York police. In contrast, adjacent Penthouse advertisements remained intact for all to see.

15 A current advert, for example, features a group of female office workers taking a collective break from work to gaze at a male construction worker removing his shirt and drinking his regular morning *Diet Coke*.

16 The inspiration for Sophie's death's head shrieking figure is reputedly said to derive from a Peruvian mummy in the *Museé de l'Homme* in Paris.

17 The tragedy of Sophie's death was also captured in another of Munch's early paintings, *The Sick Child*, using new techniques of smudging and scratching. Although derided and ridiculed when first shown, it is now acclaimed as one of the most sensitive and evocative portrayals of (childhood) illness and despair.

18 As well as the autobiographical themes of love and sexuality depicted in *The Frieze of Life*, many of *The Green Room Paintings* refer to Munch's stormy relationship with Tulla Larsen – one that ended in 1902 with a violent quarrel in which Munch shot himself in the hand. Tulla then abandoned him and married another, leaving Munch overwhelmed with bitterness and jealousy – feelings captured in vigorous brushwork and violent colours. *Self Portrait with a Bottle of*

Wine, for example, evokes the sense of loneliness and despair which Munch felt after this rupture, an event which culminated in a nervous breakdown in 1908.

19 An image which appears on the cover of Naomi Wolf's (1990) *The Beauty Myth*.

20 Perhaps the most recent example of this is to to be found in the Royal Academy's autumn 1997 'Sensations' exhibition, featuring a variety of young British artists such as Jake and Dinos Chapman, Tracey Emin, Sarah Lucas, Marcus Harvey, Damien Hirst and Rachel Whiteread.

References

Adler, K. and Pointon, M. (1993) *The Body Imaged: The Human Form and Visual Culture Since the Renaissance*, Cambridge: Cambridge University Press.

Albrow, M. (1992) 'Sine ira et studio – or do organisations have feelings?' *Organisation Studies*, 13: 313–27.

Aldersey-Williams, H. (1997) 'Drawing on real experience', *Independent on Sunday*, 14 December (Review) pp. 44–5.

Alpers, S. (1983) *The Art of Describing: Dutch Art in the 17th Century*, Chicago: University of Chicago Press.

Alvarez, A. (1995) *Night*, London: Vintage.

Anderson, R. and Bury, M. (eds) (1988) *Living with Chronic Illness: the Experience of Patients and their Families*, London: Unwin Hyman.

Anderson, W. F. (1995) 'Gene therapy', *Scientific American*, September: 96–8b.

Archer, M. S. (1995) *Realist Social Theory: A Morphogenetic Approach*, Cambridge: Cambridge University Press.

Ardes, D., Benton, T., Elliott, D. and Boyd White, I. (1995) *Art and Power; Europe under the Dictators 1930–45*, The Hayward Gallery, South Bank Centre.

Ardey, R. (1966) *The Territorial Imperative*, London: Collins.

—— (1970) *The Social Contract*, London: Collins.

Aries, P. (1976) *Western Attitudes Toward Death: From the Middle Ages to the Present*, London: Marion Boyers.

—— (1981) *The Hour of Death*, London: Allen Lane.

Armstrong, D. (1983) *Political Anatomy of the Body: Medical Knowledge in Britain in the Twentieth Century*, Cambridge: Cambridge University Press.

—— (1986) 'The problem of the whole-person in holistic medicine', *Holistic Medicine*, 1: 27–36.

—— (1987) 'Silence and truth in death and dying', *Social Science and Medicine*, 24 (8): 651–8.

—— (1993) 'Public health spaces and the fabrication of identity', *Sociology*, 27 (3): 393–410.

—— (1994) 'Bodies of knowledge/knowledge of bodies', in C. Jones and R. Porter (eds) *Reassessing Foucault: Power, Medicine and the Body*, London: Routledge.

—— (1995) 'The rise of surveillance medicine', *Sociology of Health and Illness*, 17 (3): 393–404.

Arney, W. R. and Neill, J. (1982) 'The location of pain in childbirth: natural childbirth and the transformation of obstetrics', *Sociology of Health and Illness*, 4 (1): 1–24.

Artaud, A. (1988) *Selected Writings* (ed. with an 'Introduction' by S. Sontag), Berkeley, CA: University of California Press .

Aubert, V. and White, H. (1959a) 'Sleep: a sociological interpretation I', *Acta Sociologica*, 4 (2): 46–54.

—— (1959b) 'Sleep: a sociological interpretation II', *Acta Sociologica*, 4 (3): 1–16.

Bachelard, G. (1987 [1964]) *The Psychoanalysis of Fire* (transl. by A. C. M. Ross with an 'Introduction' by N. Fryre), London: Quartet.

Bakhtin, M. (1968) *Rabelais and his World*, Cambridge, MA: MIT Press.

Balsamo, A. (1992) 'On the cutting edge: cosmetic surgery and the technological production of the gendered body', *Camera Obscura*, 28: 207–37.

—— (1995a) 'Forms of technological embodiment: reading the body in contemporary culture', *Body and Society (Cyberspace, Cyberbodies, Cyberpunk)*, 1: 3–4, 215–38.

—— (1995b) *Technologies of the Gendered Body: Cyborg Women*, Durham, NC: Duke University Press.

Barchas, P. R. (1976) 'Physiological sociology: the interface of sociological and biological processes', *Annual Review of Sociology*, 2: 299–333.

Barker, F. (1984) *The Tremulous Private Body*, London: Methuen.

Barrett, M. (1982) 'Femininity and the definition of cultural politics', in R. Brunt and C. Rowan (eds) *Feminism, Culture and Politics*, London: Lawrence and Wishart.

Barrett, M. and Phillips, A. (1992) *Destabilizing Theory: Contemporary Feminist Debates*, Cambridge: Polity Press.

Bataille, G. (1985) *Visions of Excess: Selected Writings 1927–1939* (ed. with an 'Introduction' by A. Stoekl, transl. by A. Stoekl with C. R. Lovitt and D. M. Leslie, Jr), Manchester: Manchester University Press.

—— (1987 [1962]) *Eroticism* (transl. by M. Dalwood), London: Boyars.

Battersby, C. (1993) 'Her body/her boundaries: gender and the metaphysics of containment', in Benjamin, A. (ed.) *Journal of Philosophy and the Visual Arts. The Body*, London: Academy Group Ltd.

—— (1998) *The Phenomenal Woman: Feminist Metaphysics and the Patterns of Identity*, Cambridge: Polity Press.

Baudrillard, J. (1976) *L'échange symbolique et la mort*, Paris: Gallimard.

—— (1983a) *In the Shadow of the Silent Majority*, New York: Semiotext(e).

—— (1983b) *Simulations*, New York: Semiotext(e).

—— (1988) *Selected Writings*, (ed. M. Poster), Cambridge: Polity Press.

—— (1990) *Seduction*, New York: St Martin's Press.

Bauman, Z. (1989) *Modernity and the Holocaust*, Cambridge: Polity Press.

—— (1992a) *Intimations of Postmodernity*, London: Routledge.

—— (1992b) 'Survival as a social construct', *Theory, Culture and Society*, 9 (1): 1–36.

—— (1992c) *Mortality, Immortality and Other Life Strategies*, Cambridge: Polity Press.

Baxandall, M. (1972) *Painting and Experience in Fifteenth Century Italy*, Oxford: Oxford University Press.

Bazanger, I. (1989) 'Pain: its experience and treatment', *Social Science and Medicine*, 29: 425–34.

Beck, U. (1992) *Risk Society: Towards a New Modernity*, London: Sage.

Beck, U. and Beck-Gernsheim, E. (1995) *The Normal Chaos of Love*, Cambridge: Polity Press.

Becker, H. (1982) *Art Worlds*, Berkeley, CA: University of California Press.

Beecher, H. (1959) *Measurement of Subjective Responses*, New York: Oxford University Press.

Belenky, M., Clinchy, B., Goldberger, N. and Tarule, J. (1986) *Women's Ways of Knowing*, New York: Basic Books.

Bendelow, G. (1993) 'Pain perceptions, gender and emotion', *Sociology of Health and Illness*, 15 (3): 273–94.

Bendelow, G. and Williams, S. J. (1996) 'The end of the road? Lay views on a pain-relief clinic', *Social Science and Medicine*, 43 (7): 1127–36.

—— (eds) (1998) *Emotions in Social Life: Critical Times and Contemporary Issues*, London: Routledge.

Benton, T. (1991) 'Biology and social science: why the return of the repressed should be given a (cautious) welcome', *Sociology*, 25 (1): 1–29.

Betterton, R. (1996) *An Intimate Distance: Women, Artists and the Body*, London: Routledge.

Berger, J. (1972) *Ways of Seeing*, London/Harmondsworth: BBC/Penguin.

Berger, P. (1967) *The Sacred Canopy: Elements of a Sociological Theory of Religion*, New York: Anchor Books.

Berliner, H. S. and Salmon, J. W. (1980) 'The holistic alternative to scientific medicine: history and analysis', *International Journal of Health Services*, 10 (1): 133–47.

Berman, B. (1989) 'The computer metaphor: bureaucratizing the mind', *Science as Culture*, 7: 7–42.

Bhaskar, R. (1989) *Reclaiming Reality*, London: Verso.

Birke, L. (1995) 'Our bodies, ourselves? Feminism, biology and the body', *Working Paper*, Centre for the Study of Women and Gender, University of Warwick.

Bischoff, U. (1993) *Edvard Munch* (transl. by M. Hulse), Cologne: Benedikt Taschen.

Blake, A. (1997) *The Body Language: The Meaning of Modern Sport*, London: Lawrence and Wishart.

Blaxter, M. (1990) *Health and Lifestyles*, London: Routledge.

Bleier, R. (1984) *Science and Gender: A Critique of Biology and its Theories on Women*, Oxford: Pergamon Press.

Bly, R. (1990) *Iron John: A Book About Men*, Shaftesbury: Element Books.

Bocock, R. (1976) *Freud and Modern Society*, Berkshire: Van Nostrand Reinhold Co. Ltd.

Bonner, R., Goodman, L., Allen, R., James, L. and King, C. (eds) (1992) *Imaging Women: Cultural Representations and Gender*, Cambridge: Polity Press.

Bordo, S. (1986) 'The Cartesian masculinization of thought', *Signs*, 11 (3): 433–57.

—— (1990) 'Reading the slender body', in M. Jacobus, E. F. Keller and S. Shuttleworth (eds) *Body/Politics: Women and the Discourse of Science*, London: Routledge.

—— (1993) *Unbearable Weight: Feminism, Western Culture and the Body*, Berkeley, CA: University of California Press.

Bordo, S. and Jaggar, A. (eds) (1989) *Gender/Knowledge/Body: Feminist Reconstructions of Being and Knowing*, New Brunswick/London: Rutgers University Press.

Bourdieu, P. (1977) *Outline of a Theory of Practice*, Cambridge: Cambridge University Press.

—— (1978) 'Sport and social class', *Social Science Information*, 17: 819–40.

—— (1980) *Questions de Sociologie*, Paris: Editions de Minuit.

—— (1984) *Distinction: A Social Critique of the Judgement of Taste*, London: Routledge.

—— (1990) *The Logic of Practice*, Cambridge: Polity Press.

—— (1996) *Photography: A Middle-brow Art*, Cambridge: Polity Press.

Bourdieu, P., Darbel, A. and Schnapper, D. (1990) *The Love of Art: European Art Museums and the Public* (transl. by C. Beattie and N. Merriman), Cambridge: Polity Press.

Boyne, R. (1991) 'The art of the body in the discourse of postmodernity', in M. Featherstone, M. Hepworth and B. S. Turner (eds) *The Body: Social Process and Cultural Theory*, London: Sage.

Brannen, J. and Collard, J. (1982) *Marriage in Trouble: The Process of Seeking Help*, London: Tavistock.

Brannen, J. and Moss, P. (1988) *Mothers and Daughters: A Three Generational Study of Health Attitudes and Behaviour*, London: Heinemann.

Brohm, J.-M. (1978) *Sport, A Prison of Measured Time* (transl. by I. Fraser), London: Inter-Links Books.

Brown, G. W. and Harris, T. O. (eds) (1978) *The Sexual Origins of Depression*, London: Tavistock.

—— (eds) (1989) *Life Events and Illness*, London: Unwin Hyman.

Brown, N. O. (1966) *Love's Body*, New York: Vintage Books.

Bunton, R., Nettleton, S. and Burrows, R. (eds) (1995) *The Sociology of Health Promotion: Critical Analyses of Consumption, Lifestyle and Risk*, London: Routledge.

Burkitt, I. (1991) *Social Selves: Theories of the Formation of Personality*, London: Sage.

—— (1997) 'Social relationships and emotions', *Sociology*, 31 (1): 37–55.

Burston, P. and Richardson, C. (eds) (1995) *A Queer Romance: Lesbians, Gay Men and Popular Culture*, London: Routledge.

Butler, J. (1990) *Gender Trouble: Feminism and the Subversion of Identity*, New York/London: Routledge.

—— (1993a) *Body Matters: The Discursive Limits of 'Sex'*, London: Routledge.

—— (1993b) 'Before sexual difference', in A. Benjamin (ed.) *Journal of Philosophy and the Visual Arts. The Body*, London/Berlin: Academy Group Ltd.

Buytendijk, F. J. J. (1950) 'The phenomenological approach to the problem of feelings and emtions', in M. C. Reymert (ed.) *Feelings and Emotions: the Mooseheart Symposium in Cooperation with the University of Chicago*, New York: McGraw Hill Company Inc.

—— (1962) *Pain: Its Modes and Functions* (transl. by Eda O'Shiel), Chicago: University of Chicago Press.

—— (1974) *Prolegomena to an Anthropological Physiology*, Pittsburgh: Duquesne University Press.

Callen, A. (1995) *The Spectacular Body: Science, Method and Meaning in the Work of Degas*, New Haven and London: Yale University Press.

Calnan, M. (1987) *Health and Illness: The Lay Perspective*, London: Routledge.

Cancian, F. (1987) *Love in America: Gender and Self-Development*, Cambridge: Cambridge University Press.

Cannon, W. (1927) 'The James–Lange theory of emotions: a critical examination and alternative theory', *American Journal of Psychiatry*, 138: 1319–30.

Carmichael, K. (1988) 'The creative use of pain in society', in R. Terrington (ed.) *Towards a Whole Society*, London: Richmond Fellowship Press.

Casper, M. J. (1995) 'Fetal cyborgs and technomoms on the reproductive frontier: which way to the carnival', in C. H. Gray (ed.) *The Cyborg Handbook*, New York/London: Routledge.

Chadwick, E. (1965) *The Sanitary Conditions of the Labouring Population of Great Britain: Report 1842*, Edinburgh: Edinburgh University Press.

Chadwick, W. (1990) *Women, Art and Society*, London: Thames and Hudson Ltd.

Charlton, B. (1993) 'Medicine of postmodernity', *Journal of the Royal Society of Medicine*, 86: 497–9.

Charmaz, K. (1983) 'Loss of self: a fundamental form of suffering in chronic illness', *Sociology of Health and Illness*, 5: 168–95.

Chernin, K. (1981) *Womansize: the Tyranny of Slenderness*, London: The Women's Press.

Cixous, H. (1991) 'The laugh of Medusa', in S. Gunew (ed.) *Feminist Knowledge: A Reader*, London: Routledge.

Clark, K. (1956) *The Nude: A Study of Ideal Art*, London: John Murray.

Clarke, A. (1995) 'Modernity, postmodernity and reproductive processes, ca 1890–1990, or "mommy where do cyborgs come from anyway?"', in C. H. Gray (ed.) *The Cyborg Handbook*, London: Routledge.

Classen, C. (1993) *Worlds of Sense: Exploring the Senses in History and Across Cultures*, London: Routledge.

Collins, R. (1975) *Conflict Sociology*, New York: Academic.

—— (1981) 'On the micro-foundations of macro-sociology', *American Journal of Sociology*, 86: 984–1014.

—— (1990) 'Stratification, emotional energy, and the transient emotions', in T. J. Kemper (ed.) *Research Agendas in the Sociology of Emotions*, New York: State University of New York Press.

Connell, R. W. (1983) *Which Way is Up?* Sydney/London: George Allen and Unwin.

—— (1987) *Gender and Power: Society, the Person and Sexual Politics*, Cambridge: Polity Press.

—— (ed.) (1993) 'Masculinities', *Theory and Society* 22: 5 (special issue).

—— (1995) *Masculinities*, Cambridge: Polity Press.

Connerton, P. (1989) *How Societies Remember*, Cambridge: Cambridge University Press.

Cooper, E. (1995) *Fully Exposed: The Male Nude in Photography*, London, New York: Routledge.

Corea, G. (1985) *The Mother Machine*, New York: Harper and Row.

Corea, G., Klein, R. D. *et al.* (eds) (1985) *Man-made Women: How New Reproductive Technologies Affect Women*, London: Hutchinson.

Cornwall, A. and Lindisfarne, N. (eds) (1994) *Dislocating Masculinities: Comparative Ethnographies*, London: Routledge.

Cornwell, J. (1984) *Hard-earned Lives: Accounts of Health and Illness from East London*, London: Tavistock.

Cosnett, J. (1997) 'Charles Dickens and sleep disorders', *The Dickensian*, 443, (93), (part 3): 200–4.

Cousins, M. and Hussain, A. (1984) *Michel Foucault*, London: Macmillan.

Coward, R. (1989) *The Whole Truth*, London: Faber and Faber.

Cox, B. D., Blaxter, M., Buckle, A. L. F. *et al.* (1987) *The Health and Lifestyle Survey: Preliminary Report*, London: The Health Promotion Research Trust.

Craib, I. (1988) *Psychoanalysis and Social Theory: The Limits of Sociology*, London: Harvester Wheatsheaf.

—— (1995) 'Some comments on the sociology of emotions', *Sociology*, 29 (1): 151–8.

—— (1997) 'Social constructionism as social psychosis', *Sociology*, 31 (1): 1–15.

Crawford, R. (1977) 'You are dangerous to your health: the ideology and politics of victim blaming', *International Journal of Health Services*, 7 (4): 663–80.

—— (1980) 'Healthism and the medicalization of everyday life', *International Journal of Health Services*, 10: 365–88.

—— (1984) 'A cultural account of "health": control, release and the social body', in J. B. McKinlay (ed.) *Issues in the Political Economy of Health Care*, London: Tavistock.

—— (1994) 'The boundaries of self and the unhealthy other: reflections on health, culture and AIDS', *Social Science and Medicine*, 38 (10): 1347–66.

—— (1998) 'The ritual of health promotion', in S. J. Williams, J. Gabe and M. Calnan (eds) *Theorising Health, Medicine and Society*, London: Sage.

Crossley, N. (1993) 'Body techniques and human agency in Mauss, Merleau-Ponty and Foucault', *Working Paper*, Centre for Psychotherapeutic Studies, University of Sheffield.

—— (1994) *The Politics of Subjectivity: Between Foucault and Merleau-Ponty*, Ashgate: Avebury.

—— (1995a) 'Merleau-Ponty, the elusive body and carnal sociology', *Body & Society*, 1 (1): 43–66.

—— (1995b) 'Body techniques, agency and intercorporeality: on Goffman's *Relations in Public*', *Sociology*, 29 (1): 133–50.

—— (1996) 'Body-subject/body-power: agency, inscription and control in Foucault and Merleau-Ponty', *Body & Society*, 2 (2): 99–116.

—— (1997) 'Emotions and communicative action', in G. Bendelow and S. J. Williams (eds) *Emotions in Social Life: Critical Themes and Contemporary Issues*, London: Routledge.

Csordas, T. J. (1990) 'Embodiment as a paradigm for anthropology', *Ethos*, 18: 5–47.

—— (1994a) 'Introduction: the body as representation and being-in-the-world', in T. J. Csordas (ed.) *Embodiment and Experience: the Existential Ground of Culture and Self*, Cambridge: Cambridge University Press.

Csordas, T. J. and Clark, J. (1992) 'Ends of the line: diversity among chronic pain centres', *Social Science and Medicine*, 34 (4): 383–93.

Daly, M. (1978) *Gyn/ecology: The Metaethics of Radical Feminism*, Boston, MA: Beacon Press.

Damasio, A. R. (1994) *Descartes' Error: Emotion, Reason and the Human Brain*, New York: Putnam.

Darwin, C. (1955 [1895]) *The Expression of Emotions in Man and Animals*, New York: Philosophical Library.

Davis, K. (1994) *Reshaping the Female Body: The Dilemmas of Cosmetic Surgery*, London: Routledge.

—— (ed.) (1997) *Embodied Practices: Feminist Perspectives on the Body*, London: Sage.

Davison, C., Davey Smith, G. and Frankel, S. (1991) 'Lay epidemiology and the prevention paradox: implications for coronary candidacy and health education', *Sociology of Health and Illness*, 13 (1): 1–19.

Davison, C., Frankel, S. and Davey Smith, G. (1992) 'The limits of lifestyle: reassessing "fatalism" in the popular culture of illness prevention', *Social Science and Medicine*, 34 (6): 675–85.

Dawe, A. (1971) 'The two sociologies', in K. Thompson and J. Tunstall (eds) *Sociological Perspectives*, Harmondsworth: Penguin.

Dawkins, R. (1976) *The Selfish Gene*, London: Paladin.

de Beauvoir, S. (1972 [1959]) *The Second Sex*, Harmondsworth: Penguin.

Deitch, J. (1992) *Post Human*, Amsterdam: Idea Books.

de la Mare, W. (1939) *Behold this Dreamer*, London: Faber and Faber.

Deleuze, G. and Guattari, F. (1984 [1972]) *Anti-Oedipus: Capitalism and Schizophrenia I* (transl. by R. Hurley, M. Seem and H. R. Lane, Preface by M. Foucault), London: Athlone Press.

—— (1988 [1980]) *A Thousand Plateaus: Capitalism and Schizophrenia II* (transl. by B. Mussumi), London: Athlone Press.

de Maupassant, G. (n.d.) *The Complete Short Stories of Guy de Maupassant*, London: Blue Ribbon Books.

de Montaigne, M. (1959 [1592]) *In Defense of Raymond Sebend* (transl. by A. Beattie), New York: Fredrick Ungar Publishing Co.

Denny, E. (1996) 'New reproductive technologies: the views of women undergoing treatment', in S. J. Williams and M. Calnan (eds) *Modern Medicine: Lay Perspectives and Experiences*, London: UCL Press.

Denzin, N. K. (1984) *On Understanding Emotion*, San Francisco: Jossey Bass.

—— (1997) 'Narratives of the self: co-dependency and the inner child: emotionality, meaning and gender in cyberspace', in G. Bendelow and S. J. Williams (eds) *Emotions in Social Life: Critical Themes and Contemporary Issues*, London: Routledge.

Dery, M. (1996) *Escape Velocity: Cyberculture at the End of the Century*, New York: Grove Press.

Descartes, R. (1972) *Treatise of Man* (transl. with a 'Commentary' by T. S. Hall), Cambridge, MA: Harvard University Press.

de Swaan, A. (1990) *The Management of Normality: Critical Essays in Health and Welfare*, London: Routledge.

Dewey, J. (1922) *Human Nature and Conduct: An Introduction to Social Psychology*, New York: Holt.

Diamond, I. and Quinby, L. (eds) (1988) *Feminism and Foucault: Reflections on Resistance*, Boston: Northeastern University Press.

Dingwall, R. (1976) *Aspects of Illness*, London: Martin Robertson.

Doane, M. A. (1990) 'Technophilia: technology, representation and the feminine', in M. Jacobus, E. F. Keller and S. Shuttleworth (eds) *Body/Politics: Women and the Discourse of Science*, London: Routledge.

Douglas, M. (1966) *Purity and Danger: An Analysis of the Concepts of Pollution and Taboo*, London: Routledge and Kegan Paul.

—— (1970) *Natural Symbols: Explorations in Cosmology*, London: The Cresset Press.

—— (1971) 'Do dogs laugh? A cross-cultural approach to body symbolism', *Journal of Psychosomatic Research*, 15, 387–90.

—— (1986) *Risk Acceptability According to the Social Sciences*, London: Routledge and Kegan Paul.

Douglas, M. and Calvez, M. (1990) 'The self as risk-taker: a cultural theory of contagion in relation to AIDS', *Sociological Review*, 38 (3): 445–64.

Duncombe, J. and Marsden, D. (1993) 'Love and intimacy: the gender division of emotion work', *Sociology*, 27: 221–41.

—— (1998) 'Stepford Wives? Love, intimacy and the gender division of "emotion work"', in G. Bendelow and S. J. Williams (eds) *Emotions in Social Life: Critical Themes and Contemporary Issues*, London: Routledge.

Durkheim, E. (1961 [1912]) *The Elementary Forms of Religious Life*, London: Allen and Unwin.

Durkheim, E. and Mauss, M. (1975 [1902]) *Primitive Classification* (transl. by R. Needham), Chicago: Chicago University Press.

Ehrenreich, B. (1987) 'Foreword', in K. Theweleit, *Male Fantasies Vol. 1: Women, Floods, Bodies and History*, Minnesota/Cambridge: University of Minnesota/Polity Press.

Ehrenreich, B. and English, D. (1974) *Complaints and Disorders: The Sexual Politics of Sickness*, London: Compendium.

Ekman, P. (1977) 'Biological and cultural contributions to the body and facial movement', in J. Blacking (ed.) *Anthropology of the Body*, New York: Academic Press.

—— (ed.) (1982) *Emotion in the Human Face*, Cambridge, MA: Cambridge University Press.

—— (1984) *Approaches to Emotion*, Hillsdale, New Jersey: Lawrence Erlbaum.

Ekman, P., Levenson, R. W. and Friesen, W. V. (1983) 'Autonomic nervous system activity distinguishes among emotions', *Science*, 221: 1208–10.

Elias, N. (1978 [1939]) *The Civilizing Process: Vol I: the History of Manners*, Oxford: Basil Blackwell.

—— (1982 [(1939)]) *The Civilizing Process, Vol II: State Formations and Civilization*, Oxford: Basil Blackwell.

—— (1983) *The Court Society*, Oxford: Basil Blackwell.

—— (1985) *The Loneliness of Dying*, Oxford: Basil Blackwell.

—— (1989a) 'The symbol theory (part I)', *Theory, Culture and Society*, 6: 163–217.

—— (1989b) 'The symbol theory (part II)', *Theory, Culture and Society*, 6: 339–83.

—— (1989c) 'The symbol theory (part III)', *Theory, Culture and Society*, 6: 499–537.

—— (1991) 'On human beings and their emotions: a process-sociological essay', in M. Featherstone, M. Hepworth and B. Turner (eds) *The Body: Social Process and Cultural Theory*, London: Sage.

Elias, N. and Dunning, E. (1986) *The Quest for Excitement: Sport and Leisure in the Civilizing Process*, Oxford: Basil Blackwell.

Engels, F. (1987 [1845]) *The Conditions of the Working Class in England*, Harmondsworth: Penguin.

Evans, D. (1997) 'Michel Maffesoli's sociology of modernity and postmodernity: an introduction and critical assessment', *The Sociological Review*, 45 (2): 221–43.

Falk, P. (1994) *The Consuming Body*, London: Sage.

Faurschou, G. (1988) 'Fashion and the cultural logic of postmodernity', in A. Kroker and M. Kroker (eds) *Body Invaders: Sexuality and the Postmodern Condition*, Basingstoke: Macmillan.

Featherstone, M. (1987a) 'Leisure, symbolic power and the life course', in J. Horne, D. Jary and A. Tomlinson (eds) *Sports, Leisure and Social Relations*, London: Routledge and Kegan Paul.

—— (1987b) 'Lifestyles and consumer culture', *Theory, Culture & Society*, 4: 55–70.

—— (1991) 'The body in consumer culture', in M. Featherstone, M. Hepworth and B. S. Turner (eds) *The Body: Social Process and Cultural Theory*, London: Sage.

Featherstone, M. and Burrows, R. (1995) 'Cultures of technological embodiment: an introduction', *Body & Society*, 1 (3 and 4): 1–19.

Featherstone, M. and Hepworth, M. (1991) 'The mask of ageing and the post-modern life course', in M. Featherstone, M. Hepworth and B. S. Turner (eds) *The Body: Social Process and Cultural Theory*, London: Sage.

Featherstone, M. and Turner, B. S. (1995) 'Body & society: an introduction', *Body & Society*, 1 (1): 1–12.

Feher, M., Naddaff, R. and Tazi, N. (1989a) *Fragments for a History of the Human Body, Part One*, New York: Zone.

—— (1989b) *Fragments for a History of the Human Body, Part Two*, New York: Zone.

—— (eds) (1989c) *Fragments for a History of the Human Body, Part Three*, New York: Zone.

Feine, J., Bushell, M., Miron, D. and Duncan, G. (1990) 'Sex differences in the perception of noxious heat stimuli', *Pain*, 44: 255–63.

Fineman, S. (1993) *Emotion in Organizations*, London: Sage.

Firestone, S. (1970) *The Dialectic of Sex: The Case for Feminist Revolution*, London: The Women's Press.

Foucault, M. (1973) *The Birth of the Clinic: An Archaeology of Medical Perception*, London: Tavistock.

—— (1977) *Discipline and Punish: the Birth of the Prison*, London: Tavistock.

—— (1979) *The History of Sexuality, vol. 1: an Introduction*, London: Allen Lane/Penguin.

—— (1980) *Power/Knowledge: Selected Interviews and Other Writings 1972–1977*, (ed. C. Gordon), Brighton: Harvester Press.

—— (1984a) 'Nietzsche, genealogy, history', in P. Rabinow (ed.) *The Foucault Reader*, New York: Pantheon Books.

—— (1984b [1972]) 'Preface', in G. Deleuze and F. Guattari (eds) *Anti-Oedipus: Capitalism and Schizophrenia*, London: Athlone Press.

—— (1987) *The Use of Pleasure. The History of Sexuality, vol. 2*, Harmondsworth: Penguin.

—— (1988a) *The Care of the Self. The History of Sexuality, vol. 3*, Harmondsworth: Penguin.

—— (1988b) 'Technologies of the self', in L. H. Martin, H. Gutman and P. H. Hutton (eds) *Technologies of the Self: a Seminar with Michel Foucault*, London: Tavistock.

Fox, N. (1993) *Postmodernism, Sociology and Health*, Milton Keynes: Open University Press.

Frank, A. W. (1990) 'Bringing bodies back in: a decade review', *Theory, Culture & Society*, 7 (1): 131–62.

—— (1991a) 'For a sociology of the body: an analytical review', in M. Featherstone, M. Hepworth and B. S. Turner (eds) *The Body: Social Process and Cultural Theory*, London: Sage.

—— (1991b) 'From sick role to health role: deconstructing Parsons', in R. Robertson and B. S. Turner (eds) *Parsons: Theorist of Modernity*, London: Sage.

—— (1992a) 'Twin nightmares of the medical simulacrum: Jean Baudrillard and David Cronenberg', in W. Stearns and W. Chalouplea (eds) *Jean Baudrillard: The Disappearance of Art and Politics*, London: Macmillan.

—— (1992b) *At the Will of the Body: Reflections on Illness*, Boston: Houghton Mifflin.

—— (1995) *The Wounded Storyteller: Body, Illness and Ethics*, Chicago/London: University of Chicago Press.

Frankenberg, R. (1990) 'Review article: disease, literature and the body in the era of AIDS – a preliminary exploration', *Sociology of Health and Illness*, 12 (3): 351–60.

Frascina, F. and Harris, J. (1992) *Art in Modern Culture: An Anthology of Critical Texts*, London: Phaidon Press/Open University Press.

Freud, S. (1963 [1908]) 'Civilized sexual morality and modern nervous illness', in P. Rieff (ed.) *The Collected Papers of Sigmund Freud: Sexuality and the Psychology of Love*, New York: Collier-Macmillan.

—— (1976 [1953]) *The Interpretation of Dreams*, Harmondsworth: Penguin.

—— (1982 [1930]) *Civilization and its Discontents*, London: Hogarth Press.

—— (1984 [1923]) *The Ego and the Id*, in S. Freud *On Metapsychology*, Harmondsworth: Penguin.

Freund, P. (1982) *The Civilized Body: Social Control, Domination and Health*, Philadelphia PA: Temple University Press.

—— (1988) 'Understanding socialized human nature', *Theory and Society*, 17: 839–64.

—— (1990) 'The expressive body: a common ground for the sociology of emotions and health and illness', *Sociology of Health and Illness*, 12 (4): 452–77.

—— (1997) 'Social performances and their discontents: reflections on the biosocial psychology of role-playing', in G. Bendelow and S. J. Williams (eds) *Emotions in Social Life: Critical Themes and Contemporary Issues*, London: Routledge.

Fromm, E. (1957) *The Art of Loving*, London: Allen and Unwin.

Fussell, S. W. (1991) *Muscle: Confessions of an Unlikely Bodybuilder*, New York: Poseidon Press.

Fyfe, G. and Law, J. (1988) *Picturing Power: Visual Depictions and Social Relations*, London: Routledge.

Gallop, J. (1988) *Thinking through the Body*, New York: Columbia University Press.

Gatens, M. (1992) 'Power, bodies and difference', in M. Barrett and A. Phillips (eds) *Destabilizing Theory: Contemporary Feminist Debates*, Cambridge: Polity Press.

Gehlen, A. (1988) *Man: His Nature and Place in the World*, New York: Columbia University Press.

Gerth, H. and Mills, C. Wright. (1964) *Character and Social Structure: The Psychology of Social Institutions*, New York: Harcourt, Brace and World.

Gibson, W. (1984) *Neuromancer*, London: Harper Collins.

Giddens, A. (1984) *The Constitution of Society*, Cambridge: Polity Press.

—— (1990) *The Consequences of Modernity*, Cambridge: Polity Press.

—— (1991) *Modernity and Self-Identity: Self and Society in the Late Modern Age*, Cambridge: Polity Press.

—— (1992) *The Transformation of Intimacy: Love, Sexuality and Eroticism in Modern Societies*, Cambridge: Polity Press.

—— (1994) *Beyond Left and Right*, Cambridge: Polity Press.

Gill, M. (1989) *Image of the Body*, New York: Doubleday.

Gilligan, C. (1982) *In Another Voice: Psychological Theory and Women's Development*, Cambridge MA: Harvard University Press.

Glaser, B. and Strauss, A. L. (1965) 'Temporal aspects of dying as a non-scheduled status passage', *American Journal of Sociology*, 71: 48–59.

Glassner, B. (1989) 'Fitness and the postmodern self', *Journal of Health and Social Behaviour*, 30: 180–91.

—— (1995) 'In the name of health', in R. Bunton, S. Nettleton and R. Burrows (eds) *The Sociology of Health Promotion: Critical Analyses of Consumption, Lifestyle and Risk*, London: Routledge.

Gleichmann, P. R. (1980) 'Einige soziale Wandlungen des Schlafens', *Zeitschrift fur Soziologie*, 9 (3): 236–50.

Goffman, E. (1951) 'Symbols of class status', *British Journal of Sociology*, II: 294–304.

—— (1959) *The Presentation of Everyday Life*, New York: Doubleday Anchor.

—— (1961) *Asylums: Essays on the Social Situation of Mental Patients and Other Inmates*, Harmondsworth: Penguin.

—— (1963) *Behaviour in Public Places*, London: Allen Lane.

—— (1967) *Interaction Ritual: Essays on Face-to-Face Behaviour*, Doubleday, Anchor Books.

—— (1968 [1963]) *Stigma: Notes on the Management of Spoiled Identity*, Harmondsworth: Penguin.

—— (1971) *Relations in Public: the Micro-Politics of Public Order*, London: Allen Lane.

—— (1977) 'The arrangement between the sexes', *Theory and Society*, 4(3): 301–31.

—— (1979) *Gender Advertisements*, London: Macmillan.

—— (1983) 'The interaction order', *American Sociological Review*, 48: 1–17.

Goleman, D. (1996) *Emotional Intelligence: Why it can Matter more than IQ*, London: Bloomsbury.

Good, B. (1992) 'A body in pain – the making of a world of chronic pain', in M.-J. D. Good, P. E. Brodwin, B. J. Good and A. Kleinman (eds) *Pain as Human Experience: an Anthropological Perspective*, Berkeley, CA/Oxford: University of California Press.

Gorer, G. (1955) 'The pornography of death', *Encounter*, October.

—— (1965) *Death, Grief and Mourning in Contemporary Britain*, London: Cresset.

Gray, C. H. (ed.) (1995) *The Cyborg Handbook*, London: Routledge.

Grosz, E. (1990) *Jacques Lacan: a Feminist Introduction*, London: Routledge.

—— (1994) *Volatile Bodies: Toward a Corporeal Feminism*, Bloomington and Indianapolis: Indiana University Press.

—— (1995) *Space, Time and Perversion*, London: Routledge.

Grosz, E. and Probyn, E. (eds) (1995) *Sexy Bodies: The Strange Carnalities of Feminism*, London: Routledge.

Griffiths, E. (1996) 'Hegel's Winter Collection', *Times Literary Supplement*, 8 March, pp. 20–1.

Haferkamp, H. (1987) 'Reply to Stephen Mennell', *Theory, Culture & Society*, 4: 562.

Hanna, J. L. (1988) *Dance, Sex and Gender*, Chicago: University of Chicago Press.

Haraway, D. (1991) *Simians, Cyborgs and Women*, London: Free Association Books.

Harding, S. (1986) *The Science Question in Feminism*, Buckingham: Open University Press.

Harper, P. (1985) 'The first feminist art: a view from the 1980s', *Signs*, 10(4): 762–81.

Harré, R. M. (ed.) (1986) *The Social Construction of Emotions*, New York: Basil Blackwell.

Hay, C. M., O'Brien, M. and Penna, S. (1993–4) 'Giddens, modernity and self identity', *Arena*, 2: 45–76.

—— (1991) *Physical Being: A Theory of Corporeal Psychology*, Oxford: Blackwell.

Hearn, J. and Morgan, D. H. J. (1990a) 'Men, masculinities and social theory', in J. Hearn and D. Morgan (eds) *Men, Masculinities and Social Theory*, London: Unwin Hyman.

—— (1990b) *Men, Masculinities and Social Theory*, London: Unwin Hyman.

Heim, M. (1991) 'The erotic ontology of cyberspace', in M. Benedikt (ed.) *Cyberspace: the First Steps*, Cambridge, MA: MIT Press.

Heller, A. (1989) 'Are we living in a world of emotional impoverishment?' *Thesis Eleven*, 22: 1–16.

Helman, C. (1990) *Culture, Health and Illness*, 2nd edn, London: Wright.

Herek, G. M. (1987) 'On heterosexual masculinity: some psychical consequences of the social construction of gender and sexuality', in M. S. Kimmel (ed.) *Changing Men: New Directions in Research on Men and Masculinity*, Newbury Park, CA: Sage.

Heritier-Auge, F. (1989) 'Semen and blood: some ancient theories concerning their genesis and relationship', in M. Feher, R. Naddaff and N. Tazi (eds) (1989c) *Fragments for a History of the Human Body, Part Three*, New York: Zone.

Hersey, G. (1996) 'Perspective: beauty is in the eye of a Greek chisel holder', *Times Higher*, 31 May, pp. 16–17.

Hertz, R. (1960 [1909]) *Death and the Right Hand*, New York: Cohen & West.

Herzlich, C. and Pierret, J. (1988) *Illness and Self in Society*, Baltimore/London: Academic Press.

Hevey, D. (1992) *The Creatures Time Forgot: Photography and Disability Imagery*, London and New York: Routledge.

Hilbert, R. (1984) 'The acculturation dimension of chronic pain: flawed reality construction and the problem of meaning', *Social Problems*, 31: 365–78.

Hill, M. and Tidsall, K. (1997) *Children and Society*, London: Longman.

Hite, S. (1988) *Women and Love*, London: Viking.

Hochschild, A. (1979) 'Emotion work, feeling rules and social structure', *American Journal of Sociology*, 85: 551–75.

—— (1983) *The Managed Heart: the Commercialisation of Human Feeling*, Berkeley CA: University of California Press.

—— (1989) 'Reply to Cas Wouter's review essay on *The Managed Heart*', *Theory, Culture and Society*, 6: 439–45.

—— (1990) 'Ideology and emotion management: a perspective and path for future research', in T. J. Kemper (ed.) *Research Agendas in the Sociology of Emotions*, New York: State University of New York Press.

—— (1998) 'Emotions as a way of seeing: the case of love', in G. Bendelow and S. J. Williams (eds) *Emotions in Social Life: Critical Themes and Contemporary Issues*, London: Routledge.

Hogle, L. F. (1995) 'Tales from the crypt: technology meets organism in the living cadaver', in C. H. Gray (ed.) *The Cyborg Handbook*, London: Routledge.

Holland, J., Ramasanoglu, C., Scott, S., Sharpe, S. and Thomson, R. (1990) 'Sex, gender and power: young women's sexuality in the shadow of AIDS', *Sociology of Health and Illness*, 12 (3): 336–50.

—— (1992) 'Pressure, resistance, empowerment: young women and the negotiation of safe sex', in P. Aggleton, P. Davis and G. Hart (eds) *AIDS: Rights, Risk and Reason*, London: Falmer Press.

Honneth, A. and Joas, H. (1988) *Social Action and Human Nature*, New York: Cambridge University Press.

Hughes, S. (1996) 'Perspective: soeur passing her limits: an interview with Helene Cixous', *Times Higher*, 31 May, pp. 16.

Hunt, S. M., McEwen, J. and McKenna, S. P. (1986) *Measuring Health Status*, London: Croom Helm.

Husband, C. (1982) 'Introduction: "race", the continuity of a concept', in C. Husband (ed.) *'Race' in Britain: Continuity and Change*, London: Hutchinson.

Huxley, A. (1982/[1932]) *Brave New World*, Harlow, Essex: Longman Group Ltd.

Illich, I. (1976) *Limits to Medicine – Medical Nemesis: The Expropriation of Health*, Harmondsworth: Penguin.

Ingham, M. (1984) *Men*, London: Century.

Irigaray, L. (1985a) *This Sex Which is Not One* (transl. by C. Porter and C. Burke), Ithaca, NY: Cornell University Press.

—— (1985b) *Speculum of the Other Woman* (transl. by G. Gill), Ithaca: Cornell University Press.

—— (1991) 'This sex which is not one', in S. Gunew (ed.) *Feminist Knowledge: A Reader*, London: Routledge.

Jackson, J. (1994) 'Chronic pain and the tension between the body as subject and object', in T. J. Csordas (ed.) *Embodiment and Experience: the Existential Ground of Culture and Self*, Cambridge: Cambridge University Press.

Jackson, S. (1993) 'Even sociologists fall in love: an exploration of the sociology of emotions', *Sociology*, 27 (2): 201–20.

Jacobus, M., Keller, E. F. and Shuttleworth, S. (1990) *Body/Politics: Women and the Discourse of Science*, London: Routledge.

Jaggar, A. (1989) 'Love and knowledge: emotion in feminist epistemology', in S. Bordo and A. Jaggar (eds) *Gender/Body/Knowledge: Feminist Reconstructions of Being and Knowing*, New Brunswick/London: Rutgers University Press.

James, A. (1993) *Childhood Identities: Social Relationships and the Self in Children's Experiences*, Edinburgh: Edinburgh University Press.

James, A. and Prout, A. (1990) *Constructing and Reconstructing Childhood: Contemporary Issues in the Sociology of Childhood*, London: Falmer Press.

James, A., Jenks, C. and Prout, A. (1998) *Theorizing Childhood*, Cambridge: Polity Press.

James, N. (1989) 'Emotional labour: skill and work in the social regulation of feelings', *The Sociological Review*, 37, 15–42.

—— (1992) 'Care = organisation + physical labour + emotional labour', *Sociology of Health and Illness*, 14 (4): 488–509.

—— (1993) 'Divisions of emotional labour: the case of cancer and disclosure', in S. Fineman (ed.) *Emotion and Organizations*, London: Sage.

James, V. and Gabe, J. (eds) (1996) *Health and the Sociology of Emotions*, Oxford: Blackwell.

James, W. and Lange, C. (1922) *The Emotions*, Baltimore: Wilkins and Wilkins.

Jamous, H. and Pelliole, B. (1970) 'Changes in the French University-Hospital system', in J. A. Jackson (ed.) *Professions and Professionalisation*, Cambridge: Cambridge University Press.

Jeffords, S. (1989) *The Remasculinization of America: Gender and the Vietnam War*, Bloomington and Indianapolis: Indiana University Press.

—— (1994) *Hard Bodies: Hollywood Masculinity in the Reagan Era*, New Brunswick: Rutgers University Press.

Jenkins, R. (1992) *Pierre Bourdieu*, London: Routledge.

Jewson, N. D. (1976) 'The disappearance of the sick man from medical cosmologies: 1770–1870', *Sociology*, 10: 225–44.

Johnson, D. (1983) *Body*, Boston: Beacon Press.

Johnson, H. M. (1931) *Bodily Positions in Restful Sleep*, New York: The Simmons Company.

Johnson, H. M., Swan, T. H. and Weigand, G. E. (1930) 'In what positions do healthy people sleep?' *Journal of the American Medical Association*, 94: 2058–62.

Johnson, M. (1987) *The Body in the Mind: The Bodily Basis of Meaning, Imagination and Reason*, Chicago: University of Chicago Press.

Joralemon, D. (1995) 'Organ wars: the battle for body parts', *Medical Anthropology Quarterly*, 9 (3): 335–56.

Jordan, T. (1995) 'Collective bodies: raving and the politics of Gilles Deleuze and Felix Guattari', *Body & Society*, 1 (1): 125–44.

Jordan, W. D. (1969) *White Over Black*, Harmondsworth: Penguin.

—— (1982) 'First impressions: initial English confrontations with Africans', in C. Husband (ed.) *'Race' in Britain: Continuity and Change*, London: Hutchinson.

Jordanova, L. (1997) 'Happy marriages and dangerous liaisons: artists and anatomy', in D. Petherbridge and L. Jordanova, *The Quick and the Dead*, London: South Bank Centre.

Kaplan, G. and Rogers, L. (1990) 'The definition of male and female. Biological reductionism and the sanctions of normality', in S. Gunew (ed.) *Feminist Knowledge: Critique and Construct*, London: Routledge.

Kellner, D. (1984) *Herbert Marcuse and the Crisis of Marxism*, London: Macmillan.

Kelly, M. and Field, D. (1996) 'Medical sociology, chronic illness and the body', *Sociology of Health and Illness*, 18: 241–57.

——(1997) 'Body image and sociology: reply to Simon Williams', *Sociology of Health and Illness*, 19: 359–66.

Kemper, T. J. (1990a) 'Themes and variations in the sociology of emotions', in T. J. Kemper (ed.) *Research Agendas in the Sociology of Emotions*, New York: State University of New York Press.

—— (1990b) 'Social relations and emotions: a structural approach', in T. J. Kemper (ed.) *Research Agendas in the Sociology of Emotions*, New York: State University of New York Press.

Kettenman, A. (1992) *Frida Kahlo: Pain and Passion* (transl. by K. Williams), Cologne: Benedikt Taschen.

Kierkegaard, S. (1962 [1847]) *Works of Love: Some Christian Reflections in the Form of Discourses*, London: Collins.

Kiernan, V. G. (1982) 'European attitudes to the outside world', in C. Husband (ed.) *'Race' in Britain: Continuity and Change*, London: Hutchinson.

Kimmel, M. S. (1987) (ed.) *Changing Men: New Directions in Research on Men and Masculinity*, Newbury Park, CA: Sage.

Kirk, D. (1993) *The Body, Schooling and Culture*, Deakin: University of Deakin Press.

Kirk, D. and Tinning, R. (1994) 'Embodied identity, healthy lifestyles and school physical education', *Sociology of Health and Illness*, 16 (5): 600–25.

Kirkup, G. and Keller, L. S. (ed.) (1992) *Inventing Women: Science, Technology and Gender*, Cambridge: Polity Press.

Kleinman, A. (1988) *The Illness Narratives: Suffering, Healing and the Human Condition*, New York: Basic Books.

Kotarba, J. (1983) *Chronic Pain: Its Social Dimensions*, Beverly Hills, CA: Sage.

Kristeva, J. (1982) *Powers of Horror: An Essay on Abjection* (transl. by L. Roudiez), New York: Columbia University Press.

—— (1986) *The Kristeva Reader* (ed. by T. Moi), Oxford: Basil Blackwell.

Kroker, A. and Kroker, M. (1988) *Body Invaders: Sexuality and the Postmodern Condition*, Basingstoke: Macmillan.

Kuzmics, H. (1987) 'Civilization, state and bourgeois society: the theoretical contribution of Norbert Elias', *Theory, Culture and Society*, 4: 515–37.

Lacan, J. (1953) 'Some reflections on the ego', *International Journal of Psychoanalysis*, 34: 1–17.

—— (1977) *Ecrits: A Selection* (transl. by A. Sheridan), London: Tavistock.

Laing, R. D. (1965) *The Divided Self*, Harmondsworth: Penguin.

Lakoff, G. (1987) *Women, Fire and Dangerous Things*, Chicago: University of Chicago Press.

Lakoff, G. and Johnson, M. (1980) *Metaphors We Live By*, Chicago: University of Chicago Press.

Langer, M. M. (1989) *Merleau-Ponty's Phenomenology of Perception: A Guide and Commentary*, London: Macmillan.

Langer, R. and Vacanti, J. P. (1995) 'Artificial organs', *Scientific American*, September, 100–3.

Laqueur, T. (1987) 'Orgasm, generation and the politics of reproductive biology', in C. Gallagher and T. Laqueur (eds) *The Making of the Modern Body. Sexuality and Society in the Nineteenth Century*, Berkeley, CA: University of California Press.

—— (1990) *Making Sex: Body and Gender from the Greeks to Freud*, Cambridge, MA: Harvard University Press.

Lasch, C. (1979) *The Culture of Narcissism: American Life in an Age of Diminishing Expectations*, New York: Norton.

Latour, B. (1993) *We Have Never Been Modern*, London: Harvester/Wheatsheaf.

Lawlor, J. (1991) *Behind the Screens: Nursing, Somology and the Problem of the Body*, London: Churchill Livingstone.

Lawrence, S. and Bendixen, K. (1992) 'His and hers: male and female anatomy in anatomy texts for US medical students, 1890–1989', *Social Science and Medicine*, 15 (7): 925–34.

Leder, D. (1990) *The Absent Body*, Chicago: Chicago University Press.

—— (1984–5) 'Toward a Phenomenology of Pain', *The Review of Existential Psychiatry*, 19: 255–66.

Lessor, R. (1984) 'Conscious of time and time for the development of consciousness: health awareness among women flight attendants', *Sociology of Health and Illness*, 6: 191–213.

Levin, D. M. and Solomon, G. F. (1990) 'The discursive formation of the body in the history of medicine', *Journal of Medical Philosophy*, 15: 515–37.

Lewis, C. S. (1977 [1940]) *The Problem of Pain*, London: Fount/Harper Collins.

Lippard, L. (1976) *From the Center: Feminist Essays on Women's Art*, New York: Thames and Hudson.

Lofland, J. (1978) *The Craft of Dying: The Modern Face of Death*, Beverley Hills: Sage.

—— (1980) 'Early Goffman: style, structure, substance and soul', in J. Ditton (ed.) *The View from Goffman*, London: Macmillan.

Lowenberg, J. S. and Davis, F. (1994) 'Beyond medicalisation–demedicalisation: the case of holistic health', *Sociology of Health and Illness*, 16 (5): 579–99.

Lupton, D. (1994a) *Medicine as Culture: Illness, Disease and the Body in Western Societies*, London: Sage.

—— (1994b) 'Panic computing: the viral metaphor and computer technology', *Cultural Studies*, 8 (3): 556–68.

—— (1995a) *The Imperative of Health: Public Health and the Regulated Body*, London: Sage.

—— (1995b) 'The embodied computer/user', *Body & Society*, 1: 3–4, 97–112.

—— (1996) *Food, the Body and the Self*, London: Sage.

Lupton, D. and Chapman, S. (1995) ' "A healthy lifestyle might be the death of you": discourses on diet, cholesterol control and heart disease in the press and among the lay public', *Sociology of Health and Illness*, 17 (4): 477–94.

Lupton, D., McCarthy, S. and Chapman, S. (1995) ' "Panic bodies": discourses on risk and HIV antibody testing', *Sociology of Health and Illness*, 17(1): 89–108.

Lynch, J. (1977) *The Broken Heart: The Medical Consequences of Loneliness*, New York: Basic Books.

—— (1985) *The Language of the Heart: The Human Body in Dialogue*, New York: Basic Books.

Lyon, M. (1994) 'Emotion as mediator of somatic and social processes: the example of respiration', in W. M. Wentworth and J. Ryan (eds) *Social Perspectives on Emotion*, vol. 2, Greenwich, CT: JAI Press Inc.

—— (1998) 'The limits of cultural constructionism in the study of emotion', in G. Bendelow and S. J. Williams (eds) *Emotions in Social Life: Critical Themes and Contemporary Issues*, London; Routledge.

Lyon, M. and Barbalet, J. (1994) 'Society's body: emotion and the "somatization" of social theory', in T. J. Csordas (ed.) *Embodiment and Experience: the Existential Ground of Culture and Self*, Cambridge: Cambridge University Press.

McCarthy, E. D. (1989) 'Emotions are social things: an essay in the sociology of emotions', in D. D. Franks and E. Doyle McCarthy (eds) *The Sociology of Emotions: Original Essays and Research Papers*, Greenwich, CT: JAI Press Inc.

McGovern, K. (1994) 'Applications of virtual reality to surgery', *British Medical Journal*, 380: 1053–4.

McGovern, K. and McGovern, L. T. (1994) 'Virtual clinic. The future is now', *Virtual Reality World*, March–April, 41–4.

McGuire, M. B. (1990) 'Religion and the body: rematerializing the human body in the social sciences of religion', *The Journal for the Scientific Study of Religion*, 29 (3): 283–96.

McIlvaine Parsons, H. (1972) 'The bedroom', *Human Factors*, 14 (5): 421–50.

McKeown, T. (1979) *The Role of Medicine*, 2nd edn, Oxford: Basil Blackwell.

McNay, L. (1992) *Foucault and Feminism: Power, Gender and the Self*, Cambridge: Polity Press.

—— (1994) *Foucault: A Critical Introduction*, Cambridge: Polity Press.

McNeil, M., Varcoe, I. and Yearley, S. (eds) (1990) *The New Reproductive Technologies*, London: Macmillan.

Maffesoli, M. (1995) *The Time of Tribes. The Decline of Individualism in Mass Society*, London: Sage.

——(1996) *Ordinary Knowledge*, Cambridge: Polity Press.

Mansfield, A. and McGinn, B. (1993) 'Pumping irony: the muscular and the feminine', in S. Scott and D. Morgan (eds) *Body Matters: Essays in the Sociology of the Body*, London: Falmer Press.

Mansfield, P. and Collard, J. (1988) *The Beginning of the Rest of Your Life?* London: Macmillan.

Marcuse, H. (1969 [1955]) *Eros and Civilization: A Philosophical Inquiry into Freud*, Boston: Beacon Press.

Marshall, R. (1894) *Pain, Pleasure and Aesthetics*, London: Macmillan.

Martin, E. (1987) *The Woman in the Body*, Milton Keynes: Open University Press.

—— (1994) *Flexible Bodies*, Boston: Beacon Press.

Marx, K. (1959 [1844]) *Economic and Philosophical Manuscripts of 1844*, London: Lawrence and Wishart Ltd.

—— (1967) *Karl Marx: Selected Writings in Sociology and Social Philosophy* (eds T. Bottomore and M. Rubel), Harmondsworth: Penguin.

Mauss, M. (1973 [1934]) 'Techniques of the body', *Economy and Society*, 2: 70–88.

Mayall, B. (1996) *Children, Health and the Social Order*, Buckingham: Open University Press.

Mead, G. H. (1962) *Mind, Self and Society*, 2 vols, Chicago: University of Chicago Press.

Mellor, P. and Shilling, C. (1993) 'Modernity, self-identity and the sequestration of death', *Sociology*, 27 (3): 411–32.

—— (1997) *Re-Forming the Body: Religion, Community and Modernity*, London: Sage.

Melucci, A. (1996) *The Playing Self: Person and Meaning in the Planetary Society*, Cambridge: Cambridge University Press.

Melzack, R. and Wall, P. (1965) 'Pain mechanisms: a new theory', *Science*, 150: 971–9.

—— (1988) *The Challenge of Pain*, Harmondsworth: Penguin.

Mennell, S. (1989) *Norbert Elias: Civilization and the Human Self-Image*, Oxford: Basil Blackwell.

Merleau-Ponty, M. (1962) *The Phenomenology of Perception* (transl. by C. Smith), London: Routledge and Kegan Paul.

—— (1963) *The Primacy of Perception*, Evanston, IL: Northwestern University Press.

—— (1965) *The Structure of Behaviour*, London: Methuen.

—— (1968) *The Visible and the Invisible* (transl. by A. Linglis), Evanston, IL: Northwestern University Press.

—— (1991) *The Coming* Fin de Siècle*: An Application of Durkheim's Sociology to Modernity and Postmodernity*, London: Routledge.

Mestrovic, S. G. (1997) *Postemotional Society*, London: Sage.

Metcalf, A. and Humphries, M. (eds) (1985) *The Sexuality of Men*, London: Pluto Press.

Mills, C. W. (1959) *The Sociological Imagination*, New York: Oxford University Press.

Mitchell, J. (1976) *Psychoanalysis and Feminism*, Harmondsworth: Penguin.

Mitchell, J. and Rose, J. (1982) *Feminine Sexuality: Jacques Lacan and the Ecole Freudienne*, London: Macmillan.

Morgan, D. H. J. (1992) *Discovering Men*, London: Routledge.

—— (1993) 'You too can have a body like mine: reflections on the male body and masculinities', in S. Scott and D. H. G. Morgan (eds) *Body Matters*, London: Falmer Press.

Morgan, D. H. J. and Scott, S. (eds) (1993) 'Bodies in a social landscape', in S. Scott and D. H. G. Morgan (eds) *Body Matters*, London: Falmer Press.

Morris, David (1991) *The Culture of Pain*, Berkeley, CA: University of California Press.

——(1994) 'Pain's dominion', *Wilson Quarterly*, (Autumn), 8–26.

Morris, Desmond (1967) *The Naked Ape*, London: Cape.

—— (1969) *The Human Zoo*, London: Cape.

Mort, F. (1987) *Dangerous Sexualities: Medico-Micro Politics in England since 1830*, London: Routledge and Kegan Paul.

Murphy, R. F. (1987) *The Body Silent*, New York: Henry Holt.

Murray, E. J. (1965) *Sleep, Dreams and Arousal*, New York: Appleton-Century-Crofts.

Nead, L. (1992) *The Female Nude: Art, Obscenity and Sexuality*, London/New York: Routledge.

Nettleton, S. (1992) *Power, Pain and Dentistry*, Milton Keynes: Open University Press.

——(1995) *The Sociology of Health and Illness*, Cambridge: Polity Press.

Nochlin, L. (1973a) *Realism*, Harmondsworth: Penguin.

—— (1973b) 'Why have there been no great women artists?' in T. Hess and E. Baker (eds) *Art and Sexual Politics*, Harmondsworth: Penguin.

Oakley, A. (1972) *Sex, Gender and Society*, Aldershot, Hampshire: Gower Publishing Company Ltd.

—— (1980) *Women Confined: Towards a Sociology of Childbirth*, Oxford: Martin Robertson.

—— (1984) *The Captured Womb*, Oxford: Basil Blackwell.

—— (1996) *Public Visions, Private Matters: A Professorial Lecture*, London: Institute of Education, University of London.

O'Brien, M. (1981) *The Politics of Reproduction*, London: Routledge and Kegan Paul.

—— (1989) *Reproducing the World*, Boulder, CO: Westview Press.

O'Neill, J. (1985) *Five Bodies: The Human Shape of Society*, Ithaca and London: Cornell University Press.

—— (1989) *The Communicative Body*, Evanston, IL: Northwestern University Press.

Oudshoorn, N. (1994) *Beyond the Natural Body: An Archaeology of Sex Hormones*, London: Routledge.

Parsons, T. (1951) *The Social System*, London: Routledge and Kegan Paul.

Petherbridge, D. (1997) 'Art and anatomy: the meeting of text and image', in D. Petherbridge and L. Jordanova (eds) *The Quick and the Dead*, London: South Bank Centre.

Petherbridge, D. and Jordanova, L. (eds) (1997) *The Quick and the Dead: Artists and Anatomy*, London: South Bank Centre.

Pilgrim, D. and Rogers, A. (1993) *A Sociology of Mental Health and Illness*, Milton Keynes: Open University Press.

Pinker, S. (1998) *How the Mind Works*, Harmondsworth: Penguin.

Pleck, E. and Pleck, J. H. (eds) (1980) *The American Man*, Englewood Cliffs, NJ: Prentice-Hall.

Pleck, J. H. (1982) *The Myth of Masculinity*, Cambridge, MA: MIT Press.

Pleck, J. H. and Sawyer, J. (eds) (1974) *Men and Masculinity*, Englewood Cliffs, NJ: Prentice-Hall.

Polhemus, T. (ed.) (1978) *Social Aspects of the Human Body*, Harmondsworth: Penguin.

Pollock, G. (1982) 'Vision, voice and power: feminist art history and Marxism', *Block*, 6: 6–9.

Popay, J. (1992) ' "My health is alright, but I'm just tired all the time": women's experience of ill health', in H. Roberts (ed.) *Women's Health Matters*, London: Routledge.

Pouchelle, M.-C. (1990) *The Body and Surgery in the Middle Ages* (transl. by R. Morris), Cambridge: Polity Press.

Prendergast, S. (1995) 'With gender on my mind: menstruation and embodiment at adolescence', in J. Holland, M. Blair and S. Sheldon (eds) *Debates and Issues in Feminist Research and Pedagogy*, Milton Keynes: Open University Press.

Prior, L. (1989) *The Social Organization of Death*, London: Macmillan.

Procacci, P. and Maresca, M. (1985) 'A philological study on some words concerning pain', *Pain*, 22: 201–3.

Prout, A. (1998) 'Childhood bodies: social construction and translation', in S. J. Williams, J. Gabe and M. Calnan (eds) *Theorising Health, Medicine and Society*, London: Sage.

Pultz, J. (1995) *The Body in Photography*, London: Calman and King.

Radley, A. (1989) 'Style, discourse and constraint in adjusting to chronic illness', *Sociology of Health and Illness*, 11 (3): 230–52.

—— (1995) 'The elusory body in social constructionist theory', *Body & Society*, 1 (2): 3–24.

Radley, A. and Green, R. (1987) 'Chronic illness as adjustment: a methodology and conceptual framework', *Sociology of Health and Illness*, 9 (2): 179–207.

Ratcliffe, P. (1980) *Race Relations at Work*, Leamington Spa: Warwick District Community Relations Council.

—— (1996a) ' "Race", ethnicity and housing differentials in Britain', in V. Karn (ed.) *Employment, Education and Housing among Ethnic Minorities in Britain*, Ethnicity in the 1991 Census, Vol. 4. London: HMSO.

—— (1996b) *'Race' and Housing in Bradford*, Bradford: Bradford Housing Forum

Reich, W. (1949) *Character Analysis*, New York: Farrar, Straus and Giroux.

—— (1969 [1951]) *The Sexual Revolution* (4th revised edn) (transl. by T. P. Wolfe), London: Vision Press Ltd.

—— (1983 [1942]) *The Function of the Orgasm* (transl. by V. F. Carfagno), London: Souvenir Press.

Rey, R. (1995) *The History of Pain* (transl. by L. E. Wallace, J. A. Cadden and S. W. Cadden), London/Cambridge MA: Harvard University Press.

Rich, A. (1976) *Of Woman Born*, London: Virago.

Ridsdale, L. (1989) 'Chronic fatigue in family practice', *Journal of Family Practice*, 29 (5): 486–8.

Rieff, P. (1979) *Freud: the Mind of a Moralist*, London: Chatto and Windus.

Riesman, D. (1969 [1950]) *The Lonely Crowd*, New Haven, CT: Yale University Press.

Riessman, C. K. (1989) 'Women and medicalization: a new perspective', in P. Brown (ed.) *Perspectives in Medical Sociology*, Belmont, CA: Wadsworth.

Ritzer, A. (1993) *The McDonaldization of Society*, London: Sage.

Robinson, I. (ed.) (1994) *The Social Consequences of Life and Death Technology*, Manchester: Manchester University Press.

Rose, H. (1994) *Love, Power and Knowledge: Towards a Feminist Transformation of the Sciences*, Cambridge: Polity Press.

Rose, N. (1990) *Governing the Soul: the Shaping of the Private Self*, London: Routledge.

Rowland, R. (1985) 'A child at any price?' *Women's Studies International Forum*, 8 (6): 539–46.

—— (1992) *Living Laboratories: Woman and the Reproductive Technologies*, London: Pan Macmillan.

Rubin, L. B. (1983) *Intimate Strangers: Men and Women Together*, New York: Harper Row.

Ruddick, S. (1990) *Maternal Thinking*, London: Women's Press.

Ruthven, M. (1989) *The Divine Supermarket*, London: Chatto and Windus.

Rycroft, C. (1971) *Reich*, London: Fontana/Collins.

Sacks, O. (1985) *The Man Who Mistook his Wife for a Hat*, London: Picador.

Sartre, J. P. (1962 [1939]) *Sketch for a Theory of the Emotions*, London: Methuen.

Sarup, M. (1992) *Jacques Lacan*, London: Harvester Wheatsheaf.

—— (1993) *An Introduction to Post-Structuralism and Post-Modernism* (2nd edn), London: Harvester.

Sawicki, J. (1991) *Disciplining Foucault: Feminism, Power and the Body*, London: Routledge.

Sayer, A. (1992) *Methods in Social Science: A Realist Approach*, London: Routledge.

Sayre, H. M. (1989) *The Object of Performance*, Chicago: University of Chicago Press.

Scarry, E. (1985) *The Body in Pain: The Making and Unmaking of the World*, Oxford: Oxford University Press.

Scheler, M. (1961 [1912]) *Ressentiment*, New York: The Free Press.

Scheper-Hughes, N. and Lock, M. (1987) 'The mindful body: a prolegomenon to future work in medical anthropology', *Medical Anthropology Quarterly*, 1 (1): 6–41.

Schilder, P. (1950) *The Image and Appearance of the Human Body*, New York: International Universities Press, Inc.

Schudson, M. (1984) 'Embarrassment and Erving Goffman's idea of human nature', *Theory and Society*, 13: 633–48.

Schultze-Naumburg, P. (1928) *Kunst und Rasse (Art and Race)*, Leipzig: Verlag C. H. Seemann.

Scully, D. and Bart, P. (1978) ' "A funny thing happened on the way to the orifice": women in gynaecological textbooks', in J. Ehrenreich (ed.) *The Cultural Crisis of Modern Medicine*, New York/London: Monthly Review Publications.

Seale, C. (1995) 'Heroic death', *Sociology*, 29 (4): 597–613.

Seidler, V. (1994) *Unreasonable Men: Masculinity and Social Theory*, London: Routledge.

Seidman, S. (1989) 'Constructing sex as a domain of pleasure and self expression: sexual ideology in the sixties', *Theory, Culture and Society*, 6: 293–315.

—— (1991) *Romantic Longings: Love in America, 1830–1980*, New York: Routledge.

—— (1995) 'Deconstructing queer theory or the under-theorisation of the social and ethical', in L. Nicholson and S. Seidman (eds) *Social Post-Modernism*, Cambridge: Cambridge University Press.

—— (1996) (ed.) *Queer Theory/Sociology*, Oxford: Blackwell.

Sharma, U. (1992) *Complementary Medicine Today*, London: Routledge.

—— (1996) 'Using complementary therapies: a challenge to orthodox medicine?' in S. J. Williams and M. Calnan (eds) *Modern Medicine: Lay Perspectives and Experiences*, London: UCL Press.

Sharp, L. A. (1995) 'Organ transplantation as a transformative experience: anthropological insights into the restructuring of the self', *Medical Anthropology Quarterly*, 1 (1): 6–41.

Shildrick, M. (1997) *Leaky Bodies*, London: Routledge.

Shilling, C. (1991) 'Educating the body: physical capital and the production of social inequalities', *Sociology*, 25: 653–72.

—— (1993) *The Body in Social Theory*, London: Sage.

—— (1997a) 'The undersocialised conception of the (embodied) agent in modern sociology', *Sociology*, 31 (4): 737–54.

—— (1997b) 'Emotions, embodiment and the sensation of society', *Sociological Review*, 45 (2): 195–219.

Shilling, C. and Mellor, P. (1996) 'Embodiment, structuration theory and modernity: mind/body dualism and the repression of sensuality', *Body & Society*, 2 (4): 1–15.

Simmel, G. (1969) 'Sociology of the senses: visual interaction', in R. E. Park and E. W. Burgess (eds) *Introduction to the Science of Sociology*, 3rd edn, Chicago/London: University of Chicago Press.

—— (1975) *Georg Simmel on Individuality and Social Forms* (edited by D. N. Levine), Chicago/London: University of Chicago Press.

Singer, L. (1989) 'Bodies, pleasures, powers', *Differences*, 1: 45–65.

—— (1993) *Erotic Welfare: Sexual Theory and Politics in the Age of Epidemic*, New York: Routledge.

Slouka, M. (1995) *War of the Worlds: The Assault on Reality*, London: Abacus.

Smaje, C. (1995) *Health 'Race' and Ethnicity: Making Sense of the Evidence*, London: King's Fund.

Smart, B. (1985) *Michel Foucault*, London: Tavistock.

Smith, D. (1988) *The Everyday World as Problematic: A Feminist Sociology*, Milton Keynes: Open University Press.

Smith, P. (1992) *The Emotional Labour of Nursing*, Basingstoke: Macmillan Educational Books.

Sontag, S. (1991) *Illness as Metaphor/AIDS and its Metaphors*, Harmondsworth: Penguin.

Spelman, E. (1988) *Inessential Woman: Problems of Exclusion in Feminist Thought*, Boston: Beacon Books.

Spence, J. (1986) *Putting Myself in the Picture: A Political, Personal and Photographic Autobiography*, London: Camden Press.

Springer, C. (1991) 'The pleasure of the interface', *Screen*, 32 (3): 303–23.

Stacey, M. (1988) *The Sociology of Health and Healing*, London: Routledge.

Stainton-Rogers, W. (1991) *Explaining Health and Illness: An Exploration of Diversity*, London: Harvester/Wheatsheaf.

Stanworth, M. (ed.) (1987) *Reproductive Technologies: Gender, Motherhood and Medicine*, Cambridge: Polity Press.

Stearns, C. Z. and Stearns, P. N. (1988) *Emotions and Social Change*, New York: Holmes and Meier.

Stearns, P. N. (1989) *Jealousy: The Evolution of an Emotion in American History*, Chicago: University of Chicago Press.

—— (1994) *American Cool: Constructing a Twentieth Century American Style*, New York: New York University Press.

Stearns, P. N. and Haggerty, T. (1991) 'The role of fear: transitions in American emotional standards for children 1850–1950', *American Historical Review*, 96: 63–94.

Stearns, P. N. and Stearns, C. Z. (1985) 'Emotionology: clarifying the history of emotions and emotional standards', *American Historical Review*, 90: 813–36.

—— (1986) *Anger: The Struggle for Emotional Control in American History*, Chicago: University of Chicago Press.

Stearns, P. N. and Stearns, D. C. (1994) 'Historical issues in emotions research: causation and timing', in W. M. Wentworth and J. Ryan (eds) *Social Perspectives on Emotion*, Greenwich, CT London: JAI Press Inc.

Steinberg, D. L. (1990) 'The depersonalisation of women through the administration of *"in vitro* fertilisation"', in M. McNeil, I. Varcoe and S. Yearley (eds) *The New Reproductive Technologies*, London: Macmillan.

Stenger, N. (1991) 'Mind is leaking rainbow', in M. Benedikt (ed.) *Cyberspace: First Steps*, London/Cambridge, MA: MIT Press.

Stone, A. R. (1991) 'Will the real body please stand up? Boundary stories about virtual cultures', in M. Benedikt (ed.) *Cyberspace: First Steps*, Cambridge, MA: MIT Press.

Stonor Saunders, F. (1995) *Hidden Hands: A Different History of Modernity*, London: Channel Four Television.

Strauss, A. L and Glaser, B. (1975) *Chronic Illness and the Quality of Life*, St Louis: Mosby.

Strong, P. (1979) 'Sociological imperialism and the medical profession: a critical examination of the thesis of medical imperialism', *Social Science and Medicine*, 13A (2): 199–216.

—— (1990) 'Epidemic psychology: a model', *Sociology of Health and Illness*, 12 (3): 249–59.

Sudnow, D. (1967) *Passing On: The Social Organization of Dying*, Englewood Cliffs, NJ: Prentice-Hall.

Synnott, A. (1993) *The Body Social: Symbolism, Self and Society*, London/New York: Routledge.

Synnott, A. and Howes, D. (1992) 'From measurement to meaning: anthropologies of the body', *Anthropos*, February, 147–66.

Tagg, J. (1988) *The Burden of Representation: Essays on Photographies and Histories*, Minneapolis: University of Minnesota Press.

Taussig, M. (1980) 'Reification and the consciousness of the patient', *Social Science and Medicine*, 14B: 3–13.

Taylor, B. (1993) 'Unconsciousness and society: the sociology of sleep', *International Journal of Politics, Culture and Society*, 6 (3): 463–71.

Theweleit, K. (1987 [1977]) *Male Fantasies, vol. 1: Women, Floods, Bodies and History*, Cambridge: Polity Press.

—— (1989 [1978]) *Male Fantasies, vol. 2: Psychoanalysing the White Terror*, Cambridge: Polity Press.

Tickner, L. (1978) 'The body politic: female sexuality and women artists since 1970', *Art History*, 1: 236–51.

Tiemersma, D. (1989) *Bodily Schema and Body-Image: An Interdisciplinary and Philosophical Study*, Amsterdam/Lisse: Swets and Zietlinger B.V.

Tillich, P. (1968) *Systematic Theology*, Welwyn, Herts: Nisbet.

Todd, A. D. (1989) *Intimate Adversaries: Cultural Conflict Between Doctors and Women Patients*, Philadelphia: University of Pennsylvania Press.

Tolson, A. (1977) *The Limits of Masculinity*, London: Tavistock.

Touraine, A. (1995) *Critique of Modernity*, Cambridge: Polity Press.

Townsend, P., Davidson, N. and Whitehead, M. (1988) *Inequalities in Health: the Black Report and the Health Divide*, Harmondsworth: Penguin.

Turner, B. S. (1980) 'The body and religion: towards an alliance of medical sociology and the sociology of religion', *Annual Review of the Social Sciences of Religion*, 4: 247–86.

—— (1983) *Religion and Social Theory: A Materialist Perspective*, London: Sage.

—— (1984) *The Body and Society*, Oxford: Basil Blackwell; 2nd edn (1996), London: Sage.

—— (1991) 'Recent developments in the theory of the body', in M. Featherstone and B. S. Turner (eds) *The Body: Social Process and Cultural Theory*, London: Sage.

—— (1992) *Regulating Bodies: Essays in Medical Sociology*, London: Routledge.

—— (1994) 'Preface', in P. Falk, *The Consuming Body*, London: Sage.

—— (1995) *Medical Power and Social Knowledge,* 2nd edn, London: Sage.

Turner, J. H. (1985) *Herbert Spencer: A Renewed Appreciation*, London: Sage.

—— (1996) 'The evolution of emotions in humans: a Darwinian–Durkheimian analysis', *Journal for the Theory of Social Behaviour*, 26 (1): 1–33.

Vrancken, M. (1989) 'Schools of thought on pain', *Social Science and Medicine*, 29 (3): 435–44.

Wacquant, L. (1995a) 'Pugs at work: bodily capital and bodily labour among professional boxers', *Body & Society*, 1 (1): 65–93.

—— (1995b) 'Why men desire muscles', *Body & Society*, 1(1): 163–79.

Waldby, C. (1996) *AIDS and the Body Politic: Biomedicine and Sexual Difference*, London: Routledge.

—— (1997) 'The body of the digital archive', *Health*, 1 (2): 227–43.

Walter, T. (1995) *The Revival of Death*, London: Routledge.

Walter, T., Littlewood, J. and Pickering, M. (1995) 'Death in the news: the public invigilation of private emotion', *Sociology*, 29 (4): 574–96.

Walvin, J. (1982) 'Black caricature: the roots of racialism', in C. Husband (ed.) *'Race' in Britain: Continuity and Change*, London: Hutchinson.

Warde, A. (1994) 'Consumptions, identity formation and uncertainty', *Sociology*, 28 (4): 877–98.

Weber, M. (1948) *From Max Weber: Essays in Sociology* ('Introduction' by H. H. Gerth and C. W. Mills (eds)), London: Routledge and Kegan Paul.

—— (1974) *The Protestant Ethic and the Spirit of Capitalism* (transl. by T. Parsons, 'Foreword' by R. H. Tawney), London: Unwin University Books.

Weeks, J. (1991) *Sexuality and its Discontents: Meanings, Myths and Modern Sexualities*, London: Routledge.

Wentworth, W. M. and Ryan, J. (1990) 'Balancing body, mind and culture: the place of emotion in social life', in D. D. Franks (ed.) *Social Perspectives on Emotions*, Greenwich, CT/London: JAI Press Inc.

—— (1994) 'Introduction', in W. M. Wentworth and J. Ryan (eds) *Social Perspectives on Emotion*, Greenwich, CT/London: JAI Press Inc.

Wentworth, W. M. and Yardley, D. (1994) 'Deep sociality: a bioevolutionary perspective on the sociology of emotions', in W. M. Wentworth and J. Ryan (eds) *Social Perspectives on Emotion*, Greenwich, CT/London: JAI Press Inc.

Wex, M. (1979) *Let's Take Back Our Space: 'Female' and 'Male' Body Language as a Result of Patriarchal Structure*, (transl. by J. Albert), Munich: Frauenliteraturverlag Hermine Fees.

Wiley, J. (1995) 'Nobody is "doing it": cybersexuality as a postmodern narrative', *Body & Society*, 1 (1): 145–62.

Wilkinson, R. (1996) *Unhealthy Societies: The Afflictions of Inequality*, London: Routledge.

Williams, G. H. (1984) 'The genesis of chronic illness: narrative reconstruction', *Sociology of Health and Illness*, 6: 175–200.

Williams, S. J. (1987) 'Goffman, interactionism and the management of stigma in everyday life', in G. Scambler (ed.) *Sociological Theory and Medical Sociology*, London: Tavistock.

—— (1993) *Chronic Respiratory Illness*, London: Routledge.

—— (1995a) 'Theorising class, health and lifestyles: can Bourdieu help us?' *Sociology of Health and Illness*, 17 (5): 577–604.

—— (1995b) 'Anthropomorphism and the computer virus: the latest chapter in the illness as metaphor story?' *Medical Sociology News*, 20 (2): 22–6.

—— (1996a) 'The body in question: a rejoinder to Mike Bury', *Medical Sociology News*, 21 (2): 17–22.

—— (1996b) 'The vicissitudes of embodiment across the chronic illness trajectory', *Body & Society*, 2 (2): 23–47.

—— (1996c) 'Medical sociology, chronic illness and the body: a rejoinder to Michael Kelly and David Field', *Sociology of Health and Illness*, 699–709.

—— (1997) 'Modern medicine and the "uncertain" body: from corporeality to hyperreality', *Social Science and Medicine*, 45 (7): 1041–9.

—— (1998a) 'Emotions, "hyperreality" and the "virtual" body: a critical appraisal', in G. Bendelow and S. J. Williams (eds) *Emotions in Social Life: Social Theories and Contemporary Issues*, London: Routledge.

—— (1998b) '"Capitalising" on emotions? Re-thinking the inequalities in health debate', *Sociology*, 32 (1): 121–39.

—— (1998c) 'Arlie Russell Hochschild', in R. Stones (ed.) *Key Sociological Thinkers*, London: Macmillan.

Williams, S. J. and Bendelow, G. (1998) 'In search of the "missing body": pain, suffering and the (post)modern condition', in G. Scambler and P. Higgs (ed.) *Modernity, Health and Medicine*, London: Routledge.

Williams, S. J. and Calnan, M. (eds) (1996) *Modern Medicine: Lay Perspectives and Experiences*, London: UCL Press.

Williamson, J. (1978) *Decoding Advertisements: Ideology and Meaning in Advertising*, London: Marion Boyars.

Wilson, E. O. (1975) *Sociobiology: The New Synthesis*, Cambridge, MA: Harvard University Press.

—— (1994) *The Diversity of Life*, Harmondsworth: Penguin.

Wilson, M. D. (1978) *Descartes*, London: Routledge and Kegan Paul.

Wittgenstein, L. (1968) *Philosophical Investigations* (transl. by G. E. M. Anscom), 3rd edn, Oxford: Blackwell.

Wolf, N. (1990) *The Beauty Myth: How Images of Beauty are Used Against Women*, London: Vantage.

Wolff, J. (1975) *Hermeneutic Philosophy and the Sociology of Art*, London: Routledge and Kegan Paul Ltd.

—— (1981) *Aesthetics and the Sociology of the Arts*, London: Allen and Unwin.

—— (1993) *The Social Production of Art*, 2nd edn, London: Macmillan.

Wood, M. (ed.) (1992) *Edvard Munch: The Frieze of Life*, London: National Gallery.

Woods, R. L. (ed.) (1947) *The World of Dreams: An Anthology*, New York: Appleton-Century-Crofts.

Wouters, C. (1986) 'Formalization and informalization: changing tension balances in civilizing processes', *Theory, Culture and Society*, 3 (2): 1–18.

——— (1987) 'Developments in the behavioural codes between the sexes: the formalization of informalization in the Netherlands 1930–85', *Theory, Culture and Society*, 4: 405–27.

——— (1989a) 'The sociology of emotions and flight attendants: Hochschild's *Managed Heart*', *Theory, Culture and Society*, 6 (1): 95–123.

——— (1989b) 'Response to Hochschild's reply', *Theory, Culture and Society*, 6 (3): 447–50.

——— (1990) 'Social stratification and informalization in global perspective', *Theory, Culture and Society*, 7: 69–90.

——— (1998) 'Developments in the "lust balance" of love and sex', in G. Bendelow and S. J. Williams (eds) *Emotions in Social Life: Social Theories and Contemporary Issues*, London: Routledge.

Wright, I. (1962) *Warm and Snug: A History of the Bed*, London: Routledge and Kegan Paul.

Wrong, D. (1961) 'The oversocialised conception of man in modern society', *American Sociological Review*, 26: 184–93.

Young, I. (1990) *Throwing Like a Girl and other Essays in Feminist Philosophy and Social Theory*, Bloomington and Indianapolis: Indiana University Press.

Zborowski, M. (1952) 'Cultural components in response to pain', *Journal of Social Issues*, 8: 16–30.

Zola, I. K. (1966) 'Culture and symptoms: an analysis of patients' presenting complaints', *American Sociological Review*, 31: 615–30.

——— (1972) 'Medicine as an institution of social control', *Sociological Review*, 20: 487–504.

——— (1973) 'Pathways to the doctor – from person to patient', *Social Science and Medicine*, 7: 677–89.

——— (1982) *Missing Pieces: A Chronicle of Living with a Disability*, Philadelphia: Temple University Press.

——— (1991) 'Bringing our bodies and ourselves back in: reflections on a past, present and future "Medical Sociology"', *Journal of Health and Social Behaviour*, 32 (March): 1–16.

Zolberg, V. (1990) *Constructing a Sociology of the Arts*, Cambridge, New York, Melbourne: Cambridge University Press.

Index

Note: page numbers in italics indicate illustrations

Printed in the United Kingdom
by Lightning Source UK Ltd.
122636UK00002B/184-189/A